FROM CARNEGIE TO INTERNET2: FORGING THE SERIALS FUTURE

Proceedings of the NORTH AMERICAN SERIALS INTEREST GROUP, Inc.

NASIG

14th Annual Conference
June 10-13, 1999
Carnegie Mellon University
Pittsburgh, Pennsylvania

From Carnegie to Internet2: Forging the Serials Future has been co-published simultaneously as *The Serials Librarian,* Volume 38, Numbers 1/2 and 3/4 2000.

The *Serials Librarian* Monographic "Separates"

Below is a list of "separates," which in serials librarianship means a special issue simultaneously published as a special journal issue or double-issue *and* as a "separate" hardbound monograph. (This is a format which we also call a "DocuSerial.")

"Separates" are published because specialized libraries or professionals may wish to purchase a specific thematic issue by itself in a format which can be separately cataloged and shelved, as opposed to purchasing the journal on an on-going basis. Faculty members may also more easily consider a "separate" for classroom adoption.

"Separates" are carefully classified separately with the major book jobbers so that the journal tie-in can be noted on new book order slips to avoid duplicate purchasing.

You may wish to visit Haworth's website at . . .

http://www.haworthpressinc.com

. . . to search our online catalog for complete tables of contents of these separates and related publications.

You may also call 1-800-HAWORTH (outside US/Canada: 607-722-5857), or Fax 1-800-895-0582 (outside US/Canada: 607-771-0012), or e-mail at:

getinfo@haworthpressinc.com

Women's Studies Serials: A Quarter-Century of Development, edited by Kristin H. Gerhard, MLS (Vol. 35, No. 1/2, 1998). *"Candidly explores and analyzes issues which must be addressed to enure the continued growth and vitality of women's studies. . . . It commands the attention of librarians, scholars, and publishers." (Joan Ariel, MLS, MA, Women's Studies Librarian and Lecturer, University of California at Irvine)*

E-Serials: Publishers, Libraries, Users, and Standards, edited by Wayne Jones, MA, MLS (Vol. 33, No. 1/2/3/4, 1998). *"Libraries and publishers will find this book helpful in developing strategies, policies, and procedures." (Nancy Brodie, National Library of Canada, Ottawa, Ontario)*

Serials Cataloging at the Turn of the Century, edited by Jeanne M. K. Boydston, MSLIS, James W. Williams, MSLS, and Jim Cole, MLS (Vol. 32, No. 1/2, 1997). *Focuses on the currently evolving trends in serials cataloging in order to predict and explore the possibilities for the field in the new millennium.*

Serials Management in the Electronic Era: Papers in Honor of Peter Gellatly, Founding Editor of The Serials Librarian, edited by Jim Cole, MA, and James W. Williams, MLS (Vol. 29, No. 3/4, 1996). *Assesses progress and technical changes in the field of serials management and anticipates future directions and challenges for librarians.*

Special Format Serials and Issues: Annual Review of . . . , Advances in . . . , Symposia on . . . , Methods in . . . , by Tony Stankus, MLS (Vol. 27, No. 2/3, 1996). *A thorough and lively introduction to the nature of these publications types.*

Serials Canada: Aspects of Serials Work in Canadian Libraries, edited by Wayne Jones, MLS (Vol. 26, No. 3/4, 1996). *"An excellent addition to the library literature and is recommended for all library school libraries, scholars, and students of comparative/international librarianship." (Library Times International)*

Serials Cataloging: Modern Perspectives and International Developments, edited by Jim E. Cole, MA, and James W. Williams, MSLS (Vol. 22, No. 1/2/3/4, 1993). *"A significant contribution to understanding the 'big picture' of serials control . . . . A solid presentation of serious issues in a crucial area on librarianship." (Bimonthly Review of Law Books)*

Making Sense of Journals in the Life Sciences: From Specialty Origins to Contemporary Assortment, by Tony Stankus (Supp. #08, 1992, 1996). *"An excellent introduction to scientific periodical literature and the disciplines it serves." (College & Research Libraries News)*

Making Sense of Journals in the Physical Sciences: From Specialty Origins to Contemporary Assortment, by Tony Stankus, MLS (Supp. #07, 1992, 1996). *"A TOUR DE FORCE . . . It will immeasurably help science serials librarians to select journal titles on a rational and defensible basis, and the methodology used can be extended over time and to other fields and other journals." (International Journal of Information and Library Research)*

The Good Serials Department, edited by Peter Gellatly (Vol. 19, No. 1/2, 1991). *"This is recommended for library educators, students, and serials specialists. It should be useful both to novices and veterans." (Journal of Academic Librarianship)*

Scientific Journals: Improving Library Collections Through Analysis of Publishing Trends, by Tony Stankus, MLS (Supp. #6, 1990). *"Will be of great value to science librarians in academic, industrial, and governmental libraries as well as to scientists and professors facing problems in choosing the most economical and useful journals for library collections." (American Scientist)*

Implementing Online Union Lists of Serials: The Pennsylvania Union List of Serials Experience, edited by Ruth C. Carter, MA, MS, PhD, and James D. Hooks, PhD, MLS (Supp. #05, 1989). *"This practical and very readable book provides not only a useful guide to the development and use of online union lists, but also a fine example of library co-operation and hard work." (Library Association Record)*

Newspapers in the Library: New Approaches to Management and Reference Work, edited by Lois Upham, PhD, MSLS (Supp. #04, 1988). *"Lively, varied and written with good sense and enthusiasm. Recommended for those working in or administering newspaper collections for the first time, and also those who, immersed in the problems of this seemingly intractable material, need the inspiration of solutions devised by others." (Riverina Library Review)*

Scientific Journals: Issues in Library Selection and Management, by Tony Stankus, MLS (Supp. #3, 1988). *"This book has significance for those for those who select scientific journals for library collections and for the primary users and producers of the literature as well. More works of this type are needed." (American Reference Books Annual)*

Libraries and Subscription Agencies: Interactions and Innovations, edited by Peter Gellatly (Vol. 14, No. 3/4, 1988). *"Put[s] developments in context and provide[s] useful background information and advice for those contemplating implementation of automation in this area." (Library Association Record)*

Serials Cataloging: The State of the Art, edited by Jim E. Cole, MA, and Jackie Zajanc (Vol. 12, No. 1/2, 1987). *"Really does cover an amazingly broad span of serials cataloging topics . . . Well worth its purchase price." (Lois N. Upham, PhD, Assistant Professor, College of Library and Information Science, University of South Carolina)*

Serial Connections: People, Information, and Communication, edited by Leigh Chatterton, MLS, and Mary Elizabeth Clack, MS (Vol. 11, No. 3/4, 1987). *"The essays are uniformly lively and provide excellent overviews of the aspects of serials control, from acquisition to automation." (Academic Library Book Review)*

Serials Librarianship in Transition: Issues and Development, edited by Peter Gellatly (Vol. 10, No. 1/2, 1986). *"Well-written and tightly edited . . . Specialists in the 'serials chain' and students interested in serials librarianship should give this book top priority in their professional reading lists." (Library and Information Science Annual)*

The Management of Serials Automation: Current Technology and Strategies for Future Planning, edited by Peter Gellatly (Supp. #2, 1984). *"A thoroughly documented review of the progress and problems in serials automation strategy and technology." (Information Retrieval & Library Automation)*

Union Catalogues of Serials: Guidelines for Creation and Maintenance, with Recommended Standards for Bibliographic and Holdings Control, by Jean Whiffin, BA, BLS (Vol. 8, No. 1, 1983). *"A clearly written and easily read set of guidelines . . . Recommended for library science collections. Essential where union catalogs are contemplated." (Public Libraries)*

Serials Librarianship as an Art: Essays in Honor of Andrew D. Osborn, edited by Peter Gellatly (Vol. 6, No. 2/3, 1982). *An exploration of the advantages and excellences of the manual check-in operation versus automation.*

Sex Magazines in the Library Collection: A Scholarly Study of Sex in Serials and Periodicals, edited by Peter Gellatly (Supp. #01, 1981). *"Recommended for librarians with collections that include sex periodicals, as well as for those librarians who haven't quite made up their minds and are looking for more background information." (Technicalities)*

The North American Serials Interest Group (NASIG) Series

From Carnegie to Internet2: Forging the Serials Future, edited by P. Michelle Fiander, Joseph C. Harmon, and Jonathan David Makepeace (Vol. 38, No. 1/2/3/4, 2000). *Current information and practical insight to help you improve your technical skills and prepare you and your library for the 21st century.*

Head in the Clouds, Feet on the Ground: Serials Vision and Common Sense, edited by Jeffrey S. Bullington, Beatrice L. Caraway, and Beverley Geer (Vol. 36, No. 1/2/3/4, 1999). *"Practical, common sense advice, and visionary solutions to serials issues afoot in every library department and in every type of library today. . . . An essential reference guide for libraries embracing electronic resource access." (Mary Curran, MA, MLS, Coordinator, Bibliographic Standards, Morisset Library, University of Ottawa, Ontario, Canada)*

Experimentation and Collaboration: Creating Serials for a New Millennium, Charlene N. Simser and Michael A. Somers (Vol. 34, No. 1/2/3/4, 1998). *Gives valuable ideas and practical advice that you can apply or incorporate into your own area of expertise.*

Pioneering New Serials Frontiers: From Petroglyphs to Cyberserials, edited by Christine Christiansen and Cecilia Leathem (Vol. 30, No. 3/4, and Vol. 31, No. 1/2, 1997). *Gives you insight, ideas, and practical skills for dealing with the changing world of serials management.*

Serials to the Tenth Power: Traditions, Technology, and Transformation, edited by Mary Ann Sheble, MLS, and Beth Holley, MLS (Vol. 28, No. 1/2/3/4, 1996). *Provides readers with practical ideas on managing the challenges of the electronic information environment.*

A Kaleidoscope of Choices: Reshaping Roles and Opportunities for Serialists, edited by Beth Holley, MLS, and Mary Ann Sheble, MLS (Vol. 25, No. 3/4, 1995). *"Highly recommended as an excellent source material for all librarians interested in learning more about the Internet, technology and its effect on library organization and operations, and the virtual library." (Library Acquisitions: Practice & Theory)*

New Scholarship: New Serials: Proceedings of the North American Serials Interest Group, Inc., edited by Gail McMillan and Marilyn Norstedt (Vol. 24, No. 3/4, 1994). *"An excellent representation of the ever-changing, complicated, and exciting world of serials." (Library Acquisitions Practice & Theory)*

If We Build It: Scholarly Communications and Networking Technologies: Proceedings of the North American Serials Interest Group, Inc., edited by Suzanne McMahon, MLS, Miriam Palm, MLS, and Pamela Dunn, BA (Vol. 23, No. 3/4, 1993). *"Highly recommended to anyone interested in the academic serials environment as a means of keeping track of the electronic revolution and the new possibilities emerging." (ASL (Australian Special Libraries))*

A Changing World: Proceedings of the North American Serials Interest Group, Inc., edited by Suzanne McMahon, MLS, Miriam Palm, MLS, and Pamela Dunn, BA (Vol. 21, no. 2/3, 1992). *"A worthy publication for anyone interested in the current and future trends of serials control and electronic publishing." (Library Resources & Technical Services)*

The Future of Serials: Proceedings of the North American Serials Interest Group, Inc., edited by Patricia Ohl Rice, PHD, MLS and Jane A. Robillard, MLS (Vol. 19, No. 3/4, 1991). *"A worthwhile addition to any library studies collection, or a serials librarian's working library, . . . I would recommend separate purchase of the monograph. NASIG plays too important a role in the serials universe to ignore any of its published proceedings." (Library Acquisitions: Practice & Theory)*

The Serials Partnership: Teamwork, Technology, and Trends, edited by Patricia Ohl Rice, PhD, MLS, and Joyce L. Ogburn, MSLS, MA (Vol. 17, No. 3/4, 1990). *In this forum, scholars, publishers, vendors, and librarians share in discussing issues of common concern.*

Serials Information from Publisher to User: Practice, Programs, and Progress, edited by Leigh A. Chatterton, MLS, and Mary Elizabeth Clack, MLS (Vol. 15, No. 3/4, 1988) *"[E]xcellent reference tools for years to come." (Gail McMillan, MLS, MA, Serials Team Leader, University Libraries, Virginia Polytechnic Institute and State University)*

The Serials Information Chain: Discussion, Debate, and Dialog, edited by Leigh Chatterton, MLS, and Mary Elizabeth Clack, MLS (Vol. 13, No. 2/3, 1988). *"It contains enlightening information for libraries or businesses in which serials are a major concern." (Library Resources & Technical Services)*

From Carnegie to Internet2: Forging the Serials Future has been co-published simultaneously as *The Serials Librarian,* Volume 38, Numbers 1/2 and 3/4 2000.

Cover design by Thomas J. Mayshock Jr.

Cover photo of the Seventh Street Bridge courtesy of Carnegie Library of Pittsburgh.

Library of Congress Cataloging-in-Publication Data

North American Serials Interest Group, Conference (14th : 1999 : Pittsburgh, Pa.)
From Carnegie to Internet2 : forging the serials future : proceedings of the North American Serials Interest Group, Inc. : 14th annual conference, June 10-13, 1999, Carnegie Mellon University, Pittsburgh, Pennsylvania / P. Michelle Fiander, Joseph C. Harmon, Jonathan David Makepeace, editors.
p. cm.
Includes bibliographical references and index.
ISBN 0-7890-1007-0–ISBN 0-7890-1035-6
1. Serials librarianship–United States–Congresses. 2. Serials librarianship–Canada– Congresses. 3. Information networks–United States–Congresses. 4. Information networks–Canada–Congresses. 5. Libraries–United States–Special collections–Electronic journals–Congresses. 6. Libraries–Canada–Special collections–Electronic journals–Congresses. I. Title: From Carnegie to Internet2. II. Title: From Carnegie to Internet two. III. Fiander, P. Michelle, 1964- IV. Harmon, Joseph C. V. Makepeace, Jonathan David. VI. Title.
Z692.S5 N67 1999
025.1′732–dc21 00-023223

FROM CARNEGIE TO INTERNET2: FORGING THE SERIALS FUTURE

Proceedings of the NORTH AMERICAN SERIALS INTEREST GROUP, Inc.

NASIG

14th Annual Conference
June 10-13, 1999
Carnegie Mellon University
Pittsburgh, Pennsylvania

P. Michelle Fiander
Joseph C. Harmon
Jonathan David Makepeace
Editors

The Haworth Information Press
An Imprint of
The Haworth Press, Inc.
New York • London • Oxford

Indexing, Abstracting & Website/Internet Coverage

This section provides you with a *chronological list* of major indexing & abstracting services. That is to say, each service began covering this periodical during the year noted in the right column. Most Websites which are listed below have indicated that they will either post, disseminate, compile, archive, cite or alert their own Website users with research-based content from this work. (This list is as current as the copyright date of this publication.)

Abstracting, Website/Indexing Coverage .... Year When Coverage Began

- ***CAMBRIDGE SCIENTIFIC ABSTRACTS*** **1992**
- ***CHEMICAL ABSTRACTS*** **1992**
- ***CINAHL (Cumulative Index to Nursing & Allied Health Literature), in print, also on CD-ROM from CD PLUS, EBSCO, and Silver- Platter, and online from CDP Online (fomerly BRS), Data-Star, and PaperChase. (Support materials include Subject Heading List, Database Search Guide, and instructional video.)*** **1992**
- ***CURRENT AWARENESS ABSTRACTS OF LIBRARY AND INFORMATION MANAGEMENT LITERATURE, ASLIB (UK)*** **1992**
- ***HEIN'S LEGAL PERIODICAL CHECKLIST: index to periodical articles pertaining to law*** **1992**
- ***INDEX TO PERIODICAL ARTICLES RELATED TO LAW*** .. **1992**
- ***INFORMATION REPORTS & BIBLIOGRAPHIES*** **1992**
- ***INFORMATION SCIENCE ABSTRACTS*** **1992**

(continued)

- *LIBRARY & INFORMATION SCIENCE ABSTRACTS (LISA)* **1992**
- *LIBRARY DIGEST* **1992**
- *LIBRARY LITERATURE* **1992**
- *REFERATIVNYI ZHURNAL (Abstracts Journal of the All-Russian Institute of Scientific and Technical Information)* . **1992**
- *ACADEMIC ABSTRACTS/CD-ROM* **1993**
- *INFORMED LIBRARIAN, THE. For more information visit us at <http://www.infosourcespub.com>* **1993**
- *IBZ INTERNATIONAL BIBLIOGRAPHY OF PERIODICAL LITERATURE* **1994**
- *NEWSLETTER OF LIBRARY AND INFORMATION SERVICES, China Sci-Tech Book Review, Library of Academia Sinica, 8 Kexueyuan Nanlu, Zhongguancum, Beijing 100080, People's Republic of China* **1994**
- *PASCAL, C/O INSTITUTE DE L' INFORMATION SCIENTIFIQUE ET TECHNIQUE* **1994**
  PASCAL, %Institute de L'Information Sceintifique et Technique. Cross-disciplinary electronic database covering of the fields of science, technology & medicine. Also available on CD-ROM, and can generate customized retrospective searches. http://ww.inist.fr
- *ACADEMIC SEARCH: database of 2,000 selected academic serials, updated monthly: EBSCO Publishing* . . **1995**
- *BUBL INFORMATION SERVICE. An Internet-based Information Service for the UK higher education community. <URL: http://bubl.ac.uk>* **1995**
- *CNPIEC REFERENCE GUIDE: Chinese national directory of foreign periodicals* **1995**
- *KONYVTARI FIGYELO-LIBRARY REVIEW* **1995**
- *SOCIOLOGICAL ABSTRACTS (SA) www.csa.com* **1995**

(continued)

- ***MASTERFILE: Updated database from EBSCO publishing* . . 1995**
- ***PERIODICA ISLAMICA* 1995**
- ***CURRENT CONTENTS: Clinical medicine/life sciences (CC: CM/LS) Weekly Table of Contents Service), and Social Science Citation Index. Articles also searchable through Social SciSearch, ISI's online database and in ISI's Research Alert current awareness service* 1997**
- ***JOURNAL OF ACADEMIC LIBRARIANSHIP: Guide to professional literature, the* 1997**
- ***LIBRARY AND INFORMATION SCIENCE ANNUAL (LISCA) Further information is available at <www./lu.com/arba>* 1998**
- ***FINDEX <www.publist.com>* 1999**
- ***HANDBOOK OF LATIN AMERICAN STUDIES* 1999**
- ***Microcomputer Abstracts can be found Online at: DIALOG, File 233; HRIN & OCLC and on Internet at: Cambridge Scientific Absracts; Dailog Web; & OCLC* 1999**

Special Bibliographic Notes related to special journal issues (separates) and indexing/abstracting:

- indexing/abstracting services in this list will also cover material in any "separate" that is co-published simultaneously with Haworth's special thematic journal issue or DocuSerial. Indexing/abstracting usually covers material at the article/chapter level.
- monographic co-editions are intended for either non-subscribers or libraries which intend to purchase a second copy for their circulating collections.
- monographic co-editions are reported to all jobbers/wholesalers/approval plans. The source journal is listed as the "series" to assist the prevention of duplicate purchasing in the same manner utilized for books-in-series.
- to facilitate user/access services all indexing/abstracting services are encouraged to utilize the co-indexing entry note indicated at the bottom of the first page of each article/chapter/contribution.
- this is intended to assist a library user of any reference tool (whether print, electronic, online, or CD-ROM) to locate the monographic version if the library has purchased this version but not a subscription to the source journal.
- individual articles/chapters in any Haworth publication are also available through the Haworth Document Delivery Service (HDDS).

NASIG Officers and Executive Board

1998/1999

Officers:

Steve Oberg, President, University of Chicago
Dan Tonkery, Vice-President/President Elect, The Faxon Company
Margaret Mering, Secretary, University of Nebraska-Lincoln
Geraldine Williams, Treasurer, Northern Kentucky University
Susan Davis, Past President, State University of New York at Buffalo

Executive Board:

Eleanor Cook, Appalachian State University
Carol Pitts Diedrichs, Ohio State University
Ann Ercelawn, Vanderbilt University
Jim Mouw, University of Chicago
Margaret Rioux, Woods Hole Oceanographic Institution
Frances C. Wilkinson, University of New Mexico

1999 Program Planning Committee

Pre-Conference, Plenary, and Issues Sessions:

Connie Foster, Co-Chair, Western Kentucky University

Judy Luther, Informed Strategies

Kathryn Ellis, University of Tennessee

Phillip Wallas, EBSCO Publishing

Susan Markley, Villanova University

Anne McKee, Co-Chair, Blackwell's Information Services

Workshops:

Jos Anemaet, Co-Chair, Oregon State University

Barbara Albee, The Faxon Company

Jill Emery, University of Texas, Arlington

Cameron Campbell, University of Chicago

Hui-Yee Chang, University of California, Santa Cruz

Fritz Schwartz Serials Education Scholarship

Donna M. Viscuglia, Simmons College

NASIG Conference Student Grant Award Recipients

Jennifer Dekker, University of Toronto

Susie Husted, Queens College/CUNY

Kate M. Manuel, Catholic University of America

Konstantina Matsoukas, McGill University

Edward W. Murphy, University of South Florida

Marianne Orme, Pratt University

Michelle Pearse, Simmons College

Anne F. Rasmussen, Kent College

Laurentiu Mircea Stefancu, University of Illinois at Urbana-Champaign

Horizon Award Winners

P. Michelle Fiander, Indiana University-Purdue University Indianapolis

Jonathan David Makepeace, Indiana University-Purdue University Indianapolis

June Rutkowski, Harvard College Library

ABOUT THE EDITORS

P. Michelle Fiander has been Serials Cataloger and Reference Librarian at University Library, Indiana University-Purdue University Indianapolis since July 1998. She was Cataloger and Reference Librarian at Mount Allison University, Sackville, New Brunswick from 1996-1998. Michelle received her M.L.S. (1996) and M.A. in English (1994) from Dalhousie University, Halifax, Nova Scotia. Michelle was a 1999 NASIG Horizon Award recipient.

Joseph C. Harmon is Cataloging Team Leader at University Library, Indiana University-Purdue University Indianapolis. Joseph received his M.L.S. in 1988 and his M.A. in Anthropology in 1996 from Indiana University. His publications include *Philanthropy in Short Fiction: An Annotated Bibliography and Subject Index* (1992) and "The Death of Quality Cataloging: Does It Make a Difference for Library Users?" *Journal of Academic Librarianship* (July 1996).

Jonathan David Makepeace has been Cataloger and Digital Projects Librarian at University Library, Indiana University-Purdue University Indianapolis, since August 1997, prior to which he was a cataloger/automation specialist at Louisiana State University in Baton Rouge from 1995-1997. He received his M.S. in Library and Information Science in 1994 from the University of Illinois at Urbana-Champaign. Jonathan was a 1999 NASIG Horizon Award recipient.

From Carnegie to Internet2: Forging the Serials Future

CONTENTS

ALL HAWORTH INFORMATION PRESS
BOOKS AND JOURNALS ARE PRINTED
ON CERTIFIED ACID-FREE PAPER

Introduction

As we approach the turn of the century, it seems appropriate for the library community to look back at our origins as well as forward to our future. NASIG's 14th Annual Conference, held June 10-13, 1999, Pittsburgh, PA gave us an opportunity to do these things. The theme, "From Carnegie to Internet2: Forging the Serials Future," identifies an influential individual and a powerful technology, both exerting a profound impact on librarianship. The legacy of Carnegie libraries, decades after their inception, is still with us today. The legacy of the Internet and Internet2 is in the making, but its influence, while different in kind from the influence of Carnegie's libraries, will serve the same fundamental purpose: to disseminate information and to encourage learning–bedrock goals of the library community.

The preconference sessions, one on metadata, the other on scenario building, provided a good start to the conference. The discussion of metadata helped demystify it and illuminated its practical applications, while the scenario building session suggested a strategy to help libraries plan for the future. All three plenary speakers focussed on the impact of technology on libraries. Vicki O'Day outlined the paradigm of an information ecology, arguing that the way we see, think, and talk about technology has consequences for the way we use it. William Graves encouraged us to deal with the changes wrought by the Internet in a systematic rather than random way; and Stephen Abram exhorted us to be the connection between information and the information user.

Many of the issues sessions focussed on management of full-text databases and electronic serials, including concomitant issues of licensing

[Haworth co-indexing entry note]: "Introduction." Fiander, P. Michelle, Joseph C. Harmon, and Jonathan David Makepeace. Co-published simultaneously in *The Serials Librarian* (The Haworth Press, Inc.) Vol. 38, No. 1/2, 2000, pp. 1-2; and: *From Carnegie to Internet2: Forging the Serials Future* (ed: P. Michelle Fiander, Joseph C. Harmon, and Jonathan David Makepeace) The Haworth Press, Inc., 2000, pp. 1-2. Single or multiple copies of this article are available for a fee from The Haworth Document Delivery Service [1-800-342-9678, 9:00 a.m. - 5:00 p.m. (EST). E-mail address: getinfo@haworthpressinc.com].

and budgeting. Searching, selecting, and evaluating Web resources were also discussed. Other topics included an historical look at librarianship, scholarly publishing by librarians, the evolution of distance education, and communication–between individuals and within organizations.

Workshops covered a range of topics, many of which dealt with the management of electronic resources. Aggregator databases were a hot topic, whether owned by a single institution or a consortium. Standards for electronic materials and licensing issues were also discussed. Other sessions described specific projects between universities and publishers to provide full-text electronic access to journal literature. The impact of electronic materials on public service work, and library users–especially their inflated expectations of electronic materials, formed the basis for other sessions. Despite an emphasis on digital materials and technology, a number of workshops dealt with the foundations of serials librarianship, covering the history of MARC development, and an update on AACR2 rules for serials cataloging. The work of deacidification was described in another session, reminding us that electronic materials are not the only vulnerable medium in our collections. In the context of electronic publishing, the role and definition of serial publications were explored. Surprisingly, the role of the serial, whether electronic or paper, has changed very little in the past century. The advent of the Internet heralds a dynamic method of communication unlike anything we have ever known, but the electronic serial is serving much the same purpose as the paper journals that filled Carnegie libraries.

The papers included in this volume were reported and written by NASIG members and conference attendees, as well as speakers themselves. To the speakers and reporters we'd like to extend a hearty "Thanks!" Your work is much appreciated. Needless to say, without your contributions, this volume would not be possible.

Throughout the editing process we've received support and assistance from a variety of individuals including Ann Ercelawn, our NASIG Board liaison, various members of the Program Planning and Conference Committee, Erika Linke, Conference Registrar, Nancy Deisroth of Haworth Press, and our colleagues at IUPUI University Library. Many thanks to all.

P. Michelle Fiander
Joseph C. Harmon
Jonathan David Makepeace
September 19, 1999

PRECONFERENCE PROGRAMS

Metadata Preconference

Stuart Weibel
Jane Greenberg
Robin Wendler

Presenters

Debbie Malone

Recorder

SUMMARY. Stuart Weibel discussed metadata resource recovery, focussing on the Dublin Core initiative. Jane Greenberg discussed metadata elements and search engines. Robin Wendler discussed metadata in the library and focussed on projects at Harvard. *[Article copies available for a fee from The Haworth Document Delivery Service: 1-800-342-9678. E-mail address: getinfo@haworthpressinc.com <Website: http://www.haworthpressinc.com>]*

METADATA FOR RESOURCE RECOVERY: THE DUBLIN CORE METADATA INITIATIVE

Stuart Weibel began by explaining that although metadata can take many forms, this workshop would focus on a particular type, resource

---

Stuart Weibel is Senior Research Scientist, OCLC.

Jane Greenberg is Assistant Professor, School of Information and Library Science, University of North Carolina, Chapel Hill.

Robin Wendler is Metadata Analyst, Office for Information Systems, Harvard University Library and a member of the Library Digital Initiative Team.

Debbie Malone is Head, Technical Services Department, Ursinus College, Collegeville, PA.

[Haworth co-indexing entry note]: "Metadata Preconference." Malone, Debbie. Co-published simultaneously in *The Serials Librarian* (The Haworth Press, Inc.) Vol. 38, No. 1/2, 2000, pp. 5-14; and: *From Carnegie to Internet2: Forging the Serials Future* (ed: P. Michelle Fiander, Joseph C. Harmon, and Jonathan David Makepeace) The Haworth Press, Inc., 2000, pp. 5-14. Single or multiple copies of this article are available for a fee from The Haworth Document Delivery Service [1-800-342-9678, 9:00 a.m. - 5:00 p.m. (EST). E-mail address: getinfo@haworthpressinc.com].

description metadata. This structure is needed because of the growing size of the Web, which has over five hundred million addressable pages. High consumer expectations are in conflict with primitive search tools and mechanisms. The Web as an information system is suffering because resource discovery is chaotic, organization is haphazard, and preservation is almost non-existent.

Weibel suggested that metadata, structured data about data, can help to impose order on this chaos and enable automated manipulation of resources. Challenges arise in the attempts to reconcile the tension between the functionality of metadata and simplicity of production and use. MARC is a rich and complicated metadata system, but it can be time consuming and expensive to produce. Machine production of MARC records is expanding and such records are cheaper to produce than those created by human catalogers. The drawback is that machine produced records tend to be inferior to those created by human catalogers.

A resource description community is characterized by common semantic, structural and syntactic conventions, which enable exchange of information. Libraries have used MARC and AACR2 for years, but what Weibel describes as the "Internet Commons" embraces many different resource description communities, which have different conventions. For example, museums, geographic data users, scientific data users, and the ever widening commercial sector, all need methods for describing aspects of their resources, but they also need systems that allow these different communities to talk to one another. Such interoperability requires conventions defining the semantics of each element; the structure of the record, which must be human-readable and machine-parseable, with the syntax and grammar to convey the semantics and structure.

The Dublin Core metadata set is an attempt to build an interdisciplinary consensus about a core element set for improved resource discovery. It consists of 15 elements that are all optional, repeatable and extensible, and which provide a starting place for richer description [1]. Weibel said this extensibility was analogous to nested Ukrainian dolls, which are similar but not identical. The sub-structure of Dublin Core should increase the precision of description. The modular aspect of the Dublin Core also improves its extensibility. To make his point, Weibel compared Dublin Core elements to Lego, saying that just as the Lego we used as kids can be used with today's Lego, Dublin Core elements can be used with other metadata systems.

Although unqualified Dublin Core is the simplest to use, additional detail is often required to support the needs of local or discipline-specific applications. Dublin Core will allow such specificity. Dublin Core also contains qualifiers, which specify encoding rules. For example, the unqualified statement, 2/4/1998, could be interpreted either as February 4, 1998 or April 2, 1998. A qualified statement, 2/4/1998, where the first position represents the month, the second position the day, is not confusing. In this case, some flexibility is lost, but the information is more meaningful. Weibel feels that complexity of description is unavoidable and that precision is often more important than simplicity. Dublin Core should enable the coexistence of the two.

The Dublin Core has been developed through a series of six international seminars with the seventh planned for November 1999 in Frankfurt, Germany. It has been strongly influenced by MARC/AACR2, although there are important differences in structure, detail, and focus between Dublin Core and MARC/AACR2. Substantial effort has been invested in the creation of crosswalks between the two, the CORC project at OCLC being one of these. Z39.50 standards are being maintained, with Dublin Core as the proposed cross-domain attribute set. The creator/contributor/publisher fields have been collapsed into a single abstract attribute, Name [2].

How is the Dublin Core being used today? Weibel said that there are over 100 major implementation projects today in 20 different countries. There are a number of syntax alternatives and Weibel described three of them. The simplest is embedding the metadata within the HTML document and using the Web as the infrastructure. This would be analogous to getting the catalog cards with books. The disadvantage lies in the limited structural richness; hierarchical or tree-structured data would not be supported. The second syntax alternative is XML, which is the emerging standard for networked text and data. Its disadvantage lies with its great flexibility, which interferes with interoperability. The third alternative is RDF or Resource Description Framework, which Weibel strongly favors. It provides enabling technology for richly structured metadata, and its infrastructure will be ubiquitous. Weibel foresees tighter coupling with other software applications such as word processors, browsers, image management software, database management software, etc., and automated creation of metadata.

Weibel posed the question "Can you deal in a single system with both Dublin Core and MARC?" The answer is "yes," and the example is CORC, Cooperative Online Resource Cataloging, an OCLC research project designed to provide cooperative cataloging of electronic resources using a variety of metadata standards [3]. Over 70 libraries are currently participating, with a goal of 100 libraries by the end of 1999. Users can choose to view records in either the Dublin Core or the MARC format.

Audience questions centered on the practical applications of Dublin Core, particularly if various popular search engines are using it. The answer was that not many search engines are harvesting metadata due to the tendency of some producers to load their sites with inappropriate key words in an effort to skew search retrievals. Weibel mentioned that some search engines, Northern Lights for one, are harvesting "high quality metadata that was created with good intentions." He also mentioned that some local sites are using imbedded metadata in their databases and finding it useful.

There was also good discussion of OCLC's CORC project, particularly what type of libraries are participating. Weibel noted that public libraries are underrepresented, and that it is an international effort with such institutions as the National Library of Australia and the Library of Scotland contributing. He foresees CORC becoming the Prism system for the Internet. Some participants noted that the requirement that participating libraries devote the equivalent of a half full-time staff person to the project would prevent smaller libraries from joining [4].

METADATA ELEMENTS AND SEARCH ENGINES

Jane began by arguing that the World Wide Web is in no way like a library because there is little organization, classification or selection of resources. Small segments may provide organized access to evaluated resources, but for the most part WWW is most like a library with the books thrown on the floor. She defined metadata as data that supports resource discovery and use. Resource discovery would include access points such as author, title, and subject; resource use would include information on rights management, type of format etc. In answer to the question "Is the metadata we are creating being exploited by search engine developers?" Jane would answer "yes and no."

She sees the search engine landscape as having three basic categories. The WWW, with directories like Yahoo, etc.; Intranets; and Project-oriented sites. WWW engines search the whole Web, Intranets search organization-specific resources, and Project-oriented sites search information-specific resources, such as the Digital Library Project. Jane emphasized that the boundaries between these categories are artificial; the present theory is a work in progress.

Who has access to these types of resources? WWW search engines allow anyone and everyone to search; Intranets generally allow access only to organizational members and visitors; Project-oriented sites allow access to subscribers and visitors through mechanisms such as valid IP addresses, etc.

Popular commercial WWW search engines include AltaVista, Excite, HotBot, Lycos, and Yahoo. Many of these have directories as well. Intranet engines include Blue Angel, I-Search, as well as products made by commercial engine vendors, such as InfoSeek's UltraSeek, AltaVista, and VeritySearch97. Project-oriented engines are essentially the same as engines used for Intranets. Examples include in-house engines like HotMeta and MetaWeb, but can also include off-the-shelf engines used by Intranets. The underlying purposes of search engines in each category also differ. WWW engines are designed to make money; Intranet engines are designed to facilitate organizational productivity and publicity; Project sites seek to facilitate resource discovery and use.

WWW search engines do not generally support Dublin Core or any other metadata schemes, at least publicly. The only exception being that many use the <Title> HTML tag, and HotBot and InfoSeek make use of <META NAME = keyword> and <META NAME = description> tags. The specialty or newer search engines, such as Northern Light, are beginning to take advantage of other metadata elements. When metatags are not manipulated for specific retrieval purposes, the terms in them are at least included in the retrieval algorithm. Intranets can be configured to search using Dublin Core elements, but it is far from a universal practice. The Project-specific sites are easier to configure due to their more homogenous databases. In fact, project sites are using more metadata searching than the other two categories, but it is still minimal.

Jane's handout included search examples from a project-oriented engine using the Dublin Core, HotMeta [5]. This is a product of Distributed Systems Technology Centre, DSTC, from the Queensland Government Demonstration Site. HotMeta crawls the Internet or Intranet, extracts and indexes metadata from embedded HTML metatags, and saves it in a metadata repository. The software provides interfaces to enable users to browse, find, and see the metadata stored in the repository. The result is a display in which the elements such as creator, identifier, subject and description are clearly labeled and easy to read.

For the future, Jane predicts that metadata development will continue in all three categories. She sees a critical mass probably being reached in the Project-oriented area first. With better access to information the Internet will become more productive with new profits realized. She hopes to see more cooperation between the profit and not-for-profit communities.

The discussion period focused on our need to convince our own administrators about the need to add metadata to our records now, even if search engines are not routinely harvesting it yet. When asked if records with metadata would be excluded from a search if the engine did not harvest metadata, Jane replied that it would depend on the programming hierarchy of the search engine.

RESOURCES REVEALED: METADATA IN THE LIBRARY

Robin's presentation included three main discussion points: metadata in the abstract, forces operating on libraries which are influencing what metadata they create, and ongoing projects at Harvard University.

She began by defining metadata within the context of the Harvard Library Digital Initiative: metadata is the information that makes it possible to find, access, use, and manage information resources. This definition is broad and includes non-electronic resources as well as other kinds of information needed to manage and access resources. Metadata can also be categorized based on the function it supports. The most common types are descriptive, administrative, and structural, but the boundaries are fuzzy and some metadata falls into more than one category.

Cataloging records are an example of the descriptive or intellectual metadata. This category includes traditional MARC records and also archival finding aids, museum registrars' files, etc. Descriptive metadata supports discovery and identification of resources. It is often public information, information worth sharing outside of institutional boundaries. MARC and AACR2 have served the library community well, but other communities have their own standards, such as Categories for Description of Works of Art, the Content Standard for Digital Geospatial Metadata, and the Visual Resources Association Core Categories. The Dublin Core was specifically designed to cross community boundaries and promote sharing of resources.

The second category is administrative metadata that supports the management of the resource. It can be used to determine who is allowed to use the resource and under what conditions, and who has permission to alter or delete the resource and so on. Because these have been seen as primarily local functions, there has been less pressure for standards. However this is changing; publishers' groups are actively investigating standard ways of expressing information about licensing and access rights as we move into electronic commerce.

The third major category is structural metadata, information that ties the components of a complex resource together and makes the whole useable. It may include information that supports navigation among the components of a work; for example, jumping to a particular chapter or page or switching between images and linked text.

Over the past three decades, libraries have been creating metadata in our integrated library systems. However, certain materials and functions did not fit well into the OPAC model. For example, slides, photographs, finding aids for archival materials, realia and artwork continued to be managed using manual files, as isolated word-processed documents, or in stand-alone systems. These were seen as purely local materials or completely unique items. Standard methods of describing them across institutional boundaries did not seem justified.

Now, however, due to the Internet and greater ease and availability of automation options, more types of library information are becoming available online. Archival findings aids are being converted to machine-readable form and marked up in the Encoded Archival Description format. Visual resources are cataloged with reference to standards such as the VRA Core Categories. We are creating parallel public access systems which supplement our original union catalogs. As more kinds of metadata become available online and specific communities strive to create metadata standards specific to their own needs, Robin sees tension developing between the need to construct metadata and systems that are effective within an institution vs. across institutions.

The rest of Robin's presentation was a show-and-tell demonstration of some interesting projects in which she is involved at Harvard. The first involved structural metadata and was designed to improve access to remote storage journals. Widener library needed to free up significant amounts of shelf space, and they identified 19th century European history journals as likely candidates to be sent off site. These journals had very low use and took up a good bit of space. However, they were not indexed in any Abstracting and Indexing services, and scholars used them by leafing through the volumes one by one. Some alternative form of browsing was needed.

To remedy this situation, the Digital Contents Project was established [6]. The processing staff identifies the table of contents throughout the physical volumes to be transferred and marks them for scanning. They also create structural metadata, tying the scanned images to the logical unit (e.g., volume/issue) and to the bound volumes. The Systems Office uses the metadata to create an interface that allows users to navigate among the table of contents pages for a given journal. Processing staff adds the URL for a title's TOC to the catalog record. Professors seem generally happy with this system. They can browse and recall obscure material in the comfort of their homes and offices.

The second project she demonstrated is the Visual Information Access System, which was designed to provide public access to images and objects in material culture and social history [7]. Within the Harvard system, there are many libraries, archives, and museums which hold these visual resources, and there is tremendous diversity in local cataloging practices. Many of the repositories maintain their own local systems to which there is little public access. One of the obstacles to providing a public union catalog of visual resources was the lack of a commonly agreed upon set of data elements and a way to communicate them which would support interoperability of metadata from different repositories.

The bulk of the contents of the project will come from study collections of images: visual documents or surrogates of objects. Traditional descriptive methods for library holdings have never dealt well with multiple versions of a particular item. The expression of this kind of relationship is a critical need for visual resource collections. Robin showed us a record for a self-portrait by Van Gogh. The painting was described and the record contained a series of links and descriptions for various surrogates which included slides of details of the face, the head, etc. Her handouts included print screens from the site.

The group working on the project had to agree on a common set of data elements, a record structure, and an encoding syntax. They chose a three-tier hierarchical metadata structure, in which groups of works, works, and surrogates could each be described. A task group defined a common set of data elements which can occur at any level of the hierarchy. The Systems Office developed an XML Document Type Definition for the syntax.

The last project Robin discussed was the Harvard union catalog of finding aids, OASIS or Online Archival Search Information System. The system currently contains approximately 150 of 14,000 finding aids, so there is a good bit of work to be done. The major obstacle to the development of the standards necessary to make finding aids work better in a retrieval environment is their duel nature as data and metadata. The archive community sees finding aids as documents in their own right; historical and contextual information is often created as part of writing a finding aid and its integrity should be preserved. However, if the Encoded Archival Description is viewed as a mechanism for supporting online retrieval, it needs to be open to changes such as authority control. Robins feels that archivists' concerns about the integrity of the finding aids as documents could be addressed by using different versions or editions, thus striking a balance between fluid cataloging records and the fixed nature of publications.

Now that we have all these separate catalogs, how can we help users navigate among them to find relevant materials? Robin feels that Harvard is building Stu's individual LEGOS but they are not fitting together yet. She sees two approaches to this "fit": cross system searching or issuing a single search across multiple databases, and explicit links or pointers to related metadata in different systems.

At Harvard, various kinds of descriptive metadata are created in different departments, by staff with different kinds of training, and with reference to different standards. There is little interaction between staff from various repositories. As more metadata becomes accessible online, the discrepancies become more visible while the relationships between them remain unclear. Making our resources more available will require staff members with a clear understanding of how the work we do relates to the work of others.

The discussion period focused on technical issues. When asked if OCLC's SiteSearch could be used to search both an OPAC and separate local databases with one search, Robin replied that it is not easy to do that yet. She also noted that the only integrated library system vendor that is incorporating metadata is Endeavor.

NOTES

1. "Dublin Core Metadata Initiative," [Internet, WWW], ADDRESS: http: //purl.org/ dc/

2. "The Z39.50 cross-domain attribute set," [Internet, WWW], ADDRESS: http:// www.oclc.org/~levan/docs/crossdomainattribureset.html

3. "CORC: Cooperative Online Resource Catalog," [Internet, WWW], ADDRESS: http: //purl.oclc.org/corc/

4. Additional metadata resource sites:
"Metadata: Subject Guide to International Metadata Resources," [Internet, WWW], ADDRESS: http: //www2.sub.uni-goettingen.de/metaguide/index.html; IFLA, "Digital libraries: metadata resources." [Internet, WWW], *http://www.ifla.org/II/metadata.htm*; National Library of Australia, "Meta Matters." http: //www.nla.gov.au/meta

5. Digital Systems Technology Center, "HotMeta," [Internet, WWW], http:// www.dstc.edu.au/Research/Projects/hotmeta/search.html

6. Harvard University Library, 1999, "Library Digital Initiative, Digital Contents Pilot Project (DCPP)" [Internet, WWW], http: //hul.harvard.edu/ldi/html/ dcpp.html

7. Harvard University, 1999, "Visual Information Access Catalog" [Internet, WWW], http: //via.harvard.edu:748/html/VIA.html; about the project: "Visual resources at Harvard University: Task Group Report, May 30, 1997," 1997, [Internet, WWW], http: //www.peabody.harvard.edu/VRTG/report.html; Harvard University Library, "Library Digital Initiative: VIA," 1999, [Internet, WWW], http: //hul.harvard. edu/ldi/html/via.html; specifically about the metadata: Harvard University Library, "Library Digital Initiative: Metadata in VIA," [Internet, WWW], http: //hul.harvard. edu/ ldi/html/via_metadata.html

Scenario Building: Creating Your Library's Future

Nancy Rea
Stacey Aldrich

Presenters

Jill Emery

Recorder

SUMMARY. This session consisted of an introduction to scenario planning, the process of projecting a hypothetical future, and planning for it. The meeting's facilitators provided historical and contextual information, and then facilitated a series of small group projects in which participants projected a future and planned for it. *[Article copies available for a fee from The Haworth Document Delivery Service: 1-800-342-9678. E-mail address: getinfo@haworthpressinc.com <Website: http://www.haworthpressinc.com>]*

Nancy Rea is Staff Development Coordinator, Anne Arundel County Public Library.

Stacey Aldrich is Public Library Consultant, Maryland State Department of Education/Division of Library Development and Services.

Cheryl Riley, session convener, is Serials Librarian at Central Missouri State University.

Jill Emery is Collections and Acquisitions Specialist, University of Texas at Arlington Libraries.

[Haworth co-indexing entry note]: "Scenario Building: Creating Your Library's Future." Emery, Jill. Co-published simultaneously in *The Serials Librarian* (The Haworth Press, Inc.) Vol. 38, No. 1/2, 2000, pp. 15-21; and: *From Carnegie to Internet2: Forging the Serials Future* (ed: P. Michelle Fiander, Joseph C. Harmon, and Jonathan David Makepeace) The Haworth Press, Inc., 2000, pp. 15-21. Single or multiple copies of this article are available for a fee from The Haworth Document Delivery Service [1-800-342-9678, 9:00 a.m. - 5:00 p.m. (EST). E-mail address: getinfo@haworthpressinc.com].

THE SETTING

This pre-conference session was held in the Singleton Room, a crow's nest of sorts, located at the top of one of the Engineering Departments at Carnegie Mellon University. Four tables were arranged in a semi-circle with five to six people at each table. In the center of each table was a basket of developmental toys to help establish group dynamics and a creative presence. Each table was also equipped with folders for all participants, colored squares of paper, scented markers and an easel stand with paper to facilitate taking notes as a group. The setting and arrangement of the room set the stage for the day's activities, especially the creative processes integral to Scenario Building.

Facilitator Cheryl Riley began the day by introducing session instructors Nancy Rea and Stacey Aldrich, consultants experienced in scenario planning. Both women contributed to "Maryland Libraries in the 21st Century: Scenarios for the New Millennium" (1996), which includes vision and planning statements for the Maryland public libraries. Aldrich and Rea described the work they did in Maryland, thereby providing an orientation to the topic of our workshop. Next, we were given a moment to look through the folders we had been given. Each folder contained a scenario building worksheet that defined terms; outlined steps in the scenario building process; and provided a rationale for the scenario building process.

SCENARIO BUILDING: WHAT IS IT?

Scenario planning or building is an alternative to strategic planning. Instead of finding strategic ways to continue what a library has always done, scenario planning allows a planning team to "suppose" or predict a future and see how their library can meet the needs of that future. Another way to think of scenario building is as a process of developing stories about the future and planning for this future. Plans for any given scenario must include all aspects of the scenario and should be developed for a five-year period. The steps involved in scenario building are:

- Identify a process, department, or situation.
- Identify current trends and/or developments likely to have a future impact on the process, department, or situation.

- Predict what this process, department, or situation will look like in the future, based on the impact of the trends identified.
- Of the trends identified, choose the two most important, and ensure that each is fairly specific–it's not helpful to work with very broad ideas.
- Construct a matrix to represent four outcomes of the scenario.

PREDICTING THE FUTURE–A PRACTICE RUN

Before beginning our daylong project, we were asked to practice predicting the future by imagining news headlines for June 10, 2020. The results among groups were surprisingly similar and included: Episode 9 of Star Wars Opening Tonight! Manned Mission to Mars Completed! Human Genome Project Completed! Cure for AIDS Discovered! Chelsea Clinton–Next US President of the United States! Canada, The Newest State!

We learned from this exercise that we could identify issues and trends from our present and project their future development. The basis of scenario planning, then, is to identify important current trends and issues and project how these trends and issues will change our futures. Both Rea and Aldrich were pleased with the results of the first exercise and were ready to lead us on to the practice of scenario planning. They said that while we would not come away from our session with a perfect scenario, we would learn the process of scenario planning.

OUR TEST SCENARIO: SERIALS LIBRARIANSHIP 20 YEARS FROM NOW

Our scenario building project began with a question: What is the state of serials librarianship in twenty years? Next each group member identified trends and developments s/he felt would change serials' librarianship in the future; we then eliminated duplicates within each group and among groups to finally arrive at a concise list of trends. Some of the trends identified at each table were: copyright; octopus mergers; more serials than monographs; universal access to some resources; search engines as part of every database; lack of standards;

full-text resources; distance education; the demise of ALA; consortia; outsourcing of core services; digital archiving; EDI; cost; professional staff and classified staff duties move closer together; artificial intelligence and expert systems; inconsistencies between print and electronic versions of resources; publish or perish; and many others.

Each group reported the trends it identified and posted them on a large piece of parachute silk sprayed with adhesive so that the paper would stick to it. If a group was presenting a trend that was already posted, they were asked to place it over or near the trend that already existed. The whole group was asked to narrow the trends down to the most important five. We were asked to vote for five trends we each felt would have the most significant impact on our scenario by placing colored dots on our choices. The top trends identified at this point were: direct services from publishers to end-users, archiving/back-files, full-text, lack of standards, broader resource sharing, artificial intelligence and expert systems, inconsistency between print and electronic versions of resources, privatization, publish or perish dilemma–associated with tenure, consortia, technology, and who controls publication.

To further narrow our scope and ultimately identify the top two trends, we first counted the number of colored dots on each sheet and identified the top four trends. The top four trends were who controls publication (10 votes); archiving/back-files (10 votes); full-text (10 votes); and technology (16 votes). We were then asked to place red dots next to the ones we felt were most critical. An almost three-way tie resulted between who controls publication, technology and full-text. A lengthy discussion ensued. Some felt that technology was too broad to be characterized as a trend, others felt that full-text was too narrow a focus. Aldrich and Rea noted that narrowing the trends is often the hardest part of scenario building, and continued to mediate and coach us through this process. Eventually, the group decided to narrow the topic of technology down to access issues; the issue of access was then narrowed to the electronic delivery of information. The two trends were finally established as who controls publication and the electronic delivery of information.

At this point, we were asked as a group to identify oppositional aspects of these two trends. For instance, with respect to electronic delivery of information, we noted the following set of aspects: free versus paid for, particular location versus remote access, instant availability versus delayed availability, universal versus proprietary, pull versus push, mediated versus unmediated. The oppositional aspects of who controls publications were author versus publisher, non-profit versus for profit, author versus consumer, government versus business, copyright versus not copyrighted, reviewed versus not reviewed, and scholarly versus popular. We then narrowed down the oppositional aspects of the trends to two and the results for who controls publishing were authors versus publishers. For the electronic delivery of information, we chose the oppositional aspects of mediated versus unmediated access.

We then put these oppositional aspects of our trends on a grid. The x-axis was defined between authors and publishers, while the y-axis went from mediated to unmediated information to look like the following:

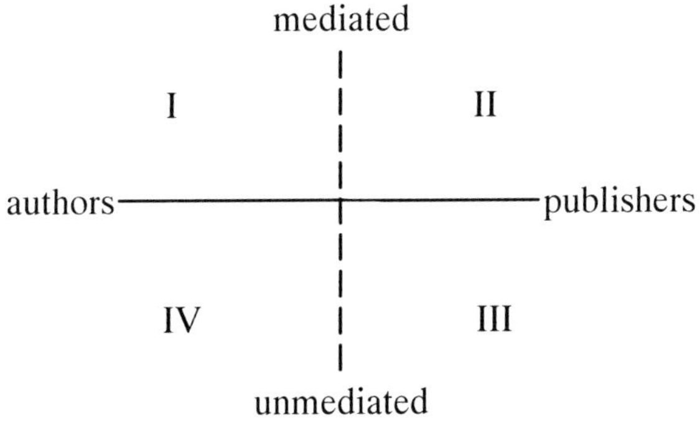

We were then asked to re-form into our original groups to go through the last steps of the exercise. Aldrich and Rea assigned a quadrant to each group. We were asked to define what each scenario might be comprised of, the trigger events that led up to this scenario, what strategies we would need to develop to survive in this particular scenario and what we would name this scenario.

The first group named themselves "Partners in Crime." Their scenario consisted of authors in control of their work with information being mediated. They defined their trigger events to be: publish or perish dies in 2010, a new Bern Convention assigns copyright to authors in 2019, and the first pre-print archive was established in 1992. This group felt that libraries in this scenario would be creating and marketing services for their patrons, increasing their subject specialization, mediating between the content and the users, partnering with the faculty/authors, and assuming the role of packaging, dissemination and archiving of information.

The second group named themselves "Back to the Future." Their scenario consisted of mediated information being controlled by publishers. They defined their trigger events to be: Copyright Laws change and place restrictions on "fair use" in 2005, technology develops to allow for more pay per view in 2001, and tenure requirements become stricter in 2010. This group felt that libraries in this scenario would be trying to find new funding models, developing knowledge systems to refine and focus use by patrons on true relevancies, depending more on abstracting services, and developing the skills of staff.

The third group named themselves "Stand and Deliver: the Development of the Information Hub." The scenario that they were grappling with consisted of unmediated access to information being produced by publishers. Their trigger events were defined as: tenure process requires publishing in top-tier publications by 2002; publishers cut a deal with the entire campus for exclusive rights to information developed there in 2005–an arrangement along the lines of the Pepsi® or Coke® arrangements today; and centralized libraries are deemed redundant in 2010. This group saw libraries as having to prove their worth through marketing, outreach and having a positive impact on the bottom line, educating the community about the economics of information and transforming the library into an information hub which controls, manages, educates and advises.

Group four named themselves "From Chaos to Consultancy." Their scenario consisted of having authors in control of all unmediated information. The trigger events they identified were: in 2001 free software is developed that allows authors to self-publish documents that are self-indexing and automatically coded for electronic delivery; desktop publishing companies flourish to assist authors with quality control, since peer-review is falling apart in 2005; also in 2005, Reed, Bowker, Elsevier, and Disney are sold to Amazon.com; in 2010 ALA disbands and NASIG becomes WAIC (World Association of Information Consultants); and in 2012 Amazon.com is sold to everything.com. The strategies they developed for libraries to survive were: libraries work with author co-ops, tenure is replaced by continuous employment contracts, libraries become personalized collections of information managed by information consultants, who are loosely federated former librarians who have joined together in private practice. This group also identified some robust strategies for libraries including the replacement of re-con projects with digitization projects, oracle type databases dominant, and information consultants replace librarians, as we know them.

CONCLUSION

In conclusion, each group recognized the following to be important in the future for serial librarianship: education of library patrons concerning publishing options and economic models; libraries must become closer partners with their universities, publishers and societies; libraries need to become micro-managers of information; and finally, libraries need to become the exclusive delivery agent for their campuses. The group liked the term "information hub" and decided that we must learn how to provide information better, faster, and cheaper to our end users. Also noted was the strong emphasis on marketing and outreach by each group. Despite the fact that each group worked with different scenarios, many of the strategies developed were the same.

Overall, Aldrich and Rea felt our scenario planning had been successful and complimented us on a planning session that ended up being well-developed and well-executed. All of the participants were enthusiastic about the exercises and the results. Someone asked how effectively this type of planning would work at everyone's respective institutions. Most of the participants felt that this type of planning could positively impact their libraries and would like to see it attempted. At this point, the morning drew to a close and lunch was served.

PLENARY SESSIONS

Moving the Network Revolution in Knowledge Management Beyond Random Acts of Progress

William Graves

Presenter

Bud Sonka

Recorder

SUMMARY. The Internet is a revolution in both human communications and resource sharing. Online interaction with ideas and other people is amplifying the effectiveness and reach of learned and learning communities. But for today's random acts of progress to evolve into systematic institutional and national progress, leaders will have to focus on technologies and professional methodologies that are scalable, manageable, and affordable. Efforts such as the Internet2 Project and the Instructional Management Systems Project have recognized the need for collective investment and action in these areas. This session reports and demonstrates recent, systematic progress that is global in scale. *[Article copies available for a fee from The Haworth Document Delivery Service: 1-800-342-9678. E-mail address: getinfo@haworthpressinc.com <Website: http://www.haworthpressinc.com>]*

William Graves is President, Collegis Research Institute and Chairman and Founder of Eduprise.com.

Bud Sonka is Head of Serial and Electronic Resources, National University Library System in San Diego, CA.

[Haworth co-indexing entry note]: "Moving the Network Revolution in Knowledge Management Beyond Random Acts of Progress." Sonka, Bud. Co-published simultaneously in *The Serials Librarian* (The Haworth Press, Inc.) Vol. 38, No. 1/2, 2000, pp. 25-30; and: *From Carnegie to Internet2: Forging the Serials Future* (ed: P. Michelle Fiander, Joseph C. Harmon, and Jonathan David Makepeace) The Haworth Press, Inc., 2000, pp. 25-30. Single or multiple copies of this article are available for a fee from The Haworth Document Delivery Service [1-800-342-9678, 9:00 a.m. - 5:00 p.m. (EST). E-mail address: getinfo@haworthpressinc.com].

GLOBAL ONLINE REVOLUTION

The Internet as information highway has become an outmoded concept. Libraries and their parent institutions must recognize the Web as a global learning infrastructure, which is a revolution in human communication and resource sharing. The communication revolutions following the advent of print and television did not change the dynamics of learning. Libraries must join in the redefinition of their parent institutions as learning communities rather than learned communities. Global reach is a two-edged sword. Your institution can reach other audiences, but the other institutions can reach your audience. This is more competitive, which is healthy.

The Web is changing campus learning communities from teaching-driven, vertical communities based on specific disciplines such as math and science to learning-driven, horizontal communities based on technology that provides just-in-time information. The aggregation of campus forces into a jointly accessible Website results from acceptance of the principle that research is learning. Some traditional academic freedoms must be compromised to merge different disciplines with different missions within the technological limitations of the Internet.

Education is in pretty good shape. More than seventy percent of all institutions of higher learning are using the Internet, and many have virtual university strategies. Society expects higher education to become more flexible in its course and curriculum offerings in order to meet the new educational needs of a learning society. Rapid changes in academic disciplines, along with rapid growth in the volume of the overall knowledge base, are fueling an increasing emphasis on lifelong learning and learning to earn. These changes, along with the rapid growth in the volume of the overall knowledge base, are driving the need for continuing education throughout a lifetime.

Most students now express tightly focused, self-selected learning objectives as consumers of instruction. This is especially the case with nontraditional learners and lifelong learners who may have legitimate educational needs not easily accommodated by either the time and place constraints of traditional, campus-based study or the time constraints of multiple-year degree offerings.

Society also expects higher education to link its curriculum offerings, its research agendas, and its public service offerings more closely to social and economic needs. These increased expectations of flexibility and relevance come at a time when new political and economic forces are making it increasingly difficult to sustain historic financial commitments to higher education. These changes dictate that the leaders in higher education optimize the collective investment in the educational constructs of the virtual university, which can both increase access to instruction and maintain the quality of learning while also containing overall instructional costs.

RANDOM ACTS OF PROGRESS

We are at that stage today when most colleges and universities are trying to build their own solutions, introducing information technology into the curriculum as an enabling tool, whether it's focused on enhancing the traditional classroom or offering instruction entirely online at a distance. Many institutions are repeating the mistake made years ago when administrative systems were automated. As we have learned, it's not just technology. It's chiefly about restructuring practices and processes.

What doesn't work so well is the idea that enough technology thrown over the transom to faculty members will result in an initiative that pays off. By and large, ad hoc, project-by-project, bottom-up activities do not work at the institutional level. Instructors and departments are creating their own Web pages without much thought for the institutional implications of these random acts of progress. Students may have to learn different interfaces for different courses and another for administrative functions. Random acts of progress need to be converted into planned progress. As a foundation for strategies to improve the quality of student learning and the convenience of instruction, institutions need to create a coherent and manageable instructional and institutional presence on the Web.

TRANSFORMATION TO LEARNING INFRASTRUCTURE

A new metaphor is needed to replace the old model of the learned teacher instructing the student. Instead, learning may be seen as an expedition, with faculty as guides, who draw maps of where to go in pursuit of new knowledge. We need a transformation from a teaching infrastructure to a learning infrastructure. What's missing on the Web is the face-to-face experience of the on-campus experience, but there is no absolute in educational quality. The old Oxford model of one tutor for one student is just not affordable in a democracy dedicated to affordable educational opportunity. Even the classroom model will diminish because of the spectrum of possibilities the Web provides.

There is more to exploiting the Web than organizing resources and guiding self-study. What's missing is the shared social construction of knowledge. At its best this shared construction is what classroom discussion is about. We're not lecturing at students or simply delivering knowledge to them; we are engaging collectively with them in their discovery of knowledge. It is important to simulate this engagement if we are going to instruct on the Web, particularly if we are going to instruct entirely on the Web and not have any classrooms at all.

We must take advantage of the Web as a communications revolution. Faculty must move beyond their fear that all teaching will be done online, that instructors will disappear from the equation and with them the human communication we all value. Perhaps teachers experienced the same fear when libraries were first built. In spite of all the knowledge now captured in a library, faculty continue to play an important role in education that goes well beyond giving students a map to the library.

The convenience of the Web outweighs the losses. Today people are interested in getting job skills, in getting training, in adult education; and they can't afford the traditional residential experience on campus. That is where this new technology is promising increased access to education.

LEARNING EVOLUTION

The Web has become today's primary window onto a range of new communications possibilities, organized principally by shared interest and only secondarily, if at all, by proximity in time or place. Nowhere are the constraints of time and place more noticeable than in today's classrooms on the same campuses that were the birthplace of the anytime, anyplace Internet. Resistance to change contributes to this phenomenon. Computers and the network infrastructure, like telephones and telephone networks, must be personally accessible to all constituencies to be useful. Campus-based networks connecting offices, classrooms, libraries, and labs must be expanded to provide remote access for off-campus users.

We have to realize when we talk about the future that higher education today is not a one-size-fits-all enterprise. There is a very valid notion of the eighteen to twenty-year-old coming to the campus as part of growing up. It's the idea of a general education, of a liberal education, of learning to work together, of being exposed to new ideas in an intimate, seminar-like way, and of the melting-pot socialization that takes place among students outside the classroom. But that's not what is happening. Today's large lecture halls don't provide that experience. But it is the ideal, and there will likely continue to be demand for that kind of experience. Graves' fear is that the tax-paying public will not support the idea. Legislatures will back away from funding public higher education, and that ideal, residential, liberal educational model will be accessible only to the rich.

Liberal education will survive and be improved in the presence of the new technologies. There are lots of other forms of educational change to consider. We all know the demographics tell us that nontraditional education, or adult education, is growing in proportion to more traditional forms of education. Technology will play a major role in providing that kind of education. Convenience is another key concept. A lot of us use technology because it's convenient. People will be looking for education with convenience, not with brand names or any other attribute, in mind.

We are preparing our students for a productive life in the next century. They will need online literacy to navigate the networks and to find the information and knowledge needed to express themselves, publish information, and communicate.

The key principles for the future will be:

- Online literacy: It has become one of the Three Rs.
- Universal access: Students, faculty, and staff have to be online literate and must be able to access the network almost any time and any place.
- Standards: Equipment, software, and training must be standardized because your tech support can only support so much.
- Life-cycle funding: Computers and other equipment need to be upgraded every three years; software needs to be upgraded frequently; funding agencies need to budget for that.
- Strategic investing: Forty to fifty percent of your enrollments are in a dozen or so of your courses; one percent of your courses are

generating almost half of your enrollments; start there with your investment in technology for maximum impact.
- Academic intranet: Design for and integrate into the academic community.
- Manage change: Serve the institutional good by planning progress.

RETURN ON INVESTMENT

Technology today is being bolted on top of everything else you do. When you do that you add to costs, and most institutions can't afford to do that. Faculty and instructional support are about seventy-eight percent of the existing costs of education. If you are going to harness technology as an integral part of the institution, you are going to have to do it as part of the transformation of instruction. That is where the money needs to come from. We cannot simply bolt information technology onto existing educational practices, if we expect to extend the reach of higher education's services to meet society's need for flexible, relevant educational services. Today's lecture-dominated, contact-hour model is a one-size-fits-all model, mass produced on an infrastructure of classrooms, chalkboards, and rigid class structures. It is an institution-centered teaching infrastructure, rather than a student-centered learning infrastructure.

Although face-to-face contact between student and instructor will continue to be important under many circumstances, we must selectively abandon the idea that the primary locus for such contact must be the classroom. The old model of the three-hour class can become one hour in class and more time spent in guided research on the Web, along with interaction and discussion through e-mail and Websites.

For institutions to go forward they need to invest in technology, but it needs to be a strategic investment, which means you have to know why you are doing it and how you plan to use the technology. Otherwise you will be managing the investment as a cost, trying to contain it. If you see that investment as a strategic asset, you'll be acting differently on it. You're going to really make the technological investment pay off in the form of a coherent and competitive instructional presence on the Web, a presence that will help secure your institution's role in the emerging knowledge economy.

Information Ecologies

Vicki L. O'Day

SUMMARY. This paper argues that the way we see, think, and talk about technology has consequences for the way we use it. The author observes that we have difficulty bringing critical sensibilities into our evaluation and use of technology; she posits three reasons for this difficulty: the rhetoric of inevitability, the limitations of partial perspectives, and the effects of metaphor. The author proposes paying attention to technology and observing the social practices surrounding its use. One good way of paying attention to technologies and concomitant social practices is to think ecologically. By positing an information ecology, we will provide ourselves with a framework for thinking about and evaluating technology, both within and outside libraries. *[Article copies available for a fee from The Haworth Document Delivery Service: 1-800-342-9678. E-mail address: getinfo@haworthpressinc.com <Website: http://www.haworthpressinc.com>]*

INTRODUCTION

The way we pay attention to technology has consequences for how we use it. In this paper, I consider different ways of seeing, thinking, and talking about technology. In particular, one good way of paying attention to technologies and the social practices that surround their use is to think ecologically. Many of the ideas discussed here are developed further in the book *Information Ecologies* [1], in which

Vicki L. O'Day is affiliated with the University of California, Santa Cruz (E-mail: oday@calterra.com).

[Haworth co-indexing entry note]: "Information Ecologies." O'Day, Vicki L. Co-published simultaneously in *The Serials Librarian* (The Haworth Press, Inc.) Vol. 38, No. 1/2, 2000, pp. 31-40; and: *From Carnegie to Internet2: Forging the Serials Future* (ed: P. Michelle Fiander, Joseph C. Harmon, and Jonathan David Makepeace) The Haworth Press, Inc., 2000, pp. 31-40. Single or multiple copies of this article are available for a fee from The Haworth Document Delivery Service [1-800-342-9678, 9:00 a.m. - 5:00 p.m. (EST). E-mail address: getinfo@haworthpressinc.com].

Bonnie Nardi and I discuss case studies of technology in libraries, schools, hospitals, and other settings. Here, the idea of an information ecology is applied to digital libraries. An expanded version of this discussion appears in *Digital Library Use: Social Practice in Design and Evaluation* [2].

The Internet and digital libraries have had (and continue to have) a profound impact on the tools and practices of librarians. Sources of information, methods for organizing and accessing information, and locations where information is found have been redefined and recombined in novel ways. In general, information is becoming more ubiquitous, more portable, and more networked.

People who use new information technologies and services need to find ways to evaluate and integrate them with imagination and insight. But it is not particularly easy to evaluate technology carefully and thoughtfully, to decide just which new tools we'll leave alone, which tools we want to pick up and use, and how to adapt new tools to the needs of our particular user communities.

Why is it hard to bring critical sensibilities into our evaluation and use of technology? I suggest three reasons and briefly discuss each in turn: the rhetoric of inevitability, the limitations of partial perspectives, and the effects of metaphor.

RHETORIC OF INEVITABILITY

The first difficulty in applying critical sensibilities to technology is that we are surrounded by a "rhetoric of inevitability," in which we hear from well-informed people that technology is either wonderful or awful. So we can choose between uncritical acceptance and total condemnation–but these are not good choices if what we want to do is think reflectively about how to use technology well without being overwhelmed by it.

It is possible to see the rhetoric of inevitability at work in the titles of several recent books, such as *The Road Ahead* [3], *What Will Be* [4], and *Beyond Calculation: The Next Fifty Years of Computing* [5]. Each title implies that the future of technology is known–at least to some people. These books are enthusiastic about the prospect of technological change, but none of them suggests that non-technologists might have a role in shaping it.

Here is an example of the rhetoric of inevitability from one of the articles in *Beyond Calculation*, by Gordon Bell and James Gray. The authors, who are engineers, make this assertion: "By 2047 . . . all information about physical objects, including humans, buildings, processes, and organizations, will be online. This is both desirable and inevitable" [6]. In this formulation, people are considered as objects, just like buildings. There is no invitation to apply our critical sensibilities to the new technological possibilities–to discuss whether and how we would like to have "all information" about ourselves online.

Technophilic and technophobic arguments have one crucial feature in common: They imply that the way technology is designed and used is not something for non-technologists to influence and shape. This is a compelling message, even when we have experience to the contrary. The most effective way to dispute the rhetoric of inevitability is simply to notice it. Watching these rhetorical moves with a critical eye is a good way of disarming them.

PARTIAL PERSPECTIVES

A second factor that complicates an engaged, imaginative process of evaluating technology is the problem of partial perspectives. People see different sides of technology and social practice, depending on their positions. Sometimes the work of some people is quite invisible to others.

Here is an example of partial perspectives from a library setting. In 1993, as part of a study of reference library practices at Hewlett-Packard's corporate library, I interviewed several clients of library services [7]. One client's work was analyzing business processes for Hewlett-Packard. He was a regular and very satisfied user of the library, and he usually interacted with the same librarian. Here is his description of his interactions:

> Let's say . . . we need to study quick response logistics, quick response team management programs. So I say, 'All right, let me go out and do a little research and find out some names that tend to come up.' . . . So I will go to Joan and I'll say, 'Joan, here is what we are studying, it is quick response logistics. Now let's make that a sort word. Now the problem with it, it's sometimes maybe considered to be a fairly new phrase, so what could be some of the components. So look under supply chain manage-

> ment. Look under order fulfillment. Look under inventory management. Look at it under logistic partnerships. Look under blah blah.' You know, all types of things like that. Usually I want fairly current data, so I will typically cut it off at 1990 or something or '91 even, coming forward . . . So it is really that simple, there has been nothing complicated about what I have done with Joan because she knows what I am after, sort of . . . I mean it's not rocket science, that's the whole thing, it is pretty basic. You know the burden is on me to define what it is that I am looking for and if I give Joan the right words. [*From an interview with a library client.*]

I also had an opportunity to interview the librarian referred to here, and not surprisingly, she had a very different characterization of the situation. She knew a great deal about her client's business activities, including the different phases of his projects and the kind of information needs that cropped up in each phase. In fact, she adapted her search strategies to his project lifecycle. She did not describe her interactions with this client as an exchange of "sort words."

Let us consider these different perspectives in light of changing technologies. It seems likely that the client in this story might have a different view of how new technologies should fit into library practice than the librarian might have. Each of these people is immersed in information access activities, but they see the same activities very differently. Paying attention to technology is not just a matter for individuals–it is clear that we need to *share* perspectives, to talk across boundaries of profession and expertise. By doing this, we can learn to see more of the complexity and richness of social practices around technology, and we can do a better job of imagining new ways of working that will really work.

CHOICES OF METAPHOR

A third factor that complicates our critical sensibilities around technology is the powerful effect of metaphor. Metaphors matter. The metaphors we use for technology guide our questions, conversations, and the criteria we set for success.

Each metaphor has something to recommend it–a particular strength to help us see technology in a different way. And of course, each metaphor also leaves something out. If we want to become more involved in active, thoughtful conversations about technology, we need to use language that promotes this kind of involvement. Below, we discuss several common metaphors to see how they work.

Tool metaphor. First, we can consider technology as a tool. This is the most common language we encounter–think about spreadsheets, drawing programs, editing programs, browsers, and e-mail programs. When we talk about a technology as a tool, it leads us to focus on accomplishing tasks and doing work. We talk about the affordances of tools–what they allow us to do. We think of tools as being under the control of their users.

Some of the key concerns that arise with tool-thinking are productivity, usability, skill, and learning. We ask: What does the tool do? Will it make me more efficient? Can it be used easily? Some of the questions that do not come up when we talk about tools are those that span broader social, organizational, and political contexts.

Assistant metaphor. Another way to think about technology is as an assistant. We often see this metaphor used in advertisements. The idea here is to visualize technology not as a material object, but as an agent that acts on your behalf while you're busy doing more important things. It takes over the drudgery of repetitive tasks. A common example is an information search agent, which keeps track of news or other information you'd like to collect on a regular basis.

This metaphor emphasizes key questions such as: Will it do what I want? Is it reliable? What are the lines of accountability? This metaphor tends to keep us focused on individual users and their wants and needs, to the exclusion of other people who might be located in the same physical or online environment.

System metaphor. Sometimes people talk about technology as a system, a complex arrangement of technological and social forces. The work of Jacques Ellul [8], Langdon Winner [9], and Neil Postman [10] follows this line of thinking. For example, a car is a familiar technology, but it is also part of a whole system of roads, gas stations, parking lots, mechanic shops, car insurance, smog checks, and many other aspects of transportation.

Systemic thinking leads us to think about our pervasive involvement with technology. It raises key concerns of technology's autonomy, neutrality, and comprehensibility. Seeing technology as a system encourages large-scale, interconnected thinking.

Questions about systems go beyond particular objects or tools to include the many different relationships they are involved in. We ask questions such as: What are the social implications of a new technology? How can we change the system? Who is responsible for it? Can we control it? These are good questions to ask, but they leave out a sense of locality–local differences and local influences. The strength of systemic thinking is in its broad scope, but if we want to take effective action, we often need to understand technologies very well in *particular*, *local* settings.

Ecology metaphor: We now turn to our metaphor of the information ecology. Bonnie Nardi and I like the ecological metaphor because it raises questions and discussions that other metaphors do not suggest. The idea of an information ecology suggests a particular way of paying attention–the ecology metaphor is good to think with.

Here is our definition of an information ecology: a system of people, technologies, practices, and values in a local setting. Key concerns are the complex interdependencies between tools and social practices and the possibility of diverse local variations and local influences. We believe the ecology metaphor offers more possibilities for local action.

For example, a library is an information ecology, with librarians, clients, books, magazines, computers, comfortable chairs for reading, and a strong value of providing access to information.

A copy shop is an information ecology, with sales assistants, computer experts, walk-in users, a variety of copiers, computers, fax machines, different kinds of paper, tools for working with paper, and a value of making it easy for people to create documents for business and personal use.

We include values because they are rarely discussed, but they are central to understanding what motivates the activities of each information ecology. If we do not ask questions about technology in light of values, it is easy to spend a lot of time and money on technological innovations that don't quite take, because it turns out they're incompatible with some of the basic principles and motivations that are at work. The way we think about this is knowing *why*, as well as knowing *how*. It is easy to dive straight into know-how discussions, and talking about values helps us remember to ask know-why questions, too.

CHARACTERISTICS OF BIOLOGICAL ECOLOGIES

There are four main characteristics of biological ecologies that we want to pay attention to in information ecologies: diversity, keystone species, locality, and coevolution. Each of these gives us ways to open our eyes and see technology in new ways. We now consider each of these ecological characteristics in turn, to see how they can help us pay attention to digital libraries in useful ways.

Diversity. Ecologies are full of different species in different niches. In an information ecology, we should not be focusing on one or two roles or one or two tools. It does not help when we talk about "the user," as if there was only one, or when we lump "users" together as if people are all doing the same thing. Any technology is used in a variety of ways, and any person engages with a variety of technologies. What would it mean to think about diversity in digital libraries? Here are some of the questions we might consider:

- Whose help is needed to make digital libraries work? What new participants might be involved in shaping content and access?
- Can we imagine new ways of reaching digital library collections, beyond the obvious home pages on the Web?
- What complementary low-tech tools are needed to complement high-tech information access tools?
- What tools or materials will help people move back and forth between the physical and digital worlds as they find and organize their information?

Locality. Another feature of ecologies is locality. Ecologies are bounded–they are not too big. In a biological ecology, we can see how species adapt to their local environment. In information ecologies, it is important to pay attention to how technology works at the local level, looking at the relationships between the particular people, activities, and values found there. Questions that arise from thinking about locality might include:

- How could a digital library collection be customized for the different information ecologies in which is it used?
- How could different digital libraries be assembled together in new ways, to suit the particular needs and interests of distinct information ecologies?

Keystone species. Another feature of ecologies is keystone species. In biological ecologies, there are sometimes species whose contributions are so central to the dynamics of the ecology that without them, the ecology would become very unstable [11]. There are keystone species in information ecologies too. In our view, these are people who fill gaps, make tools work just right for the local setting, and create bridges between people and technologies. Very often, their work is not fully visible to others. Librarians are a good example of a keystone species. So are teachers who enjoy teaching their peers how to develop curriculum using the Internet. We need to look for the keystone species in our information ecologies and make sure they are thriving. The idea of keystone species suggests several questions for digital libraries:

- What new roles can librarians play as information consultants for digital library collections and services?
- What other expert consultants are needed to enhance the experience of people who use digital libraries?

Co-evolution. Finally, we consider co-evolution. Biological species co-evolve with their neighboring species. Changes in one species or in the environment may affect other species. When a new technology is introduced to an information ecology, it is likely to have a ripple effect throughout the environment. We should anticipate mutual adaptations of tools and social practices, and also mutual adaptations of tools and other tools. The idea of co-evolution suggests a variety of questions for digital libraries:

- How can digital library tools take into account and leverage the experience of the reference interview?
- How can reference interviews adapt to accommodate transitions between self-help and assisted searches, without losing context each time?
- How can digital library tools and services adapt to the common pattern of extended, interconnected searches, which may take place over weeks or months?
- What happens to paper? How do new tools work together with old ones?
- How do digital libraries coexist with physical libraries?

CONCLUSION

The aim of this paper has been to show how ecological thinking can generate useful questions and ideas for people who work with digital libraries. The information ecology metaphor is not a new methodology–it is a way of *paying attention*, so we can develop a certain consciousness about technology and its meanings and impacts. It is a language and a set of ideas that can be integrated into different conversations–formal or informal, among people of different professions and expertise. The way we pay attention to technology is consequential. Talking about technology ecologically is a kind of intervention that works against the rhetoric of inevitability.

When we focus on technical features to make decisions about technology, we are likely to miss some of the social interconnections that shape successful practice. The successful adaptation of digital libraries calls for sustained, thoughtful conversations among librarians, publishers, software developers, and other participants in each information ecology.

In *Pilgrim at Tinker Creek,* Annie Dillard writes about the effort it takes to see what is around her:

> Seeing is of course very much a matter of verbalization. Unless I call attention to what passes before my eyes, I simply won't see it. It is, as Ruskin says, 'not merely unnoticed, but in the full, clear sense of the word, unseen.' . . . I have to maintain in my head a running description of the present . . . Otherwise, especially in a strange place, I'll never know what's happening [12].

Technology has led to the creation of some strange and interesting places. As Dillard says, we need to call our attention to what passes before our eyes, so we know what is happening and know how to make our places friendly, useful, and habitable.

NOTES

1. Bonnie A. Nardi and Vicki L. O'Day, *Information Ecologies: Using Technology With Heart* (Cambridge, Mass.: MIT Press, 1999).
2. Vicki L. O'Day and Bonnie A. Nardi, "An ecological perspective on digital libraries," in *Digital Library Use: Social Practice in Design and Evaluation*, ed. Ann Bishop, Barbara Butterfield, and Nancy Van House (Cambridge, Mass.: MIT Press, to appear in 2000).

3. Bill Gates, *The Road Ahead* (New York: Viking, 1995).

4. Michael Dertouzos, *What Will Be: How the New World of Information Will Change Our Lives* (San Francisco: Harper San Francisco, 1997).

5. Peter J. Denning and Robert M. Metcalfe, *Beyond Calculation: The Next Fifty Years of Computing* (New York: Springer-Verlag, 1997).

6. Gordon Bell and James N. Gray, "The revolution yet to happen," in *Beyond Calculation: The Next Fifty Years of Computing*, ed. Peter J. Denning and Robert M. Metcalfe (New York: Springer-Verlag, 1997), 5.

7. Vicki L. O'Day and Robin Jeffries, "Orienteering in an Information Landscape: How Information Seekers Get From Here to There," in *Proceedings of the Conference on Human Factors in Computing Systems* (New York: ACM Press, 1993).

Also, Vicki L. O'Day and Robin Jeffries, "Information Artisans: Patterns of Result Sharing by Information Searchers," in *Proceedings of the Conference on Organizational Computer Systems* (New York: ACM Press, 1993).

8. Jacques Ellul, *The Technological Society* (New York: Vintage Books, 1964).

9. Langdon Winner, *Autonomous Technology: Technics-out-of-Control as a Theme in Political Thought* (Cambridge, Mass.: MIT Press, 1977).

10. Neil Postman, *Technopoly* (New York: Vintage Books, 1993).

11. Edward O. Wilson, *The Diversity of Life* (New York: W.W. Norton and Company, 1992).

12. Annie Dillard, *Pilgrim at Tinker Creek* (New York: Bantam Books, 1974), 32.

Shift Happens: Ten Key Trends in Our Profession and Ten Strategies for Success

Stephen Abram

SUMMARY. A discussion of the future of the information professions, their work, and professional environments. The author identifies ten trends in today's world and ten strategies for success in the future. He explores the impact of these trends on marketing our libraries, our technology and ourselves. *[Article copies available for a fee from The Haworth Document Delivery Service: 1-800-342-9678. E-mail address: getinfo@haworthpressinc.com <Website: http://www.haworthpressinc.com>]*

INTRODUCTION

I once watched a robin build her nest from what was available around my yard. Her choices were interesting. She had lots of material to choose from, but kept picking up the shiny, silver tinsel from our discarded skeleton of a Christmas tree. Her nest was beautiful when done. It was also more cold, and non-absorbent, and she was never

---

Stephen Abram, MLS, is Vice President, Product Management at Micromedia Limited, an IHS Group Company in Toronto, Ontario, Canada. He recently completed a term on the SLA International Board of Directors from 1996-1999 and chaired the Association Public Relations and Strategic Planning Committees (E-mail: sabram@micromedia.on.ca).

[Haworth co-indexing entry note]: "Shift Happens: Ten Key Trends in Our Profession and Ten Strategies for Success." Abram, Stephen. Co-published simultaneously in *The Serials Librarian* (The Haworth Press, Inc.) Vol. 38, No. 1/2, 2000, pp. 41-59; and: *From Carnegie to Internet2: Forging the Serials Future* (ed: P. Michelle Fiander, Joseph C. Harmon, and Jonathan David Makepeace) The Haworth Press, Inc., 2000, pp. 41-59. Single or multiple copies of this article are available for a fee from The Haworth Document Delivery Service [1-800-342-9678, 9:00 a.m. - 5:00 p.m. (EST). E-mail address: getinfo@haworthpressinc.com].

able to successfully get her eggs to hatch. One of the morals of this story: Sometimes that which we find attracts us is not necessarily what's best for the purpose. Perhaps adopting the latest shiny technologies for our libraries and users isn't the best way to incubate knowledge and encourage the best behaviours in either society or organizations.

Let's learn from our past experiences. For example, we can ask ourselves that if one of the real end-user benefits of the information-based CD-ROM is its portability, then how portable are the CDs in library collections? Usually, but not always, there's precious little portability left after a library has got a hold of these resources. And, when we look to DVD to solve our problems with the limited storage capacity of CD, we still hit walls. DVD may be a possible solution but it's unlikely to succeed. We could acknowledge that the long-term trend is that Moore's Law of storage capacity has now been transferred to bandwidth. Why then would we would want to invest heavily in an emerging technology like DVD, which will be surpassed by distant server-based products, which can be updated more frequently and enjoy equal performance? Indeed, the entire DVD technology has been driven by the needs of movies over much else–in the same way that CD-ROM was driven by the needs of music. Wiring may drive bandwidth but does anyone actually believe that the cable, copper and glass fiber-wiring infrastructure so conscientiously built over the past century will survive the onslaught of high bandwidth, wireless technologies? Whither CD-ROM in the world of cheap or free lap/palmtops wirelessly connected to the next generation Web infrastructure through PCS wireless links? Add to this the strong trend towards enterprise and consortia content acquisition, where information users can opt-in to several pools of content through membership, enrolment, or employment, and you have the knowledge-based society, seamlessly connected to oceans of information with no need to consider alternative delivery formats. Are libraries well prepared to deal with more change and more changing technologies? Is there better positioning for the skills of librarians and information access professionals?

Rushing to adopt shiny new technologies may do nothing to forward librarians or our institutions towards our goals. Of course, we can still see a secure place for CD in the future and the transitional technologies of special drives and towers will bridge the gap. However, some library technology trends are emerging as we move into the next phase of our future. We need to acknowledge from our learning with CD-ROM experiences that long-term technological stability is a chimera. For those of us who build our library's technology and services we find that we must be mindful of the global trends or we may back ourselves into a corner, far from the mainstream of society. Below are some of my thoughts on current trends. Some may not be the most important trends since *shift happens*–but they're what's occupying my thoughts today and I want to explore in this article what impact they may have on marketing our libraries, our technology and ourselves. There is a distinct emphasis below on making the nest warm and not going for the shiny stuff too fast.

TRENDS

Trend #1: The Pace of Change Is Too Slow!

At a recent conference of information industry CEOs, the executives said that their biggest challenge was that they felt that their organizations were "boldness challenged." They explicitly felt that they weren't introducing change *fast enough*! They felt that their organizations needed to adopt more modern team strategies to involve customers in the process of rapid change, which accompanies most products of the information industry. Such involvement, the CEOs thought, would engender trust between the information industry and its clients. In the information industry, speed is an issue, and the introduction of continuous change in products and services is the norm.

What does this mean to us? Well, for one, it means that the products and services we market to our clients and users are likely to mutate from day-to-day, in both small and big ways. The ability of suppliers and purchasers to communicate these changes quickly and broadly will be difficult, if not impossible. The days of having years between Dialog I and Dialog II, or a year or more between new releases/updates of CD-ROM software are gone. Monthly and daily updates, changes and improvements to interfaces, content and terms are likely and, often, desirable. Web culture not only encourages rapid change it often demands it. As a cultural precept of the new knowledge society this presents us with some real challenges.

Trend #2: Education Is Out–Learning Is In

When did we stop calling it learning? Think about it in terms of technology and marketing. Education is something done "to" people while learning is something that people do for themselves. Indeed in many ways technology is something we also do "to" people.

When I think about marketing our technology in the "learning" context, rather than a systems or content context, I start to think about marketing a learning environment. Marketing the environment, and making the technology and content secondary, highlights what librarians create, rather than making us shills for the products we purchase. We create learning environments, and anything that doesn't enhance learning or gets in the way of learning is "bad." This perspective can drive training and orientation strategies that are holistic and based in long-term literacy skills, rather than being purely training for individual applications and products. It also makes choices related to content and interfaces easier to make.

Trend #3: The Next Generation Is Largely Composed of Next-Heads

Librarians usually are not Next-Heads; we tend to be Text-Heads. We all know that physical books stopped dominating in or around 1990 in terms of revenue and unit sales. Today the printed text represents only a small fraction of all stored data and information and, in some markets like business, it represents a very small portion of content acquisition budgets. However, de-emphasizing text has driven a further change that we need to explicitly acknowledge–the dominance of educated persons who decode and internalize "text" well is ending.

Recognizing that there are many different kinds and mixes of intelligence and learning styles, we need to be aware that text-based collection development is becoming just one tool for serving our emerging markets well. Many libraries use software like iKIOSK and Fortres to ensure that information applications like e-mail, chat, multimedia, Real-Audio, RealVideo, streaming video, and more are not accessible on public access terminals. This policy ensures that only "serious" applications are available without compromising system performance. As we move into the future, we'll have to remember that information will be coming in many ways and our traditional preference and respect for text-based information will need to be reviewed and balanced with the market's needs. The rule of introducing these emerging technologies is to match the technology to the user's needs and styles–not the provider's or intermediary's comfort level.

Trend #4: The Next Generation Is What It Needs to Be and Nothing Less

As it ages, each generation develops a culture of generational doom. In ancient Greece, Socrates bemoaned the lack of respect the younger generation had for learning; and Shakespeare wrote: "Thou hast most traitorously corrupted the youth of the realm in erecting a grammar school." The coming generations will have been trained through many means to adapt information differently. Think computer games. Their ability to enter a "problem set" virtually and solve the problem through multivariate paths, stored clues, and information prepares them well for entering bodies of "information" with problems to solve and decisions to make using three-dimensional interfaces. Play Zelda, Myst or whatever and you'll know what I mean. Apply the same navigation paradigm to a file of spreadsheets and it's amazing what insights can emerge. Topographic style interfaces like Cartia (www.cartia.com), while at first causing a level of discomfort, actually allow the user to enter an unknown body of information in a thoughtful way. In marketing technologies, we need to acknowledge our own prejudices and then respect the fact that the clients' abilities may be informed in a way ours are not.

Trend #5: Change Cannot Be Managed Generationally Anymore

Change now cycles in a hamster's life span–less than three years. In this environment, we can't expect the education system to prepare fully formed leaders, employees and citizens for the future–it just can't.

For one, anyone who has successfully completed a program of study is back at square one in about five years, unless, of course, they have developed a habit or predilection for continuous learning. For another the Boomers are, figuratively, this "pig-in-the-snake," by which I mean they represent demographically a big clump of workers needing regular re-treading on a very large scale. As marketers of technology combined with content and an environment for learning, we are well tooled and equipped to be the gurus for the "knowledge ecology." Someone needs to ensure that the environment for continuous learning is managed well. But, this is not enough. Someone also needs to communicate that this resource exists to ensure people remain successful. This will be a key role of information professionals–to create awareness of the impact that can be made on the individual who participates in the information environments we create.

Trend #6: Virtual Is a Place Not a Format

Perception is reality–if you believe something exists then you will act on that belief. Generally, most adults cannot separate belief from perception. It is clear that for information professionals and librarians, "virtuality" will dominate as an environment. Many consumers in our markets now believe that information is free, that everything's on the Web and that physical access to any information of value is now possible from home in your pajamas. The role of marketing, and the sacred trust for professional librarians, is that we must begin to introduce the truth about this situation to our users and, sometimes, our decision-makers. If we don't, we run the risk of allowing a massively transformational technology like the WWW to actually decrease intelligence in society. We run the risk of encouraging a new Dark Age. Previous transformational technologies have been the telephone and television. I leave it up to you to decide if their introduction increased intelligence in society or not. Are we serving our enterprises or society by simply championing AltaVista or Edgar, for example, at the desktop?

Trend #7: Communities of Interest Are No Longer Bounded by Geography

Most institutional structures will evolve but many will disappear. If you define yourself or your role in the context of your institutions (university libraries, public libraries, community information centers), without a strong understanding and communication of your role in that environment, then your position and place are at risk. In marketing terms, focus your efforts on what you can do well and sacrifice the benign, inadequate, or unaffordable. For example, the emerging strong trend towards distance education will not destroy every traditional educational institution but it will hurt some; new organizations will emerge while others will disappear. The role of some libraries as community centers will decline if people find networks of like-minded individuals through the Web to which they have stronger ties than those they have to their local neighborhoods. If you rely on proximity or word-of-mouth for your marketing and you can foresee that your community is no longer tied together through proximity, then carefully review your marketing strategies.

Trend #8: New Brands Are Emerging on the Web

One e-newsletter announced that Amazon, Drudge and Yahoo were the newest major brands created by the Web. There are other new content brands emerging too. What is worrisome, however, is that the traditional value-added publishers and aggregators, as they reinvent themselves for the "New World Order," run some risks. First, traditional supporters may permanently or temporarily abandon them, destroying their business models. Some content publishers may not be around by the time the lusty new, and possibly free, Web services are found to be lacking for serious research and decision support.

As for marketing a professional library, what does it say about a library that offers access through simple hyperlinking to Internet resources, just the normal stuff any patron can likely get at home anyway? If librarians are purveyors of access to free and shallow Web resources, what does that present us as over the long term? In marketing language, the library's client value proposition (what value your clients actually place on your services) has always been highest for selected access to deep information and information of high quality. As the world of information shifts you have to be able to prove to your clients that you actually have something that they can't get elsewhere more cheaply. Web links to the usual Internet resources won't cut it. Can you prove that your services are differentiated in a visible, tangible way from the Web experiences they have at home on their computers that, by the way, are more than likely better than anything available in your library? When you know the answer to this question, you know what you've got that's valuable to them.

Trend #9: Extra Pre-Millennium Work Is Stifling Change

The infamous Y2K bug is a double-edged sword. On the one hand it is stifling change and new product introduction as programming resources are shifted to re-engineer old products and system architectures. Most companies have had periods of lock-down in order to test for Y2K compliance and readiness. This has taken resources, analysis time and funding away from developing new products and services and improving others.

On the other hand, Y2K has promoted change, namely, the opportunity to replace legacy equipment and programs with new hardware and software. The result of this mass upgrading will be the most homogenous technical environment in decades. After the turn of the century, some institutions will likely continue to struggle with dated technology, but, for the most part, the environment will be greatly improved. I also anticipate the new millennium will see the largest introduction of new, and primarily Web-based, applications ever seen.

What does this mean for marketing a library's services? Training for both librarians and clients becomes one where understanding certain basics (Windows, browsers, etc.) will give the ultimate searcher a leg up. Application or content training in the absence of an understanding of the technological environment will fail. Marketing your training services will move to this environment as well–pop-up ads or click-through features leading the end-user to their learning goal will cease being only the domain of for-profit entities and will be used to communicate tips, library training events and library news. It will be equally important to focus on teaching end-users *finding* skills, while reserving the advanced *searching* skills for information professionals.

Trend #10: Every Profession's Relevance Is in Question

As librarians and information professionals, we agonize that our value as a profession is in a state of flux. Focus groups with librarians and information managers tell us that there is one overriding concern–sustaining *relevance* to our organizations in an era of constant and transformational change. This is not a matter affecting just our profession. Indeed, the Web has changed the way many professions and companies conduct business. I believe that the marketing tack for librarians to take is to return to two fundamental principles: understand the difference between intellectual and physical access; and market the librarian, not the technology.

First, we need to remember the important difference between *intellectual* and *physical* access. As librarians, we can very successfully compete on *intellectual* access activities like information coaching, training, and problem definition (remember reference interviewing!).

Over the coming years it will be more and more difficult to position our sense of place in terms of physical access. Our role as information counselors will increase as the information "appliance" becomes the norm and wireless and bandwidth advances destroy any advantage to CD or DVD collections, multimedia software, and full motion and sound services.

Second, we need to understand fully the role we play in adding value to information experiences. Unlike those few remaining bank tellers, we are not in the transaction and delivery business. Since the invention of the photocopier and other delivery technologies, we have run the risk of marketing ourselves in terms of faster and speedier delivery. But emphasizing speed neglects the key, but largely intangible, role we play in the transfer of knowledge and creation of environments for successful intellectual capital growth. We have marketed the dickens out of the latest in new technologies and have lost ground to a certain degree. We need to get back to basics by marketing the librarian, not the technology.

Back to the Bird's Nest

Now back to our robin and her nest. The robin is us. The nest is our library environment. The robin built a beautiful nest using the latest, most available and most appealing materials. But she forgot what the nest was for in the first place–to incubate the next generation to become successful participants in the ecology. PCs in libraries are meaningless without money for content and staff. The content is useless if it's not both physically and intellectually accessible. The staff programs are pointless, if they're not aimed at increasing knowledge and learning. Market the hell out of that idea–not the shiny technology.

STRATEGIES FOR SUCCESS

Before we start to think about what strategies we must undertake to be successful in the new age we must acknowledge one fact: The Information Era failed. It failed miserably. The "Information Highway" metaphor is no longer useful. It's worse than drinking water through a fire hose to receive all the information we need, all the time, anywhere! Our beloved users actually drowned as we shoved more and more information down the highway–just because it was there. We were laying roads without a map and quickly discovered that new metaphors were needed. Information isn't about travelling down a road and stopping to pick some up at predefined intersections and towns. That's a telephone or cable TV model, and it serves the interests of those industries dependent on wire and heedless of the coming wireless environment. Information is an immersion environment and the metaphor of "Information Oceans," not an "Information Highway," will redirect us as we define the future information environment and our roles in it.

We are entering the *Knowledge Era*. This is a Post-Information Age where the competitive advantage moves from information access to knowledge creation, from physical access to intellectual access. The successful services and knowledge objects will be products, enterprises and environments designed for precognition and adaptation. As you enter the Knowledge Era, your focus must go from achieving stability to continuous redefinition and reinvention, while being comfortable with ambiguity and sustained chaos. "To react is to fail; to anticipate is to succeed." We already see this in the faster cycle time for change and iteration–the compression of the concept through action continuum. Simply put, the world of right answers and facts gives way to consensus answers and informed guesses. It's the difference between learning history through memorizing dates and understanding history through synthesizing multiple viewpoints and scenarios.

As we enter the Knowledge Era, we move from the old information era, where the Gurus were those who understood the technology nuts and bolts, to one where the Gurus are those who understand and communicate innovation in a future context. Information combined with insight rules. Interestingly we see the supply and demand model of economics falling apart in the knowledge ecology, as we move to one where supply *drives* demand. The value-added, and therefore economically valuable, activities are filtering, selection, organizing, digesting, packaging, and just plain dealing with the flood of information.

Strategy #1 for Success: Know the Difference Between Data, Information and Knowledge, and Also Know That These Distinctions Are Not Enough!

Wisdom is not the end result one seeks in society. Our goal in the knowledge-based sector is to integrate the data-information-knowledge continuum to fundamentally and positively impact *behaviour* in our enterprises and society.

Data is raw facts with no context and no inherent meaning. Data only has value to end-users in context; data professionals can add this value by applying standards such as SGML, HTML, Fields, Tags, MARC; by normalizing data; and through quality control.

Information is the tangible representation of data within a specific context. In order for information to be successful, it must be useful. To be useful it must be communicated to a user, and must meet the specific needs of this user. Librarians and other information professionals can add value to information by representing data and content effectively.

Knowledge is information in context. For knowledge to exist there must be congruity between the information and the individual's context. Knowledge can only be stored in a human being. Knowledge cannot be stored on paper or in a computer; only information and data can be stored in this way.

Behaviour can be thought of as simply "decisions" that result in action, even if that action is non-action. Enterprises exist to provide an ecology for decision-making. The key success factor is intelligent, informed results that have value in proportion to the results required to meet the needs of the individual or social organization. Keeping this principle in mind, your desired strategy must be to focus your service goals on having an impact on personal and organizational behaviours and only on those behaviours which will have a strategic impact. To put it bluntly, if you focus on managing information or managing knowledge with your information skills you will not succeed as well as you might like. If having a bunch of knowledgeable people and lots of information were power, universities would be at the top of the economic food chain. They're not. To be successful in an enterprise you must focus your information services, collections and strategies on the most desired and strategically important *behaviours* in your organization. Our lesson for the millennium is that information is not enough.

Strategy #2 for Success: Spend More Time and Money on People Issues Than on Technology Issues

Spend time on markets (customer, clients, users, and students) over infrastructure. Don't focus more time on organization structure and processes than you do on market dynamics and behaviours.

Know your stakeholders. Determine your client's psychographic profile. The Dilbert team (The Boss, Dilbert, Catbert, Dogbert, Ratbert, Wally and Alice) is a fun way to help visualize and understand client needs. If that doesn't work for you, use the Simpsons or study the advertising literature for demographic profile inventories. It's not important to be perfectly right; it is important to start focusing on the market and the maps and reduce the focus on your own navel. Focus on your *Knowledge Workers*, since they hold the organization's memory and competencies. They have talents and knowledge that are under-exploited in the enterprise, and this knowledge leaves the building in the elevator every night. Look for under-exploited knowledge and then look for synergies between knowledge pools.

Strategy #3 for Success: Understand That People Are Different and Not Like You

Diversity is the norm not the exception. Learn about learning from such great thinkers as Gardner, Bloom and Piaget. A powerful tool for developing learning strategies is the Taxonomy of Intelligence and Learning Styles. It identifies seven key learning styles that are present in all people in different combinations and proportions:

1. Visual/Spatial is picture smart. People with this intelligence can think in images and pictures and develop clear visual images and representations.
2. Verbal/Linguistic Intelligence is word smart. Their talent is to think in words with highly developed auditory skills.
3. Musical/Rhythmic is music smart. They think in sounds, rhythms and patterns and sing, hum, and whistle to themselves.
4. Logical/Mathematical is number smart. These people think conceptually and are skilled in reasoning, logic and problem solving.
5. Bodily/Kinesthetic is body smart. These people can process knowledge through bodily sensation and have excellent fine-motor coordination.
6. Interpersonal is people smart. They think and process information by relating, cooperating, and communicating with others.
7. Intrapersonal is SELF-SMART. They are skilled in inner focusing and display a strong personality.

Acknowledge that there is more than one learning style. Don't indulge yourself with a strategy that assumes others learn the way you do. The powerful strategy is one that doesn't work against the diverse ways in which humans learn and adapt information. Focus on people and their diversity, and you will be more successful than if you focus on an ideal, model user.

Strategy #4 for Success: Seek the Understandable Not the Intuitive

There is no single, best interface, and "intuitive" is a word for fools. If we accept the proposition that people learn in an innumerable combination of fashions, then there will be an unlimited range of potential versions of intuitive. Search out the understandable and learnable interface–not the illusory intuitive one. By focusing on an actual interface, your evaluation will be based in reality and you will develop realistic criteria. Some interface design and evaluation principles here are:

1. You must design interfaces for humans. Humans come in many cultural types, with various levels of information literacy and differing learning behaviours. Tune the interface to the full range of users or, ideally, allow users to tune them themselves.
2. Be prepared to adapt your interface continuously. You will discover many improvements as you go along–test and launch regularly–don't keep dozens in a bucket to launch en masse.
3. Tunable interfaces for now, probably means tiers–like basic, advanced, professional, etc. Watch for interfaces in the future that learn and adapt, based on user behaviour.
4. Understand that *search* is not equal to *find*. Librarians love searching and the thrill of the hunt. End-users hate searching and want to find information. Evaluating a "search" interface for end-users, solely on its searching ability, puts the analysis in the wrong court. Evaluate its ability to quickly produce satisfying answers.
5. Support the full information continuum–identification through analysis with visible value-add. An interface that merely delivers results or answers without making it easily adaptable to the user's workflow and needs is not optimal. Recognize that we need to know what happens to the information after it leaves the service. For example, providing a comprehensive pile of annual

reports in paper is nice. But if the user must enter those numbers into a spreadsheet, we have merely provided data; we have not added value where the user could import the data into a spreadsheet.

6. Determine how you can formally integrate internal and external information. Can your users really tell the difference? Can you place the same interfaces on top of both, thus reducing the interface learning barrier?
7. Is the Intranet an extension of the library, or is the library an extension of the Intranet? There is no right answer to this question, but you really should choose one focus. This is the "enterprise portal" question where you need to decide if information access is an enterprise wide issue or a departmental one.
8. Build products and services that highlight the relevance of the librarian/information professional. The role of the librarian should be explicit, tangible, and accessible from all knowledge products. Are "you" in your interface? How easy is it to find "you" from your portal?
9. Focusing on the understandable forces you to clearly strategize in the areas of understanding–training, support, and communication. Interfaces must be understandable and as easy to train for as possible–calling them intuitive trivializes the role of librarians.
10. Manage meaning, not content. Content doesn't need strong management (it's generally managed by the content providers). Meaning is what librarians do well in interpreting resources for users. Content in context (*meaning*) is the goal.

Strategy #5 for Success: Understand the Real Needs of Your Market and the Individuals Therein

Many enterprises base their future success on either targeting future markets (those kids growing up now) or by being part of the process of teaching the future generation (schools, colleges and universities). It is common for older generations to understand the next generation poorly. This lack of a complete understanding of one's "market" drives poor decision-making.

Focus on Generation "J," the "Joystick Generation." If you're thinking that keyboards will represent the primary interface to your information products in the next decade for this multi-literate group, you're fooling yourself and fundamentally misunderstanding their skills and competencies. Watch for voice response technologies to outpace keyboards faster than predicted. Make your investments where it allows respect for the Next-Head skills they embody. Does your OPAC strategy allow for multimedia, chat rooms, and streaming video, or have you limited your future by "saving" money with lower grade PCs? Irony rules here, as the generations move through the future together, yet apart.

Strategy #6 for Success: Understand the Dynamics of Your Ecology

Ecology is the science of understanding whole environments. Focusing on our ecology is to focus on human-centered information management. Therefore, the relationships of the parts to the whole are of paramount importance. In order to effectively help people adapt information, you must immerse yourself in their information ocean; i.e., understand your "user." The shift we're experiencing right now is a refreshing move from a technology-centered focus, with the emphasis on generation, collection, and distribution, to one where the emphasis is on effective use and usefulness. The ecology is "sick" if there is not a balance between technology and people.

Strategically look at your ecology and your role in it:

1. View and map the relationships.
2. How is learning happening, and with what?
3. When does innovation and creativity occur?
4. How do they turn ideas into action?

Strategy #7 for Success: Understand the Rule of 15% and Apply It in Your Development and Evaluations

There is a significant body of research about human perception that hypothesizes that humans can only see change when it is visible and when it exceeds 12-15%. This has been tested on such diverse subjects as candlelight, music volume, added-value features, price, and job evaluation points. It used to be said that you could be successful if you did 100 things 1% better. The 15% theory would postulate that, in such an environment, no one would notice. This theory reinforces the role of strategy in setting as priorities those things and activities that really matter. Priorities for libraries should be proving to the user (actually prove!) the visible value in your products, services, and organization; and assessing whether parts of your service are at risk of commoditization–that is, services that can no longer be improved with added value features. Interlibrary loan, for example, may be at risk of commoditization since Web services such as Northern Light and Electric Library offer similar services.

Strategy #8 for Success: Be Realistic About the Adoption Cycle

The future of information professionals will be integrally tied to introducing new services, interfaces, content, products, and training to the enterprise. Each "new" thing will need to be adopted by the users and markets. Understand three classic laws of adoption:

1. There are five immutable adoption stages that EVERY individual must progress through before completing the adoption: awareness, interest, evaluation, trial, adoption. Failure to follow these steps, in order, will result in the failure of users to adopt a new idea, product, or service.
2. There are five key attributes that favour more *rapid* adoption. Feel free to ensure your initiative uses these in a Machiavellian manner. These attributes are relative advantage, compatibility, reduced complexity, trial-ability, and observability.
3. There is a classic bell curve to adoption and the individual's pattern of risk-taking behaviours:

1. Innovators	2.5%
2. Early Adopters	13.0%
3. Early Majority	17.0%
4. Middle Majority	34.0%
5. Laggards	17.5%
6. Non-Adopters	16.0%

Don't be fooled about the value of your initiative by the reactions of late adopters during the launch period. Also don't get too encouraged by innovators' excitement, until you get some feedback from the second stage early adopters. New initiatives are exciting. Don't let your strategies fail by evaluating them too early.

Principal #9 for Success: Truly Know That People Don't Want or Need Information

This may seem like librarian heresy, but people don't want information–especially in the form of articles, books, printouts, fiche, diskettes, Websites or whatever. They want usable answers, confidence and success. They want to *find* NOT *search*. With this insight you can be prepared to market to your user's real needs. We've spent decades marketing our collections and services and not vastly increasing our success. By targeting people's real needs and desires we become immeasurably more tied to their ultimate success.

As an example, research done by the great knowledge management guru, Tom Davenport, identifies the information preferences of information executives: received from people; in context; current, correct and concise; operational; about people (who got what); and external rather than internal. Note that this doesn't mention format or content but talks about attributes of the information process and experience. Enhance the information experience and you will be more successful. Enhance *only* the information and you won't get there.

Principal #10 for Success: Become a Transformational Librarian

Knowledge management targets both kinds of knowledge–tacit and explicit. Tacit knowledge is know-how. It is intangible, harder to adopt/learn, and generally more valuable. Explicit Knowledge is about "knowing that" and "knowing what." It is tangible, able to be represented, easier to distribute, manage, and control. Many other languages separate these two concepts into two words; for example, the French "savoir" and "connâitre" [1]. A transformational librarian keeps these two aspects of knowledge in balance. Over the years librarianship, on the whole, has swung too far to managing explicit information and lost touch with our more valuable professional skills of leading or being a catalyst in the creative process of creating human beings with new tacit knowledge.

In this knowledge ecology, there is an expanded role for librarians as knowledge leaders:

1. Information pruning
2. Adding context
3. Enhancing style

4. Choosing the right medium
5. Knowledge management activities; e.g., taxonomist
6. Information audits
7. Information mapping
8. Best practice databases
9. Information literacy training
10. Skills and competencies databanks
11. Information integrity and organization
12. Licensing negotiation
13. Design and customization
14. Navigators (personal and virtual)
15. Information selection and integration skills
16. Information organization (micro and macro) skills
17. Interface selection and design, combined with training skills
18. Searching, finding, and usage skills (analysis, packaging, reporting).
19. High level information literacy skills
20. From Gatekeepers *to* Gateways
21. Guide, trainer, teacher, coach
22. Team member, partner
23. Seller, marketer
24. Information Ocean organizer, designer
25. Linker, qualifier, chooser, and buyer

In short, adopt "Knowledge Positioning." Transformational librarians focus on where the transformations occur. Transformations occur for librarians and their users primarily between information and knowledge and between knowledge and behavior. It's called learning in one case and success in the other. Transformational librarians focus on the learning organization. It's a potentially huge transformational leap to move to this perspective. The Special Libraries Association calls this "Turning Information into Knowledge and Putting Knowledge to Work." Also, by focusing on ultimate behaviors, the challenge to librarians' turf by other information and data professionals is less threatening.

CONCLUSION AND NEXT STEPS

Some final tactics are needed to start on this path to the future. My top four recommended tactics are:

1. Suck up to IT–you need their competencies. It's probably your second most important strategic relationship.
2. Have lunch with your enterprise and market leaders and the entire breadth of potential users. Your success will be in understanding the user's real needs and goals.
3. Leave the library occasionally. It will only fall apart without you if you stay stuck there.
4. Walk and interpret–observe what your users are doing, NOT what they say they're doing. With messianic fervor, share your insights with your team.

It is absolutely true that librarians and information professionals have nearly all the competencies to thrive in the new knowledge ecology but "Insanity is doing things the way you've always done them and expecting different results" (Rita Mae Brown). An ecology requires a healthy climate, and we can be catalysts in the ultimate health and success of the climate of the knowledge society. Remember that it was only from the perspective of the dinosaur that climatic change was a bad thing–we mammals thought it was a pretty neat change!

NOTE

1. Editor's note: Connaître means 'to know, to be acquainted with, to make the acquaintance of.' Savoir means 'to know how.'

ISSUES SESSIONS

ACADEMIC LIBRARIANSHIP AND THE REDEFINING SCHOLARSHIP PROJECT

Academic Librarianship and the Redefining Scholarship Project

Gloriana St. Clair
Rush Miller

Presenters

P. Michelle Fiander

Recorder

SUMMARY. Following is a brief discussion of scholarship and the tenured, academic librarian. The ACRL Redefining Scholarship Project provided a context for the discussion. Librarians' scholarship is

Gloriana St. Clair is University Librarian, Carnegie Mellon University and Editor, Journal of Academic Librarianship.

Rush Miller is University Librarian, University of Pittsburgh.

P. Michelle Fiander is Cataloger and Reference Librarian, IUPUI University Library.

[Haworth co-indexing entry note]: "Academic Librarianship and the Redefining Scholarship Project." Fiander, P. Michelle. Co-published simultaneously in *The Serials Librarian* (The Haworth Press, Inc.) Vol. 38, No. 1/2, 2000, pp. 63-67; and: *From Carnegie to Internet2: Forging the Serials Future* (ed: P. Michelle Fiander, Joseph C. Harmon, and Jonathan David Makepeace) The Haworth Press, Inc., 2000, pp. 63-67. Single or multiple copies of this article are available for a fee from The Haworth Document Delivery Service [1-800-342-9678, 9:00 a.m. - 5:00 p.m. (EST). E-mail address: getinfo@haworthpressinc.com].

compared to that of teaching faculty, the impediments to scholarly research by librarians examined, and recommendations made. *[Article copies available for a fee from The Haworth Document Delivery Service: 1-800-342-9678. E-mail address: getinfo@haworthpressinc.com <Website: http://www.haworthpressinc.com>]*

INTRODUCTION

ACRL's Redefining Scholarship Project was a year-long endeavor which sought to define and describe the scholarship performed by academic librarians, with the goal of promoting the legitimacy of library research and, therefore, the legitimacy of tenure status for librarians within the academy [1]. In this session, task force members Gloriana St. Clair and Rush Miller described the Project and its methodology. The task force discussed the relationship between scholarship and tenure for academic librarians, and made recommendations for supporting librarians' research within academia.

Beginning in mid-1996, ACRL's Redefining Scholarship Project Task Force sought to analyze the types of research done by academic librarians, as opposed to teaching faculty, with the goal of solidifying "faculty understanding of the ways in which librarian research equates to research in other fields." According to St. Claire, the thesis informing the task force was that "librarians can improve their level of respect on campus by understanding how their research parallels that in other disciplines." The genesis of this thesis is the well-known feeling (or is it a fact?) among many academic librarians that, despite tenure status and academic rankings similar to those of teaching faculty, neither librarians nor their research are considered scholarly. Despite tenure status, librarians are out of the scholarly loop.

The first step in challenging these assumptions was to analyze the scholarly output of librarians. To this end, the classification system developed by Eugene Rice and elaborated by Ernest Boyer in his 1990 book *Scholarship Reconsidered: Priorities of the Professoriate* was implemented as a framework for conducting the study. Rice and Boyer contend that scholarly research falls into one of four categories: inquiry/discovery, integration, application, and teaching, with definitions as follows. Inquiry or discovery refers to investigating activities or ideas for the sake of advancing knowledge; integration, refers to scholarship which makes "connections across disciplines [or] give[s] meaning to isolated facts" [2]; application, takes the ideas and theories and applies them to real-life situations; and teaching refers to research on "improving pedagogical techniques to meet the library's role [creating] independent scholars."

Having established the categories, St. Clair then provided examples of library research topics corresponding to each category.

- *Inquiry:* research on the organization of information; user information needs; library contributions to learning; preservation and access issues; and navigating cyberspace.
- *Integration:* investigations into the application of learning theory to instructional activities; employing communications theory in the study of reference work; and applying administrative and management techniques to library services.
- *Application:* articles on best practices for benchmarking in production areas, such as shelving; or, library initiatives that did not go well. St. Claire notes that our inclination is to write about success stories while failing to report on less than successful enterprises; the result, she implies, is that we miss an opportunity to learn from each other.
- *Teaching:* developing, testing and improving pedagogical techniques to meet the library's role in teaching people to be independent scholars; exploring the effectiveness of online tutorials; best practices in Web design; and student learning styles related to a variety of techniques.

Having defined categories and identified corresponding research topics, St. Clair described an experiment she referred to as Rush Miller's Challenge. The challenge consisted of examining a year's worth of articles from *Journal of Academic Librarianship* to see how many fell into the Rice/Boyer categories. Of the 27 articles published during 1998, 12 fell into the inquiry category; 7 into integration; 4 into teaching; and 4 into application. These results tell us that library scholarship is similar to other scholarly production across disciplines. These findings are reassuring given that much library literature has the reputation, even within the profession, of being pedestrian with little new insight.

At least some library research is as scholarly as research by teaching faculty; but other factors influence the reputation of librarians within the academy. The first relates to librarian status within universities. Citing statistics from a variety of publications and reports, Miller painted a somewhat disturbing picture. While a majority of libraries accord "faculty status" to librarians, including the opportunity for tenure, librarians do not publish as much as their counterparts on the teaching faculty. Despite this disparity librarians achieve tenure in equal percentages to teaching faculty. If librarians publish less, and if publication is an important factor in granting tenure, what does this say about the tenured librarian or the system granting tenure to the librarian? Miller sees this circumstance as pointing to a disparity between the requirements for tenure and the way librarians meet them.

There are many reasons for low research output by librarians. In some institutions, those without tenure status for librarians, for example, publishing is not required. In others, publishing is not rewarded. In environments demanding publication, however, time, funding, and research skills are factors influencing librarians' publication output. Time–or the lack thereof–is a major tyrant since a typical librarian's work week is 35-40 hours with few opportunities for release time to pursue research. Funding is another problem–librarianship is not supported to the same extent as other disciplines, either within institutions or by granting agencies. Finally, and most interestingly, Miller notes that librarians are seldom socialized to the research process in general, and to research of librarianship in particular.

Poor socialization is the result of a number of factors, the most important of which may be the MLS programs which train librarians. Few programs emphasize scholarly research and writing; and sometimes those that encourage research do so in a vacuum, as they do not teach students the skills necessary to fulfill scholarly objectives. To address these circumstances, Miller, a teacher himself, says that MLS students must be shown how to do research and they must be made to feel comfortable with the process. The result should be the "socialized" librarian advocated by Miller, who can hold his or her own in academia, thereby raising the profile of librarians within the academic community.

Although there is little empirical evidence to this effect, those who advocate tenure and faculty status for librarians say that anecdotal evidence suggests that librarians with faculty status are better respected by teaching faculty. Gloriana St. Claire, for example, asserts that talking with faculty about research, theirs and yours, is a proven way to gain respect. Given this anecdotal and experiential evidence,

Miller believes that an empirical study to support these anecdotes should be undertaken. Such a study would have the goal of establishing, objectively and definitively, that faculty status and research by librarians has a measurable positive impact on service and professionalism.

Until we have evidence to support what is an implicit understanding of academic librarians–that research helps raise our profile and reputation in academic communities–Miller suggests implementing the report of the Redefining Scholarship Task Force to establish how scholarship in libraries should be utilized and recognized. Further, Miller says, library administrators must provide incentives and rewards for all kinds of research activities in order to encourage and develop it.

Discussion took place throughout the session as St. Claire and Miller made their respective presentations. Most audience members were familiar with the time restrictions that make research difficult for tenure-track librarians. A few participants observed that much of the library literature they read was not research, but reporting. Audience members also commented on their MLS education; some had been introduced to research methods and topics, while others had not. Even when research was promoted in programs, coursework undermined it, emphasizing set assignments instead. Both speakers were candid in relating pertinent experiences to the audience; their dynamic careers and activities made for an informed and encouraging presentation.

NOTES

Recorder's note: I have quoted liberally from the Power Point Slides of both Dr. St. Clair's and Dr. Miller's presentations.

1. For detailed information about the Redefining Scholarship Project, see: ACRL Institutional Priorities and Faculty Rewards Task Force, "Redefining Scholarship Project: A Draft Report," *College and Research Libraries News*, 58, no. 6 (June 1997): 414-418. The final report is available; for order information see: http://www.ala.org/news/archives/v3n20/v3n20j.html

2. Ernest L. Boyer, *Scholarship Reconsidered: Priorities of the Professoriate* (Princeton: Carnegie Foundation for the Advancement of Learning, 1990), 17-24.

3. Ibid., 18.

ELEMENTS OF STYLE FOR NEXT GENERATION SERIALS ELECTRONIC DATA INTERCHANGE

Elements of Style for Next Generation Serials Electronic Data Interchange

Robert W. Boissy
Jane Grawemeyer
Bonnie Postlethwaite

SUMMARY. *The Elements of Style* by Strunk and White has been an elegant, yet compact guide to good writing for many generations of students. This paper offers rules of thumb for next generation serials interface design, based on common mistakes made since the earliest days of electronic interfaces until today. The focus is on acquisitions-related in-

Robert W. Boissy is Manager, Standards and Interface Services, Faxon Company.
Jane Grawemeyer is Academic Product Manager, SIRSI.
Bonnie Postlethwaite is Director, University Library Technology Services, Tufts University.

[Haworth co-indexing entry note]: "Elements of Style for Next Generation Serials Electronic Data Interchange." Boissy, Robert W., Jane Grawemeyer, and Bonnie Postlethwaite. Co-published simultaneously in *The Serials Librarian* (The Haworth Press, Inc.) Vol. 38, No. 1/2, 2000, pp. 69-88; and: *From Carnegie to Internet2: Forging the Serials Future* (ed: P. Michelle Fiander, Joseph C. Harmon, and Jonathan David Makepeace) The Haworth Press, Inc., 2000, pp. 69-88. Single or multiple copies of this article are available for a fee from The Haworth Document Delivery Service [1-800-342-9678, 9:00 a.m. - 5:00 p.m. (EST). E-mail address: getinfo@haworthpressinc.com].

terfaces: ordering, invoicing, and claiming. Topics include making the decision to develop a new interface, determining functional and technical specifications, coordinating and communicating with other parties, determining the data transfer mechanism, testing, implementing, and iterative enhancements. Common mistakes in interface design and their underlying causes are explored. These causes include issues relating to lack of shared technical terminology, development resource constraints, shifting standards, and competitive barriers to interoperability. Several rules of thumb governing the design of the next generation of serials interfaces are offered as a guide to EDI style based on Strunk and White's *The Elements of Style*. *[Article copies available for a fee from The Haworth Document Delivery Service: 1-800-342-9678. E-mail address: getinfo@haworthpressinc.com <Website: http://www.haworthpressinc.com>]*

INTRODUCTION

In keeping with the theme of the 1999 NASIG conference, it seemed appropriate to look at the history of how interfaces between distinct automated systems involved with serials control have been created, and what has been learned that can be put to use in the future. As with any technology, the curious reality of what is in place today can only be understood by examination of the past. Tracing the evolution of electronic interface development, it becomes evident that the library community has a unique Electronic Data Interchange (EDI) style. This presentation is an attempt to start to codify this knowledge and provide guidance to those who will develop the next generation of interfaces.

PRE-1990s

By Bonnie Postlethwaite

The 1980s opened with the widespread practice of posting serials invoices by manual data entry to mostly mainframe-based library systems. The library community became aware that, while computers were increasing its sense of control over serials collections, the data entry burden was significant and subject to the inaccuracies introduced by rekeying of data. The concept of data interfaces was born not long afterward in the minds of both serials librarians and subscription agents.

The first interfaces were customized to particular library systems. Agents were required to create files that met the requirements of individual library systems. Many interface implementations were created for homegrown library systems, for just one library. While this approach to interface development was manifestly inefficient, it was a competitive factor in the subscription business, and it did improve workflow for orders, invoices, and claims at those select libraries that were involved. As more commercial library systems came on the market, there were more requests from libraries to interface with their new systems. Consequently, as the decade progressed, library system vendors and agents began to embrace the idea of interfaces, though still in the form of distinct proprietary formats for each system. By the mid- to late-1980s, library system vendors and subscription agents upgraded their systems, requiring additional programming. While this provided job security for programmers, it was also becoming clear to the subscription agents that the cost of maintaining this growing web of changing proprietary interfaces was becoming prohibitive. Mainframe software changes by vendors and agents had to be queued, and delays caused gaps in service for the libraries.

The early focus of interface development was on the idea of creating a special Z39 standard within a National Information Standards Organization (NISO) working group to cover serials orders and claims. To this end there was significant work on Z39.55, a protocol later abandoned as unnecessarily industry-specific[1]. Publishers, agents, and librarians, particularly corporate librarians, had a vision of standardized datasets in the library industry and looked for a model from other industries. It did not take long to discover that the wider business community had indeed been steadily developing the idea of standard, flexible, generic transaction sets for common business purposes. The emerging focus in North America was on the American National Standards Institute (ANSI) Accredited Standards Committee X12, which had been originally chartered in 1979 to develop "uniform standards for electronic exchange of business transactions"[2]. Version two, releases one, two, three, and four were published in the latter half of the 1980s. Version two, release four, was comprised of twenty-eight business transactions including: invoices, X12 transaction set identifier 810; orders, X12 transaction set identifier 850; other transactions for order status inquiry, X12 transaction set identifier 869; and order status reports, X12 transaction set identifier 870. All of these could be used for serials claims and claims responses. It was understood that preexisting proprietary data interfaces with publishers and libraries could be mapped into these generic transaction sets.

Building on the work done in proprietary interface development and in the Z39.55 effort, the Serials Industry Systems Advisory Committee (SISAC) began work on X12 transactions for serials orders, invoices, claims, and claim responses. There was reluctance and some opposition to the X12 effort, as the work of the Z39 committee had been based on MARC, the foundation for the communication of bibliographic data, while X12 was not. A distinction was drawn between the need for detailed and industry-specific standards for exchange of authoritative, permanent bibliographic data, represented by MARC, and the need for daily transmission of brief and transitory business transactions, represented by X12. An additional motivation for subscription agents to promote X12 was that publishers and corporate customers were disinclined to adopt a MARC format approach. Consequently, pilot projects were begun to promote the use of X12 standards for serials transactions as early as 1989[3]. The exchange of electronic data with publishers was seen as equally important as exchange of data with library systems. Publisher transactions included claims, claims responses, cancellations, and address changes. Library transactions included invoices, claims, and claims responses.

One result of these early projects was the realization that the coordination of the data transfer process itself was difficult if not handled through a third party, value-added network. These store-and-forward commercial networks allowed for relatively inexpensive transfer of data between electronic mailboxes on the same network or, for a higher fee, across commercial networks. The use of value-added networks (VANs) was welcomed by publishers, and by some early-adopter libraries, because the alternative was dial-up transfer, a cumbersome method requiring coordination and infrastructure. Although a welcome alternative, VANs were costly, a factor which prohibited their adoption by academic libraries. The rise of the Internet and file transfer protocol (FTP) would soon change this landscape.

The genesis of serials EDI was clearly a phenomenon of the 1980s. It would be hard to call the various interfaces developed during this time true EDI, as they were frequently not machine-to-machine. There was almost always a great deal of human intervention, and there were no standards used by everyone. Each party applied their proprietary data structures to the process of exchanging data.

Lessons Learned

Common error: Rush to develop a service without thinking through the long-term support and maintenance.
Background: The impact of software upgrades, data structure enhancements, and hardware obsolescence were not factored into the development process. Nor was the labor required to support the production version understood until too late.
Rule of thumb: Analyze workflow of all participants before committing to development.

Common error: Lack of awareness of pre-existing options.
Background: For a long time the library and publishing industries were relatively unaware of existing EDI standards and systems that could be used.
Rule of thumb: Do not reinvent the wheel.

Common error: Over-emphasize the uniqueness of the situation.
Background: The library and publishing industries were very focused on their uniqueness and did not look first at the commonalties they had with other industries for standard business transactions. They looked to MARC-based standards, which were based on archival needs, for business functions.
Rule of thumb: Think outside the box, see where you fit in the bigger picture.

Common error: Customized development for each trading partner.
Background: All data interfaces developed were proprietary between a library or a group of libraries using the same system vendor and a subscription agent or between a subscription agent and a publisher. Even in a group of libraries using the same system vendor, their specifications frequently varied, requiring built-in options or different versions.
Rule of thumb: Find commonalties, standardize data.

Common error: Electronic data, regardless of physical media, reduces human intervention.
Background: Output to a physical medium required human intervention to perform the process. There were often defects that required re-processing. Data files were frequently too large for some media, such as diskettes, creating the need for complex processes to span physical units.

Rule of thumb: Don't touch.

Common error: My programming priorities are your priorities.
Background: Little thought was given to the fact that both software and data structures change with some frequency. Ancillary programs like data interfaces need to be rewritten to accommodate such changes for all systems involved.
Rule of thumb: Inform business partners of system changes well in advance.

Common error: Assuming that all parties will always use the same equipment.
Background: Hardware obsolescence is a fact of life. If a vendor upgrades hardware or media type, it has the potential of requiring a similar upgrade by the receiving party. This may be inconvenient or impossible to accommodate at the exact time.
Rule of thumb: Plan for obsolescence.

Common error: Meetings and phone conversations can resolve all issues.
Background: Agreements, specifications, timetables all need to be in writing with formalized signoffs to avoid unnecessary programming and disagreements and delays later.
Rule of thumb: Get it in writing.

Common error: Data in any format can be transmitted to and manipulated by other systems.
Background: None of the systems involved in early data interfaces were designed with EDI in mind. Data must be very structured. In-depth analysis for data use and meaning must be done during the system design phase.
Rule of thumb: Square pegs don't fit in round holes; EDI analysts must be part of original system design.

In Memoriam

In the 1980s a number of pioneers in our profession had the vision and the conviction that data interfaces, and later EDI, could greatly benefit our work. They worked tirelessly on standards creation, policy, user education, systems design, and benefits analysis. A number of those individuals are NASIG members and they continue this large task and we all feel enormous appreciation for their work. However, one cannot discuss this period of data interfaces and early EDI without mentioning three individuals no longer with us. Mary Ellen Clapper had the vision for data moving smoothly and error-free between systems, and she worked tirelessly to develop the SICI code and other standards to bring this vision to life, all while developing those early, proprietary data interfaces. With her passing in 1988, Fritz Schwartz continued the vision until his own death in 1995, with his absolute conviction that EDI was the only way to effectively make this happen. His pioneering spirit and risk-taking has paid off for the rest of us. Susan Malowski Swanson of John Wiley & Sons was an outspoken advocate for publishers during the EDI standards creation process. The offices of John Wiley & Sons became unofficial home to SISAC. Sue passed away in January 1998. I take this opportunity to remember their significant contributions. These professionals taught me that we must take risks to make progress and that we must evaluate our missteps and not be afraid to take new paths where appropriate.

EDI IN THE 1990s: THE SIRSI EXPERIENCE

By Jane Grawemeyer

The early 1990s saw a number of experiments in the design of EDI interfaces. The most common approach was to use PC-based EDI translation software to interpret between the ASCII fixed length flat files that library, agent, and publisher systems could process and the neutral EDI format files[4]. As proprietary formats were slowly replaced, first by agent-specific X12 implementations and then by implementations based on industry-wide draft standards, there was ongoing discussion about what EDI really meant to the serials community[5]. Could the phrase electronic data interchange refer to any electronic interface, or was it confined to the ANSI X12 format? Was it necessary to use a value-added network as in the traditional corporate model of EDI, or could data transferred on tape and disk media be considered EDI? Was the exchange of MARC records a form of EDI?

By the mid- to late-1990s it was easier for a library system vendor to implement X12 EDI. The early EDI experiments and pilots had coalesced into the SISAC implementation guidelines for X12, which were published in June of 1995[6]. There was constant pressure by subscription agents to adopt EDI, and this carried over to the library customers who had seen demonstrations at professional conferences and began asking for EDI in proposals. SIRSI adopted the X12 standard and introduced the capability to send its first transaction set, the 869 for serials claims, in 1998.

SIRSI systems incorporate an EDI transaction manager, which comprises a set of programs for sending files, receiving files, building acknowledgments, and resending transactions if necessary. Developing this EDI capability involved becoming very familiar with the X12 transactions themselves, then creating new fields as needed for both the transaction data and the fixed enveloping data. Envelope data is carried in trading partner profiles, which is a variant of the traditional vendor record. The trading partner profile has enhancements to carry fixed mandatory data required by X12, plus information about the data transfer process with each agent.

The decision about how to engineer the data transfer process came up early in the design phase. Value-added networks were deemed to be an extra cost that most library customers would not be willing to shoulder, especially when Internet infrastructure was rapidly becoming ubiquitous. There was sentiment that Multipurpose Internet Mail Extensions (MIME) might provide a fast and easy method for transferring EDI data as mail attachments. However, it became clear that there were not enough trading partners who could integrate their mail-handling and EDI translation software to make this feasible. FTP was easier for customers and most agents to understand, implement, and support.

Coordinating development with subscription agents was not difficult, as most were eager to send and receive test data files. User group meetings, Website announcements, and updates to documentation were all channels for broadcasting interface news to customers and potential customers. Rules of thumb include: using a team approach to completely define the functional specifications for an interface before development begins; and building in a function that provides acknowledgments for every transmission sent or received.

GOING FORWARD WITH SERIALS EDI

By Robert W. Boissy

Start with this fact: ANSI's X12 and the United Nations' EDI for Administration, Commerce, and Transport (EDIFACT) are languages, neutral languages like Esperanto. But, unlike Esperanto, EDI messages in X12 and EDIFACT were designed as intermediary languages for the action-oriented content they convey. EDI messages are meant to be translated out of X12 and EDIFACT and into the typically more rigid and proprietary format of the receiving system before further processing begins. The fact that X12 and EDIFACT are languages allows us to talk about syntax, structure, and even style in EDI as they relate to automating business processes and workflows for serials control. In EDIFACT and X12, sentences are known as segments, and words are known as data elements. A completed document, such as an invoice, is known as a message in EDIFACT, and as a transaction set in X12.

Examples of EDIFACT sentences:

- *BGM+380+186814+31* means "I am an EDI copy of printed invoice 186814."
- *DTM+137:19980929:102* means "The invoice date is September 29, 1998."

Examples of X12 sentences:

- *BIG*990519*219327*****CI* means "I am consolidated invoice number 219327, dated May 19, 1999."
- *TDS*600**609* means "Your total list amount was $6.00. Pay me a final total of $6.09."

With that background under your belt, let us examine the impetus behind interface development. For subscription agents, the decision to develop EDI interfaces was initially based on the economics of software development. A myriad of interfaces servicing few customers was expensive. Standardizing these interfaces offered the opportunity to limit the number of supported interfaces. It became clear in the latter half of the 1990s that EDI had evolved from window-dressing to a way of doing business. Besides the economic impetus behind the development of EDI, the following factors, questions, and observations played a role:

- The competition has it, so we must have it. The competition does not have it, so we must seize the opportunity.

- Standards are the high ground, so create and promote them. But standards take a long time to develop, so implement with pilot projects and draft standards in the meantime.
- Who will get the most labor savings benefit from implementing a particular transaction? If we implement a part of a business cycle that benefits another party, will the other party implement the rest of the workflow to benefit my organization?
- Speed the flow of money. But will anyone actually pay faster just because they do not have to key an invoice?
- Decrease the overhead associated with maintaining orders. In other words, decrease manual claims processing, and decrease claims overall. Technology to automate the existing process is now mixing with ideas to prevent claims with dispatch data delivered to the library. Electronic journals should not need claims, but the question is still open.
- Listen to the clientele. Do libraries and publishers really want EDI, and are they willing to press for it, or is it deemed a benefit only to agents?
- Improve an existing interface. For example, migrate from a proprietary to a standard format, add Y2K compliant date formats, move from a media-based interface to file transfer, add acknowledgments, etc.
- It is easier to develop some kinds of interfaces than others. For example, it is easier to send data than to receive and load it. It is also easier to create an interface involving a small dataset of familiar data that is common to all potential trading partners than one involving customized datasets for each individual institution.

Implementation of a new EDI interface is sometimes a very simple decision. There are occasions when an important business opportunity involves a mandate to support EDI. Large corporations and governments are fond of such mandates. It is also true that any high volume transaction is an EDI implementation target. On the other hand, business transactions that involve a series of unstructured negotiations, or involve very large amounts of money, such as contract or license negotiations, are not normally considered for automation.

When drafting the functional requirements for an interface it is not appropriate to start with anything other than the business need itself. That is, defining the nature of what needs to be communicated to a trading partner. There is no need to immediately assume that the need is to create an electronic version of a printed business document that is normally sent via the postal service or other physical document carrier. However, in practice, most implementations do closely mirror preexisting printed document counterparts, partly because this is an easier transition to support throughout an organization, and partly because paper-based transactions have often been through many useful stages of refinement already. The important thing to define in a functional specification, however, is what will get communicated to whom and how often.

When determining technical specifications, it makes sense to start by asking whether there are relevant international, national, or industry specifications for the transaction defined in the functional specification. There is typically an X12 transaction set or EDIFACT message that is designed for the stated purpose, or can be adapted to the purpose. It is wise to ask whether there are standards for individual data elements that should be incorporated, such as ISSN, Serial Item and Contribution Identifier (Z39.56), International Organization for Standardization (ISO) currency codes and country codes, Standard Address Numbers (SAN), and the European Article Numbering Association (EAN) location code.

A typical approach to mapping EDI transactions is to assign data to elements specified as mandatory in the given standard. After this, a series of questions must be answered regarding the distinction between data which are desirable and should be sent versus data which the receiving party is able to load. For example, European practice on paper invoices is to include an itemized summary of the various forms of tax. But many library systems used by Europeans are developed in North America and few of these systems include multiple fields for tax data. In this situation, a number of questions arise. Should the tax information be sent, leaving the onus for posting it on the receiving system? Should the tax data be rolled together in a way that might allow it to be posted in some form to the receiving system? Should the sender simply ignore the question and count on the receiver to read the paper invoice accompanying the transmission?

As already mentioned, the most common approach to EDI development is to closely mirror an existing paper document. While the gut reaction to this might be that there is no reason to be tied to the paper transaction, there tend to be assumptions by service staff that all data on the familiar paper transaction is in the electronic format as well.

When these same staffers are called on to answer questions relating to electronic transactions, the closer the electronic and paper transactions resemble each other, the easier it is on the service staff and the technical staff.

Some design principles require little explanation. The debate about rich versus parsimonious messages, for example, points to the principle that one should always favor the simpler message. This does not mean sending cryptic price adjustments and claims response codes. It does mean expending effort to define a subset of codes that can be exploded out to full meaning by a receiving system to provide the system user with all the explanation necessary. Codes with defined meanings, when accompanied by dates, and perhaps other reference numbers, have a better chance of becoming universally understood within the serials community than the random free-text explanation of a given worker on a given day. Communications that use a predefined set of codes at their core, presuming these codes really do define the majority of cases within a communication type, also offer the benefit of being quantifiable. Processes that can be quantified can then be studied and refined. Free-text communication cannot be refined in this way.

While the design practice of minimizing code data in the EDI transaction set is important, it is at odds with the important tradition of sending just enough extra data to allow manual troubleshooting, should the need arise. For example, the title of a journal is not strictly necessary, since a title can be identified by an alphabetic, numeric, or alphanumeric code. In practice, however, it is helpful to have the journal title in the data so it can be pushed to an exception report in case of a mismatched invoice line or claim. The title provides a visual check against the numeric data when errors must be corrected by hand.

The header must also be considered during the design process. It contains many fields which can have an impact on the final product. Decisions must be made concerning what data will go in the header of the transaction, determining the break. That is, if you put a purchase order number in the header of an invoice, then you force all line items on the invoice to be for the same purchase order. If you put an invoice type code like debit or credit in the header then all line items must be of this type, and no consolidated invoice is possible. Again using the invoice as an example, it is also necessary to determine whether receiving systems will be able to tolerate itemization of charges and credits, as well as summarization of the same data. It may be that only itemization, or only summarization will be allowed. It is wise to limit the number of data elements in the line item area of an EDI document, as elements added here increase the size of the document exponentially. Data in the summary area is typically used to allow the receiving system to run integrity checks against the detail lines.

Another design consideration is whether and how to prevent the transmission of incomplete messages. For example, when mandatory order identifiers are missing in an invoice or claim, the EDI transaction ought not to be sent. Sending blanks, zeroes, or "not available" messages is not a great solution to this problem, as it puts the burden of data entry back on the recipient. The purpose of defining a data element as mandatory is to ensure that the recipient has the best possible chance of loading the structured data automatically.

Using the superset approach, EDI can be developed more rapidly than traditional interfaces and by staff with less computer training. This simply means that when a new outbound transaction is designed, it ought to draw from the sender's database all the possible data that one might ever think would go on that type of transaction. A non-programmer can then use translation software to generate as many flavors of that transaction as are required by trading partners. Note that this is not like the old environment of creating many proprietary formats. Instead, it is simply assigning data to a series of optional slots in a standard EDI syntax, according to the needs of the recipient. Adding new data elements to the original extract from a database is what causes development delay, so it is a better use of programmer time to output all the data that might ever be needed the first time the transaction is developed. Implementations where an EDI document is generated directly from a business application without use of translation software are not as flexible. In development terms, this "hardwired" approach is actually quite similar to the manner in which earlier proprietary formats were supported, even though the format itself is updated to be compliant with international standards. If a trading partner were to require more or less data in a given document, new programming would be necessary.

Development decisions are ultimately derived from a perception of what the customer wants. The more explicitly this is communicated, the more likely it is to be implemented. A conference special interest group was asked whether they really wanted to load claims responses automatically. Why ask? Why not just assume that people would not want to record claims responses by hand? But perhaps there are those who fear that claims responses will get lost if loaded automatically. It might get too easy not to review them. Reports of ceased titles might go unnoticed. Perhaps there is a fear that library systems will not trigger proper reports, alerts, or update issue statuses correctly. It turned out that these types of concerns did not override the need for labor savings. The response was "load 'em up!" But it does not hurt to ask.

Coordinating and communicating with other parties is a major part of any EDI interface development project. By its very nature, EDI development involves more than one organization, more than one system. There are many ways to approach EDI development projects and relationships involving libraries tend to differ from those involving the corporate world. Corporations, for example, tend to approach EDI projects in a formal, inflexible manner where contracts must be signed, deadlines met, and specifications detailed. EDI development between libraries on the one hand and system vendors or subscription agents on the other tends to be characterized by flexibility and informality.

The basis for this cooperation was the shared effort to create industry implementation guidelines by standards groups such as the Serials Industry Systems Advisory Committee (SISAC), International Committee for EDI for Serials (ICEDIS), and EDItEUR International[7], as well as the pioneering research by Clapper and Schwartz. While cooperative endeavors have forged bonds between libraries and other communities, it has also contributed to the delay between early EDI experiments from 1989 through 1996 and the critical mass of implementations reached since that time. This spirit of community and cooperation has meant that within the library world pressure for development and implementation of EDI has not been brought to bear. This dynamic is different from that seen in the corporate world, where pressure is routinely brought to bear by the partner with the most power. Despite a slow start, libraries are now involved in EDI implementation.

It is a cliché among EDI people from all industries that EDI work requires ninety-five percent business skill and five percent technology competence. The core technology is simply taking one file format and turning it into another format. But the work to build agreements on what data will be exchanged, how often, by what means, etc., is what takes the time. It is very clear that EDI implementation is work for people who want to split their time between technical and nontechnical tasks.

Cooperating to build an interface between two systems may require that one party educate and guide the other before any serious development can begin. It is rarely the case that two parties will find themselves ready to implement the same transaction at the same time unless there has been significant preparation. Cooperative technical development has been greatly improved since the widespread adoption of electronic mail. It is common to hear stories of EDI interfaces being developed after exchange of dozens and even hundreds of electronic mail messages. It is useful and important to eventually transform the informal flow of information into a specification or guideline that summarizes how the interface between two systems works. User documentation is especially important with a technology that allows data to post to a system without anyone having to key it or even monitor it. The best thing EDI partners can do is share and cross-check their internal documentation for the interface. Customers always need documentation down to the field name level and tend to count on the subscription agent to be conversant with the terminology of the library system vendor. They also expect the library system vendor to be familiar with the terminology of the agent. This is particularly critical when it comes to discussing linking numbers, the hooks from one system into another. For example, an electronic invoice from an agent to a library usually carries a unique order identifier assigned by the library system. A claim from a library to an agent will carry a unique order identifier assigned by the agent.

A critical step taken in the development of an interface is exchange of test data. Exchange of test data proves that the parties are serious about the development, and allows the receiving party to test their translation and load programs under real conditions. The best way to do this is to generate data from a production system that is of production quality, which is treated as a test by the receiving party. Ideally, the receiving party generates an acknowledgment for the transmission which gives the sender positive proof of receipt. Exchange of test data between vendors is often referred to as an alpha test. Exchange of test data between a vendor and a customer is known as a beta test. Functional specifications, technical specifications, test data, and user documentation are mutually supporting.

The final step in the development and implementation of EDI is informing all parties who can benefit from the interface that it is ready. This rollout is normally done through press releases, Websites, marketing collateral, sales calls, e-mail broadcasts, listserv postings, and conference announcements. In addition, library business partners, like subscription agents, often encourage libraries to take advantage of the EDI capabilities of their automated systems. The reason for this cross-marketing is that the subscription agent cannot exploit his system's EDI unless business partners, like libraries, do the same.

It is worth noting that the data transfer mechanism is the least important part of the development. Some library systems vendors confine their development to the creation or posting of appropriate files, and leave the choice of transfer mechanism to the library and agent. During the 1980s the main choices were reel tapes, tape cartridges, and diskettes. Other options included value-added networks and direct dial-up file transfer. Through the 1990s the choices for academic customers have related to the Internet: e-mail, e-mail attachment, and FTP. Corporate customers continue to use VANs, though FTP use is increasing. It is hard to imagine anything other than a network-based approach in the future. Many organizations are experimenting with Web front-ends to capture data to an EDI format, which is then passed through a preexisting EDI infrastructure. This is a complementary approach to traditional EDI for those customers not already committed to data maintenance on a library system. What is very clear is that no one wants to key the same data in two systems.

Shifting Standards and Barriers to Interoperability

There have always been those who relied on excuses relating to standards to delay the implementation of EDI. Typical comments relate to the slow development of standards, the existence of multiple competing standards, the idea that standards change between draft and final stages, the cost of buying standards documents, and the notion that newer standards are so flexible in design that they are difficult to implement. The important thing is to recognize these as excuses, and move on to ask the real reason why implementation has not occurred. Other organizations implement under these conditions, and are able to do so by actively participating in developing the standards.

EDI in the serials industry has already overcome major differences between independently developed systems. The real barrier to interoperability is that EDI and all future interfaces based on standards suffer from the same marketing flaw. Standards work against the grain of the commercial requirement to brand and distinguish products and services. After meeting the standard there is nothing else for a commercial entity to do. And yet this is the best of all possible worlds for the consumer, who can rely on their standards-based interface investment to carry to another vendor or agent, should they decide to make a change for other reasons. Because EDI and future standards-based interfaces are vulnerable to this marketing weakness, their continued existence will rely on the demand of consumers, and the ability of agents and publishers to show labor savings through a high volume of data traffic. In other words, it must become *the* way of doing business, not just *a* way of doing business, or an overlay to another way of doing business.

EDI STYLE

The inspiration for this paper was Strunk and White's *Elements of Style*[8], the contention being that what we have learned in twenty years of interface development in the serials industry could and should be codified into a guide for future use. It was an enjoyable exercise to attempt to match the pithy suggestions from the original with something equally concise for electronic commerce.

Strunk and White's Elements of Style	Elements of Style for Serials EDI
1. Place yourself in the background.	1. Let industry EDI standards be your guide.
2. Write in a way that comes naturally.	2. Exchange familiar data.
3. Work from a suitable design.	3. Use business and data flow models.
4. Write with nouns and verbs.	4. Send mostly numbers and codes.
5. Revise and rewrite.	5. Be committed to standards review.

6. Do not overwrite.	6. Do not change for the sake of change.
7. Do not overstate.	7. Do not send data just because you can.
8. Avoid the use of qualifiers.	8. Tag each data element with a qualifier.
9. Do not affect a breezy manner.	9. Design from basic business practice.
10. Use orthodox spelling.	10. Abide by superordinate standards.
11. Do not explain too much.	11. Use examples to explain usage.
12. Do not construct awkward verbs.	12. Construct simple transactional messages.
13. Make sure the reader knows who is speaking.	13. Use standard identification for each party.
14. Avoid fancy words.	14. Define terminology in standards documents.
15. Do not use dialect unless your ear is good	15. Use industry code lists only when necessary.
16. Be clear.	16. Be clear.
17. Do not inject opinion.	17. Limit free text notes.
18. Use figures of speech sparingly.	18. Explain EDI in relation to paper processes.
19. Do not take shortcuts at the cost of clarity.	19. Spell out your acronyms and initialisms, e.g., Electronic Data Interchange (EDI).
20. Avoid foreign languages.	20. Embrace international standards.
21. Prefer the standard to the offbeat.	21. Prefer standard to proprietary.

Parting Thoughts

- X12 is the name of a standards committee; it is not a telecommunications protocol like X.25 and X.400. So drop the dot.

- Stop transmissions lacking mandatory data before they can be sent.
- The sender is responsible for sending transmissions free from syntax errors.
- The receiver is responsible for explaining the nature of content errors to the sender.
- The sender is responsible for resending a clean transmission.
- The receiver is responsible for acknowledging transmissions received.
- The receiver should report how they are processing the data.
- For every transaction, the receiver stores one line-level sender identifier.
- For every transaction, the sender sends one line-level receiver identifier.
- Don't limit line items per transaction set or message; send all available lines.
- No range claims. One claim per issue needed. Computers don't care.
- Expect delayed service when using free-text notes. Free-text paralyzes EDI.
- An invoice is an attempt to elicit payment for goods and services. Don't build a database from an invoice.
- Your business transactions are based on what you bought, not how you catalog.
- Your business processes are only as reliable as the time you put into the technical and business agreements on which they are based.
- You are obligated to inform your trading partners well in advance of any changes to the format you will be using.
- If one company writes the specification, then it is not a standard.
- Don't create an EDI function for which there are no trading partners.
- Don't create an EDI function you cannot support.
- Read the specifications twice. Implement once.

NOTES

1. Frederick E. Schwartz. "The EDI Horizon: Implementing an ANSI X12 Pilot Project at the Faxon Company." *The Serials Librarian* 19, no. 3/4 (1991): 47.
2. Data Interchange Standards Association, Inc. *Electronic Data Interchange X12 Standards,* draft version 2, release 4 (Alexandria, VA: DISA, 1989): p. iii.

3. Schwartz, 39-58.

4. Linda Richter and Joan Roca. "An X12 Implementation in Serials: MSUS/PALS and Faxon." *Serials Review* 20, no. 1 (1994): 13-24.

Basil W. Sozansky. "NOTIS, Faxon, and University of Minnesota Libraries' Electronic Data Interchange Pilot Project for Claims." *Library Acquisitions: Practice and Theory* 18, no. 1 (1994): 123-124.

Joan Griffith. "Electronic Data Interchange: Dartmouth + Faxon + Innopac + SISAC + X12 = Serials Claims Pilot Project." *Serials Review* 21, no. 3 (1995): 33-46.

5. Sharon Cline McKay and Charles J. Piazza. "EDI and X12: What, Why, Who?" *Serials Review* 18, no. 4 (1992): 7-10.

6. Serials Industry Systems Advisory Committee. *SISAC X12 Implementation Guidelines for EDI* (New York: BISG, 1995).

7. Serials Industry Systems Advisory Committee (SISAC) develops EDI guidelines for libraries, agents, and publishers in the United States. The International Committee for EDI for Serials (ICEDIS) creates EDI guidelines for exchange of data between publishers and agents. Among other things, EDItEUR creates EDIFACT guidelines for use by all parties.

8. William Strunk, Jr., and E.B. White, *The Elements of Style* (New York: Macmillan, 1979): 66-85.

PEAK Project Overview

Maria Bonn

Presenter

Leslie Horner Button

Recorder

SUMMARY. PEAK is an experimental service providing delivery to and pricing research on the 1100+ electronic journals published by Elsevier Science. The initial data collected by the project has helped participants to understand patterns of journal use and illuminates some issues involved in pricing electronic journal delivery. Maria Bonn presented an overview of the project and its pricing structure. John M. Haar shared the experiences of the library at Vanderbilt University. Sharon Cline McKay presented a vendor's perspective on pay-per-view ar-

Maria Bonn is Library Program Development Librarian, University of Michigan.

Leslie Horner Button is Head, Serials Section, University of Massachusetts Library.

The report on the PEAK Project Overview was prepared by Leslie Horner Button and also appeared in the NASIG Newsletter, September 1999.

[Haworth co-indexing entry note]: "PEAK Project Overview." Button, Leslie Horner. Co-published simultaneously in *The Serials Librarian* (The Haworth Press, Inc.) Vol. 38, No. 1/2, 2000, pp. 89-90; and: *From Carnegie to Internet2: Forging the Serials Future* (ed: P. Michelle Fiander, Joseph C. Harmon, and Jonathan David Makepeace) The Haworth Press, Inc., 2000, pp. 89-90. Single or multiple copies of this article are available for a fee from The Haworth Document Delivery Service [1-800-342-9678, 9:00 a.m. - 5:00 p.m. (EST). E-mail address: getinfo@haworthpressinc.com].

ticle delivery. *[Article copies available for a fee from The Haworth Document Delivery Service: 1-800-342-9678. E-mail address: getinfo@haworthpressinc.com <Website: http://www.haworthpressinc.com>]*

Maria Bonn opened this workshop with an explanation of Pricing Electronic Access to Knowledge (PEAK), which is a collaborative effort for electronic journal delivery and experimental pricing research of the University of Michigan's School of Economics and the University of Michigan Library. Aware that the dissemination of information is in transition, researchers wanted to see if present models for structuring, delivering and pricing journals make sense in an electronic environment. They were also interested in learning whether new value could be created through innovative electronic product offerings, such as sophisticated searching abilities and nonlinear pricing. PEAK provides electronic delivery of over 1,100 journals published by Elsevier Science. Twelve libraries (ten academic and two corporate) agreed to participate in PEAK, and researchers developed three article bundling types to gather data across a variety of pricing models.

The first option, termed traditional, is very similar to the existing print model where the publisher decides what content will be delivered. It is the least expensive, at $4.00 per article. The second, or generalized, option allows institutions to purchase bundles of articles (120 articles per bundle at a cost of $548.00 per bundle). In this model, the user chooses the content at a cost per article of approximately $4.50. The third model is the per article option, where the individuals select what they want. This is the most expensive at $7.00 per article. Per article costs are in addition to other costs member institutions must pay.

After nearly three years of operation, the PEAK project is nearing completion. Preliminary analysis of data indicates that users tend to select more generalized, rather than specialized, materials and that many institutions initially over-estimated demand for the service. For its part the University of Michigan Library has learned what it means to be an information provider to other institutions and is not certain it can afford to continue this type of service. More information on the PEAK project is available at the following sites:

- http://www.lib.umich.edu/libhome/DLI/
- http://www.lib.umich.edu/libhome/peak

Project PEAK: Vanderbilt's Experience with Articles on Demand

John M. Haar

PEAK VERSUS SELECTION AND COLLECTION

To understand why the PEAK concept intrigued Vanderbilt, it is instructive to review how academic libraries currently acquire and supply their patrons with journal literature. First, we select the journals. As a collection development officer, I define selection as the rational act of carefully choosing those titles most likely to offer reliable scholarly and clinical information in subjects that closely match local interests. Sound selection decisions are informed by a knowledge of both subject literatures and the research and instructional programs on our campuses. Put another way, serials selection is an attempt to anticipate–one could say guess–which of the thousands of periodicals published for the academic market that faculty and students will actually want to read.

Once we select a journal, we acquire it through a subscription. We subscribe to as many journals as we can afford, and in this era of serial price inflation we can afford ever fewer. When our subscription renewal costs outstrip our ability to pay, we respond in the only way we can: we cancel subscriptions.

John M. Haar is Assistant University Librarian for Collection Development, Vanderbilt University.

[Haworth co-indexing entry note]: "Project PEAK: Vanderbilt's Experience with Articles on Demand." Haar, John M. Co-published simultaneously in *The Serials Librarian* (The Haworth Press, Inc.) Vol. 38, No. 1/2, 2000, pp. 91-99; and: *From Carnegie to Internet2: Forging the Serials Future* (ed: P. Michelle Fiander, Joseph C. Harmon, and Jonathan David Makepeace) The Haworth Press, Inc., 2000, pp. 91-99. Single or multiple copies of this article are available for a fee from The Haworth Document Delivery Service [1-800-342-9678, 9:00 a.m. - 5:00 p.m. (EST). E-mail address: getinfo@haworthpressinc.com].

The way we acquire journals is fundamentally flawed because it does not correspond to the way our patrons use them. People do not read journals; they read articles. They may have favorite journals in their fields of specialization that they carefully browse to see which articles they want to read, but one suspects that few scholars read every article in even the core journals in their specialties. For journals outside the core, they are more likely to seek particular articles they identify through cited references, indexing services, or tips from colleagues.

Every serial subscription is a package deal. When we subscribe, we buy and retain every article in every issue whether we need it or not, whether any of our users ever reads it or not. We spend considerable sums binding, shelving, and storing bound volumes that are full of literature that no one on our campus will probably ever need. Of course, it's this uncertainty that drives the entire operation: we can never be sure which articles someone will need, so we keep them all to be prepared.

This system is inefficient and wasteful, not only because scholarly journals are so expensive, but also because to obtain the literature we need libraries must buy an enormous amount of literature they do not need. If a critical mass of faculty–and that number can often be one–wishes to read some of the articles in a journal, we subscribe to all the articles in the journal because we have no choice. We have no choice because serial publication and acquisition have until very recently been bound by the limitations of paper.

At base the journal, like all periodicals, is a packaging convenience suited to paper. The journal issue is a way to bundle groups of articles for sale and distribution. Theme issues aside, in most cases the articles that compose an issue are related only in the very broad sense that they all address topics within a particular sub-discipline. Each is authored independently, and each stands on its own. But in a print-based acquisitions model, we cannot select and purchase articles; the way articles are packaged dictates how we buy and what we pay for serial literature.

PEAK AT VANDERBILT

When we at Vanderbilt learned of PEAK, we decided to participate because we wanted to see if digital content, freed from the constraints of paper packaging, offered a better way to provide our patrons with the articles they want. The PEAK pricing model we chose was attractive not because it promised a cost reduction, but because it offered the prospect that we would realize a better return on the investment we make in Elsevier journals. We might not pay less, but we would pay for journal literature that our patrons actually used. If PEAK worked, we could consider replacing the dysfunctional hit-and-miss system of subscriptions with the precision of articles-on-demand.

Vanderbilt holds print subscriptions to about 403 of the 1,175 journals in PEAK at a cost of approximately $700,000 per year. With PEAK we could offer full-text electronic content to all 1,175 journals from at least 1996 through the present. Of the three PEAK pricing options, we chose the so-called generalized subscription. Under this plan we paid an entry fee to join the program. This fee also provided open access to all Elsevier journal content published in 1996 (and earlier in some cases). We also pre-paid for packages of tokens, each token representing one article published in 1997 or 1998. Each time one of our authorized users viewed a 1997 or 1998 article, we expended one token, but–significantly, as it turned out–that article became part of the open access content from that point forward.

COST

We paid a total of $43,660 to participate in PEAK for a year. Our entry fee was $19,000, and we paid another $24,660 for 5,400 tokens, our estimate of the number of articles our users would view during a full year. This was a major investment, but in comparative terms the cost appeared reasonable. The entry fee bought access to 1996 content in all 1,175 Elsevier journals; by contrast we paid about $700,000 for 1998 content in only 403 journals. The price for each token, which purchased 1997 and 1998 articles, was $4.57. Based on data supplied by Elsevier, I roughly calculated that our cost per article in their print journals was about $8.32.

Because Elsevier discounted its prices in exchange for guaranteed revenue, we were required to purchase all our tokens before the experiment began. The project was to run for one year. If we bought too few tokens to last the year, we could not purchase more. If we bought too many, we would not receive a refund for unused tokens. This is where things got interesting. Though we had extensive use data on our print journals, we had no way to know how many articles our patrons read–and thus no way to predict how many tokens they might use in an electronic journal aggregation. Predicting token usage was a risky shot in the dark.

USE DATA

PEAK also promised to supply use data at a greater level of detail and across a larger number of journals than that offered by any other aggregator at the time. We would learn, for instance, the total number of individuals who logged onto the database and the numbers of articles opened in each journal.

As an experiment, one of PEAK's objectives was to gather highly specific use data. Thus it imposed demands on our patrons that we would have found unacceptable in other databases. Though we worked with PEAK to make its authentication procedure relatively easy for users to navigate, we anticipated that the procedure would probably discourage some potential users. I think it is fair to assume that the character of PEAK's usage was somewhat different from that of other electronic journal aggregations, but we cannot know exactly how different–or whether the difference significantly skewed the use data we obtained.

PEAK required patrons to register and be assigned passwords. We all know how this negatively influences patron response and complicates user education, and indeed this was a major cause of confusion in the first months of the study. The requirement was understandable in an experimental context. Passwords enabled PEAK to anonymously track use by individuals. It also enabled registered users to access the database from any Internet protocol address and through any Internet service provider.

PEAK required us to send them a list of authorized users (with e-mail addresses) that they could use to validate persons attempting to register. After stipulating a written privacy guarantee, we decided to use the university's Web-based personnel directory as the source for this list. Because the directory offers listed persons the option of removing themselves from the list, it provided us with a means of withholding information about persons who did not wish to make their names and e-mail addresses public. Anyone excluded in this way could request that they be added to the list immediately, and we also sent updated lists monthly to keep up with personnel arrivals and departures. Our first authorized user list included only faculty, staff, and graduate students; we omitted undergraduates for fear that their inclusion might cause us to expend our tokens too quickly; we were soon to learn how naive we were.

The registration procedure was somewhat complicated, so we created our own introductory Webpage with an explanation of the experiment's purpose and content and, we hoped, clear step-by-step registration instructions. All the links to PEAK from our homepage routed users through this introductory page. This step appears to have been very worthwhile. The page has received an average of almost 800 hits per month. We also added a special PEAK mailbox, linked from this page, to answer user queries. The mailbox averaged three to five messages per week during the year; the average for the first few months was considerably higher. Early on, many questions reflected user confusion about PEAK's e-mail response to patrons' registration requests. The messages seemed to indicate that credit card numbers were required to access the database; this was part of a deal with an Internet banker. After PEAK clarified that credit card numbers were optional–patrons could use them to purchase articles for themselves–most of the mailbox queries came from persons excluded from the authorized user lists. Once we verified their institutional affiliation, we added their names to the list.

Our first important discovery about electronic journal usage came as a consequence of our attempts to promote PEAK on campus. We began with a media saturation campaign. We sent letters to deans and department heads about the service and asked them to inform their faculties. At least one dean sent letters to every faculty member and graduate student in his school. We also featured PEAK links on our library homepages and placed an article in the university's faculty-staff newspaper. Early feedback indicated that we had reached some, but not nearly enough, of our intended audience. After three months we had expended only 281 of the 5,400 tokens we thought we would need for an entire year, an average of 97 per month.

At this point we determined to expand our promotional effort in two ways. First, we modified catalog records for most of our 403 Elsevier print journals by adding URLs for their PEAK counterparts. Second, we added links to all 1,175 PEAK titles to our Web e-journal list. Over the next three months we expended an average of 205 tokens per month, more than doubling the usage of the first quarter. Surely word of mouth contributed to this increase, but it seems clear that established finding aids like the catalog and homepage were more effective in promoting the service than publicity blitzes like letters and newspaper articles. Given what we ultimately learned about the high use of journals that we do not hold in print, we might conclude that the Web list was a more successful promotional tool than the catalog, a lesson that could be applied to other journal aggregations.

Despite the upturn in usage, it soon became clear that we had grossly overestimated the number of tokens we would need. This was our second discovery–and an expensive one. We permitted undergraduates to register once we realized that expending tokens too quickly was the least of our worries. Usage continued to increase, but we ended 1998 with slightly over 2,800 tokens expended, only 52% of the amount we bought. Other PEAK participants with generalized subscriptions overbought to a similar degree.

While we may have overpaid for our tokens, the usage data we gleaned has been well worth our investment. PEAK has taught us more about how serial information is used than any collection assessment project we have ever undertaken. We learned not only which journals our patrons used, but also how many articles in each journal they used and how often they used each article. Moreover, because PEAK statistics covered over seven hundred titles that we do not hold in print, we could to some extent evaluate how successfully we anticipated our users' information needs in selecting our 403 subscriptions from Elsevier's universe.

Here are some of our findings based on data from fourteen months of PEAK usage. Elsevier's publications are, as we know, heavily weighted toward science, technology, and medicine. But within this focus area not all disciplines on our campus availed themselves of PEAK in equal measure. University of Michigan librarians segmented PEAK journals into thirteen broad subject clusters. Three clusters related to our engineering programs included 29% of all PEAK journal titles. The number of tokens–read articles–used in these clusters represented almost 48% of total token usage. In no other clusters was there such a strong positive differential between percentage of content and percentage of usage.

This may be due to the fact that our engineering program at Vanderbilt is comprehensive, but our engineering periodical collection is not.

Each school or college funds its own library operations, and the School of Engineering has not been able to support its library adequately. Thus, information-starved engineers quickly recognized PEAK as a dream come true (we have testimonials to this effect). Their use may have been disproportional to other disciplines better served by our print collections, but it was clearly proportional to their need.

The two clusters with the highest negative content-usage differential were life sciences and health sciences. They also included 29% of journal titles, but represented only about 18% of token usage. The likely reason is that our medical library, concerned about encouraging user dependence upon a service that was to last only a year, chose not to publicize PEAK heavily. They did not add PEAK title links to their catalog or to their Web e-journal page. Publicity and promotion do make a difference.

Like all use studies, PEAK helped us assess how accurately we anticipated users' needs in selecting print serials. But it added a significant dimension that print-based use studies could not. In-house studies can tell us which titles in the collection patrons do not use. Within the parameters of the Elsevier universe, at least, PEAK provided important corollary information: Which titles not in our collection did patrons want to use?

As a measure of the quality of our selection decisions, PEAK offered some sobering data. Our patrons used tokens representing articles in 637 journals. Of those 637, we subscribed to 289, or 45%. We did not subscribe to 348, or 55%. Of the 403 journals in the PEAK database to which we subscribed, 114 (28%) were not used. Of the thirty most heavily used PEAK journals, we did not subscribe to fifteen.

Obviously our selection could have been better, but it was not as inept as these figures make it appear. Of those fifteen titles in the top thirty that we lacked, no fewer than twelve were engineering journals. Much of the gap between what we owned and what people wanted to read was not the result of ill-informed selection decisions, but a consequence of insufficient funding in a journal-dependent discipline. PEAK has given us powerful empirical data to support our appeals for budget enhancements in engineering.

One question PEAK could help answer is whether patrons use print and electronic journals differently. If so, the difference might explain the gap between our journal selections and PEAK statistics. We compared PEAK data to a study of print journal usage in our Science and Engineering Library during the 1997-98 academic year. For science and engineering journals the usage patterns were generally similar. Many of the most highly used print titles, like *Chemical Physics Letters* and *Journal of Chromatography*, were among the most highly used PEAK titles. There were, however, some mysterious anomalies. For instance, *Tetrahedron*, *Tetrahedron Letters*, and *Journal of Organometallic Chemistry*, all very highly used in print, were far from the top of the PEAK usage list. One possible reason: PEAK issues were often posted online weeks after their appearance in print, another necessary consequence of the project's experimental nature. For readers of high-demand journals this delay may have been unacceptable.

The most fascinating and enlightening PEAK statistics are those that relate to the acquisition of articles as an alternative to the acquisition of subscriptions. In all of 1998, Vanderbilt patrons opened 2,808 Elsevier journal articles published during 1997 and 1998. They opened many of these articles multiple times, but they used only 2,808 unique articles. Based on a PEAK article count, I estimate that Elsevier publishes about 160,000 articles a year. Thus, of 1,175 PEAK journals, Vanderbilt patrons looked at less than 2% of the total content.

We subscribe to 403 Elsevier journals. Let us assume that these subscriptions equal approximately one third of Elsevier's content. This means that we subscribed to far more content than our patrons needed. Given that we subscribed to fewer than half the PEAK journals our patrons used, we provided far less content than they wished to read. Would we not have spent our money more effectively had we bought the 2,808 articles they read, rather than subscriptions to 403 journals containing thousands of articles no one on our campus cared to read?

PEAK reported not only how many tokens our users expended. We also learned how many times users viewed articles represented by tokens. This statistic remained remarkably consistent from month to month. The number of times articles were viewed equaled 2.7 times the number of tokens used. This means that, on average, patrons used each of the 2,808 articles 2.7 times. Thus while they used only a minuscule portion of PEAK's content, they tended to use that portion repeatedly. Other PEAK participants experienced similar patterns of repeat usage, some with higher and others with lower ratios.

Of course we cannot know if this pattern also holds true in print journal usage. But if it does, it lends new meaning to the concept of "high-use" journal. High use, as reported in re-shelving studies, probably does not mean that every, or even most, articles in a journal issue or volume are in high demand. It is more likely to mean that multiple patrons read a relatively small number of articles. If we can believe what PEAK tells us, most of the articles even in "high-use" periodicals go unread.

Our experience with PEAK was positive enough that we agreed to renew our participation into 1999. We have seen enough, however, to believe that articles-on-demand may be a viable model of electronic journal delivery. It is not risk-free. Costs could be unpredictable and could fluctuate from year to year. It might even be necessary to ration the service at times. But we have to appreciate that we ration journal delivery now by subscribing only to a portion of every publisher's output. No matter how intelligently we select this portion, we will inevitably fail to provide every article our users want.

We should probably not assume that buying articles will cost us less than buying journals. There is no incentive for publishers to sell us articles at a price that is lower than what we now pay for subscriptions. But even if our costs do not decrease, or even if they increase slightly in exchange for access to a publisher's complete database, we can at least have the consolation of knowing that we are spending our money more efficiently, because we are purchasing only what patrons use. Moreover, we are saving on binding, shelving, and storage costs, and we are meeting our patrons' serial information needs much more effectively than we ever could through subscriptions.

By offering our patrons access to a publisher's complete journal database we in effect allow them to do the selection. While bibliographers may recoil at that notion, it is hard to object to a system that frees us from trying to guess what patrons will read and liberates us from paying for a dozen articles in order to provide users with the one they may want. We could offer both the highly specialized articles requested by one individual as well as the popular articles sought by the many. Articles' links to their journals could become exclusively a bibliographic convenience, a means of identification. They could be freed from their physical and fiscal ties to their parent publications, and they could be bought and stored the same way they are used: one at a time.

E-Business for E-Journals: Article Pay-per-View

Sharon Cline McKay

INTRODUCTION

As part of the presentation on the PEAK Project, the comments that follow offer the vendor's point of view in providing electronic journal articles on a pay-per-view (PPV) or transactional purchase basis. These comments are intended to apply in a generic way to articles available to be purchased in this manner from any publisher.

THE PLAYERS

Libraries, publishers, subscription agents and other service agencies all play a part in serving users and enabling them to gain access to articles in e-journals. If the user does not have access through a personal or institutional subscription, many publishers are now making articles available for single purchase. Library staff time can be saved by having users search for their own articles and avoid using interlibrary borrowing services, which are staff-intensive. Because of the availability of many e-journals via pay-per-view over the Internet, broader access can be provided for users who may be remote from the

---

Sharon Cline McKay is Director, Academic Sales, Western Region, The Faxon Company, Inc.

[Haworth co-indexing entry note]: "E-Business for E-Journals: Article Pay-per-View." McKay, Sharon Cline. Co-published simultaneously in *The Serials Librarian* (The Haworth Press, Inc.) Vol. 38, No. 1/2, 2000, pp. 101-105; and: *From Carnegie to Internet2: Forging the Serials Future* (ed: P. Michelle Fiander, Joseph C. Harmon, and Jonathan David Makepeace) The Haworth Press, Inc., 2000, pp. 101-105. Single or multiple copies of this article are available for a fee from The Haworth Document Delivery Service [1-800-342-9678, 9:00 a.m. - 5:00 p.m. (EST). E-mail address: getinfo@haworthpressinc.com].

library. It is possible to limit access to pay-per-view by type of user, such as faculty, graduate students, researchers, etc. A goal for libraries in providing access to pay-per-view for their users is better access for the same or less money.

Publishers may be concerned about online branding of their product; that is, making sure the user knows the name of the publisher providing the material. In order to bring this information to the user's attention, some publishers require a separate logon, which causes administrative problems for library staff and presents hurdles for users. Publishers may also be wary of selling articles one at a time for fear that this may cause them to lose revenue from their subscription base, if libraries cancel subscriptions in favor of buying individual articles. However, it's possible that publishers may experience an increase in income because of users now accessing the articles whereas they wouldn't otherwise have access if a subscription were required. If libraries provide pay-per-view access to their users for titles to which they have decided not to subscribe, this could represent additional revenue for publishers.

Subscription agents and other types of providers can provide pay-per-view as an alternative to traditional services, thus providing broader access more directly to users. These providers tend to view pay-per-view as an enhancement of existing product offerings to their primary clients–libraries.

Users tend to want access to everything (and they want it *now!*). The typical user does not know which publisher's journals will provide the information needed. The ability to search across publishers and journals to retrieve relevant information is the ideal. Remote access is needed for convenience, to avoid having to physically go to the library, and in some cases it is necessary because of the user's circumstances or location.

Both users and library staff prefer IP access. IDs and passwords are too hard to manage and too easy to share, reducing the effectiveness of their purpose, which is preventing unauthorized access to a system. Assigning and tracking IDs and passwords for several thousand users is too time-consuming and difficult for library staff, and some refuse to use any system that isn't available via IP.

Publishers currently known to be offering pay-per-view access to a total of approximately 600 electronic journals are:

- Adis International
- American Institute of Physics
- Arnold
- Blackwell Science
- Kluwer Academic Publishers
- NRC Research Press
- Professional Engineering Publishing (formerly Institution of Mechanical Engineers–IMechE)
- Royal Society of Chemistry

APPLICATIONS

Typically, high-priced journals and/or low-use journals are good candidates for accessing via pay-per-view. Library staff can easily provide access to disciplines not specifically covered by their collection through this means. Occasional and unaffiliated users can also be served, without compromising existing budgets or collection development policies.

Current awareness/alerting services can be provided through many services that provide pay-per-view and subscription-based access. A user can arrange to be alerted when a new issue of one or more selected journals has been released, whether or not subscriptions have been placed. The user may also select a search strategy to be run against all new data loaded, regardless of the journal source. An e-mail notification is sent whenever a new issue of selected journals or new content matching the saved query is loaded. From within the text of the e-mail, the user can click on a hyperlink to a specific article from the table of contents (TOC) of a selected journal or from the saved query result list to retrieve an article of interest. The article can then be viewed on user's desktop if a subscription exists, or ordered via pay-per-view options.

COLLECTION DEVELOPMENT

Collection development professionals in libraries are accustomed to selecting an entire universe of materials, based on carefully devised programs and policies, with the purpose of supporting their institutions' primary focuses and disciplines. On the other hand, users are able to control their own selections of articles within that universe. With the option of pay-per-view, a user can go beyond the universe and select articles of interest from a broader base of information. It will be interesting to see how this new avenue of access to information affects existing collection development policies and practices. Library professionals may find that the titles they have selected are not as close to meeting their users' needs as they had expected.

PRICING

Most publishers are currently charging a flat fee regardless of the length of articles. This fee ranges from $12.00 to $20.00. However, some publishers set their charges based on the article's length, in which case the fee can range up to $40.00. In almost all cases, delivery of an article to the desktop in electronic format is cheaper than fax, and the quality of the image is much better. The article can be printed, in color if applicable, and saved on disk, further making the online delivery more desirable than fax. Both of these actions are subject to publishers' usage restrictions, of course.

Some publishers offer bundles of articles as a purchase option, such as a pre-determined number of articles from any of the journals published and ordered within a specific time period for a fixed price. Bundles can provide a discount off the price of single articles. However, the money must be paid in advance, and generally no refunds are given for articles not ordered.

Payment options can include:

- Credit cards
- Institutional
- Deposit accounts
- Billing accounts
- Maximum purchase limits per user or group
- Per article
- Per journal title

REPORTS

Services offering pay-per-view can automatically track purchases and provide managers with reports of useful statistics, reflecting total purchases from each journal (as well as from each publisher). The manager can then easily compare the total paid for individual articles versus the subscription price if the institution had purchased the journal in that manner. Selection decisions for the following year can then be revised based on actual usage of journals rather than predicted usage.

LONG-TERM CONCERNS

E-journals are extremely useful to those users who are located remotely from the library. They are also a convenient way to provide coverage of marginal titles or disciplines related to the core collection. However, several issues of concern to librarians have not yet been resolved. One issue is what is sometimes called "package" sales, or the requirement of some publishers for libraries to buy an entire package of titles without the ability to choose only those journals of greatest interest. Each library must evaluate the total cost of this type of package deal compared to the ease of access and broader coverage. If the library would otherwise be spending less money to purchase only a few titles from that publisher, but would not have electronic access, it must decide whether access to the entire list of journals, as well as the electronic access, is worth the extra money.

The implications of pay-per-view access on collection development policies and procedures must also be examined and evaluated. Allowing users to choose articles from a broader selection of journals than those specifically chosen by librarians may show that desired materials differ from collected materials. If this is the case, a greater portion of the institution's resources may shift from subscription to pay-per-view. The effect this shift may have on publishers' revenues is hard to predict. If publishers experience a decline in overall revenues from the familiar and traditional subscription model, they will probably raise prices. If, however, they see a wider distribution of readership because of greater accessibility without the commitment of a subscription purchase, it will be a win-win situation. Dare we predict that journal prices could actually go down?

UNIFIED SEARCHING OF LOCALLY MOUNTED AND DISTRIBUTED WEB JOURNALS

The American Physical Society and the TORPEDO Ultra Project

Robert A. Kelly

SUMMARY. Since 1993, the American Physical Society (APS) has been seeking ways to provide new offerings to our library customers. In anticipation of the development of new offerings we started an experiment in 1994 with the U.S. Naval Research Laboratory (NRL) in Washington, D.C. During the NRL TORPEDO experiment it became apparent that there was a need for APS to develop a new service for consolidators and integrators. Our intent is to capitalize on our electronic deliverables, our commitment to SGML, and the persistent linking into our wrappers. We are developing a subscription to make available full-text SGML, minus the figures and APS added links, of APS published articles. *[Article copies available for a fee from The Haworth Document Delivery Service: 1-800-342-9678. E-mail address: getinfo@haworthpressinc.com <Website: http://www.haworthpressinc.com>]*

Robert A. Kelly is Director, Journal Information Systems, American Physical Society.

[Haworth co-indexing entry note]: "The American Physical Society and the TORPEDO Ultra Project." Kelly, Robert A. Co-published simultaneously in *The Serials Librarian* (The Haworth Press, Inc.) Vol. 38, No. 1/2, 2000, pp. 107-111; and: *From Carnegie to Internet2: Forging the Serials Future* (ed: P. Michelle Fiander, Joseph C. Harmon, and Jonathan David Makepeace) The Haworth Press, Inc., 2000, pp. 107-111. Single or multiple copies of this article are available for a fee from The Haworth Document Delivery Service [1-800-342-9678, 9:00 a.m. - 5:00 p.m. (EST). E-mail address: getinfo@haworthpressinc.com].

Since its beginning, the objective of the American Physical Society has been to advance and diffuse the knowledge of physics. As a society of physicists we have an interest in serving the current and evolving needs of our community, the authors and readers of our journals, and theoretical and experimental physicists. Since 1993 one of our motives for moving our journals onto the Internet has been to exploit the technology and develop services based on the content that we have published and will publish for our current community as well as to explore opportunities in new communities.

Since 1995 we have published all but one APS journal online for current awareness, as well as providing print as an archival medium. The one exception is *Physical Review Special Topics: Accelerators and Beams* (PRST-AB) which is a free, solely electronic, peer-reviewed journal. Laboratories that conduct research in accelerators and beams sponsor PRST-AB. The APS journals Webpage, http://publish.aps.org/, contains links to our online offerings and information about our journals.

Our goal is to develop services based on the published article, with the bibliographic information, the wrapper, as the electronic anchor point. In 1995 we decided that the titles, authors, and abstracts of all electronic articles would be available for browsing on the World Wide Web. Journal top pages and issue tables of contents are there for browsing and to facilitate access to articles. All other services, e.g., searching across the collection, linking out, linking to different formats of the full-text, etc., are available for a fee. The collection of fees is mainly by subscription. However, we are considering other fee-based revenue opportunities.

In 1997 we started developing a methodology that will encourage and aid others in linking to the wrappers of our articles. The LinkManager software was released, providing a Persistent Uniform Resource Locator (PURL), using the terminology used by authors, to link into our content. In addition several other physics publishers have initiated a wrapper concept. By the end of 1999 we should have cross-linking between publisher sites for most of the online physics research literature.

Information on linking into the wrappers for APS articles is available at http://publish.aps.org/linkfaq.html. Construction of the Uniform Resource Locator (URL) requires the appending of the journal name, volume, and page or article number to *http://publish.aps.org/*

abstract/. An example from *Physical Review D* is available at http://publish.aps.org/abstract/PRD/v55/p1/.

In 1993 APS committed to producing journals using the Standard Generalized Markup Language (SGML). The initial approach was to use SGML for the production of journals and to set the stage for online distribution. This was a replacement for the various typesetting systems that were used, and the Document Type Definition (DTD) defined in the International Organization for Standardization (ISO) 12083 standard was selected. All APS journals are now produced in this fashion, and we will continue to format articles from SGML. However, it is recognized that the power of SGML is also in its use as a feed to databases, and we are redesigning the DTD to make the SGML easier to port into a database for subsequent use.

Subsequent use has been tested as part of the Digital Library Initiative (DLI) that APS is participating in with the Grainger Engineering Library at the University of Illinois at Urbana-Champaign (http://dli.grainger.uiuc.edu/). Several nonprofit publishers have been providing SGML of their journals since 1995. The DLI experiment showed that it is possible to normalize and integrate SGML files from multiple publishers into a searchable database. It was not easy and started us thinking about redesigning the DTD.

A second technical component of the DLI experiment was to develop a methodology to dynamically format the SGML files at the user's Web browser. We were unable to use the SGML for browser display, mainly due to the complexities of formatting equations with the current browser technology.

Extensible Markup Language (XML), a new phase in the evolution of SGML, was introduced in 1998. Browser manufacturers can build their browsers to dynamically format XML files, including equations. Internet Explorer 5, from Microsoft, is XML-enabled. Other browser manufacturers are expected to follow.

Dynamically converting the SGML into XML for display is an example of subsequent use and will provide a third format, along with Portable Document Format (PDF) and PostScript, to deliver articles. XML articles will take full advantage of the internal tagging structure, including internal and external linking and the dynamic display of complex equations. The DLI experiment has been extended and has been successful in the formatting of equations. I anticipate that we are a year, at most two years, away from the introduction of XML articles into our services portfolio.

At the 1996 NASIG Annual Conference I presented a joint experiment with the NRL where APS would deliver content to NRL for subsequent use[1]. The American Physical Society delivered unbound copies of *Physical Review E* and *Physical Review Letters* as well as text files containing the titles, authors, and abstracts of the articles. The articles were scanned using Optical Character Recognition (OCR), loaded into the NRL's TORPEDO, and offered for use by scientists within the lab. The experiment is a success and opened our eyes to future developments.

APS's Physical Review Online Archive (PROLA) project, http://prola.aps.org/, described in my 1996 presentation, has reached its first stage, containing *Physical Review* articles from 1996 back to 1985. We are starting the second stage that will load PROLA with *Physical Review* articles back to 1970, *Physical Review Letters* articles back to 1958, and *Reviews of Modern Physics* articles back to 1928. It is our intent to load PROLA back to the beginning of *Physical Review* in 1893. As an indicator of our intent, we have loaded volume 1, series 1, July 1893 through May 1894. We will fill the gap.

As stated earlier, the APS provides print copies of its journals to subscribers as archival copies. A subscription to any of our journals includes access to the collection, a database, for the duration of the subscription, as well as the delivery of printed archival copies. We will continue to provide print issues and possibly develop other media to satisfy the archival needs of libraries. The development of our online services will be an expansion of our services into a database paradigm where access will be available to subscribers. Our current thinking is that we will position our collection as an overlay or underlay to other data service providers.

All APS journal articles in the database will be linked to references cited in the article, if they are online. Articles will also link forward to citing articles that are in our online service and to unpublished information. Currently we link to the Los Alamos archive and to the archive at the Stanford Linear Accelerator Center, with more sites to be added.

During the NRL TORPEDO experiment[2] it became apparent that there was a need for APS to develop a new service for consolidators and integrators. Our intent is to capitalize on our electronic deliverables, our commitment to SGML, and persistent linking into our wrappers. We are developing a subscription to make available full-text SGML, minus the figures and APS added links, of APS published articles. Subscribers, mainly integrators and consolidators, will be able to build a search index from APS SGML and SGML from other publishers. They will also be able to build a Table of Contents (TOC) and bibliographic information for browsing and then link to the APS article wrapper for full-text and APS services. The success of the DLI at the University of Illinois indicates that this is feasible.

We have already started with OhioLINK and will develop a similar offering with the NRL's TORPEDO Ultra project. As institutions, consolidators, and integrators start to provide services in support of searching across multiple Web journals, APS will be there to support these efforts and the information needs of the physics community.

NOTES

1. Robert A. Kelly, "Digital Archiving in the Physics Literature: Author to Archive and Beyond–The American Physical Society," Co-published simultaneously in *The Serials Librarian* 30, no. 3/4 (1997): 163-170; and: *Pioneering New Serials Frontiers: From Petroglyphs to Cyberserials*. ed. Christine Christiansen and Cecelia Leathem (New York, N.Y.: The Haworth Press, Inc., 1997): 163-170.

2. Laurie E. Stackpole, "TORPEDO Ultra: Unified Searching of Locally Mounted and Web-based Journals," To be co-published simultaneously in *The Serials Librarian* 37, no. 1/2, 3/4 (2000); and: *From Carnegie to Internet2: Forging the Serials Future*, ed. P. Michelle Fiander, Joseph C. Harmon, and Jonathan David Makepeace (New York, N.Y.: The Haworth Press, Inc., 2000).

The U.S. Naval Research Laboratory and the TORPEDO Ultra Project

Laurie E. Stackpole

SUMMARY. The U.S. Naval Research Laboratory (NRL) library provides its users in four geographic locations with digital library services including over five hundred electronic journals. The InfoWeb information system and gateway serves as a single point of access to these services. InfoWeb includes the TORPEDO Ultra digital library initiative, the library's Web-based SIRSI Unicorn catalog, a locally mounted *Web of Science: Science Citation Index Expanded* database, and Contents-to-Go, a custom-developed current awareness and document delivery service. TORPEDO Ultra provides institutional researchers with a unified way to search all of the library's digital collections, whether these materials originate from a commercial publisher, such as Elsevier; an association publisher, such as the American Physical Society; or a government publisher, such as NRL. TORPEDO Ultra also provides an infrastructure that enables databases that have traditionally served as pointers to documents to now deliver that content directly. In a future release, TORPEDO Ultra will enable end user scientists to search and link to journals residing on publisher Websites at the same time that they are searching locally mounted electronic journals. *[Article copies available for a fee from The Haworth Document Delivery Service: 1-800-342-9678. E-mail address: getinfo@haworthpressinc.com <Website: http:// www.haworthpressinc.com>]*

INTRODUCTION

The Naval Research Laboratory serves as the U.S. Navy's corporate research institution. Employees in four geographic locations enjoy

---

Laurie E. Stackpole is Chief Librarian, U.S. Naval Research Laboratory's Ruth H. Hooker Research Library.

[Haworth co-indexing entry note]: "The U.S. Naval Research Laboratory and the TORPEDO Ultra Project." Stackpole, Laurie E. Co-published simultaneously in *The Serials Librarian* (The Haworth Press, Inc.) Vol. 38, No. 1/2, 2000, pp. 113-122; and: *From Carnegie to Internet2: Forging the Serials Future* (ed: P. Michelle Fiander, Joseph C. Harmon, and Jonathan David Makepeace) The Haworth Press, Inc., 2000, pp. 113-122. Single or multiple copies of this article are available for a fee from The Haworth Document Delivery Service [1-800-342-9678, 9:00 a.m. - 5:00 p.m. (EST). E-mail address: getinfo@haworthpressinc.com].

twenty-four-hours-a-day, seven-days-a-week access to databases, information products, reference tools, technical reports, and journals. Services are available to researchers working in their offices, at home, or while travelling through a Web-based information system and gateway called InfoWeb (*http://infoweb.nrl.navy.mil*). InfoWeb was developed by the Ruth H. Hooker Research Library at NRL to meet the information needs of thirty-five hundred federal staff members and about fifteen hundred on-site contractors located in Washington, D.C., Bay St. Louis, Miss., and Monterey, Calif. InfoWeb services are also available to NRL's parent organization, the Office of Naval Research (ONR) in Arlington, Va.

DIGITAL LIBRARY CONTEXT

InfoWeb serves as a single point of entry to the NRL digital library. It not only provides Web access to the library's online catalog, it also facilitates researcher-library communication through the use of online request forms, e-mail links to staff, and a suggestion box.

InfoWeb provides employees with an organized approach to finding information that is openly available on the Web, eliminating the frustration of finding thousands of hits in response to a Web search. The library has organized frequently requested information into broad subject categories: computer support, government information, Internet directories, and science resources. Library staff mine the Web for sites that contain information of particular interest to NRL researchers. InfoWeb links are then created and annotations are added so that researchers know in advance what they can expect to find at each site. Every month an automated program checks links to be sure they are active. In addition, the library staff continually adds new sites and re-evaluates those that are on the system to be sure that they are not outdated. This information is accessible outside NRL and is heavily used by other libraries and end users in government, academia, and the general public.

The InfoWeb resources most in demand by the NRL community are those that the library licenses or pays for. These include databases that the library provides by linking to external Websites and those that the library mounts locally on its own servers. Examples of licensed databases that reside on remote sites are the Institution of Electrical Engineers (IEE) *INSPEC* database covering physics, electrical engineering, electronics, computing and control, and information technology, as well as OCLC *FirstSearch*, providing access to more than forty databases in all subject areas. Locally mounted databases include *Science Citation Index Expanded* and the NTIS database of government publications.

DIGITAL LIBRARY IMPLICATIONS

While online library catalogs and databases are prerequisites for a digital library they are not sufficient to qualify a library as digital. Because they most frequently serve as pointers to documents they do not meet the fundamental goal of the digital library, which is to deliver the full content of library materials to the desktop.

One way in which libraries can create content and ultimately share it on an enterprise-wide basis is by digitizing institutional publications that are not protected by copyright. The NRL library has been scanning its technical reports collection since 1989 and has converted about 180,000 reports (nine million pages) to a digital format. Because most of these reports have limitations on dissemination they are currently available only within the library, to staff and authorized users. As the library begins to provide services over a secure network, access to all of this content will become more widely available. At this time the full content of some six thousand unrestricted reports is openly available through InfoWeb, either through a search of the library's Web-based catalog or through the TORPEDO Ultra digital repository.

A more typical way of providing content for access by library users is to license it. For example, NRL has a license with Elsevier Science permitting it to mount electronic versions of journals on a local server for institutional access. Elsevier was the first publisher to offer electronic journal subscriptions on a commercial basis with a 1996 offering that included 1995 backfiles. The NRL library was an early implementer of this service and currently has over two hundred Elsevier journals archived in TORPEDO Ultra and available to the user community through InfoWeb.

Cooperative agreements are another approach to building digital content and can help minimize the risk for both publishers and libraries in testing the digital waters. The *Technology Transfer Act of 1986* provides the authority for government organizations and other types of organizations to enter into a Cooperative Research and Development Agreement (CRADA). The NRL library recently completed a CRADA with the American Physical Society (APS) that resulted in the creation of a ten-year digital archive called Physical Review Online Archive (PROLA). Under the terms of this agreement, much of the PROLA content is also mounted locally at NRL. The NRL Library and the American Institute of Physics (AIP) recently signed a similar CRADA agreement, which will expand the AIP's Web-based journal offerings and provide NRL users with access to seventeen new, locally mounted journals going back to 1992.

In addition to locally mounted content, the NRL library provides InfoWeb links to over 280 journals that reside on remote sites. Examples include the publications of scholarly associations, such as the American Chemical Society, as well as journals produced by commercial publishers, such as Springer-Verlag.

DIGITAL LIBRARY REPOSITORY

TORPEDO Ultra is the key component of the NRL digital library initiative, storing the library's digital content and providing search and retrieval capabilities for accessing it. TORPEDO Ultra has been developed by the NRL Library to provide end users with the ability to browse and search its rapidly growing digital collection. This collection currently consists of six thousand technical reports, two thousand NRL press releases, ten thousand NRL-authored articles and conference papers, and over two hundred thousand articles from more than two hundred journals. The total size of this collection is well over two million pages.

TORPEDO Ultra allows users to browse the library's digital holdings in much the same way that users browse a library's physical stacks. For example, a TORPEDO Ultra browse lets users find a specific article by selecting a particular journal from an alphabetic or subject list of journals, selecting a volume from the list of available volumes, selecting an issue from the list of issues in that volume, and finally selecting the article from the table of contents for that issue. Users can also search individual journals, groups of journals, reports, or the entire collection. For its search engine TORPEDO Ultra relies on a commercial off-the-shelf search engine called RetrievalWare from Excalibur Technologies. With RetrievalWare users can perform field searches, e.g., for all articles by a certain author, or they can search the full-text of digital documents. RetrievalWare facilitates retrieval by permitting different types of full-text searches. A concept search allows users to define terms using an online dictionary. Concept searches can be refined, for example, by instructing the system to find *climate* only in its meteorological sense. Concept searches can also be expanded by instructing the system to find terms that are even loosely related to the search term. A pattern search uses a patented algorithm, adaptive pattern recognition processing, to find near matches and is useful in compensating for errors in optical character recognition scanning. A Boolean search option is also available. Search results for concept and pattern searches are presented in a user-defined sort, with the default set for relevance ranking so the best hits are displayed first.

Once users identify an article or report they're interested in, they can display it in Portable Document Format (PDF) using the Adobe Acrobat Reader. There are currently two types of PDF files in TORPEDO Ultra, those that have been produced from scanned, bit-map images (wrapped PDF) and those that have been generated as part of the publication process (distilled PDF). All PDF files added to TORPEDO Ultra are optimized by the library for fast retrieval and enhanced with thumbnails of all pages to facilitate document navigation.

PROVIDING ACCESS TO FULL-TEXT

While TORPEDO Ultra provides NRL with a true digital library, it serves another, equally important, function. Because TORPEDO Ultra documents are stored with a Uniform Resource Locator (URL) based on the bibliographic characteristics of the document, they can be readily fetched by other databases in use by NRL and ONR researchers. TORPEDO Ultra therefore provides the underpinning for content by enabling a broad range of library resources. *Content-enabling* refers to providing links to full-text documents. The library has capitalized on this TORPEDO Ultra capability and is in the process of content-enabling three of its most heavily used services, its Web-based catalog, its locally mounted *Science Citation Index Expanded* database, and an e-mail journal alerting service, Contents-to-Go.

The library has added URLs to its online catalog for some six thousand technical reports and ten thousand other NRL-authored publications that are available digitally in TORPEDO Ultra. This provides end users performing a Web-based catalog search with immediate access to the full content of NRL technical reports and publications. Activating a hyperlink that says "Full Content" launches the Acrobat Reader and displays the PDF image of the first page of the report along with thumbnail page images. A similar process takes catalog users to digital holdings of journals that are in the TORPEDO Ultra collection. In the case of journals, clicking on the hyperlink connects users to the journal in TORPEDO, where they can browse digital holdings or perform a search.

One of the most frequently used InfoWeb databases is *Science Citation Index Expanded* produced by the Institute for Scientific Information (ISI) and mounted at NRL for the use of all employees served by a consortium of four federal science libraries known as the National Research Library Alliance. NRL is currently working with ISI to add hyperlinks to those articles in *Science Citation Index Expanded* that are stored in TORPEDO Ultra. As new articles are added to TORPEDO Ultra, identifying information and URLs will be sent via File Transfer Protocol (FTP) to ISI and automatically added to the next weekly database update installed by NRL. A user searching the citation database will see a "Full Text" button for any article that is stored digitally in TORPEDO Ultra. Clicking on the button will display the PDF file. Authorizations built into the database display the button only to users that are permitted to see a particular article, allowing each consortium member to customize its digital holdings and enter into individual license agreements with publishers. In phase two of this project, links to the ISI bibliographic record will be added to TORPEDO Ultra metadata to enable users to link to article references in the citation database and display the cited article in TORPEDO Ultra. In a third phase, links will be added to journals licensed by consortium members for access from publisher Websites.

One of the most popular digital services the NRL Library has offered over the past several years is called Contents-to-Go. In the beginning, Contents-to-Go had no digital content at all. It combined an automated e-mail alerting service with old-fashioned document delivery, i.e., photocopies sent via interoffice mail.

Here's how Contents-to-Go works. The library subscribes to electronic tables of contents for all journals in its collection. The tables of contents, which are e-mailed to a library mail server, are automatically redistributed to users who have subscribed to the service for specific journals. An InfoWeb interface allows users to select as many journals as they want by clicking a check box. Subscribing requires a user to enter a valid e-mail address, which enables the subscription module to automatically build the mailing lists. No staff intervention is required at any time. Users can add or subtract journals whenever they choose. The e-mail messages that go out to users have customized headers explaining how to request copies of articles, using the e-mail reply function.

An interim step in adding digital content to Contents-to-Go was to add a URL to the header of e-mailed tables of contents for those journals that are stored digitally. This URL takes users into the TORPEDO Ultra system where they can then browse or search for the specific article in which they are interested. Similarly links have been added to Contents-to-Go e-mail messages that take users to journals that are available from publisher Websites. The library will, in the very near future, provide users with the ability to link from the e-mailed table of contents to each individual article in TORPEDO Ultra. This will be accomplished by replacing vendor tables of contents for those journals that are part of TORPEDO Ultra with tables of contents automatically created by the TORPEDO Ultra system each time a new journal issue is added. These system-generated, e-mailed tables of contents will incorporate URLs for each article providing users with enhanced access to digital journal content.

HARDWARE CONFIGUATION

InfoWeb, *Science Citation Index Expanded*, and TORPEDO Ultra run on a Sun Enterprise 4000 server under the Sun Solaris operating system. Documents are stored on a Sun Storage Array RAID Level 5 array, which also accommodates the nearly one full terabyte of online storage required by the Citation Index. The library catalog system runs on a separate Sun system, a Sun Ultra 170. Network access to restricted InfoWeb services is controlled by Internet Protocol (IP) filtering, using Unix Transmission Control Protocol (TCP)-wrappers and IP address ranges.

ADVANTAGES OF TORPEDO ULTRA

TORPEDO Ultra provides a number of advantages to NRL researchers over other Web-based journal retrieval systems from individual publishers or content aggregators by:

- permitting users to take advantage of NRL's excellent network infrastructure, which provides high speed connectivity and near instantaneous access to locally mounted content;
- integrating access to digital content, regardless of whether that content is produced by a commercial publisher, a scholarly association, or a government agency;
- offering a common interface for browsing and searching digital collections, facilitating access and fostering user productivity;
- creating a local archive for journals and other digital publications, thereby assuring future availability of critical research information;
- providing an internal infrastructure for reliably and permanently content-enabling other library databases and services; and
- bringing system enhancements under local control, enabling the library to provide NRL scientists with a product customized to meet their specialized needs.

FUTURE DEVELOPMENT

One of the primary goals of TORPEDO Ultra is to provide users with a single interface for searching the electronic journals of many publishers. For locally archived journals, as well as other materials, this goal has been met. However, for those journals that are resident on publisher Websites, users continue to encounter many diverse approaches to browsing and searching, which vary widely from publisher to publisher. Since any given subject area is usually represented by the journals of multiple publishers, it is not uncommon for users to need to be conversant with the protocols of seven or eight different publishers. The library has created a hyperlinked alphabetical journal list in InfoWeb to enable users to finesse the need to associate a journal with its publisher. However, users are still, for the most part, limited to searching across journals produced by a single publisher or hyperlinking from references to articles that are part of that publisher's archive.

While NRL anticipates implementing agreements with many more publishers for local journal archiving, in some cases it finds that publishers will agree to provide access to digital journals only from their own Website. In the beginning, the rationale for this resistance appeared to be the fear of losing control over copyrighted content. However, more recently NRL is finding that publishers, particularly those that have invested heavily in enhancing their Web journal offerings, are increasingly reluctant to allow libraries to load journals locally. Examples of common publisher enhancements are links from references to records in auxiliary databases or digital archives, forward and backward hyperlinking to citing or cited articles, and links to external Web sites. The availability of an enhanced hyperlinked Web journal appears to cause publishers to view digital versions of the printed publication as inferior products, which they are hesitant to provide to libraries.

TORPEDO Ultra offers a solution to the problem of simultaneously searching or browsing journals on remote Websites along with locally mounted publications. Implementing this solution requires that the journal content, which would remain on the publisher Website, be indexed in TORPEDO Ultra. Users could then browse or search TORPEDO Ultra and click on a hyperlinked title to display the full document in PDF regardless of whether it resides locally or on a remote server. NRL is currently exploring two approaches to provide users with such unified searching of locally mounted and distributed documents. Both approaches, which will probably both be available as publisher options, achieve the same end result. They provide the two types of data required by TORPEDO Ultra: bibliographic records for fielded searching and display and access to the full-text for indexing purposes.

In the first approach, which is currently being tested with the American Physical Society, the publisher has provided sample article content in Standard Generalized Markup Language (SGML) format. The intent is for NRL to extract bibliographic data from the delivered SGML file and to index the full-text of the entire article for searching. An alternative approach, to be tested later this year with the American Institute of Physics (AIP), will allow NRL to use a RetrievalWare spider to index journal content on the AIP Website. The publisher will provide associated bibliographic data from the AIP SPIN database for use in TORPEDO Ultra.

CONCLUSION

The NRL Library has made significant progress in providing its user community in four geographic locations with a single point of access to information needed to support scientific research. Locally mounted and remote databases and publications are available to researchers through a Web-based information system and gateway known as InfoWeb. In addition to linking users to journals on publisher Websites, InfoWeb serves as the portal to a local digital repository with sophisticated online browse and search capabilities, called TORPEDO Ultra. Over two hundred journals from three publishers are currently available for browsing or searching through TORPEDO Ultra. In addition, these journals are linked from the library's catalog, a locally mounted *Web of Science* database, and a journal alerting service, providing a spectrum of content-capable services. In support of its goal to provide users with a unified approach to retrieving journal content regardless of location, the library has developed and is testing a strategy to link users to journals that reside on publisher Websites through a TORPEDO Ultra browse or search.

BIBLIOGRAPHY

Atkinson, Roderick D., and Laurie E. Stackpole. "TORPEDO: Networked Access to Full-Text and Page-Image Representations of Physics Journals and Technical Reports." *The Public-Access Computer Systems Review* 6, no. 3 (1995): http://info.lib.uh.edu/pr/v6/n3/atki6n3.html.

Atkinson, Roderick D., Laurie E. Stackpole, and John Yokley, "Developing the Scientific-Technical Digital Library at a National Laboratory," In *Digital Libraries: Current Issues, Digital Libraries Workshop DL '94, Newark, NJ, USA, May 1994, Selected Papers*, ed. Nabil R. Adam, Bharat K. Bhargava, and Yelena Yesha (Berlin: Springer, 1995), 265-279. (Reprinted at: http://infoweb.nrl.navy.mil/NRL_publications/digital_library_94.html)

THE EVOLUTION OF DISTANCE LEARNING ENVIRONMENTS: SHIFT HAPPENS

The Evolution of Distance Learning Environments: Shift Happens

Jean S. Caspers
Lawrence C. Ragan

SUMMARY. Communications technology provides the opportunity to construct learning environments where the learner is separated by space or time. This opportunity creates new challenges for how instruction is delivered at a distance as well as how to provide the necessary support services for the learner. This session will explore the impact of going online and discuss the shifts that occur in the role of the instructor,

Jean S. Caspers is Outreach and Instruction Librarian, Oregon State University's Valley Library.

Lawrence C. Ragan is Director of Instructional Design and Development, Penn State University's Distance Education/World Campus.

[Haworth co-indexing entry note]: "The Evolution of Distance Learning Environments: Shift Happens." Caspers, Jean S., and Lawrence C. Ragan. Co-published simultaneously in *The Serials Librarian* (The Haworth Press, Inc.) Vol. 38, No. 1/2, 2000, pp. 123-133; and: *From Carnegie to Internet2: Forging the Serials Future* (ed: P. Michelle Fiander, Joseph C. Harmon, and Jonathan David Makepeace) The Haworth Press, Inc., 2000, pp. 123-133. Single or multiple copies of this article are available for a fee from The Haworth Document Delivery Service [1-800-342-9678, 9:00 a.m. - 5:00 p.m. (EST). E-mail address: getinfo@haworthpressinc.com].

learner, and institutional support services including access to library resources. The issue of how libraries provide distance learners with services and resources equivalent to those provided for students and faculty on campus will also be addressed. This will be addressed in the context of the new *ACRL Guidelines for Distance Learning Library Services*. *[Article copies available for a fee from The Haworth Document Delivery Service: 1-800-342-9678. E-mail address: getinfo@haworthpressinc.com <Website: http://www.haworthpressinc.com>]*

INTRODUCTION

Distance education has recently been heralded as both the savior and death of higher education as we know it. For many, distance education provides the opportunity to participate in advanced academic study while remaining fully engaged in work and family. For others, the mere thought of offering meaningful programs of study without ever seeing or meeting the student violates the core tenets of higher education as a social and cultural change agent. Regardless of on what side of the debate one stands, the reality of learning anytime, anyplace presents a series of both academic and organizational challenges for educational and corporate institutions alike.

Traditional correspondence distance education programs, built upon a history of print delivery and surface mail systems, have been operating quite successfully for over one hundred years. Systems and services have evolved to address the needs of the distance student from course registration, materials delivery, lesson tracking, and grade assignment to advising and career counseling. Many courses offered through traditional distance education programs became self-contained study systems complete with reading packets and laboratory kits. Students progressed independently through their courses successfully achieving their academic goals without ever having to step on the hallowed soils of the granting institution.

With the advent of a wide range of electronic communications technology, a not-so-subtle change has occurred in the distance education landscape. Two of the barriers of the traditional model of distance education can now be adequately addressed. The complaint of the isolated learner has been rectified by on-line electronic communities. Using computer-mediated communications systems and the World Wide Web, communities of learners can now be created that operate academically and even socially on a par with their residential education counterparts. The same electronic technology addresses the issue of time delays to complete a transaction between the learner and the institution. With the introduction of these technologies come new challenges. Students engaged in an on-line course of study need ready access to all of the services of a traditional institution. Groups of learners need to be able to share work, collaborate on assignments, and dynamically engage in dialogue with peers whose only linkage is a thin copper wire. Institutions will need to assess the impact of providing learners at a distance the same services and support systems necessary to make the student's learning experience a success.

CATEGORIES OF SHIFT

When considering the infrastructure necessary to create and support an online community of learners, four categories of issues need to be addressed. Academic curriculum programming defines the course of study opportunities made available for the distance education student. Technological infrastructure and delivery mechanisms create the parameters of possibilities for content delivery, communications systems, individual and group projects and assignments, and evaluation and assessment methods. Administrative services necessary to support students and faculty online need to be considered and barriers resolved. Finally, access to institutional resources are a vital part of the learner's interaction with the institution. Due to the nature of the audience for this paper, this last category will deal specifically with library services.

Each of these categories presents significant opportunities and limitations that require adequate and systematic attention. If not addressed the student will experience frustration and failure when interacting with a system biased towards a residential education model. For example, when faced with a failed modem connection on the Friday evening before the big project is due, the student told "Your call is important to us so please call back between 8:00 a.m. and 5:00 p.m. Monday through Friday EST for technical support" will unlikely be willing to return to the sponsoring institution for additional coursework.

Category 1: Academic Shift

It's all academic. That is, ultimately what attracts the adult learner to a course of study is the potential to gain a degree or certificate that serves as advancement criteria in a field of work. The attractive aspect for most adult learners engaging in this course of study through distance education is that it can be accomplished without leaving the home or workplace. As we have learned more about the needs of the adult lifelong learner, we've come to understand and appreciate the promise of distance education to serve the population of adult learners who need further academic credentials for career advancement.

Academic programs offered online need to address several fundamental questions in order to attract, service, and retain students. Several of these questions challenge the core mission of the institution and fundamentally change the direction and focus of the organization:

- How does access to new audiences, not bound by geographic location, change the mission and direction of the institution?
- What will be the academic programs proposed for delivery via distance education?
- Are the programs relevant to workers employed in industry?
- Does the program have value to the student as a necessity to advance in his or her career?
- Is there a real or perceived sustainable audience for a specific program of study?
- Is there an academic expertise available within the institution to design, develop, and deliver this program via distance education?
- Are there adequate faculty resources to develop and instruct the academic curriculum?
- Is the program one which has value in the marketplace?

Category 2: Technological Shift

One of the driving factors behind the renewed interest in distance education is the development of online systems that enable students to access resources, engage in dialogue within learning communities, and complete assignments and quizzes from the convenience of their home or workplace. Although many of these systems have existed for years, the convergence of digital and analog media along with improved delivery speeds provides the capacity for the development of accessible and effective learning environments. The one remaining factor for creating the ultimate online environment, that of systems predictability, simply won't wait for resolution as more and more institutions and corporations are going online and letting the technology catch up.

Most institutions have in place a technological infrastructure designed to support the local computing and telecommunications needs of the academic community. Lab facilities and technical help desks are familiar sites on campus. Providing access to the same level of resources online can prove challenging and require appropriate planning and funding. Before the assumption is made that this same infrastructure is capable of supporting the distance learning community, several key questions need to be addressed:

- What is the principle technology system to be used in the distance education endeavor?
- How does the proposed system differ from the technological resources made available to resident students?
- Does the online community have access to adequate support and services to establish and maintain the necessary connection and delivery performance?
- What are the defined performance standards for operating and course delivery systems? Will these standards require additional staffing and operating hours?
- Will the same technical service organizations be responsible for supporting resident instruction and online activities?
- What is the degree of technical failure acceptable to the institution providing online access to academic programs?

Category 3: Administrative Shift

Most institutions have been designed, staffed, and maintained to serve a resident student population. Planning the significant adjustments to administrative systems is a key factor to the success of the online program. In some cases, these systems are relatively easy to adjust to accommodate for interacting and servicing distance students. In other cases, administrative and institutional policy may serve as a barrier to serving the distance students and advancing them through the system. One example is the question of financial aid for distance learners. Many of the criteria for students eligibility reference time on task, intensity of study, and time to completion. For the adult learner returning to academic studies while continuing full-time employment, these criteria inhibit student access to these funding resources.

Many institutional policies support requirements for student physical presence for completing a transaction. To receive a student computing account for example, students must present ID and signature at the computing facility. Policies like these need to be revisited for the distance learner. An institution's view of the traditional student may need to be broadened to accommodate for the returning adult learner taking a full load of six credits.

Several of the key questions that need attention in this category include:

- What systems and services are in place to successfully support a student through on-line course registration, lesson and grade tracking, advising and counseling services, and degree or certificate awards?
- Do these systems and procedures accommodate for the dynamics of the distance learner? (For example: longer completion dates, residency requirements, and course load requirements.)
- Have budgetary and financial systems been created to manage and track registrations, department allotments, and program expenses and income?
- Have financial arrangements been established that support the establishment and maintenance of the on-line system?

Category 4: Access Shift: Library Services

As an institutional resource, the library is arguably the heart of any institution of higher learning. And as an organization in itself, the library aptly demonstrates the ongoing academic, technological, administrative, and access-related shift to serving distance learners.

LIBRARIES AND ACADEMIC CURRICULUM

The academic library grows in direct response to the curriculum of its institution. Students and faculty expect to find materials in their library relevant to their studies. Thus faculty members mounting distance delivered courses must naturally consider this question: When I send students to the library, where will they go?

For distance learners, especially those who have not spent time on the campus of a university or college, the most obvious library may be the local public library, or that of a college in their home town. This fact then gives rise to additional questions. Will a student's local library have collected the materials needed to support the curriculum? Will students have access to the full range of services they would receive at their home institution's library, including interlibrary loan and library instruction?

To assure affirmative responses to these and other related questions distance learners must be supported by their own institution's library. And perhaps more to the point, distance learners must have access to library services and resources equivalent to those provided for students on campus. This idea of equal access is the underlying principle promoted by the Association of College and Research Libraries' (ACRL) *Guidelines for Distance Learning Library Services*, revised in July 1998.

First approved in 1981, the guidelines have long served as a foundation for academic libraries providing services to learners off campus. Following an introduction, definitions of terms, and a philosophy section, the guidelines outline recommendations for management, finances, personnel, facilities, resources, services, documentation, and library education as they pertain to distance education library services. The guidelines are intended to complement and support the ACRL standards for two-year colleges, college libraries, and university libraries.

TECHNOLOGICAL INFRASTRUCTURE

The library, like most other organizations, is affected profoundly by technological change. Patrons on-site and those at a distance can both search catalogs and indexes, check on their own borrowing records, place holds, ask reference questions, and read encyclopedia and journal articles from their desktops. Interlibrary loans can be placed online, and if the service exists, materials from their library can be requested for delivery to their homes. These services, once in place, can become relatively routine tasks for library staff.

Library instruction and reference services for the distance learner, however, require more ongoing creativity. For example, when library instruction is identified as a need within, say, a biology course such instruction should be designed for the online environment and technology system used to deliver the biology course. This may demand the development of new skills by instruction librarians working in collaboration with faculty or instructional designers to integrate library research instruction into the course. Generic approaches to library instruction such as Web tutorials, videotapes, or workbooks may enhance efficiency of delivery particularly if the students are referred to these tools strategically at points when they will put the skills taught to use immediately. It is also critical that students have access to reference librarians to reinforce the instruction within the context of their own research.

When providing reference support for distance learners, some unique questions must be answered. Are reference staff trained to expect distance learners may call? Are all the reference staff aware of the services available for distance learners, e.g., if a distance learner's call comes in while the designated distance education librarian is unavailable, can the reference staff on duty coach the distance learner to reconfigure her browser to use the proxy server? Have reference staff had appropriate orientation so they will direct distance learners to the Web forms for placing materials orders?

ADMINISTRATIVE ISSUES

Many libraries have responded to distance education initiatives on their campuses by designating a distance education librarian. Often this is part of a librarian's duties, consuming anywhere from one-tenth to one-half of the position. Some libraries hire a full-time distance education librarian, and some fully staff a separate unit to serve distance learners. Some libraries share the designated librarian with the distance education unit on campus, splitting the salary between them. The librarian so designated needs to report to two administrations, that of the library and that of the distance education unit. If there are branch campuses involved there may also be administrators at the branch to which the librarian must report.

And just as the need for an administrative framework designed for distance learners is apparent, equally apparent is the need to examine systems relevant to such administrative issues as student tracking and program funding. Here again, key questions must be raised and answered. Are students in continuing higher education programs enrolled through the central register so that they are identified as valid students in the central database or by the proxy server which facilitates electronic access to licensed databases? Is funding for distance delivery of library services designated and specifically identified within the originating institution's budget and expenditure reporting statements? Is funding sufficient to cover the type and number of services provided the distance learning community and sufficient to support innovative approaches to meeting student needs?

ACCESS TO APPROPRIATE LIBRARY RESOURCES

And finally services offered by the library to its clientele on campus must be equally accessible to the distance learner. To provide this access, issues of licensing, patron authentication, inter-library cooperation, and student orientation must be addressed. Have license agreements with database vendors been written to accommodate the needs of remote users? Has a system been devised to authenticate distance learners for electronic access to resources? Have arrangements for students to access other libraries via formal or informal arrangements been made? Have distance learners been oriented so they are aware of how to use available services from their institution's library?

CONVERGENCE IN THE VIRTUAL ENVIRONMENT: DISTANCE DISAPPEARS?

In the virtual library environment service demands converge for both the distance student and the student on campus. The learner connecting to the virtual library from two thousand miles away and the student connecting from a dorm on campus or within the library's building are experiencing virtually the same environment. As the expectations of online users become articulated, the core services of libraries will change in response. A higher percent of full-text databases will be made available so researchers and students can find more of what they need in the current literature without leaving their offices, laboratories, or homes. Electronic reserves will become more commonplace. The current confusion about copyright restrictions involving electronic formats will be better understood. Software and hardware facilitating visual as well as audio interactive communication in real time will become as ubiquitous as the telephone and will be used both for local and long distance communication. The basic equipment for fast and reliable connections to the Internet will improve and prices will probably drop as more citizens go online for commerce. As these changes evolve, many more library services for distance learners as compared to students on campus will be identical.

What will not be solved electronically is the researcher's need to explore the physical archive. For example, Oregon State University has over 1.7 million volumes of printed materials which have been collected over decades to support the OSU curriculum. As in many institutions there is a backlog of materials, particularly older proceedings and other serials, which have not been converted to the electronic catalog. In this way the virtual users on campus, in the library building, or at a distance are in an identical situation if they do not consult with library staff. Without interaction with librarians it would be reasonable for the user to conclude that the library does not own materials which do not appear in the catalog.

Creative responses to the information needs of students are best supported by faculty and librarian teams working collaboratively, both as teachers and as advocates to the administration in support of their students.

CONCLUSION

It is heartening to see professionals in distance education providing services to distance learners that are as robust as those provided for traditional, on-campus students. The future success of distance education programs may well depend upon the responsiveness in real terms to fulfillment of that most basic principle as promoted in the ACRL *Guidelines for Distance Learning Library Services*[1], "Members of the distance learning community are entitled to library services and resources equivalent to those provided for students and faculty in traditional campus settings."

NOTE

1. Association of College and Research Libraries. "Guidelines for Distance Learning Library Services." *College and Research Libraries News* 59, no. 9 (1998): 689-694. (Also available online at *http://www.ala.org/acrl/guides/distlrng.html*)

SUGGESTED READING

Larry C. Ragan. "Good Teaching Is Good Teaching: An Emerging Set of Guiding Principles and Practices for the Design and Development of Distance Education." *Cause/effect* 22, no. 1 (1999).

Looking Back

Donna K. Cohen
Karen A. Schmidt

Presenters

Jennifer L. Edwards

Recorder

SUMMARY. The presenters provided a reflective look back on libraries and serials librarianship in the 20th century. First they took a look at Andrew Carnegie, who donated thousands of libraries to communities and educational institutions. Then they highlighted the people and processes that have shaped serials librarianship and acquisitions work. *[Article copies available for a fee from The Haworth Document Delivery Service: 1-800-342-9678. E-mail address: getinfo@haworthpressinc.com <Website: http://www.haworthpressinc.com>]*

Donna K. Cohen is Associate Professor and Head of Acquisitions, Rollins College.
Karen A. Schmidt is Director of Collections and Assessment, University of Illinois at Urbana-Champaign.
Jennifer L. Edwards is Serials Cataloger, MIT Libraries.

[Haworth co-indexing entry note]: "Looking Back." Edwards, Jennifer L. Co-published simultaneously in *The Serials Librarian* (The Haworth Press, Inc.) Vol. 38, No. 1/2, 2000, pp. 135-138; and: *From Carnegie to Internet2: Forging the Serials Future* (ed: P. Michelle Fiander, Joseph C. Harmon, and Jonathan David Makepeace) The Haworth Press, Inc., 2000, pp. 135-138. Single or multiple copies of this article are available for a fee from The Haworth Document Delivery Service [1-800-342-9678, 9:00 a.m. - 5:00 p.m. (EST). E-mail address: getinfo@haworthpressinc.com].

Donna Cohen looked back at Andrew Carnegie and his role in providing thousands of libraries to communities and educational institutions. Over his lifetime, Carnegie gave almost $400 million, over 90% of his wealth, toward philanthropic activities. These gifts included $48 million toward the establishment of free public libraries. Less well known were his contributions to 108 academic libraries. Cohen provided a brief biography of Carnegie and focused her presentation on these academic libraries. Her interest in these particular libraries began with her awareness of the existence of a Carnegie library (now used in another capacity) on her campus at Rollins College in Florida.

Andrew Carnegie came from Scotland as a child and settled in Allegheny, Pennsylvania, now a part of Pittsburgh. By his late 20s, Carnegie was working in the steel industry and amassing his wealth. As a child working in the mills, he was one of many poor boys invited to use Colonel Anderson's private library of 400 books, which led to his lifelong interest in libraries. In 1889, Carnegie wrote his famous treatise, *The Gospel of Wealth*, in which he outlined his philosophy of philanthropy and of the administration of wealth. Carnegie felt that those who have wealth should give it away to benefit society. He listed the best fields of philanthropy, noting that the best public use of money is the establishment and development of libraries. As a condition of his donations, he demanded matching funds, believing that this would lead to a mass "leveling-up" of society. Carnegie was much criticized for his philanthropic work because, it was said, his wealth was based on the work of the poor and he was giving away money just to increase his own fame.

In 1901, Carnegie retired to devote himself full-time to philanthropic efforts. Among his lesser-known donations, Carnegie funded Melvil Dewey's efforts in developing a simplified spelling board. His money also developed a pension fund for academic faculty, which eventually became TIAA-CREF. Today, Carnegie is most recognized for his library gifts. The Carnegie Foundation stopped funding the building of libraries at the advent of World War I.

By the turn of the century, changes in education led from lecture and recitation to the university model, with more emphasis on libraries and collections. In 1905, a formal announcement was made that Carnegie would be funding libraries for academic institutions and outlined the procedures required for requesting a gift. The process involved very detailed forms and included letters from trustees, faculty, students, and college presidents. Carnegie's secretary, James Bertram, was the one who actually selected which institutions were to get the gift of a library. Most of these were small struggling colleges, including African-American institutions, but not the well-known universities. Cohen noted that one bias Carnegie had was that no church-supported schools were to receive a gift. As with other gifts, institutions were required to raise matching funds, some requiring 3-4 years to raise the money. For some colleges, the library was the first permanent building on campus, and provided the opportunity to have the institution's first, full-time, trained librarians. Some colleges receiving a library gift included: Earlham College, University of North Carolina, Converse College, Juniata College, Fisk University, and Syracuse University.

Beyond providing matching funds, there were no restrictions on the buildings themselves. There was no requirement that Carnegie's name appear on the building, nor did the building have to remain as a library. In fact, only 2 libraries continue to serve in their original capacity today. The architecture of the buildings varied, depending on the location, style of other buildings on campus, and the architect (Carnegie recommended architects Edward Tilton or Henry Whitefield). The buildings included large reading rooms, seminar rooms, rooms for instructional use, and the newest styles of library furniture. With the new emphasis on research and investigation, room for growth of book collections was included in the design of the buildings. An endowment was also established to ensure a planned development program for collections.

Karen Schmidt took a light-hearted look back at the development of serials librarianship over the years, with an emphasis on changing technologies for serials acquisitions work. Schmidt first gave a brief history of serials librarianship. The first recognized serials textbook, written by a secretary in 1930, surveyed academic libraries and established who was responsible for periodicals check-in, keeping ledgers, etc. The 1930s was the decade in which serials came into being as an issue. A debate started at this time about how to organize serials in libraries. In 1935 an essay was published proposing that serials be a separate department.

Schmidt then showed slides of changing technology. Beginning in the 1890s an adjustable book holder provided a public display, so that people could find material on their own. She highlighted the changes in serial check-in, starting with ledgers, then 3 × 5 cards, then the Kardex with its pocket cabinets, and now automated procedures. Other tools highlighted included: the Bates date stamp, the cataloger's camera (used to create records from the printed National Union Catalog), an electric eraser from 1949, a magazine drill, examples of different types of bindings, and periodical displays. She also showed a picture of an early bookmobile, a converted old truck, noting that ALA had guidelines for such conversions. To show that some things never change, Schmidt included a picture of a microfilm reader from the 1960s, which looks the same as the ones today.

ONE HUNDRED PERCENT COMMUNICATION

One Hundred Percent Communication

Mary Devlin

Presenter

Carol D. Green

Recorder

SUMMARY. Effective communication is essential for professional and personal success. The main cause of difficulty among colleagues, with vendors, or with customers comes from communication breakdowns. We think we have spoken clearly, only to find what we thought we said wasn't what was heard. Then there's the rest of communication, the ninety-three percent that's nonverbal. Mary Devlin explains how we can transform interactions with others by enhancing verbal and nonverbal communication and rapport. *[Article copies available for a fee from The Haworth Document Delivery Service: 1-800-342-9678. E-mail address: getinfo@haworthpressinc.com <Website: http://www.haworthpressinc.com>]*

Mary Devlin is Principal of Mary Devlin Associates.

Carol D. Green is Serials Librarian, University of Southern Mississippi.

[Haworth co-indexing entry note]: "One Hundred Percent Communication." Green, Carol D. Co-published simultaneously in *The Serials Librarian* (The Haworth Press, Inc.) Vol. 38, No. 1/2, 2000, pp. 139-141; and: *From Carnegie to Internet2: Forging the Serials Future* (ed: P. Michelle Fiander, Joseph C. Harmon, and Jonathan David Makepeace) The Haworth Press, Inc., 2000, pp. 139-141. Single or multiple copies of this article are available for a fee from The Haworth Document Delivery Service [1-800-342-9678, 9:00 a.m. - 5:00 p.m. (EST). E-mail address: getinfo@haworthpressinc.com].

Mary Devlin began with a discussion of verbal and nonverbal channels of communication, which can be broken down into percentages. Surprisingly only seven percent of all communication is through words. Fifty-five percent of nonverbal communication is physiological, such as gestures, facial expression, or movement. Thirty-eight percent is vocal, such as tone and vocal expression or quality.

With verbal communication we are consciously thinking about what we are saying. Nonverbal communication conveys a larger amount of meaning than verbal communication yet it is mostly unconscious. At this point Devlin moved on to the main objective of her presentation, how to consciously use forms of verbal and nonverbal communication to build rapport with other people.

Rapport is an unconscious part of communication but is much more than body language. It is the ability to see another's point of view and is critical to communication and understanding. Rapport is the most important part of interaction.

Devlin said that people like people who are similar to themselves. Pulling a volunteer from the audience, she demonstrated how mirroring physiological traits like gestures, posture, or facial expressions during communication can build rapport. Vocal tonality, speed, quality, and volume can also be matched. For example, when communicating with a person who is upset or angry, if you can match their vocal quality but lessen it slightly, then rapport will happen.

Rapport can also be reached through language. Individuals fall into one of three categories or representation systems according to their preferred modes of thinking and expression, i.e., visual, auditory, or kinesthetic (feeling). Those in the visual category think in pictures and use visual words such as *look*, *see*, or *show*. Auditory individuals are more influenced by voices and sounds. They may talk to themselves internally and use auditory words like *hear*, *tell*, or *listen*. Kinesthetic individuals relate their internal emotions into external feelings. They use kinesthetic words like *feel*, *handle*, or *touch*. The types of predicates (verbs, adverbs, adjectives) people use will give a clue to how they communicate. Rapport can be reached by matching the predicates and speech patterns of the person with whom you are talking.

How can you tell if you've reached rapport with another person? Indicators include a feeling of comfort and ease; color change, e.g., a slight blush, either in yourself or the other person; and being able to lead the person and have them follow what you're doing.

During the presentation, Devlin had audience members pair off and conduct communication exercises. This was followed by an enthusiastic discussion of the results. Devlin concluded with a question and answer session. Participants were given a handout that included an outline of the program, a bibliography, and examples of representation systems and language.

. . . AND I'LL HAVE THAT ORDER WITH A LICENSE ON THE SIDE, PLEASE

Vendors and Licenses: Adding Value for Customers

John Blosser

SUMMARY. The author argues that vendors have an opportunity to add value to their electronic products by assisting libraries in establishing licensing agreements, and by providing information online to reduce the amount of subscription-associated paperwork currently the norm in libraries. He then outlines a library wish-list of value-added vendor services. *[Article copies available for a fee from The Haworth Document Delivery Service: 1-800-342-9678. E-mail address: getinfo@haworthpressinc.com <Website: http://www.haworthpressinc.com>]*

INTRODUCTION

Periodical and book vendors have traditionally provided print materials to library collections, but this tradition is changing as most ven-

John Blosser is Serials Cataloger and Acquisitions Librarian, Northwestern University Library.

[Haworth co-indexing entry note]: "Vendors and Licenses: Adding Value for Customers." Blosser, John. Co-published simultaneously in *The Serials Librarian* (The Haworth Press, Inc.) Vol. 38, No. 1/2, 2000, pp. 143-146; and: *From Carnegie to Internet2: Forging the Serials Future* (ed: P. Michelle Fiander, Joseph C. Harmon, and Jonathan David Makepeace) The Haworth Press, Inc., 2000, pp. 143-146. Single or multiple copies of this article are available for a fee from The Haworth Document Delivery Service [1-800-342-9678, 9:00 a.m. - 5:00 p.m. (EST). E-mail address: getinfo@haworthpressinc.com].

dors now also include electronic resources in their product offerings. Although they provide the resource, the licensing agreement, an integral part of the electronic resource purchase, is generally left to the library. Licensing workshops are a great help in educating the brave souls who must deal with licensing agreements, but licensing agreements are nonetheless approached with trepidation by many librarians and staff. Given that most libraries approach licensing hesitantly, vendors could provide a great value-added service by supporting at least the routine processing of licenses. What follows are suggestions for value-added services related to licensing agreements which vendors could supply.

VENDORS AS MIDDLEMEN

Vendors could act as the middle-men between libraries and publishers, and work to standardize the format, language, definitions, and general conditions specified in licensing contracts. Such help is needed to overcome problems of poor contract layout and design and differences between legal language and plain English. Vendors, because they deal with electronic products daily, could develop expertise in licensing while libraries will either not have the personnel to devote to licensing, or will deal with so few electronic products that expertise will be difficult to develop.

Points for negotiation in licensing agreements between publishers and libraries: permission to use electronic materials for document delivery or inter-library loan; permission for libraries to archive electronic resources; and changing language in the license which would put the library at risk of liability due to patrons' misuse of electronic resources.

ONLINE SUBSCRIPTION AND LICENSING INFORMATION

Vendors possess information which is valuable not only to them, but to their customers. This information could be shared with their library customers via an online information site. Such an online resource could include: licensing agreement; billing information; product updates–including database descriptions; registration information such as passwords and customer numbers; technical and support information; and approved IP addresses and/or domain names. If such information were provided online, how much simpler to update IP addresses by sending changes to one vendor, rather than to many publishers. Vendors might also facilitate renewals to both print and electronic versions of a subscription with the publisher. This service would be very valuable because often the connection between the print subscription and the "free with print" electronic version accompanying it are not associated on invoices. When this happens, re-registration is often necessary. Online information detailing a library's subscription information, including free electronic versions of print resources, might help prevent renewal problems presently experienced with such package subscriptions. In lieu of such online support, many libraries are keeping paper files duplicating the information held by vendors. It seems ironic for libraries to maintain a growing body of paper file folders for electronic resources, the "new wave" of the publishing future. Permitting online registration for groups of titles would also be a help to libraries. Presently, some vendors offer notification schemes, but the library must register for each title individually with the publisher.

INCORPORATE PATRON USAGE GUIDELINES IN ELECTRONIC RESOURCE

It would be nice if the electronic resources themselves prominently displayed the restrictions of use in clear, concise language for the end-user to read. Such messages would help educate the end-user. Librarians cannot monitor all patrons while they use databases, and privacy considerations make it difficult for librarians to query patrons on the use they are making of a database. Consequently, clear messages within electronic resources might help libraries fulfill their role of advising users of their responsibilities when using the material.

LICENSING EDUCATION

While vendors may eventually be able to make a greater contribution to libraries' management of electronic resources, where can librarians go for help now? There are many valuable workshops, such as those given by the Association of Research Libraries throughout the year, and those given at conferences, like the recent 4th European Serials Conference in Manchester, England, and, of course, those provided at NASIG's annual conference. A helpful listserv is LIBLICENSE-L (liblicense-l@lists.yale.edu) which moderates discussion on licensing issues. The listserv team has developed software which is available to librarians, vendors, and publishers to help them create, revise or adapt existing licenses and is available at: http://www.library. yale.edu/~llicense/software.shtml.

Licensing: A Publisher's Perspective

Eileen Lawrence

SUMMARY. The author describes the publisher's experience in creating licensing agreements for electronic products; discusses the complexity of understanding and learning to create licensing agreements; and outlines criteria that should be included in a license. *[Article copies available for a fee from The Haworth Document Delivery Service: 1-800-342-9678. E-mail address: getinfo@haworthpressinc.com <Website: http://www.haworthpressinc.com>]*

INTRODUCTION

The first time I looked at a Chadwyck-Healey license agreement for purchasing full-text databases, I must confess that I felt *something* resembling fear–even if it was just fear about when I would ever have time to digest such a document and truly understand it. At that time, someone else in our company had responsibility for negotiating license agreements with our customers. Lucky for me? Not really, because that distance between the document and me did not lessen my anxiety. I would watch one of our databases going out into Libraryland in the form of a tape or CD, with all that carefully digitized and marked-up data, knowing that the customer would own the rights to use that data . . . *forever.* I'd think about the meaning of the words I'd

---

Eileen Lawrence, Vice President Sales, Chadwyck-Healey Inc.

[Haworth co-indexing entry note]: "Licensing: A Publisher's Perspective." Lawrence, Eileen. Co-published simultaneously in *The Serials Librarian* (The Haworth Press, Inc.) Vol. 38, No. 1/2, 2000, pp. 147-153; and: *From Carnegie to Internet2: Forging the Serials Future* (ed: P. Michelle Fiander, Joseph C. Harmon, and Jonathan David Makepeace) The Haworth Press, Inc., 2000, pp. 147-153. Single or multiple copies of this article are available for a fee from The Haworth Document Delivery Service [1-800-342-9678, 9:00 a.m. - 5:00 p.m. (EST). E-mail address: getinfo@haworthpressinc.com].

seen on the license–words such as "in perpetuity" and "without limit in time." The feeling was not unlike that of watching one's child walk to school alone for the first time.

As with most things in life, we tend to be afraid of the unknown. So I decided to take on the job of negotiating licenses with customers, and it continues to be my responsibility today. Licensing is still a complex issue, but as I got to know our own document, and as I grew to understand the needs and wishes of my customers, the anxiety went away. The task has become at least neutral, if not enjoyable–another opportunity to get to know customers, share information, and shake hands over a mutual creation.

FEAR OF LICENSES

What is everyone so afraid of? Certainly licensing issues are not trivial. For libraries, the fear is that the Licensing Police will show up and do very bad things; libraries don't want to be held legally and financially responsible for contract violations made by users, and they can't peer over users' shoulders, practically or legally. Publishers are afraid that their painstakingly created data will be misused, resold, or copied–that what they've created to sell may not remain saleable. Both of us become intimidated by the process itself. We wish that the license could be written in plain English, but then we suspect the document won't hold up in court if it's not in proper Legalese. And if only licenses didn't take up *so much of our time*!

Counteracting these concerns are a few reassuring facts for publishers. Librarians are by nature protectors, defenders, and nurturers of information. We're not in a tug of war with each other, but rather on the same side of the table, working together to achieve practical and comfortable solutions. And, despite all else, librarians do want publishers to survive and thrive, so that we can continue to provide the information that you need in order to do your jobs. Also, at Chadwyck-Healey we enjoy a high level of mutual trust with our customers. So we've won the game together before we even begin.

What do licenses protect? Can they be created simply and fairly for both sides? At Chadwyck-Healey, there are two ways in which we give libraries access to our data. If you purchase the data outright, you're really purchasing a license to use the data forever, within the terms of the agreement. You pay a one-time fee, and because we're turning over a magnetic tape or CD, the license agreement must be carefully negotiated; the data is passing in physical form into the library's hands, with substantial and long-lasting rights. This kind of agreement is longer and more complex, because the stakes are higher.

The other means to our data is through a renewable subscription. If it's a microform subscription, there's little to worry about. The data behaves like paper and is covered by existing law and familiar expectations. A microform collection can be lent like a book, for example. If it's a Web subscription–and here's our brave new world–things become more complex again. A Web subscription can't be lent, but rather must be used only by authorized users at the subscribing site. Otherwise, the publisher would sell one subscription to Library A, who could "lend" it via the library's home page, and the publisher would never be able to sell another subscription. This is simple common sense.

There's a word that begins to emerge at this point in the discussion, a word that floated toward me at just the right time about a year ago. I was attending the ARL licensing workshop for publishers, and it was shortly after I took on the licensing responsibilities at Chadwyck-Healey. I was still trying to understand a lot of new material, and the responsibility seemed very "capital R." I wondered if a wrong word or misplaced comma could cause irreparable damage to my company. I was swimming upstream against strange terms such as "indemnification" and "force majeure" and the difference between "arbitration" and "mediation," and then that word came floating toward me like a life raft: *reasonable*.

I learned from the workshop leader that I didn't have to specify exactly what percentage of the database could be copied onto a temporary storage medium. Instead, the license could say "a reasonable amount." And I didn't have to strike fear into my customers' hearts by requiring that they take every imaginable measure to ensure compliance by all their users. Instead, the license could require that the library take "reasonable measures." And this word *reasonable* would be understood in a court of law. Things began to take on a quality of common sense.

WHAT WE DO AT CHADWYCK-HEALEY

So I've come around to believing that we don't have to be lawyers to work together on these documents. We just have to agree on what's reasonable. Can a subscription vendor help us? Things have become relatively easy and comfortable, so at Chadwyck-Healey we don't feel as if we need help right now. But I came here today to listen with an open mind. And of course, just when things get comfortable something changes. Here's how we're handling licenses at the moment, along with some ideas for where we're headed, and some thoughts on how a vendor might help.

First, we believe that our licenses should not be secret. We've tried to make them simple, and we're happy to make them public. Our full-text license agreement is posted on the liblicense Website at Yale, and I'm happy to send copies of both our documents–the full-text purchase agreement and the subscription agreement–to any one who would like them.

The full-text license agreement is the only one for which we require a signature. That's because the library is purchasing the rights to use the data forever, so the publisher has more to lose. The data has to be carefully protected because it will be in the library's possession, and because the customer has extensive rights–including the right to mount our data behind the library's own interface along with other publishers' data, the right to modify the SGML markup, and so forth. This document is four pages long in Times New Roman 11, with double spaces between each of the sixteen clauses, and with a lot of white space and sixteen bold headings taking up a good amount of the document. I tell you all of this so that you understand that we've created something that is not a monster.

Customer feedback regarding this license agreement is very positive. Generally, in the case of a single institution, the document comes back to us with no more than a few requests for changes, and we are happy to accommodate all reasonable requests. Consortia may pose more challenges, and the more members in the consortia the more need for customizing, but this is nothing that time can't take care of. Tomorrow I'll be finalizing a license agreement with a very large statewide consortium, and the document will have been amended to the satisfaction of both parties with about an hour of phone time and one 10-item list of change-requests by the consortium's attorney. The list of change-requests took no more than 10 minutes for me to approve; they were quite reasonable. Customizing this full-text license agreement for other groups has been more complex, but I've never experienced a situation in which Chadwyck-Healey and the consortium hit an impossible impasse. Only once in the two years that I've handled licensing have we had to consult an attorney for advice, and that was for wording of one sentence.

We have further simplified the full-text license agreement by having it be a one-time effort. Once a customer signs the agreement, we never have to revisit the task. When the customer purchases additional databases, we simply add an amendment (signed by both parties) adding the new database to the agreement.

In contrast to our full-text license agreement, our subscription license agreement is only three pages long, and we don't require a signature on this document. That's because there's less at risk when we give a library access to our data via the Web, or through a CD subscription that is updated quarterly. If we learn that the library is misusing our data, we have easy recourse–we can simply turn off Web access or stop shipping the CD updates. (Of course, we would never do this except in an extreme case, and after giving the library notice of the violation and reasonable time to remedy the situation. At Chadwyck-Healey we have never had to take such action.) In some instances, the library's policy is to require that this document be signed, and then we're happy to do so–and this may involve some changes to the document before the library will sign. But here again, customer feedback tells us that we're on the right track; usually there are only a handful of minor changes needed. And I repeat–we will accommodate all reasonable requests.

Why has the process become relatively painless for us? Perhaps because our documents are fairly comfortably aligned with the *Principles for Licensing Electronic Resources* [1] drafted in July of 1997. Moving on from those guidelines, we take the experience learned from each contract exercise and shape the document to make the next contract negotiation easier for the customer. One of our major consortia, for example, wanted one unified document, combining the full-text purchase agreement and the Web license agreement. It took some time to hammer out, then we had a timesaving template that other consortia have since found useful. We also saw that some items kept popping up on the list of requested changes, indemnification and governing law, for example, and we can now very quickly execute those changes in very little time.

FUTURE PLANS

My summer project, about to be pulled off a very old back burner, is to rework our license agreements as samples, formatted with two columns. On the left will be the language of the agreement itself, and on the right, the translation into plain English along with our rationale. This sort of sample license will eliminate some of the mystery and can indicate to our customers where and how we are able to accommodate the most frequently requested changes. I also would like to see our license agreements posted on our Website–they're not there, which was a surprise to me as I prepared for this session. Our Web subscription guidelines should be built into the products as well. Also planned is a further simplification of the subscription agreement. I know that it could be even shorter and simpler, and this too is one of my summer projects.

I doubt that there will ever be one all-purpose license agreement, because the considerations vary so much from sale to sale. We have to consider the products, the library, the user level, and other variables. For example, if we're licensing the *Patrologia Latina*, a database of medieval literature written in Latin, we won't be concerned about a major university's distance learners who are using workstations at their local community college. But if it's a database of twentieth century American poetry, we will be concerned. The language will have to be crafted carefully to ensure that only the distance learners from the major university have access, unless the community college chooses to subscribe as well. And there are other issues–concerns particular to the institution, an individual lawyer's preferences, and various special considerations.

But there also will always be the basics: What is being protected and in what format? Define *authorized user*. Define *site*. Specify number of users. Say clearly what the users can and cannot do with the data, with the software. Explain the warranty, the guaranteed percentage of up time. Explain what will happen if the license terms are breached, how the publisher will let the library know, and how much time the library will have to remedy the breach. Explain the rules for remote access. If it's a consortium, list the member libraries. For these "givens," we might be able to come up with a standard outline and standard language that forms a contract *foundation*. Then we can customize, building on the foundation, as needed.

Can a subscription agency play a role? The feeling at Chadwyck-Healey has been that we don't want to put another layer of complexity between the customer and ourselves. We will always need to review proposed license changes, so we might as well be talking directly to our customer from the start. There is already an excellent source for standard language on the liblicense Website, language we're comfortable with. On the other hand, some libraries may not want to have to search the liblicense site and do the work of modifying our license. Libraries may welcome the efforts of a subscription vendor that crafts a generic license that meets library and publishers needs.

CONCLUSION

Our full-text purchase agreement should remain our personal, living, evolving document that we work on directly with our customers, because of the complex issues surrounding ownership and the unique needs of each library. But for Web subscription agreements, we want to do what is most useful to our customers. If they would like the help of a vendor, we'll take a close and open-minded look at the proposals. As long as the basics are covered and our data is protected, we're amenable to any format. Most of all, we don't want to make the process more complicated than it is. If vendor participation adds unnecessary or time-consuming steps in the process, we'll be reticent. But if it makes things easier and faster, we'll join the chorus of *hoorays*.

NOTE

1. *Principles for Licensing Electronic Resources.* Members of the Working Groups contributing to this document include: Robert Oakley, American Association of Law Libraries; Trisha L. Davis, American Library Association; Brian Schottlaender, American Library Association, ALCTS/CMDS, Chief Collection Development Officers of Large Research Libraries; Karen Butter, Association of Academic Health Sciences Libraries and Medical Library Association; Mary Case, Association of Research Libraries; John Latham, Special Libraries Association. *Editor's note.* The document is available at the Special Libraries Association Website: http://www.sla.org/govt/diglic59.html

Subscription Agent and Publisher Initiatives

Jan Peterson

Presenter

Jodith Janes
P. Michelle Fiander

Contributors

SUMMARY. Jan Peterson outlined vendor's concerns in creating licensing agreements and described services that may be developed and offered by vendors. *[Article copies available for a fee from The Haworth Document Delivery Service: 1-800-342-9678. E-mail address: getinfo@haworthpressinc.com <Website: http://www.haworthpressinc.com>]*

Jan Peterson reminded the audience that print differs greatly from electronic resources. Aside from copyright restrictions, print materials, once purchased, require no special attention or contracts. Electronic materials, on the other hand, require negotiations, license agreements, usage restrictions, local registrations, identification of end-users, and multiple pricing models–bundled, pay-per-view, etc. In addition to the

Jan Peterson is Vice President, Publisher Relations and Content Development, Dawson/Faxon Information Services Group.

Jodith Janes is a librarian at the Cleveland Clinic Alumni Library.

P. Michelle Fiander is Cataloger and Reference Librarian, IUPUI University Library.

[Haworth co-indexing entry note]: "Subscription Agent and Publisher Initiatives." Janes, Jodith, and P. Michelle Fiander. Co-published simultaneously in *The Serials Librarian* (The Haworth Press, Inc.) Vol. 38, No. 1/2, 2000, pp. 155-156; and: *From Carnegie to Internet2: Forging the Serials Future* (ed: P. Michelle Fiander, Joseph C. Harmon, and Jonathan David Makepeace) The Haworth Press, Inc., 2000, pp. 155-156. Single or multiple copies of this article are available for a fee from The Haworth Document Delivery Service [1-800-342-9678, 9:00 a.m. - 5:00 p.m. (EST). E-mail address: getinfo@haworthpressinc.com].

complications involved in acquiring electronic materials, vendors, publishers, and libraries are debating the very meaning of acquisition as suggested by the access versus ownership debate.

Major concerns regarding the licensing of electronic materials include a lack of standard definitions within agreements, questions of enforcement obligations, archival rights, perpetual access, and privacy issues. It is unlikely that these concerns will be easily or quickly solved. As distributors of information, agents have, in some cases, been by-passed by library consortia, which deal with redistribution of information themselves. To avoid being by-passed, subscription agents must seek ways to help their clients. Involvement in licensing agreements is one way to offer this help.

The generic Standard License Agreement initiative, spear-headed by John Cox, of Jon Cox Associates, UK, and in association with five other subscription agents, is one example of the type of service agents can and will offer. This standard licensing agreement will function as a template which can be modified to accommodate the various requirements and demands of academic, corporate and special libraries.

Services offered by Faxon Inc. to electronic resource customers include: approved IP addresses, contact people, consortia membership, and licensing details, such as number of workstations and/or simultaneous users for individual resources. They also offer a License Depot organized by publisher and title, with links to publishers' sites. The next step is to customize this interface for clients and to archive license agreements.

Searching and Access to Full Content on the Web, or, We've Got Documents and Publications, Now What?

Mark Wasson
Ray Daley

SUMMARY. Explores solutions for providing researchers with access to full content in next generation resources–those that are multi-disciplinary, index heterogeneous sources of content and access digital and non-digital resources. This paper describes the tools and processes used by LEXIS-NEXIS to put text data online, focussing on the process of normalizing unlike data to create large files for efficient, effective searching. It also looks at how similar techniques may be applied to different types of data, including documents and other materials outside LEXIS-NEXIS' warehouse, in order to increase the breadth of content to which search and retrieval processes can apply. *[Article copies available for a fee from The*

Mark Wasson is Senior Architect, LEXIS-NEXIS, a Division of Reed Elsevier plc.
Ray Daley is Product Consultant, LEXIS-NEXIS, a Division of Reed Elsevier plc.

[Haworth co-indexing entry note]: "Searching and Access to Full Content on the Web, or, We've Got Documents and Publications, Now What?" Wasson, Mark, and Ray Daley. Co-published simultaneously in *The Serials Librarian* (The Haworth Press, Inc.) Vol. 38, No. 1/2, 2000, pp. 157-163; and: *From Carnegie to Internet2: Forging the Serials Future* (ed: P. Michelle Fiander, Joseph C. Harmon, and Jonathan David Makepeace) The Haworth Press, Inc., 2000, pp. 157-163. Single or multiple copies of this article are available for a fee from The Haworth Document Delivery Service [1-800-342-9678, 9:00 a.m. - 5:00 p.m. (EST). E-mail address: getinfo@haworthpressinc.com].

Haworth Document Delivery Service: 1-800-342-9678. E-mail address: getinfo@ haworthpressinc.com <Website: http://www.haworthpressinc.com>]

INTRODUCTION

The strengths of LEXIS-NEXIS in normalizing unlike data to create large group files for efficient and effective searching are well known in the information industry. We collect data from a variety of publishers and vendors and in a variety of different formats, and process and package the data in ways that allow our customers to use the same search engine and the same queries to retrieve information from across this collection. In order to accomplish this, we rely on a number of strategies for standardizing this content in terms of document structure, keyword searching, and document enhancements.

BASIC DOCUMENT PREPARATION

Overview. Historically, documents have been the core components of a digital library. Documents can be articles, memos, abstracts, driver's license records, court cases and so on. And, historically, documents have been the "information containers" that we standardize, structure, analyze, and enhance, all with the help of "metadata," which is defined as descriptive information about a document and its content.

We license content, or obtain it through other means from a variety of sources and formats. We could store data from each source separately in order to maintain those source-specific differences, but that would leave it up to the information consumer–our customers–to search each source individually. In order to help them search across sources, we needed to break the database barrier. This involves standardizing the documents across databases; assigning metadata to documents that can be used in accessing and manipulating documents; assigning metastructures to the databases in order to control document presentation, and creating search systems that exploit the metadata and metastructures in order to help information consumers access and manipulate documents.

The primary function of our document preparation steps–our data fabrication process–is to collect documents from a number of publishers and vendors, to standardize the format and content of those documents in order to facilitate search and retrieval, and to update those documents to our online warehouse.

Collection and Conversion. Publishers and other vendors license content to LEXIS-NEXIS. As part of our partnerships with content suppliers, they send us regular feeds of texts, usually tied to their publication cycle. Our first task is to standardize the data's basic markup. Our collection and conversion process collects documents from these vendors and converts the publisher's markup language to our proprietary Variable Input String Format (VISF) markup language.

VISF was quite useful when it was first deployed, and in spite of some limitations (not the least of which is its proprietary nature) it continues to serve us well. However, SGML and now XML have growing followings, and there are a number of advantages to moving to a more common markup language. We are moving some data and products to XML to take advantage of its increased flexibility and the data integration support that XML provides.

Editing. Once a document has been converted to a common markup language, the heart of our data fabrication process begins: we are ready to edit and clean up the document. Depending on data volume, license restrictions, copyright issues and other factors, we may edit the document for any of a number of reasons. This may include the need to correct typographical and data transmission-induced errors, to clean up the document structure, to replace previous versions of some document, or to annotate documents with enhancements that our products and services can exploit. These tasks are accomplished through a number of processes, both manual and automatic.

Update. Update is the process of putting data online so that it can be searched. The update process uses database-specific metastructure and design information, stop word lists and other information to determine which parts of a document should be made searchable. The text of the document is stored in a database-file system. Searchable keywords are added to an inverted file that underlies both our Boolean and natural language search engines.

At update, a copy of the data can also be routed to other processes in order to support Web-based and other non-online products and features. These additional processes may be too slow for regular update, or perhaps they should only apply to a small number of documents.

Search and Retrieval. Scale and optimization issues notwithstanding, search and retrieval basically make use of rather straightforward inverted file technologies. The terms in a search query are found in the inverted file, and the locations where they occur in our databases are identified from there. A process that interprets the query structure and search operators is then used to reduce the set of potentially matching documents to those that actually do match the query.

Discussion. For any given document or publication, the steps in our data fabrication process are generally well defined. The real complication comes not from this basic process, but rather from our need to adapt this process to the volume and variety of sources that LEXIS-NEXIS covers. Although we do a lot to standardize the structure, format, and markup language of the content we put online, there are numerous publication-specific variations of this. At a broad level, the publication-headline-body structure of many news documents is not at all appropriate for the case name-citation-opinion structure appropriate for case law. We use a combination of database designs and source specification modules to control publication-specific document preparation needs. These allow for a lot of variation in how different sources are structured, processed and displayed while still maintaining critical standardization.

DATA ENHANCEMENTS

Overview. The primary goal of the basic data fabrication process is to take data in the format that publishers provide and put it online in a standard, searchable format. This focuses on standardizing content in a physical sense–supporting consistent structure, keyword searching and search functionality across sources. However, a document is not simply a list of typed characters. Documents present information. Data enhancements systems do for the information found in a document what our basic data fabrication process does for its form: standardize it to make the information more accessible. Examples of data enhancements include document categorization, key term extraction, summary generation, and fact extraction.

Categorizing Documents for Libraries and Indexing. One of the most common data enhancement processes is the document categorization process; that is, determining which topics the document is about. Depending on how the results are used, variations of the document categorization process support controlled vocabulary indexing, classification, and routing. Fundamentally they all do the same thing. They create a mapping between a set of documents and a set of topics, so that all the documents that map to some specific topic can be delivered to an information consumer who is interested in that topic.

Technical Approaches. LEXIS-NEXIS has deployed several document categorization systems and processes, most of which are variations of our Term-based Topic Identification [1] and NEXIS® Indexing [2] systems. The Carnegie Group has deployed categorization systems at Reuter's [3]. These systems are similar in that a domain expert builds a definition of a topic that is appropriate for the technology. The system then applies it across thousands or millions of documents in order to identify and select documents that are relevant to the topic. Selected documents can be marked up with a searchable topic identifier that online customers can use in their searches.

Document Participation in Multiple Products. One way to help break the database barrier is to have documents participate across products and services. To do this we could create a separate copy of a document for each product in which it participates. Given the volume of documents available on LEXIS-NEXIS (and now the Web), this would be a costly proposition, especially when documents can participate in numerous products. Through the use of topical metadata, a single document can be marked with one or more tags that specify all the products in which the document participates. Because there is data and metadata consistency across databases, the retrieval tools that help present products to customers can draw upon documents in thousands of databases and present them as if they were from a single database.

METADATA

Metadata is data about data. In the context of an online information provider, metadata consists of interesting attributes, features, and descriptors about a document and its content. From a search standpoint metadata includes the inverted file that makes searching on the data collection possible. Publisher-assigned attributes, such as publication name, section and date, and data enhancements results, including topic indicators and summaries, are also metadata. Metadata can support improved retrieval, better source selection, information visualization, trend analysis, and knowledge discovery.

This of course depends on capturing the right metadata. Data fabrication and enhancement processes play a key role here. The results of a document categorization process, for example, can be used to support the clustering of related documents. When monitored over time, we have found that it can be used to monitor the news for "hot" or emerging topics [4].

Metadata also provides a means to connect very different kinds of data. As a feature representation model, it can store features about a document or features that describe an image. A robust metadata model thus can provide us with the means to search, retrieve, and link information not just across documents, as we currently do today, but across a variety of data types.

BREAKING THE DATABASE BARRIER

A database is a collection of items stored on a computer. In the context of online information providers such as LEXIS-NEXIS, those items are documents. By imposing a consistent, searchable structure on documents with the help of document preparation and enhancements processes, we can make those documents easier for end users to access, even when those documents are from a number of different sources.

Database consistency is more easily achieved when a single company or service prepares all the data, than when there is the level of competition we see in today's information market. Information consumers themselves differ in the importance they place on factors, such as data availability and timeliness, source coverage, editorial enhancements, search and retrieval functionality, and their data integration needs. Information providers will seek to differentiate themselves from their competitors as they go after their targeted markets, even though it is standardization rather than differentiation that helps information consumers break the database barrier. As consumers are confronted with an ever-increasing number of information sources, data types that include image and audio in addition to text, and information providers that range from the traditional online services to the Web, we should recall the lessons learned when text alone dominated: the ultimate differentiating feature may very well be how easily and seamlessly we integrate the data and fit it into the information consumer's environment.

NOTES

1. Sharon Leigh, "The Use of Natural Language Processing in the Development of Topic Specific Databases," in *Proceedings of the Twelfth National Online Meeting*, New York, N.Y., May 1991.
2. David Schmeer and Cynthia Sidlo, "Automatic Topical Indexing at LEXIS-NEXIS," in *Proceedings of the Nineteenth National Online Meeting*, New York, N.Y., May 1998.
3. Philip Hayes, "Intelligent High-Volume Text Processing Using Shallow, Domain-Specific Techniques," in *Text-based Intelligent Systems*, ed., Paul Jacobs (Hillsdale, N.J.: Lawrence Erlbaum Associates, 1992).
4. Mark Shewhart and Mark Wasson, "Monitoring a Newsfeed for Hot Topics," in *Proceedings of the ACM SIGKDD Conference on Knowledge Discovery and Data Mining*, San Diego, Calif., August 1999.

DEVELOPING A WEB COLLECTION: SELECTION AND EVALUATION

Developing a Web Collection: Selection and Evaluation

Rick Lawson
James Testa
Angela Hitti

Presenters

Joseph C. Harmon

Recorder

SUMMARY. This panel brought together members of the library, secondary publishing, and Web aggregator community to discuss the elements each uses in establishing and building a collection of Internet

---

Rick Lawson is Vice President, Co-Founder, HealthGate Data Corporation.
James Testa is Senior Manager, Editorial Development, Institute for Scientific Information.
Angela Hitti is Vice President, Editorial, Cambridge Scientific Abstracts.
Joseph C. Harmon is Cataloging Team Leader, IUPUI University Library.

[Haworth co-indexing entry note]: "Developing a Web Collection: Selection and Evaluation." Harmon, Joseph C. Co-published simultaneously in *The Serials Librarian* (The Haworth Press, Inc.) Vol. 38, No. 1/2, 2000, pp. 165-167; and: *From Carnegie to Internet2: Forging the Serials Future* (ed: P. Michelle Fiander, Joseph C. Harmon, and Jonathan David Makepeace) The Haworth Press, Inc., 2000, pp. 165-167. Single or multiple copies of this article are available for a fee from The Haworth Document Delivery Service [1-800-342-9678, 9:00 a.m. - 5:00 p.m. (EST). E-mail address: getinfo@haworthpressinc.com].

resources for their users. *[Article copies available for a fee from The Haworth Document Delivery Service: 1-800-342-9678. E-mail address: getinfo@haworthpressinc.com <Website: http:// www.haworthpressinc.com>]*

Rick Lawson began with information on HealthGate Data Corporation. Founded in 1994, HealthGate has emerged as a leading source of reliable, objective healthcare information on the Web. Its target users include healthcare professionals, patients, and health-conscious consumers. HealthGate licenses content for healthy-living e-zines and for over 200 journals. Content is also distributed through four product lines.

Several factors enter into HealthGate's evaluative process. These include: the need for the information; the most effective delivery channel; competitors' offerings; the uniqueness of the information; the need to fill gaps in current content; and whether to license, form a cooperative arrangement, or create new content. Technology is used whenever possible to add value to the information. Clinical Advisory and Editorial boards oversee the review process.

James Testa of the Institute for Scientific Information (ISI) talked about the evaluation of Websites for inclusion in the Institute's new product, *Current Web Contents* (CWC). ISI decided to use existing staff with varied expertise to initially select the material, while peer review and citation analysis would be used in the evaluative process. Criteria for inclusion in CWC are: accuracy; authority; currency; navigability and design features; applicability and content; scope; audience level; and quality of writing. ISI welcomes suggestions for inclusion. A more detailed analysis of the evaluation criteria can be viewed at *http://www.isinet.com/hot/essays/23.html*.

Angela Hitti began with a brief description of Cambridge Scientific Abstracts (CSA). CSA is a secondary publisher of biological, aquatic, environmental, materials, sociology, and engineering sciences for the academic community. The purpose of CSA's *Web Resources Database* is to complement CSA's existing services. Excluded from the database are e-journals, conference proceedings, conference calendars, ephemera, protein sequence, gene sequence search results, sites with an obvious political agenda, or simple lists of other sites.

Human evaluators sift through possible sites, with authorship as the primary selection criteria. Typical Website authors include: government agencies, colleges and universities, organizations, associations, and companies, but rarely individuals. Indexing uses thesaurus terms, common keywords, and geographic and taxonomic terms. Frequent updating is needed to avoid dead links and to meet their clients' need for timely, accurate information. Hitti concluded with a reminder that quality database creation requires an investment in editorial staff, software engineering, Web design, and customer service.

Academic Issues in E-Journal Selection and Evaluation

Hal P. Kirkwood

E-JOURNAL SELECTION AND EVALUATION

An array of issues and problems has arisen from the increase in electronic access to resources, databases, and publications. Electronic journals are no different. Electronic journals present a new and old challenge to academic librarians. The format and delivery is new while the need for careful selection and evaluation is old. Timeliness has been (or should be) greatly improved, while there are continued questions of access vs. ownership. The selection and evaluation process is especially challenging for reference librarians and bibliographers. Several questions must be asked and answered; and then the ramifications of those answers must be dealt with.

The necessity of virtual space management and the challenge of effectively providing access to electronic publications temper the "excitement" in owning and accessing a collection of journals that take up no real space and, in some cases, have no apparent costs. Individual universities are gathering and organizing their own separate collections of electronic journals. These lists often include e-journals to which the university subscribes, as well as freely available electronic publications. All of these collections, and others like them, have their

---

Hal P. Kirkwood is Assistant Management and Economics Librarian, Purdue University.

[Haworth co-indexing entry note]: "Academic Issues in E-Journal Selection and Evaluation." Kirkwood, Hal P. Co-published simultaneously in *The Serials Librarian* (The Haworth Press, Inc.) Vol. 38, No. 1/2, 2000, pp. 169-174; and: *From Carnegie to Internet2: Forging the Serials Future* (ed: P. Michelle Fiander, Joseph C. Harmon, and Jonathan David Makepeace) The Haworth Press, Inc., 2000, pp. 169-174. Single or multiple copies of this article are available for a fee from The Haworth Document Delivery Service [1-800-342-9678, 9:00 a.m. - 5:00 p.m. (EST). E-mail address: getinfo@haworthpressinc.com].

own criteria and selection process. There was significant overlap among, yet noticeable omissions from, each list; thus, a comprehensive list of available electronic journals remains elusive.

The University of Waterloo (*http://library.uwaterloo.ca/Ejournals*) provides access to a selection of e-journals by alphabetized title and general subject area. The University of Houston (*http://info.lib.uh.edu/wj/webjour.html*) provides access to their selection of e-journals by alphabetical order only. Virginia Tech (*http://db.lib.vt.edu/ej_public/ej_show.show_searchform*) provides a more detailed subject breakdown as well as a keyword search option. These universities have chosen to provide a separate list of electronic journals. Purdue University and the University of Tennessee-Knoxville have both chosen to integrate their electronic journals directly into their Web-based OPACs.

Some universities are involved in consortia arrangements to organize e-journals. The Committee on Institutional Cooperation (The Big Ten, plus the University of Chicago) has created a large collection of e-journals, which may be searched by topic or title (*http://ejournals.cic.net/index.html*). The Colorado Alliance of Research Libraries (*http://www.coalliance.org/ejournal/*) has created a similar site with access points by title, LC Subject Headings, and Colorado e-journals.

The four primary issues, in this author's view, are selection, evaluation, organization and usage. These issues are all interrelated when dealing with any resource and this holds true with e-journals as well.

SELECTION

Selection becomes the first hurdle to overcome when building an e-journal collection. Decisions must be made as to whether there will be an exclusive or an inclusive selection criteria. Will the collection contain only subscription-based publications or will it include only freely available Web publications? Or will there be some combination? And how will these different publications, with potentially different access methods, be managed?

What is the faculty/user acceptance and knowledge of e-journals? And what kind of marketing is planned to inform users of this collection? Yes, marketing is relevant within the context of selection. It is potentially wasteful to collect and organize resources that are invisible to your users.

Is it an electronic version of a print journal or is it truly an enhanced electronic journal? Does this matter? This issue is especially problematic as more e-journal Websites provide access to special sections or unique tools. How are these items or functions to be cataloged (if at all) and how are they to be presented to the users within the reference setting?

The University of Houston (*http://info.lib.uh.edu/wj/webjour.html*) provides a clear indication of the selection process for e-journals in their collection. They have chosen to select only scholarly publications with significant portions of the content available online. This way, users can at least have some grasp as to what they will and will not find.

EVALUATION

Evaluation moves beyond simple selection into a critical analysis of the content of an e-journal. Relevancy, quality, accessibility, cost, language, consistency, and stability are the significant factors involved in evaluation. Is the content of the e-journal relevant to the collection as a whole? Is it relevant to your users? Does it contain scholarly information? Is it peer-reviewed, and by whom? These questions must be answered before any collection is undertaken. Guidelines and policies should be in place so that there is a coherent plan to acquire e-journals.

What methods of access are available? Is access IP filtered or password protected? And will this influence the decision to select the publication? It should, for if accessibility is problematic, users will be discouraged from using the resource. Will you pay, and how much? And how will you handle access to electronic versions of print journals to which you already subscribe? Will you choose English language only? Does this match your print collection selection process? And if not why not? There is often an undeniable difference between collection development in the electronic and physical worlds. Academic librarians should try to maintain a level of consistency between these two areas, as it will become increasingly difficult to separate them neatly.

Is the e-journal published on a recognizable schedule? Does the site seem stable, or is there a feeling that the location may lack permanence? There is always the fear with free Web-based information that it will be here today and gone tomorrow. But this is becoming less and less of a problem; sites are becoming more stable. You can determine with some level of confidence the stability and consistency of a site.

ORGANIZATION

What access will you be providing to your collection of e-journals? How will they be organized within the context of your other resources and Websites? Will you create a separate browsing list? Or will you include them in your OPAC, or both? What are the ramifications of updating, cataloging, and managing these separate collections? Will the separate list be alphabetical or subject-specific? How will you integrate these journals into your overall journal collection?

How searchable is the journal? Is it searchable through the publisher's proprietary collection? Is it searchable as a single journal? Are the articles included in major relevant indexing and abstracting services? This is especially important when the journal contains specific articles that are online only or if the entire journal is online. Users may not be willing or interested in searching an article database and then searching another, possibly relevant, journal separately. They will not waste the time. Separate collections only confuse the user; terms like JSTOR, Elsevier, Springer, and free Web e-journals simply become library jargon to users and are summarily ignored.

As journal publishers provide access to e-versions of their journals, and as other freely available Web publications increase in number and scope, there is a definite risk of marginality. The fragmentation of the journal will continue to be a problem without a ready solution. Especially if we choose to not include them in the library catalog alongside our print publications.

USAGE

Is the faculty using these journals? Have they gained acceptance in the departments and schools that are most relevant to subject matter? Are there any barriers for using these journals, such as the need for additional software? How troublesome will this be to manage for the user and the library?

Access to special tools and features becomes problematic, especially when users are unaware of them. How will the user find these relevant functions in a timely manner? Is it the library's job to provide access to these special functions and tools?

The lack of indexing by professional indexing services is also a problem affecting usage. Students today want single, one-stop shopping for their research needs. It becomes tedious for the students when the library provides access to a multitude of lists, collections and databases without any explanation of why they are separate.

CHALLENGES

This paper and presentation does not purport to have the answers. Obviously it raises many more questions than answers. Decisions regarding e-journal collection and organization must be made on a local level to fit with each library's policies, goals, and objectives.

The issues raised are not the only ones to consider when selecting e-journals. Archiving is an issue. If the free e-journal ceases publication, will the organization have "acquired" the publications? A process for archiving these articles will need to be set up, or the information may be lost forever. This could be handled within a group of libraries to defray the storage costs and to distribute the work. Internet Trend Watch for Libraries (http://www.itwfl.com/), a solely electronic journal, is a good example of an electronic publication that is no longer in production but has been indexed in commercial databases. It is now no longer available on the Web. Prior to its disappearance I copied the entire site. The question now is, what do I do with it? What can I do with it?

There has been some discussion that there is no need for journals, and that the article will become the primary means of publishing information. Full-text databases are already diminishing the importance of the journal. This issue brings in many other ramifications for academic libraries too numerous to go into here. The continuing availability of alternate publishing opportunities, such as free, Web-based journals, university presses, independent publishers, the students and faculty themselves, adds to the many facets of dealing with e-journals.

My view is biased from the standpoint of a reference librarian. Perhaps some of these issues are not as important to technical service or technology departments. Regardless of one's point of view, e-journals will continue to grow in number, value, and usage. Librarians will need to resolve the issues discussed here sooner, rather than later. The management of our collections and the growing volume of electronic information will continue to present new challenges and issues for our libraries. Effectively dealing with this changing environment is how librarians can add value for our users.

SELECTED BIBLIOGRAPHY

Boyce, Peter B. "It is Time to Become Discriminating Consumers," *Against the Grain*, vol. 9, no. 5, 1997, p86-87.

Ford, Charlotte E. and Stephen P. Harter. "The Downside of Scholarly Electronic Publishing: Problems in Accessing Electronic Journals Through Online Directories and Catalogs," *College & Research Libraries*, vol. 59, no. 4, 1998, p335-346.

Hamaker, Chuck. "Chaos-Journals Electronic Style," *Against the Grain*, vol. 9 no. 6, 1997-98, p90-91.

Hudson, Laura and Laura Windsor. "Providing Access to Electronic Journals: The Ohio University Experience," *Against the Grain*, vol. 10, no. 3, 1998, p1, 16, 18.

Keenan, Stella. "Electronic Publishing: A Subversive Proposal, an Even More Subversive Proposal, and a Counter Argument," *Online & CDROM Review*, vol. 20, no. 2, 1996, p93-94.

Moothart, Tom. "Providing Access to E-journals Through Library Home Pages," *Serials Review*, vol. 22, Summer, 1996, p71-77.

Rees, Louise B. and Bridget Arthur Clancy. "Cataloging Electronic Journals: Learning to Weave the Web," *Internet Reference Services Quarterly*, vol. 3, no. 3, 1998, p29-43.

REDUCING JOURNAL COSTS THROUGH ADVERTISING: EXPLORING THE POSSIBILITIES

Additive Change: Unobtrusive Advertising for Academic Journals

Casey Slott

SUMMARY. The issue of commercial advertising in academic journals is complex and controversial. It is complex because its implications reveal deeply embedded conceptions of the academy and the marketplace both traditionally and in this historical moment. It is controversial because those same implications promise that change is what this historical moment foreshadows, and change has a way of impacting the norms of tradition. The question then becomes, is there a way to synthesize these conceptions of the academy and the marketplace, perhaps in the form of unobtrusive advertising? This article considers the notion of additive change, developed by Ronald C. Arnett and Pat Arneson, as a concept for thinking through the serials crisis in

Casey Slott is Instructor of Communication, Duquesne University.

[Haworth co-indexing entry note]: "Additive Change: Unobtrusive Advertising for Academic Journals." Slott, Casey. Co-published simultaneously in *The Serials Librarian* (The Haworth Press, Inc.) Vol. 38, No. 1/2, 2000, pp. 175-185; and: *From Carnegie to Internet2: Forging the Serials Future* (ed: P. Michelle Fiander, Joseph C. Harmon, and Jonathan David Makepeace) The Haworth Press, Inc., 2000, pp. 175-185. Single or multiple copies of this article are available for a fee from The Haworth Document Delivery Service [1-800-342-9678, 9:00 a.m. - 5:00 p.m. (EST). E-mail address: getinfo@haworthpressinc.com].

academia and the marketplace. *[Article copies available for a fee from The Haworth Document Delivery Service: 1-800-342-9678. E-mail address: getinfo@haworthpressinc.com <Website: http://www.haworthpressinc.com>]*

INTRODUCTION

In the academy it is no surprise that our current historical moment is characterized by a deficit of resources. Academia in contemporary American society is facing a continuing financial shortfall that not only raises questions of its economic stability but also its role in higher education. Amidst an environment of fiscal constraint and technological orientation, academic administrators, librarians, and scholars are debating the questions that will impact the academy's most precious resource going into the 21st century, i.e., scholarship[1]. What will become particularly important to understand is the way in which scholarly communication must adapt to the particular needs and concerns of the academy functioning in the information age.

It is interesting to note that the system of scholarly communication has remained practically unchanged since the time of Gutenberg[2]. But that system is changing rapidly. Part of what is driving the change is the limitless outgrowth of computer technology, networks, and communication software, which present paper-based systems with non-paper alternatives for the publication of academic research[3]. Also, the expense of acquiring information is increasing. This is perhaps best exemplified in the continuing escalation in the cost of serials. The reason for this is not mysterious. Funding to universities is eroding and so is the purchasing power of university libraries[4]. Libraries are being forced to cancel journal subscriptions to meet tighter budgetary demands. The entire scholarly community is now experiencing a sense of urgency, as it seeks to find ways to overcome what has been called "a bleak economic outlook"[5].

The information age has brought with it the possibilities for the practice of scholarly communication in a new information environment. Yet, what can be done to counter the serials crisis? This is a question that demonstrates both a general and a specific problem. The general problem is the tension between the academy and the marketplace. It is a tension illustrative of the traditional role of universities as autonomous social institutions, sometimes critical of private sector concerns, and the role it must now function in as it shares similar concerns with the marketplace. The more specific problem is the rising cost of academic journals. Perhaps, we are called to embrace this historical moment and commit ourselves to respond in our own way to the changing marketplace. This article considers the notion of additive change, developed by Ronald C. Arnett and Pat Arneson, as a conceptual for thinking through the serials crisis in academia and the marketplace[6].

ADVERTISING IN THE ACADEMY AND THE MARKETPLACE

Is advertising a practical method for reducing the subscription prices of academic journals? The question presupposes that publishers of academic journals will earn money to offset production and distribution costs if they sell space to advertisers. Savings would then be passed on, presumably, to subscribers. Most academic journals currently accept some form of advertising. However, a distinction must be made between advertising accepted by academic journals and advertising accepted by trade journals oriented to academic disciplines. Advertising functions differently in these two types of publications.

For example, *Journal of Applied Communication Research* is a representative academic research journal that appeals mostly to a scholarly audience. *Public Relations Quarterly* is a journal that targets both an academic and a trade audience. Academic journals publish primary research by scholars in a particular academic discipline for consumption by a mostly academic audience. A trade journal oriented to an academic discipline is characterized less by research and more by news, features, and announcements germane to both academics and practitioners. Each of these journals attracts and accepts different types of advertising for different purposes.

The typical academic journal in the humanities generally accepts advertising related to academic programs, new book announcements, and services connected to the discipline. An advertising manager for this type of academic journal might consider these types of advertising as serving the best interests of the membership. Perhaps one way to describe this kind of advertising is as noncommercial, since it is not geared toward profit making.

Trade journals, however, are often associated with a commercial publisher in business to make a profit. Although the journal may serve the interests of an audience affiliated with the academy, its advertising policies are less exclusive. *The Chronicle of Higher Education*, for example, serves the academic community with news, relevant features, and announcements, and sells advertising space to major commercial entities such as AT&T and nationally recognized insurance providers.

From the publishing perspective of the academic journal, the issue of advertising has been to align its purpose with the most appropriate kind of advertisement and advertiser. A compelling question to ask, then, is whether a major commercial marketer would be appropriate to advertise in a non-commercial academic journal. This is the question that draws the distinction between academia and the private sector, since the space in academic journals has traditionally been considered sacred space and not commercial space. It has been sacred space because it is the primary medium in which scholars present their work free of non-scholarly influences. Kenneth Field in the *Canadian Journal of Communication* underscores the sanctity of the academic journal and its perceived immunity from the marketplace:

> It is almost a rule of thumb that consideration for tenure and promotion includes an examination of one's record of publications, either of monographs or articles, by publishers or in journals that are considered the most important in the particular field of study. It is not surprising, then, that many academics give little thought to the implications of this kind of system. This imperative provides the perfect environment for a profit-making publishing industry working with an audience that is captive and thus more or less immune to market pressures[7].

The history of scholarly publishing suggests that academic publishers maintain the integrity of publications by presenting messages that are in concert with the scholarly tone of the material featured. Following this principle, an article on crisis-management models in organizations would not be flanked by an advertisement for Burger King or Nike. Such an advertisement would seem to conflict with the perception of scholarship as inviolable and noncommercially motivated. Such advertising might be seen as manipulative, subversive, corruptive, and encouraging consumerism. For advertising to become an accepted approach to reducing journal costs its perceived benefits must outweigh its perceived harms. There are a number of issues that need to be addressed before commercial advertising can become a viable means of reducing academic journal subscription costs.

An academic publishing firm in tune with its clientele in higher education might consider advertising to reduce expenses because it understands both the economic and cultural benefits of advertising. Advertising as a tool can contribute to the economic growth in the service of authentic human development. Advertising of products and services that satisfy needs of the scholarly community can help to better inform community members. By supporting material of outstanding intellectual quality advertising can make possible the continued production of research knowledge[8]. Advertising can enable the presentation of non-commercial information in unobtrusive ways. Corporate sponsorship of public television programming is one example where private sector business entities support the production and presentation of socially relevant information in a non-commercial format without compromising the tone of the message.

Advertisers have traditionally targeted mass audiences to optimize both the reach of the message and potential customer base. Yet, the 1990s have been characterized by a strategic move to pinpoint specific audiences with more personalized messages that reflect a marketer's greater sensitivity to the needs and concerns of that audience. If theoretical justification is needed to support a move toward advertising in academic journals, advocates will find it in the notion of niche marketing. Niche marketers will offer only products and services within a narrow range, but the products and services advertised will not extend beyond the needs of the audience[9]. In this model, the needs of the scholarly community must be considered within both a practical and rhetorical framework. In other words, products and services must be specific for the academic audience, such as pedagogical software or an academic placement service. Niche marketing is a viable strategy for advertising in academic journals when there are marketers who have identified the scholarly audience as the target market for their products and services.

Those opposed to the notion of advertising in academic journals fear that advertising might affect academic publishing and perhaps the academy itself. Advertising suggests a linking of the university to a corporate impetus and its tools of technology, in order to fully exploit the benefits of the knowledge quest[10]. Perhaps academic and critic

Sven Birkerts most eloquently advanced the heart of this opposition. In the *Gutenberg Elegies* Birkerts states that

> as a culture, as a species, we are becoming shallower and giving up on wisdom, the struggle for which has for millennia been central to the very idea of culture. What is our idea, our ideal, of wisdom these days? Who represents it? Who even invokes it? Our postmodern culture is a vast fabric of competing-isms; we are leaderless and subject to the terrors, masked as freedoms, of an absolute relativism[11].

Fear is the primary issue behind opposition to change in scholarly communication, whether advertising, corporate affiliation, or Internet publication. John Unsworth in *Journal of Scholarly Publishing*, describes this as "the fear of pollution when the subject is scholarship–the fear of 'losing our priestly status in the anarchic welter of unfiltered, unrefined voices.' When the subject is the library, the fear expressed is 'the fear of disorientation–that we will lose our sense of the value of the past'"[12]. Each one of these fears is grounded in an assumption that the academy is becoming shallower and that, as stakeholders in the academy, we should be looking for ways to redress this degradation.

The focus of this article is the distinction between the pure academic journal defined by its content and the trade-like journal that offers more than scholarship. A further distinction is necessary, however, in order to identify journals and the disciplines they represent. For some disciplines might be more compatible to private sector marketing concerns.

Some critics, analyzing medical journals that utilize advertising, adhere to a position that advertising does work[13]. Technical journals may be more likely to court advertisers, particularly those that produce the latest technology-related products. The humanities, however, at least since the 19th century, have found themselves in much the same position as modern art, in which any social function is denied at least in the sense of defining itself against the principles of business and financial profitability[14]. The humanities have nurtured their resistance to the marketplace and frequently place themselves as naysayers to pragmatic concerns. Concerns in the sciences over university-corporate linking arrangements have generated anxiety over the issue of research. Some academics worry about colleague secrecy over research activities, research objectives skewed to corporate sponsorship concerns, and the subversion of the research process itself[15].

Corporate intrusion into the sacred space of education was best documented with the Channel One partnership between business and the educational community. Channel One supplies a twelve-minute, commercially sponsored TV news program for high school students. Schools receive $50,000 worth of communication technology for airing Channel One. Critics maintain that schools should remain commercial-free zones where "students' minds can not be auctioned off to the highest corporate bidder"[16].

Arguments against the notion of advertising in journals symbolize the broader mistrust that the academy and parallel institutions have for the corporate world. Other opponents believe the issue simply requires a common sense understanding of the essence of the medium. Carolyn Wood, Vice-President of Order Fulfillment at the University of Toronto Press asserts that marketing scholarship as though it were something else will not work. Wood recalled how a marketer for a carmaker once asked her why the University of Toronto Press didn't use a media buyer for their advertising. Wood tried to imagine an account executive high-fiving her colleagues when she landed the contract for their half-page ads in *Canadian Journal of Economics*[17].

ADDITIVE CHANGE AS A CONCEPTUAL BRIDGE

The issue of commercial advertising in academic journals is complex and controversial. It is complex because its implications reveal deeply embedded conceptions of the academy and the marketplace both traditionally and in this historical moment. It is controversial because those same implications promise that change is what this historical moment foreshadows, and change has a way of impacting the norms of tradition. The question then becomes, is there a way to synthesize these conceptions of the academy and the marketplace, perhaps in the form of unobtrusive advertising?

Additive change accepts the narrative importance of each competing discipline and simultaneously works to expand its domain by asking significant value questions. Additive change does not attempt to destroy or substitute in order to create change; instead it takes what exists and builds upon its foundation[18]. The notion of additive change, applied to the issue of the academy and the marketplace, is perhaps most meaningful when understood as relationship. This alternative emerges as a rephrasing of the question, "Can advertising be a viable means of reducing the subscription price of journals?" When applying the metaphor of additive change, the more appropriate question becomes, "What relationships must be formed to address the serials crisis that defines our historical moment?"

The idea of unobtrusive advertising embodies the pragmatic scope of additive change for it offers a marketing alternative that works with embedded assumptions of advertising in a way that builds mutually beneficial relationships for both the academy and the marketplace. Unobtrusive advertising, in this model, extends the notion of advertising to include most promotional activity that seeks to build relationships that add to the already existing belief foundations of the academy and the private sector. Again this model outlines a pragmatic solution to the complex divisions between academia and the corporate world.

Additive change recognizes the substance of relationship building as the key component in problem solving, since change can occur naturally when one builds upon what is already there. "New life can emerge without putting relationships at risk"[19]. Otherwise a response of "Yes, we must advertise in academic journals," or, "No, we must save the sacred space of the academy," becomes a kind of "imperialistic act of substitution, where one idea is simply advanced over another"[20]. Substitutional change is not additive change since it does not value the importance of relationships in seeking change (it merely projects an idea. What are the relationships that we must forge in the marketplace for the academy to adequately affect the serials crisis?

One significant example that provides some direction is intellectual sponsorship. Sponsorship is not a new thing; in fact partnerships go back fifty to one hundred years with some symphony orchestras. According to Leonard Kniffel in *American Libraries*, 1990s-style partnerships between corporations and nonprofits are still defining themselves[21]. The concept of intellectual sponsorship for scholarly publishing can be executed the same way advertising is done. In other words, an organizational sponsor will purchase advertising in the academic journal. Yet the type of advertising it represents will be different from pure commercial advertising. The rationale that drives this potential relationship is the notion that academic journals mostly represent the good name of the discipline and the reputation of the publication.

As a possible partner to organizational or corporate sponsors, academic journals present an opportunity to be associated with a good cause or socially relevant mission. For this to happen, academic publishers will have to become more proactive in their pursuit of corporate sponsors. Corporate sponsors understand that their good name in the community means good money[22]. Sponsors of academic publishing must have a stake in the scholarly community for this to work; otherwise there is no marketing benefit. Corporate sponsorship will function as intellectual sponsorship when both the academy and the marketplace are visibly entering into a relationship for mutual enhancement. This is additive change. For the publisher, intellectual sponsorship will only succeed when it can endorse the sponsoring company.

The rise of place-based advertising is further evidence of the convergence of the academy with the marketplace. Place-based advertising allows the demographics of the target audience to be controlled by the location in which the message is delivered[23]. In universities, for example, Modern College Television is a place-based advertising kiosk featuring music videos and commercials. Kiosks are placed strategically throughout the campus to reach the very specific college audience[24]. The notion of place-based advertising shows a willingness by higher education to satisfy the needs of a primary market through a commercial entity.

CONCLUSION

Additive change offers the possibility to engage in mutually beneficial relationships that bridge the ideological differences between the academy and the marketplace. We have established that our historical moment represents a time of enormous economic and technological urgency. New ways of thinking about marketing in the academy necessitate the consideration of new marketing relationships to overcome economic limitations. Relationships that address the unfolding orientation to technology might also offer the academy enough leverage to integrate new marketing strategy with a responsible and pragmatic adaptation to technology.

Advertising, like all communication, has its limitations. Advertising in academic journals must emanate as a mutually beneficial commitment to explore the potential rewards of alternative marketing strategies that recognize a changing worldview. Advertising alone, however, is not sufficient to solve the serials crisis. Additive change demands that building strategies are not limited to one foundation[25]. It is apparent in the age of information that the information cyberstructure, the Internet, will prove to be a historical world event. David Abrahamson in *Journalism and Mass Communication Quarterly* has suggested that it is possible that at least part of our nation's future will in some way be influenced by the evolution of the Internet. It seems fitting that scholars, teachers, librarians, and industry professionals should help shape that future[26]. Kenneth Field, in *Canadian Journal of Communications*, believes that, as scholars become connected to the Internet and involved in electronic communication, they will see the enormous benefits to be had[27].

Additive change is not a science, an economic model, or marketing stratagem in itself. It is a communication philosophy that discerns the importance of building on already existing foundations of human enterprise through the process of story building. Stories are constructed of people, their needs, and their concerns, the way they go about solving the problems they encounter.

The academy and the marketplace have traditionally represented competing narratives within a larger worldview. Additive change recognizes the contributions of both the academy and the marketplace and asks value-laden questions. What are the values that can be added to each foundation, in an information age of limited resources? What are the relationships that must be constructed in this marketplace shaped by evolving technology? The relationships the academy and academic publishers must develop are those that enhance the quality of scholarly communication.

NOTES

1. Richard Nimijean, "And What About Students? The Forgotten Role of Students in the Scholarly Communication Debate," *Canadian Journal of Communication* 22, no. 3/4 (1997): 179-180.

2. Kenneth Field, "Faculty Perspective on Scholarly Communication," *Canadian Journal of Communication* 22, no. 3/4 (1997): 162.

3. Ibid.

4. Ibid.

5. G. Blumenstyk, "Bleak Outlook Forces Many States to Seek More Revenue from their Public College Students," *Chronicle of Higher Education*, 6 March 1991, A26-27.

6. Ronald C. Arnett and Pat Arneson. *Dialogic Civility in a Cynical Age: Community, Hope, and Interpersonal Relationships* (Albany, N.Y.: SUNY Press, 1999), 103-123.

7. Kenneth Field, "Faculty Perspective on Scholarly Communication," *Canadian Journal of Communication* 22, no. 3/4 (1997): 163.

8. Pontifical Council for Social Communications, "Ethics in Advertising," *Vatican's Report on Social Communication* (1994): 628.

9. Donald Parente, Bruce Vanden Bergh, Arnold Barban, and James Marra. *Advertising Campaign Strategy: A Guide to Marketing Communication Plans* (Ft. Worth, Tex.: Dryden Press, 1996), 7.

10. Howard Buchbinder and Janice Newson, "Social Knowledge and Market Knowledge: Universities in the Information Age," *Gannett Center Journal* 5 (1991): 20.

11. Sven Birkerts, "The Fate of Reading in an Electronic Age." *New Letters* 60, no. 4 (1994): 111-112.

12. John Unsworth, "Electronic Scholarship; or Scholarly Publishing and the Public," *Journal of Scholarly Publishing*, October 1996, 5-6.

13. Ned Matalia, "Journal Advertising Works! Three Studies Say So!" *Medical Marketing and Media*, May 1994, 12.

14. John Unsworth, "Electronic Scholarship; or Scholarly Publishing and the Public," *Journal of Scholarly Publishing*, October 1996, 8.

15. Howard Buchbinder and Janice Newson, "Social Knowledge and Market Knowledge: Universities in the Information Age," *Gannett Center Journal* 5 (1991): 21.

16. K. Tim Wulfemeyer and Barbara Mueller, "Channel One and Commercials in Classrooms: Advertising Content Aimed at Students," *Journalism Quarterly* 69, no. 3 (1992): 729.

17. Carolyn Wood, "Marketing Scholarly Publishing Monographs as Lite Beer," *Journal of Scholarly Publishing*, July 1997, 220.

18. Ronald C. Arnett and Pat Arneson, *Dialogic Civility in a Cynical Age: Community, Hope, and Interpersonal Relationships* (Albany, N.Y.: SUNY Press, 1999), 106-109.

19. Ibid., 109.

20. Ibid.

21. Leonard Kniffel, "Corporate Sponsorship: The New Direction in Fundraising," *American Libraries*, November 1995, 1023.

22. Ibid., 1024.

23. J.P. Cortez, "Media Pioneers Try to Corral On-the-Go Consumers," *Advertising Age*, 17 August 1992, 25.

24. Matthew P. McAllister, *The Commercialization of American Culture* (Thousand Oaks, Calif.: Sage Publications, 1996), 73-74.

25. Ronald C. Arnett, and Pat Arneson, *Dialogic Civility in a Cynical Age: Community, Hope, and Interpersonal Relationships* (Albany, N.Y.: SUNY Press, 1999), 109-110.

26. David Abrahamson, "The Visible Hand: Money, Markets, and Media Evolution," *Journalism & Mass Communication Quarterly* 75, no. 1 (1998): 17.

27. Kenneth Field, "Faculty Perspective on Scholarly Communication," *Canadian Journal of Communication* 22, no. 3/4 (1997): 164.

Exploring the Possibilities in the Print and Electronic Worlds

John Tagler

SUMMARY. In this session, the speakers explores the feasibility of significantly expanding the number of space advertisements that appear in primary research journals. The program topic responds to an oft-held belief among librarians that publishers should more aggressively sell space ads in scientific journals, thereby shifting a sizeable portion of income from subscriptions to advertising and lowering subscription prices to libraries. As the shift from print to electronic is a prevailing trend among readers of scientific journals, the paper also explores the considerations involved in selling advertising in electronic journals, drawing parallels to the print world and pondering the possibilities of the new medium. *[Article copies available for a fee from The Haworth Document Delivery Service: 1-800-342-9678. E-mail address: getinfo@haworthpressinc.com <Website: http://www.haworthpressinc.com>]*

INTRODUCTION

There is a perception among many librarians that publishers of scientific, technical, and medical (STM) journals could readily reduce the subscription prices of their journals by selling advertising. As a representative of a large STM publisher, I cannot estimate the number of times this suggestion has been presented to me as a panacea for high journal subscription prices.

John Tagler is Director of Corporate Communications, Elsevier Science.

[Haworth co-indexing entry note]: "Exploring the Possibilities in the Print and Electronic Worlds." Tagler, John. Co-published simultaneously in *The Serials Librarian* (The Haworth Press, Inc.) Vol. 38, No. 1/2, 2000, pp. 187-197; and: *From Carnegie to Internet2: Forging the Serials Future* (ed: P. Michelle Fiander, Joseph C. Harmon, and Jonathan David Makepeace) The Haworth Press, Inc., 2000, pp. 187-197. Single or multiple copies of this article are available for a fee from The Haworth Document Delivery Service [1-800-342-9678, 9:00 a.m. - 5:00 p.m. (EST). E-mail address: getinfo@haworthpressinc.com].

If the solution were that simple, publishers would have begun vigorously pursuing this revenue stream long ago. Indeed, if certain STM publishers were as avaricious as is sometimes suggested by librarians, would these very same publishers ignore a potentially lucrative source of income? It's doubtful.

In reality, the inclusion of advertising in the economic model of some STM journals–and it really applies to a small percentage of journals fitting a specific profile–can be a major economic consideration. For these select titles the income from advertising can equal or exceed the income from subscriptions, and, in such cases, the advertising revenue results in a lower subscription price paid by all subscribers including institutions, individuals, and, in many cases, society members. Many of us in STM publishing have experience in ad sales for some of our journals, and we would be delighted if ad sales applied more widely across the board. For the majority of STM journals, however, most circulation is to libraries and advertising income has little or no impact on the economic picture.

As we migrate from print to the digital environment for delivery of scientific information the question about growing advertising revenue in order to reduce subscription prices is raised anew. Before there is too much excitement about the possibilities, it is necessary to understand how advertising works in the STM print journal environment. There are fundamental forces that will carry over into the digital realm. Web advertising is still a nascent industry, but there are some exciting new possibilities that could adjust the economic model. The technologies are still developing, and demographic and usage patterns are still evolving, but at this juncture it is interesting to at least explore some of the possibilities that this emerging medium offers.

WHAT ARE ADVERTISERS LOOKING FOR?

Advertisers are a savvy and discriminating lot. They speak with their spending power and, like librarians, their funds are limited. There are very specific criteria that advertisers use in deciding where to put their advertising dollars. The options outdistance the money available, so advertisers opt for proven outlets.

In assessing the STM journals field, advertisers are usually looking for titles with large circulations. In comparison to consumer magazines, of course, most STM journals cannot really lay claim to large numbers. A very select handful of scientific serials exceeds one hundred thousand subscribers, while a modest number range between fifty thousand and one hundred thousand. Most of the titles at this end of this spectrum are either general interest science publications or professional journals affiliated with large societies. In both cases the majority of subscriptions are sold to individuals or included with society membership. A good example would be *Science*, which is published by the American Association for the Advancement of Science, where a subscription to the journal is included with society membership. According to a 1999 issue of *Standard Rate and Data, Science* has a circulation slightly over 150,000, of which approximately eighty-eight percent are society members.

As the circulation levels decline, as a rule so, too, do the number of advertising pages. Scientific journals within the range of twenty-five thousand to fifty thousand subscribers can have healthy advertising sales, as these titles are frequently society-affiliated, often in professional or medical specialty fields. When the journals are oriented toward a clinical audience, they attract readers who write prescriptions and buy medical devices. The same rules apply for titles with circulation levels between five thousand to twenty-five thousand, but below the twenty-five thousand level the number of interested advertisers declines and those who advertise in the journals expect a good match between reader and product. But bear in mind that advertisers are attuned to the journal's editorial quality, reader demographics, and the buying power of the readers, so even promising circulation numbers do not necessarily guarantee advertisers.

Any title below the five thousand subscription level has little chance of having a significant advertising revenue stream, or a level of advertising that can alter the journal's economic model and substantially reduce the subscription price. Most scholarly research journals have circulation levels in range of four hundred to fifteen hundred, with most of those subscriptions sold to libraries. Virtually the entire revenue stream for these titles is from subscriptions, with most journals of this type having no space ad income whatsoever.

Once the targeted audience has been narrowed to a subject specialty and the advertiser has accepted the notion of modest circulation, advertisers are looking for readers who are decision makers and in a position to spend money. Among scientific disciplines, the strongest fields are medicine and chemistry; to a lesser extent there are also some ad sales possibilities in areas like computer science and business/management. Medicine is particularly strong because pharmaceutical companies and, to a lesser extent, medical device, equipment, and instrumentation manufacturers can sell their products to practicing physicians. Chemistry journals also are attractive to advertisers selling equipment, instruments, and materials to the laboratory or bench scientist. At the other end of the spectrum of scientific study, ad sales are weak in theoretical research areas such as physics and mathematics.

Advertisers also want to know the reach of the publication, and they want profiles of the readers' demographics. Many of the STM journals with healthy circulation levels are society publications and, quite often, societies are protective of their members' confidentiality and members are often reticent about divulging much personal information. So it may be difficult to provide advertisers with the demographic details they require.

ADVERTISING CHALLENGES POSED BY STM JOURNALS

People read different types of serial publications in very different ways and, in fact, even the distribution patterns vary among these periodicals, e.g., consumer magazines vs. professional journals vs. scholarly research journals. Magazines and professional journals are usually delivered to an individual's home or office or purchased at newsstand while most scholarly research journals are delivered to libraries. The personal subscription is often browsed cover to cover and usually in a relaxed setting. The users flip through most pages. Readers often do not read each article but scan through each issue and are generally exposed to the advertising.

In contrast, the scholarly research journal is mostly delivered to the library. In the best situations, copies are on display in reading rooms and readers who come into the library browse through the issue. Some institutions circulate journal issues but this is often an imprecise and untimely method of current awareness. The majority of researchers select their desired articles based on table of contents services, bibliographic citations, or word of mouth. Photocopies of articles are requested from the libraries or copies are obtained through document delivery services or interlibrary loans. In such situations there is little cover-to-cover browsing, and, in fact, many readers never physically see or touch an issue.

Most scholarly research journals also have an international spread of readers. While this is attractive to authors and readers, it is less appealing to advertisers. A basic tenet of advertising is that readers represent a targeted buying block. But when journals with relatively small circulations are further subdivided into different groups–with different languages, professional practices and cultural barriers–the homogeneity of the supposed targeted audience becomes quite fragmented. It is not difficult to imagine that there are subtle but importance differences in the ways medicine is practiced in North America and Europe and Asia, so one would expect physicians in these regions to have very different response levels to the same advertisement. National restrictions apply on advertising for many products, particularly pharmaceuticals. So even in the potentially lucrative pharmaceutical advertising market, a drug may have a different brand name in different countries or may have been approved in some markets but not others. Some countries have different regulations over advertising practices. For example, advertisements running in Germany cannot mention competitors. Hence, it is often necessary to print split runs of journals–one for domestic distribution (usually in the United States) and another for international circulation. The latter may indeed carry some advertisements, but these are often fewer in number and may be image ads which are often given lesser priority in many space advertising budgets since advertisers want to see an immediate return on or response to their advertising investment.

As has been noted previously, many journals with substantial circulation figures are affiliated with societies. While society affiliation may bring increased circulation numbers, many societies are quite specific as to the type and content of the advertisements they will accept. Some allow information ads or professionally related products but restrict consumer goods or anything out of scope of the society's area of specialty. Societies may also specify where space ads can appear in a journal, and one often finds ads clustered in the front or back of an issue. Sometimes there are ad wells scattered in the editorial pages. Such situations where space ads are grouped together are not advantageous as this positioning does not offer high exposure to individual advertisements. Many societies review all advertisements before publication and reject those felt to be inappropriate, and in some instances a society may refuse advertisements altogether.

THE IMPORTANCE OF CONTEXT

Another suggestion that has been widely bandied about is the notion that STM publishers should expand their scope beyond the traditional industry-related advertisers and pursue consumer goods advertising. If advertising space in STM journals is difficult to sell to the industry-specific advertiser, it is even more difficult to sell to consumer media companies. They are accustomed to dealing in millions of subscribers or, at the very least, hundreds of thousands. Even the seemingly healthy STM professional journals with tens of thousands of subscribers are not on the consumer media's radar screen. The oft-proffered, pass-along circulation numbers that libraries mention do not impress these advertisers. The numbers are too small and the profiles of readers too diffuse. Consumer products advertisers have access to sophisticated research information which is not usually available for STM titles. How successful have libraries been in having readily available data on their user populations for collection assessment purposes? In most instances it has been necessary to undertake labor- and time-intensive special user studies to assemble such data. If libraries have traditionally had a tenuous grasp on exactly who their readers are, how many they number, and what they are reading, there is certainly insufficient data to satisfy an advertiser's requirements.

Advertisers have found that context and editorial environment are very powerful forces in readers' uptake of advertised products. Readers respond to different publications for different types of goods and services, i.e., people do not traditionally turn to society or scholarly journals for the same types of products they would get from a travel or news magazine. So while a physician might browse his or her specialty journal for drug or equipment ads, there is less likelihood of responding to ads for cars, travel, or fragrances.

At Elsevier Science several years ago we conducted an interesting experiment in this direction. As the publisher of more than a dozen professional journals in various medical specialty fields we have considerable experience in selling advertising space for these titles. We felt our collection of medical specialty journals would be attractive to luxury goods advertisers in light of the demographics of the combined readership of these titles, i.e., doctors in high income brackets. A journal package was developed whereby we guaranteed advertisers multiple ad placements in these journals to a readership of one hundred thousand doctors. The package was pitched to luxury goods and travel industry advertisers, but it met with little success. The campaign was eventually abandoned.

By way of example outside the framework of STM publishing, several recent issues of *Variety*, a weekly professional magazine published by Cahners, a sister company to Elsevier Science in the Reed Elsevier group, were circulated to the North American Serials Interest Group attendees present at the concurrent session. *Variety* has some impressive demographics with a weekly circulation of thirty-five thousand with an average household income of $450,000. Also, it is more readable for the lay person than most STM professional journals. A review of recent issues of *Variety* revealed that the advertisements were almost exclusively representative of the entertainment industry. There were a few ads from hotels, airlines, and limousine companies, clearly pitched to the transient nature of the entertainment industry, but the importance of context was very evident in the profile of advertisers for the issues circulated.

A QUICK NOTE ON SPACE AD PRICES

Librarians often ask what the costs are for one-page advertisements in an STM journal. As a general rule, a journal with a circulation around one thousand to two thousand, having perhaps an even split between library and individual subscribers, will charge between $850 and $1,000 for a black-and-white, full-page advertisement. A professional journal in a medical specialty area with a circulation between ten thousand and thirty thousand costs up to $5,000 for a four-color, one-page advertisement.

THE PROMISE OF ADVERTISING IN THE WEB ENVIRONMENT

The digital environment holds promise for attracting advertising in totally new ways. As a first consideration, the medium is no longer limited by the circulation of one or even a cluster of journals. Publishers can guarantee a minimum/maximum number of hits over a fixed period of time, and they can offer a number of options:

- link space ads to hits to something other than a single journal title, e.g., link ads to table of contents services;
- link space ads to hits in a subject cluster of journals or perhaps to customized profiles of journals in a database;
- link space ads to hits to keyword searches, e.g., each time a word is used in a search; or
- link space ad to hits of specific articles.

The electronic files are seeing more use than paper journals which means that advertisers linking ads hits to specific criteria have the potential of exposing their product to a wider audience than was ever possible in print. For example, within the first six months of Science-Direct® becoming available in 1999, subscribing libraries reported use of the electronic files to be at least ten times greater than the use of the paper editions of the same titles. That is a significant increase in the number of people seeing an issue of a journal or an individual article.

The Web offers more targeted audiences and more customizability than does print. BioMedNet requires users of its free services to register and profile themselves. At present, people seem more willing to provide this kind of profile information in the electronic format than is traditionally found in print. But will this openness last or is it characteristic of the early entrants in this incipient industry?

WHAT TYPES OF ADS ARE AVAILABLE TO WEB ADVERTISERS?

There is still a lot of new ground to be covered in exploring the possibilities of Web advertising. Currently banner ads, formatted as either banners or icons, seem the most prevalent. Most offer the option to click for more content or rich media, e.g., audio, video, animation, or three dimensional. There are, however, certain inherent limitations in the present banner ad format. In a banner ad containing an icon, how does the advertiser attract attention for the reader to click for more data? There is very limited space for text or imagery that can effectively catch the reader's attention. Compare the limitation of an icon with the effect of turning a page in a print journal and seeing a full-page ad where there are far greater possibilities in terms of text and imagery.

Admittedly, the Web ad offers the option to click for rich media, but users are turning to the Web environment to improve the speed of information delivery. Rich media involves more time to download. Web users and Website owners are not always happy with the delays required to display the elaborate files.

Another option is sponsorship, where a company wants to use a Website to subtly call attention to itself or its programs by creating an association between the Website owner, its readers, and the company or brand advertiser. Since this is an ongoing association, the Website will most likely require that the banner ad or tag line be discreet. The ad may also be used for market surveys or interactive marketing, and in most situations the sponsor is allowed to send a limited number of e-mails during the course of the contract. Sponsorship arrangements usually involve a long-term commitment, e.g., six months to one year, and are likely to involve a substantial financial commitment. In order to get this type of investment from an advertiser, however, the Website must be a proven, high-use site and be able to offer convincing data that the users are an ideal target audience for the sponsor.

There are also interstitial ads, images or messages that pop onto the screen for a few seconds when a particular page is retrieved. This approach, however, can be annoying to users, especially on a fee-based service. E-mail advertising, or push technology, is probably the most established form of Web advertising and is a successful method of reaching highly targeted, registered audiences. This approach is particularly attractive as it can include multimedia features and links to Websites. But both interstitial ads and push technology are in early stages of implementation and it remains to be determined how receptive and responsive the audience for these will be in the long term.

SELLING THE WEB ENVIRONMENT TO ADVERTISERS

Despite the early enthusiasm for this new advertising medium, it is still early in its evolution. There is little quantitative or qualitative data on users and patterns, particularly because Web usage is growing exponentially and new entrants have very different profiles than the early Web users. By contrast, the direct mail industry is long established and has a tradition of critical analysis, much of it developed by trial and error over many years' practice. Within two to three years there should be much more quantitative data on Web advertising, and media buyers should become more informed and confident about spending their advertising dollars effectively.

In selling online ads, the initial approach has been to invite existing and loyal advertisers, rather than pursuing new advertisers. The STM publishers have tended to offer the new medium to known advertisers. There is the sense that both sides feel more comfortable in moving into the new medium together. Many Websites have offered introductory ad rates or offer online ads at a slight premium above the print advertising rates because of uncertainty about the demographics. The STM publishers and their advertisers are taking an experimental approach in a new medium. Publishers have also encouraged advertisers to be more creative and innovative in designing Web ads. There are few defined criteria at this point, so it is a good time to try to push the envelope to determine what new approaches will attract users' response.

The Web also holds the prospect of greater customizability than the print environment. Matching a product and its interest group could be linked via any number of criteria, from targeted e-mail to high-traffic pages. There is also the possibility of sponsorship ads linked to specific articles. A good example of this could be a new approach in how pharmaceutical companies distribute article reprints. By posting articles on the Web might pharmaceutical companies eliminate the need for paper reprints? Or are there distinct audiences to be reached through the different distribution channels and would it still be necessary to distribute paper copies? Only time and experience can tell.

OBSTACLES IN THE IMPLEMENTATION OF WEB ADVERTISING

While the group attending this session at the North American Serials Interest Group annual conference was interested in the possibilities of advertising revenues altering the economic models in STM journal publishing, the notion may not be equally embraced by all users. There remains the possibility of user resistance. If customers are paying for an electronic service, what level of advertising presence are they willing to tolerate? A good comparison is the low threshold of tolerance for advertisements at the cinema or on airplanes. How many of us have heard boos at movie theaters when advertising comes on the screen? When consumers are paying a fee for a premium service, they are less receptive to anything perceived as an intrusion. Hence, if scientists were to tolerate significant presence of advertising in a Web-based, full-text service, they would probably expect to see substantial cost savings to make the intrusion palatable. Would publishers be able to attract sufficient advertising revenue to alter the economic model?

There is also the prospect of librarian resistance. A number of listservs have already circulated discussion about advertising on purchased services and the library community in general is not especially enthusiastic. A number of librarians have recommended inclusion of a disclaimer about any library endorsement of advertised products.

In order to implement a sophisticated Website advertising package that would provide all the bells and whistles that might attract advertisers, considerable investment in software development is necessary. There are exciting possibilities for customizing ads, tracking usage, and reporting back; but at this juncture, when so much effort is devoted to getting systems up and running, advertising understandably takes a lower priority. Also, users are currently very open and responsive in the Web environment, but is this likely to change, with users becoming more reticent about their profiles and blocking out electronic advertising? Habits can change suddenly, particularly if there is a change in perception from the Web being the domain of a somewhat exclusive group to just another source of irritating intrusions from advertisers. This may be a particularly sensitive issue for users who turn to the Web for speed and functionality, only to be confronted with space ads at every turn.

CONCLUSION

Advertising plays an important role in the economic picture for some scientific journals, but it is unlikely that publishers of primary research journals can attract appreciable new sources of advertising revenue in print journals. The transition to the Web, however, opens up some new advertising opportunities. The flexibility and customizability of the online environment offer options for advertisers that were inconceivable in the print medium, but Web advertising is still a nascent industry. It is unclear at this time exactly how much the habits of readers and advertisers will change, and in which directions they will go as electronic mediums evolve.

The Journal as a Provider of Community Services

John Cox

SUMMARY. As electronic journals continue to evolve, the traditional roles of the journal will change. One of these roles will be the journal as a community service provider. Community-based services, directed at journal reading scholars, are being developed and are changing the nature of scholarly communication. These new services raise issues of quality, archiving, identification, and pricing of electronic journals. *[Article copies available for a fee from The Haworth Document Delivery Service: 1-800-342-9678. E-mail address: getinfo@haworthpressinc.com <Website: http://www.haworthpressinc.com>]*

THE SCHOLARLY ENVIRONMENT

Scholarly communication is in a process of transformation. None of us will be untouched. It used to be conducted by telephone, letter and

John Cox is Principal, John Cox Associates (E-mail: John.E.Cox@btinternet.com).

[Haworth co-indexing entry note]: "The Journal as a Provider of Community Services." Cox, John. Co-published simultaneously in *The Serials Librarian* (The Haworth Press, Inc.) Vol. 38, No. 1/2, 2000, pp. 199-209; and: *From Carnegie to Internet2: Forging the Serials Future* (ed: P. Michelle Fiander, Joseph C. Harmon, and Jonathan David Makepeace) The Haworth Press, Inc., 2000, pp. 199-209. Single or multiple copies of this article are available for a fee from The Haworth Document Delivery Service [1-800-342-9678, 9:00 a.m. - 5:00 p.m. (EST). E-mail address: getinfo@haworthpressinc.com].

conference. Its results appeared in books and journals which libraries could afford to collect on a comprehensive basis. Published scholarly information was readily available to its specialist readership. But this began to change in the 1970s.

The rapid expansion of university education in the 1960s and 1970s was matched by abundant resources for scientific research, and for libraries that collected the results of this research. In the 1990s there are twice as many scientists in research as there were in 1975. Twice as many papers are published per year than twenty years ago [1]. There are more journals than ever before. At the same time, library budgets have increased at only a fraction of the rate. The number of journal subscriptions has steadily decreased as rising prices have led to cancellations. Ready access can no longer be guaranteed.

Higher education itself is changing. After two decades of expansion, the funding environment has changed. The expectations of customers (i.e., students) are changing, as more adults seek qualifications and as the demand for lifelong or continuing education and off-campus studies increases. Universities have imported business techniques such as mission statements that wax lyrical about learner-focussed programs, customized personal learning, distance learning, linked programs and flexible delivery. Universities market themselves to potential students, and compete fiercely with each other. Many expect their faculty to be entrepreneurial in a way inconceivable only a generation ago. This change is not confined to the United States; it is commonplace throughout the western world.

THE KNOWLEDGE-BASED ECONOMY

We are all part of the knowledge-based economy, which includes the media, publishing, software, database, education and financial communities. The online industry in all its forms is strongest in the USA, but the rest of the world is following. It has quadrupled in size in ten years. Seventy per cent of online information is bought by the business and financial communities. But the biggest growth is in mass-market consumer transactions, which will continue to grow at a considerable rate, as evidenced by the following:

- The growth in Internet users: It is estimated that there were 36 million at the end of 1997, and that there will be 142 million in 2004 [2].

- The penetration of PCs: By mid-1998 there were 35.6 PCs per 100 people in the USA, 25.5 in Canada, 27.8 in Australia, 20.1 in the UK, and 18.3 in Germany [2].
- The stock market values of Internet companies such as Yahoo!, Amazon.com, e-Bay, AOL and others.
- The increased spending on Internet-based information services: $7 billion in 1990 to $13 billion in 1998. It is forecast to grow to $17 billion by 2001 [3].

THE PRINTED JOURNAL AND ACADEMIC EXPECTATIONS

The first recognisable scientific journal, *Philosophical Transactions*, was founded in 1665. The Royal Society established its key components as a scientific journal:

- Communication–regular publication of new results
- Quality control–peer review
- Priority–date-stamping the published work
- Ownership–identifying the author and establishing intellectual property protection

If you add the need to deposit the work in the "archive" of scholarly literature, it is clear that the specification of the modern journal has changed little over the succeeding three and a half centuries. It continues to serve as part of the certification process and provides a permanent record of research and scholarship that is fixed and authoritative.

Nevertheless, printed journals are unable to meet many of the demands now being placed upon them as the result of a number of factors:

- It is not only faculty and students on campus that need access to literature, but also distance learners, alumni, and others working with the university.
- Budgets no longer allow for coherent collection management other than on a cooperative, multi-institutional basis.
- Purchasing consortia negotiating licenses for their members that require 'bulk' prices, performance standards and archiving requirements.
- Printed journals no longer meet the needs of all disciplines, simply by virtue of increased specialization and complexity. The hu-

man ability to assimilate information in traditional forms has been outpaced. Technology is not an end in itself, but it provides the means to deal with such complexity.
- Some academics now believe that certification of scholarship should be decoupled from publication because of technological changes.

Universities are demanding affordable prices, an increasing role for universities and societies in the publishing process and a new deal on intellectual property. They are, at last, asserting their buying power, and will eventually ignore publishers who are not responsive to the needs of the academy.

These controversies are merely symptoms of the breakdown of traditional scholarly publishing. They have even made the Press. The *New York Times* ran a story on SPARC, entitled 'Soaring journal prices spur a revolt in scientific publishing'; it reported that *PhysChem-Comm*, the Royal Society of Chemistry's electronic journal, will sell for $350 and compete directly with Elsevier's *Chemical Physics Letters*, which costs over $8000 [4]. The problem with SPARC is that it simply introduces more journals. There is no evidence that authors will move wholesale from a high-impact, successful journal of choice to a new, unknown title, albeit at a much lower price. Things in the academy do not move quickly or in a coordinated fashion.

THE REQUIREMENTS OF TODAY'S SCHOLARSHIP AND RESEARCH

When I started in publishing in the late 1960s, the phrase of the moment was the "invisible college": comprised of scholars who, wherever they were based, shared a common research interest. They communicated by letter and telephone. The formal results of scholarship were published in printed journals and monographs. The importance of conferences grew with the advent of mass jet air travel. Then the introduction of the telex, and then the fax in the early 1980s, opened up new communications opportunities. E-mail and the Web are creatures of this decade, but have truly transformed communication. The invisible college has become visible and identifiable; and it expects information and communication products to confer benefits similar to those available from Web-based resources.

The desktop PC and the Net enable the busy researcher to communicate with his colleagues, analyze data using complex visualization tools and marshal a wide range of resources from the desktop. The formal journal literature is only a small part of this, but has the potential to form the centerpiece of community information services.

Researchers are beginning to apply market thinking to their choice of information services. They demand personalized services accessible wherever they are. They demand transparent access to a range of information sources, and the capacity to influence the presentation and the content of information consumed. They demand interaction with colleagues in a collaborative environment, but there is a gulf between expectations and capacity to deliver. We are still in the horse and cart stage of this technology. Effective filtering mechanisms and sophisticated metadata are still primitive. But the gap is closing.

THE GROWTH OF CONTENT-BASED SERVICES

There are already examples of content-based services in the scholarly arena to indicate what is possible in the future:

- *Perseus,* a digital library of the classics, demonstrates the limitations and relative inaccessibility of print on paper, as compared with an electronic environment that facilitates the analysis of documents with complex visualization tools [5].
- *Stoa* is an electronic publishing system for refereed scholarship in the humanities designed to be accessible to wide public audiences. Such an initiative adds to the pressure to break the link between publication and certification for tenure [6].
- *LANL*, the Los Alamos pre-print server, has shown how popular these services are; it has generated 102,000 submissions since August 1991, and attracts nearly 600,000 connections per week [7].

Services are also being developed by traditional publishers, both commercial and non-profit, to serve both the academic and professional user:

- *Science* is developing services on the Net to complement the weekly journal. Much is at stake for the AAAS (American Association for the Advancement of Science). *Science* is a 118-year-old weekly, with a circulation of 158,000 and revenues of $40 million a year. It has been available on-line with *High Wire* since 1995. It has now launched two Web sites: a news site and a science-graduate career-development site. The long-term view is that an on-line *Science* can be "knowledge environment" with the appropriate tools, visuals and content. Its on-line revenues are less than $1 million a year, with a great risk of jeopardizing existing journal subscription and advertising revenues. Parts of the Website are free which, ironically, appears to generate print subscriptions.

- *ChemWeb* features a library of chemical journals; databases of abstracts, chemical structures and patents; a searchable and reviewed database of Web resources; MDL's (MDL Information Systems, Inc.) *Available Chemicals Directory*; a "shopping mall" for software, equipment and books; a jobs page; and a conference diary [8].
- *BioMedNet* contains similar features for the medical and biosciences: MEDLINE, an online magazine, a job exchange, a database of relevant Web sites, a bookshop and 100 journals from which articles may be purchased [9].

Both *ChemWeb* and *BioMedNet* are products of Elsevier Science. Reed Elsevier does not confine its electronic publishing to scholarly works, or even to publishing in its general sense. As well as *Science Direct* for the academic community, it has developed *Lexis-Nexis* for the legal and business communities, *Air Transport Intelligence* for the travel business and *Estates Gazette Interactive* for the property market.

RETHINKING THE PUBLISHING PROCESS

Experience is a great teacher. Even though we are at the very beginning of the electronic revolution, it is clear to many of us in publishing that our traditional ideas and processes need to be re-engineered. Electronic publishing introduces broader content, new information tools, speed, linking mechanisms, cost reductions, and, particularly important, new buying points and more flexible business models.

It is far more important to understand and experiment with new values that can be added to information than to argue about technology. The technology is important only as a means to an end. We have spent the last five years discussing the relative merits of competing technologies: PDF, HTML, *RealPage*, SGML, etc. I have always thought this has been profoundly stupid, because it has enabled both librarians and publishers to avoid the strategic management issues underlying the transition to an electronic publishing environment. Now at least one Internet services company, CatchWord, has recognised this. CatchWord will now output more than 300 journals in any format: its own *RealPage*, PDF, XML, as well as VML, PGML and SVG. The customer chooses.

Scholarly publishers have traditionally been driven by their authors, and have rarely listened to librarians until recently. Librarians, judging by comments made by faculty editors and authors I have dealt with, seem to operate on a different agenda to that required by their patrons. In the new world, customer service and feedback becomes vital. Both of our professions must develop new skills such as information filtering, customer profiling, seller qualification and knowledge sharing. We have to understand the "context" in which content is used. Success lies in offering information that adds value to the user's decisions and activities. Context, not content or technology, is the key. Publishers and librarians have no excuse not to work together to define how information products and services are put together and delivered.

At a conference hosted by the UK Department of Trade and Industry [10], Nigel Stapleton, Joint Chief Executive of Reed Elsevier drew a distinction between e-business and e-commerce. E-commerce is about buying and selling; Amazon.com is a good example. But e-business is not just about transactions. The importance of context drives e-businesses to respond to customer needs with effective customized information systems and products. He illustrated the distinction as follows:

• *E-commerce:*	• *E-business:*
• Transaction oriented	• Customer management oriented
• Cost-based (i.e., cost reduction)	• Revenue-based (i.e., revenue growth)
• Dis-intermediated	• Re-intermediated

Publishers are likely to find it difficult to make the transition from producing and handling static and inflexible printed products, to producing and handling dynamic, flexible electronic products.

NEW BUSINESS MODELS

Recovering the investment made in all this activity is the great imponderable. Part of the Web culture is that information is free. The Web is now the property of the whole community, not just the academy, and cannot be insulated from business activity that is fundamental to western society. There is a fundamental issue that remains to be established, and it can be framed by the following questions: What will be provided free, and what must be paid for? These questions are currently being addressed by the publisher of *Science*. We do not know yet where to draw the line between academic or research-friendly indexing or linking on the one hand, and the core journal content for which payment is required, on the other.

I suspect that more and different pricing models will give users and librarians much more choice. We have an escape from the straightjacket of the individual journal subscription price. All the 'bulk' deals negotiated by consortia have already seen to that. The future may offer much more, including:

- Pre-payment for access at the article level; Elsevier has been testing this model with the University of Michigan in its PEAK project [11].
- Package pricing by discipline or sub-discipline; this may be single publisher offerings, or aggregations of multi-publisher materials.
- Transactional, or pay-by-the-drink, models similar to document delivery.
- The database, or Pay-TV, model, where the subscription provides access to a core collection of titles, including back volumes, for a set period–usually a year–at the end of which access is denied unless the subscription is renewed.
- Micro-pricing, where payment becomes due every time an item of information is accessed; the item might be a diagram, table or paragraph, and access might be downloading, printing or simply viewing for more than a set period of time. There could be many types of access, but the unit price per access will be low.

PRESERVING THE SCHOLARLY RECORD

With the opportunities that I have described come challenges: name and version control, document integrity, authentication and preservation. I want to comment on two issues related to the location of on-line literature, and access to such literature as part of the eternal scholarly record.

Finding stuff: Indexing on the major Web search engines such as AltaVista, Yahoo! and Excite has evolved under the auspices of software developers and business people rather than librarians. They lack precision, editorial control, and search power. For example, a user looking for "German Financing Companies" does not know whether to look under "German" or "Financing" or "Companies." This is only one example of many indexing problems that were solved by librarians using the Dewey Decimal System over 100 years ago.

To find the information they need researchers use many tools, most of which are available in the library. But they use on-line databases rather than the library OPAC, simply because the OPAC's information on electronic resources is patchy. The fault lies with libraries who have not articulated exactly what bibliographic information is needed, and with publishers who do not think to systematically inform libraries about developments in their products or even changes in URLs. Publishers must help libraries to maintain their effectiveness as information navigators, or the orderly distribution of information from author to reader will crumble.

Preserving stuff: Historically, university libraries, many of which date back to the Middle Ages, have taken responsibility for archiving the scholarly record. The electronic environment complicates matters, and "archiving" is not consistently defined throughout the world.

We must clarify what needs to be archived. Scholarly papers and monographs in printed form are coherent and self-defining. But behind formal publication lies a range of material that is available electronically, including critiques and conferences facilitated by the Internet, links to other resources, and other exchanges between scholars as well as grey literature and raw data. Where do we draw the line?

To me, the archive only becomes an issue when it exists only in electronic form, or if it has ceased to be available from conventional sources through a publisher or aggregator. Given the small communities of researchers to which each individual archive may be relevant, and the efficiency of technology, maybe only one archive copy will be needed–probably in the country where the publication originated. This points to a role for national libraries analogous to their responsibility for legal deposit in the print domain.

RE-ENGINEERING THE PROCESS

Publishers make products out of ideas using their skills in quality management, presentations, marketing, distribution and subscription management. They need to re-skill themselves in copyright and licensing management. Universities are now asserting control over copyright, as they already do over patents. Ways must be found to manage issues of both authors' and users' rights to facilitate the widest access to material consistent with maintaining the integrity of the product.

Much research and experimentation is needed in structuring information and designing formats for easy location, retrieval, and viewing on the screen. Every publisher needs to be involved with every librarian in the development of standards such as the DOI (Digital Object Identifier), in creating better metadata, and in the economic and cultural issue of archiving.

There needs to be a change in culture. Competition must be tempered with cooperation. The future lies in partnerships and alliances. Scholars need access to a single coherent and complete corpus of literature. Publishers have to accept that they must work together to provide their electronic content, often associated with secondary databases, through a single point of access. The challenge is to maintain the authority and integrity of the individual article, and the revenue needed to bring it to life, while providing simple, uncluttered access to readers.

NOTES

1. In 1975, 2.64 million scientists in the USA are estimated to have published 312,200 articles; in 1995, there were 5.74 million scientists and 577,100 published articles: Carol Tenopir and Donald W. King, "Trends in Scientific Scholarly Journal Publishing in the United States," *Journal of Scholarly Publishing* vol. 28, no 3 (1997).

2. Source: eStats, sourced from Department of Trade & Industry, London, 1998.

3. Source: Veronis Suhler & Associates, Inc. New York. (www.veronissuhler.com)

4. Carol Kaesuk Yoon, "Soaring prices spur a revolt in scientific Publishing," *New York Times*, December 8, 1998, sec F, p. 2.

5. The Perseus Project is "an evolving digital library of resources for the study of the ancient world and beyond." (http://www.perseus.tufts.edu)

6. The Stoa: A Consortium for Electronic Publication in the Humanities. (http://www.stoa.org)

7. LANL: Automated e-print archive of Los Alamos National Laboratory: (http://www.lanl.gov)

8. Chemweb: A site containing journals, databases and other resources related to chemistry. (http://www.chemweb.com)

9. BioMedNet: The Internet Community for Biological and Chemical Researchers. (http://www.biomednet.com)

10. "Reed Elsevier and electronic content," *Scholarly Communications Report, No 26* December 1998. This newsletter, ISSN 1364-5064, is an excellent source of news and conference reports.

11. PEAK: Pricing Electronic Access to Knowledge. A joint project of the University of Michigan and Elsevier Publishing. (http://www.lib.umich.edu/libhome/peak)

WORKSHOPS

Impact of Bundled Databases on Serials Acquisitions in Academic Libraries

Konny Thompson
Rayette Wilder

Workshop Leaders

Leslie Horner Button

Recorder

SUMMARY. The proliferation of electronic resources appears to have created a shift in some values traditionally held by collection development and serials librarians. This workshop presented results of an informal survey conducted by the presenters and discussed some changes and trends that affect serials librarians in particular. *[Article copies available for a fee from The Haworth Document Delivery Service: 1-800-342-9678. E-mail address: getinfo@haworthpressinc.com <Website: http://www.haworthpressinc.com>]*

The acquisition of databases has long been a part of the serial landscape. It started with Dialog, a luxury in its time, where librarians

Konny Thompson is Chair of Materials Management and Acquisitions Librarian, Gonzaga University.

Rayette Wilder is Electronic Resources and Reference Librarian, Gonzaga University.

Leslie Horner Button is Head of the Serials Section, Acquisitions Department, University of Massachusetts Library, Amherst.

[Haworth co-indexing entry note]: "Impact of Bundled Databases on Serials Acquisitions in Academic Libraries." Button, Leslie Horner. Co-published simultaneously in *The Serials Librarian* (The Haworth Press, Inc.) Vol. 38, No. 3/4, 2000, pp. 213-218; and: *From Carnegie to Internet2: Forging the Serials Future* (ed: P. Michelle Fiander, Joseph C. Harmon, and Jonathan David Makepeace) The Haworth Press, Inc., 2000, pp. 213-218. Single or multiple copies of this article are available for a fee from The Haworth Document Delivery Service [1-800-342-9678, 9:00 a.m. - 5:00 p.m. (EST). E-mail address: getinfo@haworthpressinc.com].

performed mediated searches for users. Dialog was not considered a serial, was not cataloged, and was typically paid for from other budget lines. Then came indexing and abstracting services, such as Magazine Index, where patrons could initiate their own searches. These products were considered serials, paid for from serials funds, and were added to library catalogs. With the advent of the Web, electronic resources emerged slowly at first. Some initial offerings, First Search and JSTOR for example, were bundles. As the Web became more sophisticated and robust a greater variety of resources evolved. Librarians faced dilemmas over which electronic resources they should add to collections, as well as whether they should add titles in bundled databases to library catalogs.

The presenters drew an analogy between bundled aggregates and monographic blanket orders. With a blanket order a library agrees to purchase everything published by a particular publisher. If the library chooses well, the blanket order meets a variety of needs, including time saved on selection and ordering. The question arises: how many libraries check all materials supplied on a blanket order to ascertain whether the content fits library needs? What happens when the publisher says they will supply everything except one particular title, which must then be ordered separately? With blanket orders librarians rely on the publisher to tell us what is appropriate for our collections.

The same can be said for aggregated databases, although aggregates do provide value-added features. These features include the ability to search for a variety of resources in one product, a single interface to search a variety of resources, flexible article delivery that permits users to save information to e-mail or disk, and usage statistics. There are disadvantages too. Each aggregate has its own interface and overlapping journal coverage. Aggregators control the content. Libraries have little say about what content is delivered, much less archived.

The presenters conducted an informal survey to identify trends and point to some thought processes that are part of acquiring aggregates. The survey, currently available online at http://www.gonzaga.edu/e-pubs/handout.html, contained fourteen questions and was distributed to six listservs: ARL-EJOURNAL, WEB4LIB, COLLIB, SERIALIST, ACQLIST, and DIG-REF. They received thirty-two responses from a wide range of institutions. The first three questions established the following. Based on the job titles given by respondents, the presenters believe that 37.5% of the respondents were administrators and 62.5% were librarians. Sixteen respondents were from institutions with less than a five thousand full-time equivalent (FTE) student population, five had between five thousand and ten thousand FTE, and ten had ten thousand or more FTE. The serials budgets of respondents ranged between $7,100 and $4 million. According to graphs presented there was no correlation between the FTE student population and the size of the serials budget. Neither was there a correlation between these factors and the number of databases available at the respondents' libraries.

The fourth question asked how many bundled aggregates were subscribed to and requested that they be listed. The answers ranged from a low of two to a high of forty-six, with an average of 8.83. The top seven databases subscribed to were FirstSearch, ProQuest, Lexis/Nexis Academic Universe, Expanded Academic ASAP, EBSCOhost Academic Search Elite, JSTOR and ABI/Inform.

The fifth question focused on whether additional funding had been allocated to pay for the bundled databases and whether databases were paid from the serials budget or from another budget line. Sixteen respondents received no new money, while sixteen respondents received additional funds. Eleven institutions paid for databases from the serials budget, fifteen institutions paid for them from a separate budget line, two combined funds from the serials budget and a separate budget to pay for databases, and four institutions did not respond. The presenters concluded that libraries appear to be finding the funds to pay for these resources out of existing funds.

The sixth question asked who negotiated license agreements. Seventeen respondents reported librarians conducted negotiations, fourteen said it was administrators, and in one instance no one did so. The seventh question asked whether the respondent's institution participated in consortial purchasing. Thirty-one of them did, one did not.

The eighth question concerned whether purchasing power for paper serials had been reduced as a result of purchasing full-text databases. Seventeen responded that there had been no reduction. The presenters questioned this result, since five of the institutions did not receive new funding. The presenters concluded that the respondents misunderstood the question or that the respondents' institutions had used funds that the respondents were unaware of. Fifteen respondents indicated they had lost purchasing power.

The ninth question inquired what portion of titles in a bundled product the respondent would choose, if able, to order on an individual basis. Twelve respondents did not answer this question. The presenters believed these individuals did not answer because it cut to the heart of how difficult these resources were to unbundle. The remaining answers ranged from two percent to one hundred percent, with the average indicating 40.83% of the titles would have been selected. The presenters thought this percentage might be high, with respondents putting a good face on what they had purchased.

The tenth question asked if the respondent's institution had a policy for purchasing bundled products. Twenty-three of the respondents had no policy, six used existing collection development policies, and three had a specific policy. The eleventh question asked respondents about their familiarity with the International Coalition of Library Consortia (ICoLC) guidelines for purchase of electronic materials and whether their institution had adopted them in dealing with these purchases or whether they had developed their own guidelines. Seventeen respondents were familiar with the ICoLC guidelines. Of these seventeen, nine complied or supported them, four did not, and four did not respond. Two of the seventeen had adopted these guidelines as policy, two had adopted them somewhat, four had not, and one did not answer.

The twelfth question inquired whether the institution had developed their own guidelines for accepting licenses. Eleven did not answer, ten had no guidelines, two used someone else's guidelines, eight had guidelines, and one was working on them. As to what had influenced these institutions to follow guidelines or set their own standards, sixteen did not respond, two indicated a workshop, and the remainder gave varying answers, e.g., they were using Cal State's policy. The thirteenth question asked whether technological capabilities were considered when ordering bundled databases and all respondents indicated they were.

The final question inquired if print subscriptions were cancelled when bundled databases were acquired. Eleven respondents said they had not cancelled any. Twenty-one said they did or had plans to cancel. As for why print was not cancelled, answers ranged from a concern about archiving, to impermanence of information in electronic format, to a lack of confidence in electronic materials. Where print was cancelled, the respondents indicated that they dropped print indexes, titles that were duplicates, titles for which the electronic form was an acceptable substitute, or titles for which the timeliness of information was improved with the electronic version. Some simply indicated that they cancelled print titles to pay for electronic products. When asked if their institution had policies or guidelines in place for how they would handle a database dropping full-text coverage, twenty-three did not, one did not but was working on it, six did not respond, and two said they had, with one of the two just accepting the loss as its policy.

ANALYSIS OF SURVEY RESPONSES

The survey raised many questions regarding bundled databases. What are we paying for, and what do we want? The answers to these questions depend on the particular bundled database. In some cases it may be more cost effective simply to purchase individual titles, assuming this is an option. According to the presenters, the survey identified an attitude shift that has taken place in both collection development and serials. First, bundled databases have changed the selection and review process. We are no longer reviewing items on a title by title basis. This runs counter to methods we operated under in the past, where librarians were very cautious about which serials to add because of budget implications. There are interface and search capability issues, which are as important as the content. Who among us has had training to balance these considerations in database selection? With these products we appear to be paying for low use titles where we may have cancelled their print counterparts. Why do we appear to ignore this? Are we prepared to allow entire runs of serials to disappear when we do not have policies to deal with publishers removing content?

Coupled with the concerns outlined above, the presenters said that the survey raised questions about measures of excellence. Aggregates add large numbers of materials to our collections. Is more better? What about the loss of diversity within collections as materials overlap? Will aggregated collections actually become our core serial holdings? While it is true that one order for an aggregate adds many titles and there is no shelving, binding, or other physical maintenance for these resources, what about maintaining access? Maintaining electronic access may require as much work as maintaining physical access. Computer technicians may replace shelvers and bindery clerks. Does the catalog no longer define our collections? If it does not, do we still need a catalog or can we simply create a Webpage with links to various resources? Is it an either/or proposition between aggregates and the catalog?

According to the survey, fifty percent of the respondents had more money to spend, and slightly more than forty-six percent indicated this gave them more purchasing power. If these percentages are true, the presenters claim that they belie Association of Research Libraries (ARL) statistics on Service Trends in ARL Libraries 1991-1997 (http://www.arl.org/stats/arlstat/1997_t1.html). The ARL statistics indicate that interlibrary loans have risen fifty-eight percent during this same time period, while serial and monographic purchases and support staffing levels declined. Libraries are changing, and we are making these changes with fewer staff. In the future, when aggregates are perceived as requiring less maintenance, we may again forego staff in some areas to gain computer technicians.

CONCLUSION

The presenters closed by stating that libraries are moving away from an ownership model toward an access model. This new model will require a different set of skills. For example, licensing experience may be sought more than it already is. The journal model may evolve into an article model, where no library staff intervention is necessary and there is unlimited delivery of articles for the life of the license negotiated. As for serials departments, we are dealing with aggregates, but we are treating them in a manner analogous to blanket orders as opposed to traditional print serials. The quality and quantity of bundled databases should be considered during their evaluation despite the difficulty of that task. There is little doubt that there will be changes in the way we acquire aggregations. Librarians in the future may be working closely with vendors to choose various options for electronic delivery, such as pay-per-view. When that happens, the function of serials librarianship itself will change.

There was a discussion period following the presentation during which several themes emerged, including the importance of peer review as a means of validating content, regardless of format, and user demand for information available at a moment's notice.

The Pricing Implications of Site and Consortia Licensing into the Next Millennium

Simon Inger
Taissa Kusma
Barbara McFadden Allen

Workshop Leaders

Sandra Barstow

Recorder

SUMMARY. Several pricing models exist for providing access to electronic journals. Models may be based on the composition of a package of resources, the size of the purchasing institution, or other factors. Libraries combining to form consortia may realize pricing benefits. In this workshop these factors were considered from the perspectives of the access provider, the publisher, and the consortium, with feedback from librarians. *[Article copies available for a fee from The Haworth Document Delivery Service: 1-800-342-9678. E-mail address: getinfo@haworthpressinc.com <Website: http://www.haworthpressinc.com>]*

Simon Inger is Managing Director, CatchWord.
Taissa Kusma is Director, Electronic Product Development, Academic Press.
Barbara McFadden Allen is Director, Committee on Institutional Cooperation (CIC).
Sandra Barstow is Head of Acquisitions, University of Wyoming Libraries.

[Haworth co-indexing entry note]: "The Pricing Implications of Site and Consortia Licensing into the Next Millennium." Barstow, Sandra. Co-published simultaneously in *The Serials Librarian* (The Haworth Press, Inc.) Vol. 38, No. 3/4, 2000, pp. 219-224; and: *From Carnegie to Internet2: Forging the Serials Future* (ed: P. Michelle Fiander, Joseph C. Harmon, and Jonathan David Makepeace) The Haworth Press, Inc., 2000, pp. 219-224. Single or multiple copies of this article are available for a fee from The Haworth Document Delivery Service [1-800-342-9678, 9:00 a.m. - 5:00 p.m. (EST). E-mail address: getinfo@haworthpressinc.com].

SETTING THE SCENE

Simon Inger introduced the workshop with a discussion of the economics of migrating from a print journal environment to an electronic journal environment. The initial costs for publishing print journals are less than those for publishing electronic journals, with production costs rising for print journals as subscriptions increase. In the world of electronic journals, however, while initial costs are higher, largely due to software and hardware requirements, additional subscriptions do not increase the costs of production to the extent they do in a print environment. In other words, the cost curve for an electronic journal is relatively flat regardless of the number of additional subscribers. For a journal available in both paper and electronic formats, the total cost of production will decline as the number of paper subscriptions decreases, making it advantageous to the publisher to promote electronic journals once the start-up costs are met.

Inger asked a number of questions to "set the scene" for the session. He first asked how many of the participants' libraries had access to electronic collections; most of the audience had such access. He then asked how many libraries had arranged consortial access to electronic collections; again, a majority of the audience had such arrangements. Inger's final question was whether the libraries who dealt with consortia felt the service was better or worse than going it alone; most thought service was better, a few were undecided, but none thought it worse. In both sessions, participants felt that "bundled" database purchases provided access to more electronic resources. The morning group felt that the extra access provided added value to the product, and could increase demand while reducing cost. The afternoon group disagreed with this assessment.

A PUBLISHER'S PERSPECTIVE

Taissa Kusma spoke about licensing and pricing models from the publisher perspective. The goals of publishers of electronic journals include expanding the readership of journals; maintaining the revenue stream; participating in an orderly transition from print to electronic format; adding value to electronic journals by providing search capability and links to other online resources; and developing new services for subscribers.

The costs of electronic journals include the online system and service; user support; licensing; and increased production costs. Some publishers have initially underestimated these costs. Kusma disagreed with Inger's characterization of the cost curve for an electronic journal as basically flat. She pointed out that while it is true that additional users can be added to an online distribution system at little additional cost, at some point the system's capacity will be reached, necessitating major system upgrades before additional users can be adequately supported. This situation would be depicted by a steep jump in the cost curve followed by flattening at a somewhat higher level.

Kusma described some of the pricing models in use by publishers of electronic journals. Over the last five years various publishers have experimented with different models, which are being refined based on feedback from librarians. In the next few years the most effective models should prevail. Pricing models include the following:

- Online access is included with the print at no extra cost.
- Online access is provided as an add-on to the print, for an additional cost.
- Print is provided as an add-on to the online, at an extra cost.
- The price of online access is based on various factors such as the size of the institutional subscriber, based on FTE students, for example; the number of subscriptions held by the institutional subscriber; or the number of simultaneous users able to access the online product.

One problem with using the size of the user community to determine the cost of the electronic product is that size alone does not indicate the probable amount of usage. The Carnegie Classification is more meaningful because it provides a way of inferring the type of use, since some institutions have more potential users than other institutions with the same size user base. Print holdings are not a good basis for estimating pricing, since they measure the strength of the library, not the number of users. Pricing by number of simultaneous users tends to inhibit use of the product, which is undesirable for both the publisher and the users.

Kusma discussed the advantages and disadvantages of various ways of licensing electronic products. Licensing individual journals lets the library limit access to a specific set of titles, but results in a higher unit cost. Licensing a package of journals provides a possible benefit to users, in that the unit cost tends to be lower and in many cases access to additional resources is provided at no extra cost to the subscriber. However, some of the librarians in the audience questioned whether the added access was actually providing added value, since the extra titles were not required for curriculum support and would not have been purchased if they had not been included in the cost of the package. Consortial licensing provides benefits of reduced licensing and billing costs, increased readership, and lower unit cost for the items. However, there is less contact between the publisher and the library and less opportunity to customize the offerings. Members of a consortium that opts out of a particular package may have to go to a new consortium in order to obtain that package.

A LIBRARY CONSORTIUM'S PERSPECTIVE

Barbara McFadden Allen, representing a library consortium's point of view, began her talk by stating that she would not be talking about the academic publishing chain, nor would she be talking about the current budgeting situation for academic institutions. Her purpose was to discuss consortia pricing models, such as those mentioned earlier, and incentives to consortial arrangements.

Consortial pricing provides benefits to libraries and to publishers. For the libraries, there is the feeling of safety in numbers in selecting which packages to purchase, and the individual members, when banded together in a consortium, have more influence on use/pricing. Few individual libraries have the legal, collection, and systems know-how to arrange package deals on their own. For users it is almost impossible to judge the value of a package and figure out how it will be used, resulting in what seems to be, in Allen's words, "mystical, cabalistic pricing." For the publishers, the advantages of dealing with consortia include greater and faster market penetration, wider exposure for their authors' works, and a single price and invoice for the whole group.

Consortia also have drawbacks. Consortial pricing may not provide any advantage for a multi-campus university or for a library with multiple branches, because some publishers treat these entities as a consortium. A large institution may be able to negotiate a better financial arrangement with a publisher separately, but may be required to participate in the consortium for political reasons. A consortium is only as fast as its slowest member. The members give up their ability to customize the packages and to influence platform and delivery issues. There is the possible loss of clout for the library director, since the provost or other administrator may want a decision-making role in the consortium. It may be more difficult to negotiate license agreements. Finally, participation in a consortium may be disruptive to the relationship between the vendors and publishers of the electronic resources versus the serials, acquisitions, and collection development staff in the libraries.

Allen pointed out that there is no perfect model yet. Libraries are becoming more market-savvy, and licensing agents may play a role in future development. Librarians are talking on campus about shaping the future of how library services are offered, with faculty and librarians working together to determine the mix of electronic versus print resources. A dose of common sense is called for. If users do not need the item, pricing will not make or break the decision; content is much more important. Libraries need to act rationally and invest wisely, while publishers are responsible for setting and meeting revenue targets.

DISCUSSION

Librarians' thoughts. The librarians in the audience were asked to consider a variation on the print pricing models of the past. Beginning with the idea of a multiple copy print subscription model, and assuming that electronic resources provide improved access for a more disparate user base, is it valid to calculate the price based on the potential user population? In the print world, higher demand for a particular title has historically been addressed by purchasing more than one subscription to the journal. However, this model does not seem to be valid in arguing for higher prices for online access. Access cost based on the size of the campus community is not fair because most institutions have a known number of users in a specialized field and it is that user base which should be considered in setting the cost of the electronic product.

The discussion shifted to a consideration of the value of the journals in a package, whether electronic or print. A price quotation for a package can be expressed in terms of the total FTE, or the same cost can be restated in terms of the number of probable users of the product. Few libraries are prepared to say what their actual prices (interpreted in terms of use) have been over the past several years, so it is difficult to say if the electronic packages are a good value in comparison to the print version. With the electronic products it is possible to measure actual usage, either on a per-article basis or on the basis of which titles in a package are receiving the most use.

Publishers' thoughts. Next, Inger asked some questions of the publishers in the audience. On the subject of the cost of dealing with a consortium versus dealing with the individual libraries, it was felt that it is cheaper to deal with a tight, well-organized consortium that supports centralized billing. Some questions on sales and marketing elicited the response that there is potential to increase market size and profitability for the social sciences and humanities publishers, with somewhat less potential for the STM (science/technology/medicine) publishers since this area has been explored more thoroughly already. Small publishers do not have a large enough sales force to take advantage of some of the new opportunities. Pricing electronic resources based on the cost of their print counterparts is a model that cannot be sustained indefinitely; there needs to be a transition from this model to use-based pricing. The publishers felt that the price should be based on actual use. It was also felt that the aggregator model has potential, and it was noted that subscription agents are involved in working on such arrangements.

A unique feature of the workshop was the use of colored tags to identify categories of audience members, so the presenters could determine the sources of the various points of view. Assigning the tags to the audience members was challenging because some people felt that the designated groups did not fit their particular situations. Participants were asked to select the tag which best approximated their actual function. It was also interesting to see that there were almost no audience members from public or community college libraries, but quite a few from universities of various sizes. There also seemed to be many publishers and subscription agents in the audiences at both sessions. This mix made the discussions quite animated.

EDITOR'S NOTE

Power Point slides of each of the three presenter's presentations are available at: http://www.catchword.com/simon.htm

Managing Multiple Media and Extraordinary Expectations

Carolyn L. Helmetsie
Randall M. Hopkins

Workshop Leaders

Kay G. Johnson

Recorder

SUMMARY. In this workshop, the challenges and strategies associated with providing both print and electronic resources for users are discussed. The case study of the NASA Langley Research Center was used to discuss the unique challenges faced by special federal libraries in providing multiple media and managing user and administrator expectations. *[Article copies available for a fee from The Haworth Document Delivery Service: 1-800-342-9678. E-mail address: getinfo@haworthpressinc.com <Website: http://www.haworthpressinc.com>]*

NASA LANGLEY RESEARCH CENTER

Carolyn Helmetsie began by giving an overview of the NASA Langley Research Center and its Technical Library in Hampton, Vir-

---

Carolyn L. Helmetsie is Librarian, NASA Langley Research Center.
Randall M. Hopkins is Account Services Manager, EBSCO Information Services.
Kay G. Johnson is Assistant Professor, Original Cataloger, University of Tennessee, Knoxville

[Haworth co-indexing entry note]: "Managing Multiple Media and Extraordinary Expectations." Johnson, Kay G. Co-published simultaneously in *The Serials Librarian* (The Haworth Press, Inc.) Vol. 38, No. 3/4, 2000, pp. 225-231; and: *From Carnegie to Internet2: Forging the Serials Future* (ed: P. Michelle Fiander, Joseph C. Harmon, and Jonathan David Makepeace) The Haworth Press, Inc., 2000, pp. 225-231. Single or multiple copies of this article are available for a fee from The Haworth Document Delivery Service [1-800-342-9678, 9:00 a.m. - 5:00 p.m. (EST). E-mail address: getinfo@haworthpressinc.com].

ginia. In March 1915, Congress established the National Advisory Committee for Aeronautics (NACA). Its purpose was to "supervise and direct scientific study of the problems with flight with a view to their practical solution." The Langley Research Center was established in 1917, and was named after Samuel P. Langley, the distinguished scientist of flight. Langley remained the only NACA research center until 1941, when the Lewis Research Center (later renamed for John Glenn) was established in Cleveland, Ohio. The formation of eleven other centers followed the creation of the National Aeronautics and Space Administration (NASA) in 1958.

Collections. The Langley Technical Library has the largest collection of aerospace research materials within NASA, and its over 2 million documents include the most complete collection of NACA documents in existence. Langley has approximately 70,000 book titles, 800 current journal subscriptions, and access to over 300 full-text electronic journals. The library's collection is especially strong in the areas of aeronautics, space engineering technology, engineering, structural mechanics and materials, physics and chemistry, electronics and control, atmospheric science, computer science, and management.

Staff. The current library staff consists of twelve civil service employees, who are responsible for overall policy and management of documents, reference, serials, interlibrary loan, document delivery and oversight of a classified section. The support service contract staff of twelve employees are responsible for acquisitions, cataloging, circulation, and journal and bindery support.

Multimedia collections. The library's multimedia collections include a card file containing information on the earliest writings on aeronautical activities. This manual collection is not indexed anywhere else in the world and is accessible only at the library. Print and microfilm remain important collections, with some microfilm dating back to the 1800s. Many of these early collections remain relevant today.

Online catalog. In the early 1980s, NOTIS software was purchased to provide a shared catalog for the NASA libraries' consortium. Despite great expectations and the libraries' best efforts, only the basic online public catalog became available. In 1989, Langley independently purchased a SIRSI STILAS system.

Langley was named the lead center for the Scientific and Technical Information (STI) Program in 1995. The STI Program requested that

Langley implement STILAS for the consortium in 1996, and the system was renamed NASA GALAXIE. The fifteen NASA libraries now have a true shared online catalog, with such benefits as desktop access and links to scanned images from Langley's photo archives.

DigiDoc. In 1991, the Langley Technical Library implemented DIGital DOCuments, or, DigiDoc. DigiDoc is a document storage and retrieval system, developed in-house, which works in conjunction with NASA GALAXIE to deliver the electronic full-text of approximately 9000 NACA and NASA technical reports. NASA GALAXIE provides the search engine and metadata for each full-text report. Each record is linked to the PDF-file DigiDoc display and uses the Adobe Acrobat Reader plug-in.

Changes at the library. Many factors in the 1990s forced significant changes in the library's operations. A reorganization of the Langley Research Center resulted in the loss of Branch status and re-assignment under the Chief Information Office. Budget cuts forced the library to drastically cut serials subscriptions and rely more on document delivery and interlibrary loan. Because of severe space shortages, the library purchased moveable shelving and sent most of their printed serial volumes to surplus. In short the library has fewer staff and less space, money, and resources–the library does more with less.

Acquisitions process. The complexity of the federal government's procurement system creates many purchasing challenges. When Helmetsie first came to Langley, only foreign subscriptions were purchased through a vendor. Domestic subscriptions were purchased directly from over 300 publishers. Because the government will pay only in advance with an invoice, it was difficult receiving publications from publishers requiring a check instead of a government purchase order. In an effort to improve this situation, Helmetsie obtained a contracting officer certificate. Since 1988, Langley has purchased most books and serials through the Federal Library and Information Program (FEDLINK), a consortium of federal agency libraries.

Electronic journals. Langley has multiple strategies for the purchase of electronic journals. A purchase can be negotiated directly with the publisher or purchased through a vendor. Dollar amounts have to be considered, because different rules apply to different dollar amounts. The library also has to consider whether the publisher or vendor has a Government Service Administration (GSA) account.

Consortia are Langley's best option for purchasing electronic journal subscriptions. In 1994, NASA aeronautical libraries, consisting of Ames, Dyrden, Glenn and Langley, formed the UniLibrary under Project Reliance. The purpose of UniLibrary is to maximize services by the institutions, preserve critical capabilities, and improve customer satisfaction. Langley is also working with the Library Services Alliance of New Mexico, of which Los Alamos is a member. The UniLibrary is planning to test access to over 1,100 Elsevier journals through Los Alamos this summer.

Electronic journal access strategies differ from purchase strategies. Helmetsie outlined several journal access strategies. Electronic journals can be accessed from the publisher, but the library is dependent on the publisher for archiving. Electronic journals can be loaded onto a library's server with the publisher's permission; however, this is costly, and requires system expertise. Access via a consortium provides potential cost savings, because libraries share data loaded onto a server. Each library pays an access fee, but does not need to maintain the data locally.

Each library must determine the best options for its local needs, perhaps utilizing a combination of purchase and access strategies. For example, core titles that are used heavily may be best loaded directly onto the library's server. High cost, low use titles may be best purchased directly from the publisher or accessed through consortia. Meanwhile, users have their own expectations for electronic journals. They expect full-text delivery, free of charge from a single interface.

Concluding remarks. In conclusion, Helmetsie recommended the following collection development strategies for managing multiple media. First, every library needs to leverage its collection with other libraries. Second, it is important to educate users about print and electronic issues, including licensing agreements and the costs of Internet resources. Third, management must also understand collection development costs. Fourth, a library's collection must transcend institutional changes. Finally, the library needs to develop strong advocacy, so it can remain active and strong by capitalizing on its strengths.

ELECTRONIC SERIALS IN FEDERAL LIBRARIES

Statistics. Randall Hopkins works with about 200 federal government libraries and has observed them grappling with coexisting print and electronic resources. He compiled statistics on the state of electronic serial availability in select federal libraries. For the collections studied, 24.9% of the libraries' current serials are available online from the publisher. An additional 2.0% is available from the publisher in CD-ROM, for a combined figure of 26.9%. The purchase of full-text databases such as those offered by EBSCO and other companies can add another 8.7% to the electronic percentage of the overall collection. In total, these federal library collections could have as much as 35.6% of their target collection in electronic format. This means that 64.4% of their active subscriptions are available only in print.

Print v. electronic titles. Research materials from 1978-1981 are generally available only in print. It is unlikely that federal libraries will pay again for electronic access to older volumes they already own in printed format. Overall, currently published materials are also largely available only in print. EBSCO has added 2600 online journals to their title database in the last 12 months–an astounding number; certainly, electronic publishing is taking off exponentially. However, in the same period 8100 print titles were added. Publishers continue to generate significant material in print format, and EBSCO continues to add print titles faster than electronic at a ratio of three to one. There are tens of thousands of publishers, and it is unlikely they will migrate to one electronic solution.

Print continues to be a big part of library collections, and it is a challenge to handle print simultaneously with electronic publications. It is a particularly big challenge in the federal government, where the user community is divided between those who are very interested in desktop access and those who prefer print or simply prefer escaping to the library. On the flip side of the user community are the library managers. Management expects libraries to provide free information online and assumes that authentication is done by some third party. Unfortunately, these expectations are not based in reality.

The challenge for libraries is to mediate the gap between electronic and print, mediate a divided user community, and mediate the gap between reality and expectation. The promises of electronic information are very real. Processing time, search ability, and ubiquity of information are all huge advantages to researchers. On the other hand, we have the realities and difficulties of setting up and administering online material. Meanwhile, staff numbers and budget totals are being cut, and users are frustrated when the Web goes down or is not as robust or as fast as they would like.

User education. Hopkins observes that libraries that have successfully handled these challenges seem to have reverted to remembering that libraries are, firstly, service organizations. Libraries that do this recognize the importance of educating the users about the economic and technological realities of information access. It is critical for the users to recognize that the popular conceptions of the Web are not accurate. The importance of staying in touch with the user community cannot be underestimated. Those who prefer the print may be the ones who hold the purse strings. The library, therefore, needs to avoid alienating the users who pay for the services.

Managing user expectations. Steps are being taken by federal government libraries in terms of strategically positioning themselves between management, user expectations, and the reality of multiple media. The first is to survey the users to determine what they want and need. Surveys allow the library to determine how to help users, and also tell the users that the library is interested in their needs. The second strategy is to integrate online and traditional materials in an OPAC. The Web-based OPACs can link to full-text, and may ultimately provide a single search interface. A single search interface eases the user's frustrations of having to search several sources to find Internet resources. Third, some libraries are scanning local documents and providing them online. This is much easier to do if the organization owns the copyright or the information is in the public domain. It is particularly valuable to scan documents that are used heavily or routinely.

Partnerships and managing multiple media. Finally, partnerships are key to managing multiple media. Partnerships between libraries, publishers, and vendors can help management understand the complexities of multiple formats. Reports from vendors, for example, can show how much information is electronic. Vendors can offer services and provide information about what can be done and what cannot be done. Society publishers are often willing to form alliances with libraries specializing in similar subject disciplines.

Concluding remarks. Hopkins concluded by asking the workshop participants how they manage the expectations of their patrons, as well as the expectations of management, in terms of dealing with multiple media. A lively discussion followed the well-received presentations.

The audience discussed the challenges of user education. Many felt that management tends to be the least sophisticated users of electronic resources. Many users do not understand that Internet information can be unreliable. There are also challenges to providing materials, when user interests conflict with the mission of the institution. Libraries are coming up with their own creative solutions to supplying multiple media and mediating user and management expectations.

Push Technology: Applications for Scholarly Communications and Information Management

Amira Aaron
David R. Fritsch
Workshop Leaders

Paula Sullenger
Recorder

SUMMARY. This paper discusses the history of push technology, its current state, the technology required for success, and its future potential. Portals and Intelligent Software Agents, current methods of developing push technology, are described. *[Article copies available for a fee from The Haworth Document Delivery Service: 1-800-342-9678. E-mail address: getinfo@haworthpressinc.com <Website: http://www.haworthpressinc.com>]*

Amira Aaron began her presentation by saying: push is not dead. Although recent proprietary applications of push have failed, push is alive and has potential. Librarians and publishers need to take advantage of this potential and develop it. The alternative is to leave push in

---

Amira Aaron is Director of Academic Services, The Faxon Company.
David R. Fritsch is Director of Business Development, The Faxon Company.
Paula Sullenger is Serials Acquisitions Librarian, Auburn. University.

[Haworth co-indexing entry note]: "Push Technology: Applications for Scholarly Communications and Information Management." Sullenger, Paula. Co-published simultaneously in *The Serials Librarian* (The Haworth Press, Inc.) Vol. 38, No. 3/4, 2000, pp. 233-236; and: *From Carnegie to Internet2: Forging the Serials Future* (ed: P. Michelle Fiander, Joseph C. Harmon, and Jonathan David Makepeace) The Haworth Press, Inc., 2000, pp. 233-236. Single or multiple copies of this article are available for a fee from The Haworth Document Delivery Service [1-800-342-9678, 9:00 a.m. - 5:00 p.m. (EST). E-mail address: getinfo@haworthpressinc.com].

the hands of technologists and business people who have driven its development so far.

Aaron defined push technology as a process by which content providers send information to the computer desktop in a format immediately accessible to the user. Users can customize or personalize a selection of information to be "pushed" to them at set intervals without having to repeatedly make requests or perform searches. Current push technologies include e-mail alerting services, Web channels, and proprietary applications such as PointCast, an Internet news service [1]. So far these applications have been largely commercial: PointCast is supported by advertising; various businesses use e-mail and Web channels to learn about or retain customers, or provide them with information; and there are many entertainment Web channels.

Applications valuable to libraries have been limited to e-mail table-of-contents (TOC) alerts, virtual updates to software, serial publication updates, and customer service applications. But if libraries are not fully exploiting push, it's not because they are unfamiliar with it. Aaron notes that push strategies are familiar to the library community, and that librarians have always pushed information using available technology such as telephones and fax machines. What is unfamiliar to the library community today is the new push technology, which goes beyond phones and faxes and is only a few years old. These new push technologies include Portals and Intelligent Software Agents (ISAs).

PORTALS

Portals are gateways that pass the user on to other destinations. Yahoo! and Netscape are well-known general portals. General portals allow users to set up a home base, which can be personalized to individual needs. Portal providers try to attract and retain a specific audience. Portals often use push channels to deliver information to their users, and may provide access to search engines, utilities, news and advertising.

Another type of portal is the vertical, or niche, portal, which is focused on a particular topic or user community. Niche portals allow for more targeted advertising. Portals, general or niche, have three main functions: research, transactions, and communications. While transactions and communication are well served by portals, research is not. Research is the weakest functional area of most portals, although Aaron thinks that non-commercial scholarly societies are in a good position to develop vertical information portals. Aaron feels that librarians should also be designing portals and helping to select and evaluate push applications for their clients.

INTELLIGENT SOFTWARE AGENTS

David Fritsch spoke about Intelligent Software Agents (ISAs) and their role in developing push technology. Like Aaron, he acknowledges that push has not yet lived up to its expectations. For example, PointCast did very well at first, but then almost went out of business [1]; and OCLC discontinued its Alerts Service. Examples of ISAs include NetMind, which notifies users of changes in competitors' Websites; and MicroSoft's "smirking paper clip" which offers advice and guidance when using MicroSoft's products. Despite limited current applications, Fritsch feels the future is promising.

Fritsch blames the limitations of current ISA applications on a lack of bandwidth, and software that is "too dumb" to handle user terminology. By "dumb software" Fritsch means software which cannot distinguish between meanings of words or which cannot automatically search synonyms. For example, an Internet search on "cars," using any one of a number of available search engines, would not necessarily find relevant information that is cross-listed under "automobiles"; and a search on "jaguar" would retrieve information on the car and the animal. Intelligent Software Agents, which Fritsch defines as push technology plus intelligence, might be the solution to these problems.

According to Fritsch, successful ISAs should be: reactive/proactive and autonomous/adaptable at the same time; capable of inference or induction; mobile–able to jump from network to network; and able to communicate and collaborate with other agents. Additional requirements for developing real ISAs are: agent name servers to map machine names to locations; and a common communication language to express the structure and content of messages which include more than just text. There have been attempts at a common language, such as Knowledge Query and Manipulation Language (KQML) and the FIPA Agent Communication Language, but there is no standard at the level Fritsch believes is necessary. Although ISAs are not at the stage where they can meet the above requirements, research continues. If ISAs fulfill their promise the economic implications will be significant.

CONCLUSION

There are existing and potential benefits of properly developed push technology. Presently, it overcomes information overload; releases users from the need to check for updates; aggregates content on the desktop; and allows content providers usable feedback on user behavior. Potentially, it will enable content providers to reach specific targets, and lead to customized information delivered in a real-time environment.

There are also many concerns about push. Who selects the content and what are their qualifications? What is the quality of that content? Librarians are concerned with users' tendency to accept what is given to them with little evaluation. Many users see the abundance of advertising as a major drawback. Privacy is also a big issue. The development of portals and ISAs may improve push technology, but only time will tell.

NOTES

1. Editor's note: For a history of PointCast see: Linda Himelstein and Richard Siklos, April 26, 1999 "The Rise and Fall of an Internet Star," *Business Week*, Issue 3626, p88, 4p. Available: Business Source Elite from EbscoHOST; ADDRESS: http://www.epnet.com/ "In 1996, before Yahoo!, Excite Inc., and others, PointCast recognized the power of delivering personalized information over the Net. Its software allowed consumers to customize news automatically through the push technology. Selected content would be culled from the Web and delivered to an individual's computer screen–all for free. PointCast made its money from advertisers. [But] problems began to arise with PointCast's technology. Customers had begun to complain that the service was slow. It also was causing traffic jams on corporate networks because bandwidth was not big enough to carry all the information that users wanted. Customers began to abandon the service in favor of new offerings from the likes of Yahoo! and Excite."

Printed Back Volumes and Issues: A Thing of the Past?

Glenn Jaeger
Tracey Clarke
Carol MacAdam
Janet Fisher
John Fobert

Workshop Leaders

Naomi Kietzke Young

Recorder

SUMMARY. With all the recent interest and discussion regarding electronic journals, it would be easy to get the impression that printed volumes are becoming obsolete. Five representatives from various aspects of the serials information chain (back issue vendor, archivist of electronic journals, journal publisher, and librarian) explore the continuing importance of the printed archive, and describe their vision of the future coexistence of electronic and

---

Glenn Jaeger is President and Co-Founder, Absolute Backorder Service.
Tracey Clarke is Vice-President and Co-Founder, Absolute Backorder Service.
Carol MacAdam is Associate Director of Library Relations, JSTOR.
Janet Fisher is Associate Director, Journals Publishing, MIT Press.
John Fobert is Serials/Document Delivery Librarian, Roger Williams University.
Naomi Kietzke Young is Periodicals/Microforms Librarian, Southern Methodist University, Dallas, Texas.

[Haworth co-indexing entry note]: "Printed Back Volumes and Issues: A Thing of the Past?" Young, Naomi Kietzke. Co-published simultaneously in *The Serials Librarian* (The Haworth Press, Inc.) Vol. 38, No. 3/4, 2000, pp. 237-241; and: *From Carnegie to Internet2: Forging the Serials Future* (ed: P. Michelle Fiander, Joseph C. Harmon, and Jonathan David Makepeace) The Haworth Press, Inc., 2000, pp. 237-241. Single or multiple copies of this article are available for a fee from The Haworth Document Delivery Service [1-800-342-9678, 9:00 a.m. - 5:00 p.m. (EST). E-mail address: getinfo@haworthpressinc.com].

paper formats. *[Article copies available for a fee from The Haworth Document Delivery Service: 1-800-342-9678. E-mail address: getinfo@haworthpressinc.com <Website: http://www.haworthpressinc.com>]*

The workshop opened with Glenn Jaeger and Tracey Clarke explaining why and how a back-issue vendor can still be useful to libraries. Jaeger said that, among currently published journals, approximately 150,000 are available exclusively in print, compared to only 4,000 exclusively electronic journals. Based on these numbers, we can assume that the print journal will not be disappearing from libraries soon. Experience shows that coexistence is the most likely outcome; electronic journals may turn out to be much like microforms, supplementing print collections rather than replacing them.

Using their own business, Absolute Backorder Service, as an example, Jaeger and Clarke outlined the current state of the back-issue industry. Sales of single-issues and of recent-backfiles have risen sharply in the last 2-3 years. Back volumes, especially those published within the past 3-5 years, are still important. Operating as friendly competitors, vendors often operate like a "junkyard for journals." Like junkyard managers, vendors keep an eye on each other's wares and may be able to deal amongst themselves or refer customers to a competitor when they cannot fill a request. By incorporating electronic technology such as Web pages of specific inventory lists, vendors are able to fill orders more efficiently. Jaeger also described other available vendor services, such as appraising the value of collections for insurance purposes, or appraisal of library gifts.

Carol MacAdam began her presentation by reviewing the history of the JSTOR program. Originally begun with a grant from the Mellon Foundation, JSTOR was seen as a partial solution to the problems of diminishing library stack space for bound volumes, the increasing fragility of older volumes, and the difficulties for publishers inherent in maintaining a printed archive. Unlike some other full-text archives, JSTOR uses imaging to reproduce the original journal, cover to cover and page by page, insuring access to editorial notes, letters to the editor, and even advertisements, which can be very important to historical research.

JSTOR is an archive of the complete back runs of journals, and participation in JSTOR is not contingent upon a library's maintaining subscriptions to the current issues. JSTOR is priced on a sliding scale;

libraries pay for the service according to their college's or university's Carnegie class, so that small academic libraries pay less than large research institutions. JSTOR estimates that it would cost libraries approximately $450,000 to replicate their archive in microform.

While JSTOR is well regarded in the serials world, and has been held up as a model for the future by many, it cannot continue to be the only such project. MacAdam pointed out that in 3 years, the project has only been able to reproduce 100 journals completely. This is partially because of the nature of serials; project organizers had to deal with missing and damaged issues and volumes, as well as title changes, splits and mergers that changed the size and scope of the project. MacAdam announced that the project would continue to expand, incorporating more scientific and medical content.

Looking to the future of paper and electronic archives, she used the analogy of TV and radio, where the dominance of one form over the other may change, but both remain important. An electronic archive does not–and perhaps should not–preclude a paper archive. Who will be the providers of future electronic archives? While there are many new archives being mounted by journal publishers for their own recent back issues, proprietary software and search engines may hinder access for end users. JSTOR strives to be a cooperative project with librarians, scholars, and publishers. To avoid jeopardizing publishers' revenue streams from current subscriptions, JSTOR has negotiated a "moving wall" of 3-7 years with each publisher before electronic archiving takes place. Journal issues are made available in JSTOR only behind the moving wall.

Janet Fisher of MIT Press agreed that many editors are enthusiastic about JSTOR and similar efforts. She described the many problems editors face in providing a stable print archive. The contracts publishers sign with printers allow for "long or short runs" and more or fewer copies of a journal than the exact number contracted. Because of this, journal issue supplies may be exhausted shortly after publication, or excess issues may linger in warehouses for years. Even if there is heavy demand for a sold-out issue, reprint runs frequently cost more than the original. There is little advantage for the publisher in maintaining a large inventory of journal back files. Journal runs are priced at the time of publication; therefore, the journal inventory is less valuable than a similar inventory of books. Warehouse staff dislike inventories of loose journal issues because they are more difficult to store and to access than bound monographs.

Fisher said that publishers, and especially university press publishers, are in an increasingly vulnerable financial position. Publishers already maintain electronic files in a variety of formats, including the author's source file, files with editing codes, and the files used by the typesetters; all these must be retained, along with their supporting software. Changing institutional priorities or financial pressures could cause publishers to jettison large archives. The best solution may be a combination of the aggregator-driven and the publisher's archive.

Agreeing with the previous speakers, Fisher said that print still has a long future in the research community. She cited an internal study of the Massachusetts Institute of Technology's computer science faculty, two-thirds of whom agreed they would gladly publish in an electronic journal–*if* that journal were also available in paper.

John Fobert concluded the workshop by sharing the perspective of a serials librarian in an academic library. He, too, asserted that print and electronic serials are complementary forms, serving different needs. Libraries are in some cases reinstating print runs previously canceled in the initial enthusiasm for full-text services. He gave several reasons for this.

Database vendors or publishers may remove titles from electronic collections, or change the depth of indexing for a title. When such databases form an increasing part of a library's collection, the librarians lose control over selection and retention of specific journals. This changing coverage in full-text sources makes it difficult to predict what print archives will be needed. Furthermore, access to an electronic archive is uncertain if the subscription is canceled. While an alternate source for the journal may be found, the extent of coverage may differ in electronic products. When the loss is realized, alternate back files, whether in print or microform, may be prohibitively expensive, or simply unavailable.

Fobert reminded us that print and digital formats are not the only two options for journal back files. While not a favorite with library patrons, microforms are still an enduring preservation format. And because most patrons do not have their own microform reading equipment, there is a lower theft and mutilation rate than for print.

Electronic formats are subject to change, and the life span of electronic products is not yet known; many older electronic formats are no longer readable with current technologies. We do not know how long current formats will be supportable, or what kinds of hardware and software upgrades will be necessary to access the digital archives of tomorrow.

Early proponents of electronic journals spoke of "the paperless library," but reality shows that full-text journal collections require a substantial investment in printers and paper. He also argued that printed volumes and photocopiers require less instruction to use than electronic journals, and that bound volumes promote more browsing (and more serendipity) than do search engines. However, once library patrons have begun using electronic archives, they may be unwilling to use other types of resources. Fobert believes that students who are searching an online source may ignore any citations that do not come with associated full text.

This session was enjoyable and energetic. All presenters agreed on the continuing importance of printed serials, and of the necessity for cooperative action between libraries, scholars, publishers, aggregators, and vendors to find the best balance of solutions for the future. The comparison of the integration of electronic formats into journal collections with the integration of microforms is an interesting one. It leaves open the question of whether electronic formats or print format will become the "new microform"–in other words, the format most patrons would rather avoid.

This workshop also raised several other questions. Do library users pass over valuable materials if their retrieval is more difficult? Are they willing to repeat the same search in a variety of proprietary publisher databases to make sure they have covered their topic thoroughly? How can the cost of creating and maintaining archives be shared within the research community? These areas deserve further exploration and study.

The Elsevier-WebLUIS Connection: A Florida Venture and Adventure

Michele Newberry
Elaine Henjum
Carol Drum

Workshop Leaders

Beth Guay

Recorder

SUMMARY. WebLUIS is a Web version of the NOTIS/LUIS software that the Florida Center for Library Automation (FCLA) began developing for the State University System (SUS) of Florida libraries in 1996 as a replacement for its traditional OPAC. WebLUIS was developed to allow direct linking from citation-to-full-text. In early 1997 several of the SUS libraries decided to license the full-image version of Elsevier science journals, to be stored and delivered over the Web by FCLA. The workshop was divided into three topics of discussion: consortial issues, technical realities, and Public Services experiences. *[Article copies available for a fee from The Haworth Document Delivery Service: 1-800-342-9678. E-mail address: getinfo@haworthpressinc.com <Website: http://www.haworthpressinc.com>]*

Michele Newberry is Assistant Director, FCLA.
Elaine Henjum is Database Coordinator, FCLA.
Carol Drum is Chair, University of Florida Marston Science Library.
Beth Guay is Serials Cataloger, University of Maryland, College Park.

[Haworth co-indexing entry note]: "The Elsevier-WebLUIS Connection: A Florida Venture and Adventure." Guay, Beth. Co-published simultaneously in *The Serials Librarian* (The Haworth Press, Inc.) Vol. 38, No. 3/4, 2000, pp. 243-248; and: *From Carnegie to Internet2: Forging the Serials Future* (ed: P. Michelle Fiander, Joseph C. Harmon, and Jonathan David Makepeace) The Haworth Press, Inc., 2000, pp. 243-248. Single or multiple copies of this article are available for a fee from The Haworth Document Delivery Service [1-800-342-9678, 9:00 a.m. - 5:00 p.m. (EST). E-mail address: getinfo@haworthpressinc.com].

FLORIDA CENTER FOR LIBRARY AUTOMATION

Michele began the discussion with a brief description of the services performed by the Florida Center for Library Automation (FCLA) to the State University System (SUS) of Florida libraries:

- Management of all ten library OPACs, with access to ten million bibliographic records.
- Acquisitions, catalog maintenance, authority control, circulation, and electronic course reserves services.
- Access management to a number of database services licensed from commercial vendors.
- Access management to 25 million locally stored bibliographic records for content of some abstracting and indexing (A & I) databases, including ERIC, MEDLINE, *Ulrich's*, and the Elsevier journals collection.

Michelle explained that FCLA maintained a single catalog with a set of redundant indexes for all ten SUS university libraries. She also noted FCLA's involvement in the publication of the electronic serial, *Florida Entomologist*. Issues are scanned, indexed, and enhanced with metadata by FCLA.

CONSORTIAL ISSUES

What issues faced this consortium in its effort to provide Web-based delivery of the full content of the Elsevier journals collection? First, should data be duplicated or shared? The rich history of collaboration, both SUS wide and SUS library wide, led to the decision to store a single copy of the data on one server. In theory, ownership of one copy of the data would require one license, one liaison with the publisher, and one "problem solving agent." It would enhance the potential for collaborative collection development.

How should licenses be set up? Rather than a single license, the ultimate arrangement was for six separate licenses, one per participating member, requiring six different services of the data content. The reality was that separate licenses were easier to negotiate *within* an institution. Further, who negotiates the license agreements among separately governed, yet jointly ruled (by the Board of Regents) institutions? Michele said that she found it hard to explain to vendors that the groups wanting the products were unable to commit the funds.

Other licensing issues? Provisions are needed for the case of consortium members dropping out. One provision that was made: all members have perpetual access to the data obtained throughout the period of the license agreement. However, Michele pointed out, in order to permit access to data by former consortium members, the system must be able to identify the data received during a given period. A system must be developed for this purpose.

The Florida Elsevier licenses allow:

- access to the electronic version of the print;
- authorized users to search, view, browse, print and download full-text;
- authorized users to access remotely via secure procedures;
- onsite walk-ins to qualify as authorized users;
- articles to be distributed in course-packs and in online course reserves;
- no inter-library loan (ILL) or other systematic distribution.

Elsevier is now willing to allow ILL, on the condition that the lending library keeps and supplies ILL statistics.

The Florida license fees include the base print costs; and a 9.5% cap on annual increases is guaranteed. The fees for electronic access amount to 7.35% of the print costs. Incremental access fees for titles not held in print (e.g., one consortium member accesses electronic titles held in print by another consortium member) amount to $9,500 for the first 500 articles, plus a per article charge beyond 500. For print journals that migrate to electronic format only, the provision allows a charge of 90% of the print price.

Michele concluded the section on consortial issues with discussion of the rationale for local content development. She explained that SUS of Florida operated under a 1992 five-year-plan mandate to deliver full-text electronically. Next, the prohibitive cost of utilizing commercial servers led to taking advantage of the infrastructure already in place: the search engine/user interface, and digital library collaboration with IBM (use of IBM digital imaging software to support a digital library). Finally, the SUS libraries were committed to "some semblance of ownership as opposed to renting content."

TECHNICAL REALITIES

Elaine led the next workshop section on technical realities. She introduced challenges facing the consortium, such as: providing access and security; devising search and retrieval mechanisms; creating a citation database with links to full-text; developing full-text technical detail; and managing data.

Access, she explained, is provided via the WebLUIS homepage, the homepage of the participating member's library, and the URL link from the OPAC record for the journal. Security is provided via validation of IP address or library patron IDs. Search and retrieval capability are supported via an A to Z journal titles list, a subject categories Webpage (based on content from the vendor), an author/title/subject/keyword search page, tables of contents pages, and an advanced search page (ISSN, CODEN, system load date, etc.).

Next, Elaine explained that the WebLUIS Elsevier journals database is a citation database laid over the journal content. Descriptive and structural metadata arrives with the full-text of the article (in PDF). The metadata is then mapped to a MARC record, which provides hierarchically ordered links in the following order: full-text of the article; its table of contents; all other issues of a particular title; and all journals in the collection. Elaine guided the audience through the process with a citation to an article in the *Archives of Oral Biology.*

Discussion of the full-text technical details ensued. Early versions were produced from the scanned page image, stored in TIFF format. Later, TIFFs were wrapped into PDF, then into distilled PDF which provided better image quality, and allowed the Acrobat search functionality within the documents. A thumbnail accompanies every page; if not supplied by Elsevier, the loader software creates one.

Elaine concluded her discussion by noting the data management issues. There were the claiming issues–some discs received (the content from Elsevier sent on CD-ROM) were missing titles; some lacked individual issues. There were the cataloging issues–the example given was of a title changing while the accompanying metadata did not. There were the technical issues–PDFs that don't open, PDFs that are blank, PDFs with incorrect character sets. There were issues from a mixed bag–the metadata lacking the article analytics, i.e., there was no link from the article to its parent journal.

PUBLIC SERVICES' PERSPECTIVE

Carol led the final section of the workshop. She began with a note of appreciation to her colleague, Rich Bennet, Electronic Access Services Coordinator at the University of Florida, for his assistance in putting the presentation together. She then began discussion of the Elsevier-WebLUIS connection from the Public Services point of view. She explained that users, familiar with its format, don't yet see it as an index, but as a way to search for articles in specific journals. Training, and a good deal of it, has succeeded in educating users as to the nature of the database.

A user survey was designed and executed to discover user satisfaction and problems using the database. One hundred twenty responses (from a non-scientific sample) were received. Of those, in reference to overall satisfaction, 17% of respondents were "thrilled," 36% were "very pleased," 26% were "satisfied," and 21% were "dissatisfied." Of the respondents included in the satisfied patron category, 17% were undergraduates, 46% were graduate students, 25% were faculty, and 12% were staff. Of dissatisfied users, 28% were undergraduates, 36% were graduate students, and 36% were faculty.

Carol noted that the comments among satisfied and dissatisfied users were the same. In fact, both groups identified the time lag from print publication to electronic availability as being a problem–the biggest problem. Other user problems with the database included problems with the software (the interface; loading Acrobat), and with the Web browser (inability to use Internet Explorer; using the browser "Back" button as opposed to the system navigation keys).

Next Carol provided use statistics showing that the database received 436 hits through its initial year (1997), 45,359 hits in 1998, and through March 1999, 33,522 hits. Additionally, she touched upon the variety of management reports that can be generated by the system: number of articles viewed by year, number by year and month, number by institution, number by journal title, year and month, etc. She noted the potential of these reports for use in collection development.

Finally, Carol discussed the next steps in the Elsevier-WebLUIS connection. License renewals come due in January 2000. Enhancements desired are links from other A & I databases, from Engineering Index, for example, to the Elsevier database. Progress is desired in using the management data in collection development, in more timely delivery of content, and in expanding the venture to other publishers' full-text.

DISCUSSION

The presentation induced a wave of questions from the audience. First, how was the service marketed or introduced to users? Carol answered that a "What's new?" feature on the UF home page, bibliographic instruction, and the reference desk were the introductory avenues. Next came a more philosophical question–what were the implications of locally mounting and managing such a big, ever-expanding database? Carol answered that the way technology changes will affect the future of the data. Michele, in turn, stated that massive data storage is quite different from storage on a floppy disc. She said: "We've moved data on a continuous basis since we started." She then added that PDF is good for providing an "authentic" version of the journal content.

Next question: how well did the metadata map to MARC? Elaine answered that MARC records don't conform to the national standard. Other questions drew these responses: Elsevier doesn't supply the metadata for newsletters, thus no access. In the case of three book reviews to a page, for example, perhaps only the first and the last reviews might be indexed. In reference to the time lag problem, some of the titles were expected to migrate to electronic version preceding print.

The questions and answers moved to discussion of access fees and negotiation among the consortium members. The four institutions of SUS of Florida that don't need the resource don't want to share in the cost. Carol summed up by acknowledging the timeworn dilemma–publishers are interested in increasing revenue, while libraries have budgets that do not increase in proportion to the increase in journal prices.

AACR2 and You: Revising AACR2 to Accommodate Seriality

Jean Hirons
Les Hawkins

Workshop Leaders

Pat French

Recorder

SUMMARY. Jean Hirons and Les Hawkins presented an overview of the proposals contained in *Revising AACR2 to Accommodate Seriality: Report to the Joint Steering Committee for Revision of AACR2*, submitted in April 1999. The proposals address change and additions to the cataloging rules which govern the creation of bibliographic descriptions for serials and other continuing publications, as well as general revisions to the code. *[Article copies available for a fee from The Haworth Document Delivery Service: 1-800-342-9678. E-mail address: getinfo@haworthpressinc.com <Website: http://www.haworthpressinc.com>]*

BACKGROUND

The initiative to revise the serials rules grew out of recommendations adopted at the 1997 International Conference on the Principles

Jean Hirons is CONSER Coordinator, Library of Congress.
Les Hawkins is Senior ISDS Cataloger, National Serials Data.
Pat French is Serials Cataloger, University of California, Davis.

[Haworth co-indexing entry note]: "AACR2 and You: Revising AACR2 to Accommodate Seriality." French, Pat. Co-published simultaneously in *The Serials Librarian* (The Haworth Press, Inc.) Vol. 38, No. 3/4, 2000, pp. 249-256; and: *From Carnegie to Internet2: Forging the Serials Future* (ed: P. Michelle Fiander, Joseph C. Harmon, and Jonathan David Makepeace) The Haworth Press, Inc., 2000, pp. 249-256. Single or multiple copies of this article are available for a fee from The Haworth Document Delivery Service [1-800-342-9678, 9:00 a.m. - 5:00 p.m. (EST). E-mail address: getinfo@haworthpressinc.com].

and Future Development of AACR held in Toronto. Following the conference, the Joint Steering Committee (JSC) asked Jean Hirons to develop rule revision proposals. She set up four task groups to work on various issues in order to develop specific proposals for changes to the code. The report to the JSC grew out of the work of these groups and was scheduled for discussion at the 1999 American Library Association (ALA) and International Federation of Library Associations (IFLA) annual conferences. A Machine-Readable Bibliographic Information (MARBI) discussion paper was also prepared for consideration at the 1999 ALA conference. The proposals were to receive the widest possible distribution and discussion prior to the JSC's fall 1999 meeting. The presentation at NASIG was part of this plan.

The goals of the proposed revision are sevenfold: (1) include new rules for integrating resources; (2) accommodate seriality throughout the code; (3) harmonize AACR2 with ISBD(S) and ISSN; (4) take a more holistic approach to the cataloging of continuing resources; (5) focus on identification rather than transcription; (6) focus on constants rather than variables; and (7) provide rules that take advantage of and acknowledge the current environment of online catalogs and cooperative cataloging.

Four major areas of change were identified to accomplish these goals: (1) type of publication (defining continuing resources) and defining new rules for new types of resources; (2) the concept of major and minor changes in relation to the need to create a new catalog record; (3) description (chief source and prescribed sources, titles, publishing statement, item described); and (4) organization of the code.

TYPE OF PUBLICATION

A central idea underlying all the proposed changes is the limitation imposed by AACR2 in its division of all publications into just two categories: monograph or serial. This division has never accommodated loose-leaf publications well. But the real impetus for change is the fact that electronic publishers are now creating resources, which cannot be described or managed within these strictures. Databases and Websites in particular do not fit into the current AACR2 definitions for monographs and serials. Here a monograph is described as a publication in any medium that is complete or intended to be complete in a finite number of parts. A serial is defined as a publication in any medium issued in successive parts bearing numeric and/or chronological designations and intended to continue indefinitely. One of the most characteristic aspects of databases and Websites is their dynamic nature; they are neither finite nor do they have discrete successive parts. Rather, they are "continuing"; i.e., subject to ongoing updating and/or revision but not necessarily through the addition of discrete parts.

The report to the JSC recommends that the concept of "continuing" be built into the code so that a broader range of non-finite publications (i.e., seriality) can be accommodated throughout the rules. Using "continuing" as an umbrella term to encompass successively issued (e.g., serials, series) and integrating resources (i.e., databases, Websites, most loose-leafs), it proposes a new model of publication types of bibliographic resources.

"Finite" publications are resources where the basic work is complete in one or more parts, but which may be supplemented over time (such as many loose-leafs and multi-part monographs); they would receive monographic cataloging treatment with provision for describing their supplemental aspects. New rules for describing the supplemental (i.e., additive) elements of "finite" publications would need to be added to the code. Adele Hallam's *Cataloging Rules for the Description of Loose-leaf Publications* could serve as the basis for some of the new rules.

"Continuing" publications are resources, wherein there is no single basic unit. Instead the entire work continues indefinitely either through successive issues or by new content being integrated into the whole work over time. The cataloging approach to continuing publications would emphasize their serial, or continuing, nature and would accommodate both classic successively issued serials and open-ended integrating resources such as databases and Websites. In order to bring both types of continuing resources under the same set of rules, the AACR2 definition of a serial would need to be revised to read, "Serial-A bibliographic resource issued in a succession of discrete parts, usually bearing numeric and/or chronological designations, that has no predetermined conclusion." By relaxing the definition of a serial in this way, dynamic resources without issues can be treated as serials so long as they have parts which can be cited (such as individual articles), and unnumbered publications such as monographic series could be cataloged as serials also. Electronic journals, which have individual articles, or parts, would be cataloged as successively issued serials.

The existing rules for successive entry cataloging accommodate those continuing resources with successive issues (whether numbered or not). The rules do not handle integrating resources well, however, because they rely on the presence of a persistent title presented on a permanent chief source for bibliographic description. The dynamic element of databases and Websites defies this type of cataloging treatment on practical grounds because a new record is needed every time the title changes. As the title or its presentation changes online, there is often no remaining trace of the former title and no record at the site that it ever existed. Furthermore, the frequency with which some sites change makes creating new records to reflect these changes a very burdensome task. For this reason, the report to the JSC proposes that when changes occur in the title, statement of responsibility, or edition areas of integrating resources, these fields in the record be changed to reflect the current descriptive information with appropriate notes and added entries, following the latest entry technique. This would apply to any type of electronic resource, including electronic journals, which does not retain the earlier form of title at its site. However, if an electronic journal changes title but retains earlier issues online with the former title, a new successive entry record would be prepared. The MARBI paper also proposes that a new fixed field code "2" be defined to identify records updated using this new application of the latest entry technique.

What Bib Level code should be used for integrating resources? The MARBI paper identifies three possibilities: (1) Continue using the current Bib Level codes. Code loose-leafs and Websites as monographs, and databases and electronic journals as serials. This option would have minimal impact on library systems. (2) Change the definition of code "s" to mean "continuing" and use one code for all continuing resources. If this were done, many existing records would need to be re-coded and there would be a major impact on CONSER, MARC, OCLC, RLIN, etc. (3) Define a new Bib Level code for integrating resources, keeping finite and continuing integrating resources together. This option would require major changes to systems and MARC.

MAJOR AND MINOR CHANGES

Under AACR2, a new record is created when a title change occurs. In practice, there are other changes (such as a change in physical format) for which Library of Congress Rule Interpretations (LCRIs) also call for a new catalog record. The report to the JSC proposes that AACR2 adopt the language "Major change" and "Minor change," to more fully delineate situations requiring a new record, and that they be listed in the introduction to the descriptive rules so that catalogers have a single place to look for guidance on updating records. This would bring the code in conformance with the terminology used by ISBD and ISSN, and would also provide for the ability to accommodate certain changes on the latest entry records for continuing resources.

Under the proposed definition, major changes which would require a new successive entry record would include changes in a serial title, physical format, or corporate body name used as main entry heading or uniform title qualifier. A change in title would be considered major only when it occurs within the first three words of the title (rather than the first five), with the exception of articles, prepositions or conjunctions. The following types of changes in title words would not be considered major: changes in the representation of title words after the first three that do not change the meaning (such as *Best Restaurants in Arlington* to *Best Restaurants in Arlington, Virginia*); changes in the representation of words (e.g., spelled out form vs. abbreviated); the addition, deletion or rearrangement of the name of the issuing body anywhere in the title (if the name of the body actually changes, this would be major); the addition or deletion at the end of a serial title of a generic word such as "journal" or "bulletin"; an addition, deletion or change in punctuation; or changes in the order of titles when it is given in one or more language on the piece. For successively issued resources, major title changes would result in a new record; minor changes would be reflected in the title proper or ignored when truly insignificant. For integrating resources, all changes, whether major or minor, would be noted on the existing record according to latest entry technique.

Minor changes outside of the title would include changes in the wording of an edition statement (e.g., "World-wide ed." to "International ed."); change of place of publication used as a uniform title qualifier; and a serial designation which begins again with the same form of numbering already used. This last proposal would harmonize AACR cataloging practice with current ISSN practice.

DESCRIPTION: CHIEF SOURCE AND SOURCES OF INFORMATION

Expanding the cataloging rules to address all types of continuing resources also necessitates some changes in the concepts of chief and preferred sources of information, because a single stable source on an identified issue is often not available. Basing the description solely on the earliest issue in hand for any type of continuing resource also does not adequately describe the resource as it evolves over time. The report to the JSC proposes a more holistic approach towards bibliographic description to provide for recording information found on the latest issue when it varies.

Specifically, it proposes that the title, statement of responsibility and edition statement be recorded from the latest piece or latest online iteration at the time of cataloging for all continuing resources. The prescribed source of information would depend on the type of resource. For printed and other non-print, non-electronic resources, the current list of preferred sources found in AACR2 would continue to be used. For electronic journals, the entire online resource would be used, with preference given to titles presented in association with the latest article or issue, if issues exist. For remote integrating resources (databases, Websites, etc.) the title screen, home page, main menu or other prominent pages would be preferred. For loose-leafs the title would be based on the latest title page or title page substitute.

When there are changes in the title, statement of responsibility, or edition areas of an integrating resource, these areas would be updated with the earlier information moved to notes and added entry fields. If a major change occurs in the title of a successively issued serial, a new record would be made. If, however, the title change is minor (as defined above), the title proper (245) would be updated in the existing record and the earliest form of the title would be recorded as a uniform title. For example, if a hypothetical journal entitled *Anatomy* changed to *Anatomy journal*, the 245 field would be changed and a new uniform title with the earlier form would be added to the record:

130 0 Anatomy

245 00 Anatomy journal

The uniform title would become a permanent identifying access point for *Anatomy*. If subsequent minor title changes occur the title proper would be changed and added entries would be made as appropriate. In this way, *Anatomy journal*'s earliest form is provided as a stable means of unique identification and its latest iteration is provided in the title proper to identify its current form.

The proposal also recommends that the earliest and latest publisher information be recorded in the existing record by updating the publishing statement. Options for recording and coding the variations include: (1) Define new subfields in the 260 field to carry the earliest/latest information (for example, 260 $jNew York, NY: $kPergamon.–$i[originally $aBoston: $bHolt], $c, 1987-); (2) Create separate 260 fields, possibly with some new form of coding for retrieval; (3) Define a new 26X field for the latest form of publishing information. [Note: The MARBI paper was subsequently revised to include only the second option with suggested use of indicator values or subfield 3.]

ORGANIZATION OF THE CODE

The fourth area of recommendations addresses structural aspects of AACR2 itself. Specifically, the report suggests that a new introductory chapter be added which defines publication types (e.g., finite, continuing, integrating, serial) and provides guidance on the type of description to create for each one. Further, it proposes that AACR2 chapters be reorganized according to ISBD areas of the description rather than by format type. This would permit a more complete integration of the concept of seriality throughout the code. Lastly, there could be a third new part created which addresses relationships between works and manifestations.

CONCLUSION

This presentation was given twice at NASIG and each session was well attended. The speakers took questions at two designated points in the presentation, which gave attendees an opportunity to clarify their understanding of the new concepts and comment on their application. Overall, the audience response was very positive. The nature of the questions and comments indicated that there was widespread admiration for the impressive intellectual work that went into developing the proposals. There also appeared to be a consensus that the proposals to the JSC would provide practical solutions for some of today's most challenging problems in serials cataloging.

Dear Abby/Dear Abbott

Tina Feick
Keith Courtney
Karen Cargille
Mike Markwith

Workshop Leaders

Stephen D. Corrsin

Recorder

SUMMARY. Following rave reviews for the 1998 "Dear Abby/Dear Abbott" workshop, it was decided to offer this session once again. The panel of experts represented the various sectors of our industry–librarians, publishers, and subscription agents–giving participants the chance to answer a number of burning questions. *[Article copies available for a fee from The Haworth Document Delivery Service: 1-800-342-9678. E-mail address: getinfo@haworthpressinc.com <Website: http://www.haworthpressinc.com>]*

Feick opened the session by stating that there would be "No outline, no handouts, zero preparation," and that there would be just one

---

Tina Feick is Vice President, Blackwell's Information Services.
Keith Courtney is Director, Taylor and Francis Ltd.
Karen Cargille is Head, Acquisitions Department, University of California, San Diego.
Mike Markwith is Chief Executive Officer, Swets and Zeitlinger, Inc.
Stephen D. Corrsin is Head of Cataloging, Technical Services and Systems, Wayne State University.

[Haworth co-indexing entry note]: "Dear Abby/Dear Abbott." Corrsin, Stephen D. Co-published simultaneously in *The Serials Librarian* (The Haworth Press, Inc.) Vol. 38, No. 3/4, 2000, pp. 257-261; and: *From Carnegie to Internet2: Forging the Serials Future* (ed: P. Michelle Fiander, Joseph C. Harmon, and Jonathan David Makepeace) The Haworth Press, Inc., 2000, pp. 257-261. Single or multiple copies of this article are available for a fee from The Haworth Document Delivery Service [1-800-342-9678, 9:00 a.m. - 5:00 p.m. (EST). E-mail address: getinfo@haworthpressinc.com].

ground rule: no bashing of anyone, present or absent. The crowd consisted largely of librarians, with a significant number of vendors but only a few publishers.

Question: Libraries get large amounts of unsolicited materials, sometimes free, sometimes with invoices that come separately; how should these be handled? It's especially irritating when librarians think the materials are free but invoices subsequently appear, demanding payment.

Answers: Treat these materials as low priority selection decisions. Also, remember that, according to the *U.S. Postal Code*, it's never necessary to pay for unsolicited materials, even if retained.

Question: Which librarian typically makes decisions about purchasing aggregator databases?

Answers: Collection development staff in consultation with the local systems office usually make such decisions. Also, these are increasingly becoming consortial purchases.

Question: How are libraries handling e-journals available for free, on a trial or test basis?

Answers: Some libraries simply put these into the regular workflow, cataloging them like anything else. A publisher then asked: how long a trial do you need? Librarians answered variously, but agreed that at least a semester is needed; think of all the work that goes into processing a title, even if the final decision is not to retain. Publishers or vendors should let libraries know the plan for such publications well in advance, including information about subscription costs for future years; there is no such thing as a pleasant surprise in this sort of situation. It was interesting that some of the same issues arose as with the unsolicited titles, mentioned above. In any case, these free trial e-journals represent a significant amount of work for libraries, proving that nothing is really free.

The discussion segued into the problem of the increasing workload for librarians imposed by electronic materials, including not only new e-journals but also purportedly free add-ons. A publisher confirmed that purportedly free electronic titles are not in fact free. In the case of "free" electronic add-ons to print titles, the price for the electronic version is actually bundled into the price of the print. The problem in the electronic environment is that everything is new, fluid, and unstable, and we need to develop a working colloquy among all parties–librarians, publishers, and vendors. One librarian also responded that we must all talk more within our own libraries. It was suggested that there is more anger now than there used to be in libraries, including (for example) between acquisitions departments and selectors. Librarians in general often feel overwhelmed; serials librarians in particular feel "hammered." Given this, let's think about where we would rather be, and how to get there. Librarians need to talk more and, in particular, tell publishers what they want.

Question: What about keeping a print copy for archival purposes? Some libraries feel they must keep archival copies. A publisher followed this with a question about electronic archiving; evidently several major library systems are developing e-archives.

Question: A librarian reports that a publisher asked to have copyright notices attached to terminals in the libraries where their titles are being used, in the same way that copyright notices are placed on photocopiers. Is this appropriate?

Answers: Not many libraries have encountered this demand. There was general agreement that this is unusual and unrealistic.

Question: Are many libraries dropping print subscriptions in favor of electronic ones?

Answers: Some major print subscription cuts are taking place at many institutions. Other libraries are not necessarily dropping print titles, but not ordering new print titles either. Some are dropping duplicate print orders, or print indexes. In general, the pattern is that money is being consciously moved, in several ways, from print to electronic materials. A positive example is the California Digital Library, which aims to develop ways for their libraries to comfortably reduce print subscriptions.

Question: Concerns were expressed about publisher-aggregator relationships, and how difficult it is to keep up with changes in these packages. In response, librarians expressed resentment over demands from their administrations for "uncoordinated, thoughtless" cutting. There is a great deal of extra work involved. There is also sometimes an edge of panic in this "electronic transition."

Question: What do libraries do when full-text has been promised in an aggregation, but the full-text is not available?

Answers: Don't look on these packages as archival copies, or as full substitutes for print versions. These aggregations should be viewed as easy to use extras, but they are not typically full substitutes.

Question from a publisher: Have librarians tried dealing directly with publishers rather than through vendors?

Answers: Yes, selectors often prefer direct orders. However, serials librarians prefer working through vendors. This can lead to internal splits and conflicts over control within the libraries. Also, some publishers will not let agents handle their electronic titles. It's uncertain what exactly vendors can do in the area of licensing, because this matter is between the publisher and the library, regardless of vendors' involvement in, for example, the ordering or invoicing processes. Considerable hope was expressed for standard licensing and continued or extended involvement by vendors. In general, serials librarians feel that publishers often don't know how to work with libraries.

Question: What is the future for vendors and subscription agents?

Answers: The vendors still have a place. Vendors can't sign the license for electronic materials on behalf of a library, but they should be able to do more in the area of license administration. Most librarians who responded prefer to deal with vendors, appreciating what they do and the time they save for acquisitions librarians in many ways.

Another thing vendors might do when they handle the order for an electronic title is to keep the library informed as to when the subscription starts and the title is actually available. However, librarians feel they can't rely fully on vendors for this yet. Or rather, the whole electronic area is still so new that librarians aren't certain of the questions to ask, to obtain what they want and need.

A vendors' group is actively trying to create generic site licenses. They are now meeting and drafting, and will vet examples with librarians and publishers as soon as possible. (There was general approbation for this news.) But this doesn't really apply for aggregated products or databases.

Question: What about libraries placing claims for individual print issues, when they subscribe to both print and electronic versions? Why bother to claim these issues?

Answers: Most libraries will claim missing print issues regardless of whether they also have full electronic versions. But claiming is a strain on libraries just as much as on vendors and publishers. In fact the same old claiming headaches persist. Are publishers paying attention to claims? Are libraries claiming inappropriately? A vendor suggested that a very high percentage of claims are unnecessary. The information requested (about, for example, a delayed issue) is available in the vendors' or publishers' Websites; librarians should be able to access these directly.

Question: Are the electronic aggregations being used successfully? Are readers using them? Are they growing or dying out?

Answers: In some ways, consortia are stepping into the aggregators' roles. "Wherein lies the future of aggregated database products?" Do publishers see them as entry to new markets, or as threats to their subscriptions? That's the rub. The benefit of aggregations is that they offer a single front end for a large number of titles. Libraries say that while aggregations are convenient and popular among users, they are also vulnerable when budgets are tight. It was again pointed out that some publishers won't let vendors or aggregators handle their e-materials.

CONCLUSION

The rise of electronic titles has unsettled the serials world enormously. Many librarians feel swamped, as users' demands grow ever greater. Vendors are trying to ensure that they have a suitable place in this new world. Publishers have new and demanding responsibilities as well. However, more positively, there seems to be a growing sense from all players that we're all in this together, and can work together to find solutions.

Hybrid Methods of Desktop Journal Article Delivery

R. James King

Workshop Leader

Amy K. Weiss

Recorder

SUMMARY. This presentation demonstrated a method of delivering journal tables of contents and journal articles to a geographically dispersed user population. Users of the Ruth H. Hooker Research Library of the Naval Research Laboratory are able to have selected tables of contents e-mailed to them. URLs are given in the e-mail header if the journal is available electronically. If not, users can request photocopies of articles by replying to the e-mail. The system is set up to require minimum maintenance from library staff. *[Article copies available for a fee from The Haworth Document Delivery Service: 1-800-342-9678. E-mail address: getinfo@ haworthpressinc.com <Website: http://www.haworthpressinc.com>]*

NAVAL RESEARCH LABORATORY: THE ENVIRONMENT

R. James King began his presentation with a description of the Naval Research Laboratory's environment. The Naval Research Labo-

---

R. James King is Acting Associate Librarian for Information Technology, Naval Research Laboratory, Washington, DC.

Amy K. Weiss is Principal Cataloger, Appalachian State University, Boone NC.

[Haworth co-indexing entry note]: "Hybrid Methods of Desktop Journal Article Delivery." Weiss, Amy K. Co-published simultaneously in *The Serials Librarian* (The Haworth Press, Inc.) Vol. 38, No. 3/4, 2000, pp. 263-267; and: *From Carnegie to Internet2: Forging the Serials Future* (ed: P. Michelle Fiander, Joseph C. Harmon, and Jonathan David Makepeace) The Haworth Press, Inc., 2000, pp. 263-267. Single or multiple copies of this article are available for a fee from The Haworth Document Delivery Service [1-800-342-9678, 9:00 a.m. - 5:00 p.m. (EST). E-mail address: getinfo@haworthpressinc.com].

ratory, which has its main campus in Washington D.C., performs basic research in the areas of physics, chemistry, electronics, oceanography, meteorology, and space sciences. The Ruth H. Hooker Research Library delivers digital library services to approximately 2,500 federal researchers and on-site contractors at the main campus. There are smaller branches at the Stennis Space Center in Mississippi and in Monterey, California. The library also provides information services to the NRL's parent organization, the Office of Naval Research, based in Arlington, Virginia.

This large and geographically dispersed user community meant that there was a need for remote access to library services. The library began delivering information directly to researchers' desktops in 1992. At that time the library developed a system called InfoNet, which provided Telnet access to CD-ROMs held by the library, and also to Internet resources such as library catalogs and the FirstSearch databases. The library had ambitious plans to index the entire Internet for their users, but quickly discovered that, even with the aid of strong search engines such as Lycos and Yahoo, this was an impossible task, and the project was discarded.

In 1993, the library began to develop a Web-based image document system called TORPEDO, which was to give users access to over 100 full-text journal titles. However, the library was conscious of the fact that its 1000 print titles were accessible only to those local users who were willing to come to the library. To remedy this shortfall, the library developed Contents-To-Go, an e-mail-based table of contents service. This service was implemented in 1996.

CONTENTS-TO-GO

The library's journal vendor, Dawson, provides the library with tables of contents from the library's journal subscriptions. Dawson sends all of the information to a single e-mail address on the library's server. The server then points the message to a filtering program which checks the sender field to confirm that the information is from Dawson, and checks the destination, which is the journal list, and passes the message to a parser. The parser removes non-relevant data and formatting and adds the NRL's custom header and footer. The added information tells users how to request photocopies of articles, or explains how to access full-text, and explains the restrictions on photocopying of articles. Users are allowed no more than 2 articles per journal because of copyright restrictions.

Users request the table of contents service through the library's Website. They are presented with an alphabetical list of all journals for which a table of contents is available. Users enter their e-mail address, and click on the titles for which they wish to receive tables of contents. Users can easily add new titles or remove titles from their profiles without mediation by library staff. The alerts come to users' desktops in the form of e-mail. Essentially, the Contents-To-Go system is a group of individual mailing lists with a Web interface. The mailing list server software used at NRL is Majordomo, which is a freeware product based on Perl, but any electronic list software could be adapted for similar use.

If users wish to receive a journal article, there are several possible scenarios. If the journal is available on a publisher's Website, there is a URL in the table of contents header which points to the Website. If the journal is mounted locally in the TORPEDO Ultra system, which includes over 200 locally mounted full-text journals, the URL in the table of contents header links to the journal directly in a browse mode. If the journal is not available electronically, the user can request a photocopy of the article. Users send e-mail to a default reply address; a library technician receives the requests, locates the articles, and then sends the articles to requesters through the Laboratory's mail system. Photocopies of articles are supplied within 48 hours.

The system has been set up so that it requires minimal maintenance or input from library staff. Users manage their own accounts. King described the user interface as "brain-dead simple" and non-threatening, so that users seldom if ever need assistance. Systems staff make sure that messages get to the users and remove invalid e-mail addresses. An e-mail alias has been created which subscribes to every title in Contents-To-Go, which allows the systems administrators to monitor the flow of information in the system. Error messages also are redirected to an alias for analysis.

User statistics. Contents-To-Go has steadily increased in use since its implementation. King reported that feedback about the service has been consistently positive. The library keeps usage statistics on the subscription interface, the number of users, and the number of articles, pages, and requesters of photocopied articles. The library is able to keep use statistics on use of electronic journals which have been locally mounted, but is not able to keep statistics on usage of other full-text sources such as publishers' Websites. At the end of April 1999, there were 461 users subscribed to the Table-of-Contents service, with profiles ranging in size from 1 to 228 titles.

Information from Contents-To-Go statistics has been used in conjunction with other types of usage statistics to justify collection decisions such as canceling or retaining journals. Since Contents-To-Go contains only journals in the library's collection, low interest in the table of contents for a journal can suggest low interest in the journal itself. Conversely, a high interest journal might be added to the list of journals that the NRL has mounted digitally in their local system.

Future enhancements include plans for HTML mail, which would allow for direct links to articles without having to display the URLs in the table of contents headers, plans to add full-text newsletters, and integrating the Contents-To-Go service with other journal lists. The latter will integrate Contents-To-Go with the library catalog, the serial holdings list and other journal lists currently maintained separately on the library's Webpage. This integration will allow tables of contents to be requested from multiple locations, including from within the library catalog, and the dynamic updating of all lists.

DISCUSSION

After completing his presentation, King opened the floor for discussion of how other libraries were providing table of contents and journal articles to users' desktops. Several members of the audience had experience with offering document delivery services in various forms.

While the NRL library has created its own table of contents service for its own journal holdings, other librarians reported that they use commercial services (UnCover was mentioned) as a way to offer access to journals to which their libraries did not subscribe. Faculty are allowed to set up profiles which allow them to receive a certain number of table of contents alerts, or they are allowed to choose a certain number of terms that the system will seek in tables of contents, so that specific article citations are delivered to the desktop. There was discussion of preferred approaches to alerts. Faculty seem to prefer the traditional table of contents, because they are familiar with this format, and because it allows for serendipitous discovery of articles that might be missed using a keyword approach. One librarian stated that businesspeople who use her library's table of contents service prefer the keyword approach since it allows for targeting relevant topics.

Issues surrounding the "pay-per-view" concept were discussed. Who pays and how payment is assessed were the two major issues. User authentication was seen as a major issue, presumably both for the information providers and for institutions that might bear all or part of the user costs. In the case of very expensive journals with few interested users, having the user pay for requested articles was seen as a possible option for providing access without having to pay for a full subscription, but most of the participants were uncomfortable with a system which presupposed charging users. Pay-per-view systems, which bypassed the library entirely, were not discussed.

There was a brief discussion of copyright issues regarding the distribution of tables of contents. King said that their tables of contents are provided by a vendor which, in turn, has a contract for data entry with the British Library. The tables of contents used in Contents-To-Go are not exact images of the journals, so publishers' proprietary formats are not transmitted. There was a question about staffing levels at the NRL library. The systems staff currently consists of seven people. King admitted that some initiatives were slowed by lack of staff; for example, Contents-To-Go has had the same interface for two years.

Altogether this was an interesting presentation about a simple and workable solution to the problems of distributing current awareness information and providing information to users who either cannot or will not use the library.

Deacidification of Journals: Saving the Past and Present for the Future– You Mean Publishers Aren't Using Alkaline Paper?

Jeanne Drewes
Kristine Smets

Workshop Leaders

Cheryl Riley

Recorder

SUMMARY. Jeanne and Kristine provided a historical overview of the paper deterioration process, summaries of surveys examining the pH of journals and monographs, and four different types of deacidification processes. The deacidification program at the Milton S. Eisenhower Library at Johns Hopkins University is presented in detail. Particular em-

---

Jeanne Drewes is Assistant Director for Access and Preservation, Michigan State University Library.

Kristine Smets is Monograph Copy Cataloging Coordinator, Milton S. Eisenhower Library, Johns Hopkins University.

Cheryl Riley is Associate Professor and Serials Librarian, James C. Kirkpatrick Library, Central Missouri State University.

[Haworth co-indexing entry note]: "Deacidification of Journals: Saving the Past and Present for the Future–You Mean Publishers Aren't Using Alkaline Paper?" Riley, Cheryl. Co-published simultaneously in *The Serials Librarian* (The Haworth Press, Inc.) Vol. 38, No. 3/4, 2000, pp. 269-276; and: *From Carnegie to Internet2: Forging the Serials Future* (ed: P. Michelle Fiander, Joseph C. Harmon, and Jonathan David Makepeace) The Haworth Press, Inc., 2000, pp. 269-276. Single or multiple copies of this article are available for a fee from The Haworth Document Delivery Service [1-800-342-9678, 9:00 a.m. - 5:00 p.m. (EST). E-mail address: getinfo@haworthpressinc.com].

phasis is placed on the workflow at the library and the procedures used at the deacidification facility. The four steps of the deacidification workflow are: identification, deacidification, recording the action in the library management system, and physically marking the volumes. The challenges at the Eisenhower library are keeping in-house costs low and limiting user-impact. *[Article copies available for a fee from The Haworth Document Delivery Service: 1-800-342-9678. E-mail address: getinfo@haworthpressinc.com <Website: http://www.haworthpressinc.com>]*

INTRODUCTION

Acquisition librarian Ladd Brown introduced Jeanne and Kristine to the group attending the morning workshop session. Jeanne Drewes is currently Assistant Director for Access and Preservation at Michigan State University. Prior to this she was Head of Preservation at Johns Hopkins University. She is co-editor of the Greenwood Press book *Promoting Preservation Awareness in Libraries: A Sourcebook for Academic, Public, School and Special Collections*. Kristine Smets is Monograph Copy Cataloging Coordinator/Original Cataloger at Johns Hopkins University. Jeanne opened by admitting her pleasure at the Thursday night opening session when the Provost of Carnegie Mellon University mentioned spending money for the deacidification of journals. She acknowledged her appreciation that the premier school for computer science had such an encouraging commitment to the preservation of paper-based materials.

HISTORICAL OVERVIEW

Jeanne first provided a historical overview of the paper deterioration process. Acidic paper is a direct result of the movement from cotton rag to wood pulp as the primary material for paper. The problem with paper produced between 1840 and 1950 is that the chemicals used to break down the wood fiber remain in the paper and continue to work. This is why we have the brittle book problem (known in preservation circles as the "inherent vice"). Other factors that contribute to paper degradation are air pollution, temperature, humidity, and the natural aging process. Deacidification is one way to preserve printed knowledge.

Although not reported in the library literature, Jeanne is aware of three surveys examining acidity of journals. The earliest survey was conducted by the National Library of Medicine (NLM) using *Index Medicus* titles, and was completed in 1987. NLM was so successful in convincing publishers to utilize alkaline paper that alkaline journal receipts rose from four to 49% between 1987 and 1991 [1]. At the University of Michigan, Shannon Zachary, a library science student, examined the journals in the Library Science and the general collection in 1993. The results of the Zachary study indicated that library journals were more alkaline than general journals, but were still 20 to 30% acidic [2]. Drewes, in 1996, conducted a random sample of ten percent of the journals in the Milton S. Eisenhower Library at Johns Hopkins University. Current periodicals are divided between science and humanities so Drewes compared the materials using those two categories. The resulting data indicate that 43% of the humanities and 27% of the science journals were acidic (clay-coated and super-calendered papers were excluded). In contrast, only 10-20% of monographs were acidic, and these were primarily foreign materials. Circumstantial evidence suggests that the high demand for paper to maintain serial production schedules results in the use of available paper regardless of its acidity.

DEACIDIFICATION

Jeanne explained four different processes available to deacidify materials. The first process is a fluid aqueous alkaline solution using calcium hydroxide. The process dips a single sheet of paper into a liquid solution. It is very expensive and requires unbinding the material and processing it sheet-by-sheet. A second method, DEZ, is a gaseous process that utilizes diethylene zinc. The AKZO Company performed this process, but closed its plant in 1994. A third option, provided by Wei T'O in Canada and Battelle in Germany, is a liquid/phase alkaline organic solution. The fourth method, Bookkeeper, is a liquid/phase solid matter. This procedure uses magnesium oxide suspended in an inert solution to neutralize the acid and leave an alkaline buffer. The license for the Bookkeeper process is held by Preservation Technologies Incorporated (PTI).

Not all printed materials are ideal candidates for deacidification. Materials printed on clay-coated and super-calendered papers are typically excluded. Kristine brought examples of both types of paper for workshop participants to examine. Printers use a clay-coating paper for higher definition printing. Clay-coated paper deteriorates more slowly as the coating creates a barrier against air pollution. Clay-coating also prevents the magnesium oxide from penetrating as well so the efficacy of deacidification is reduced. Similarly, super-calendered paper, paper placed under high-pressure rollers for a smoother surface, has similar limitations for the magnesium oxide penetration. These processes do not prevent the need for deacidification, but the paper does deteriorate at a slower rate.

DEACIDIFICATION AT JOHNS HOPKINS

The Milton S. Eisenhower Library is the main research library of Johns Hopkins University. It has a collection of 2.4 million printed volumes, 14,000 serial subscriptions, 3.5 million microforms, more than 200,000 maps, and audiovisual, manuscript, and archival resources. The library management system (LMS) is currently Horizon; it was NOTIS prior to 1997. The Preservation Department and the Cataloging Department together manage the deacidification process. The Preservation department includes seven full time staff plus student assistants. The department consists of the Commercial Binding Office, Preparation Unit, and the Book Repair Unit. The Cataloging department has six senior staff members, 16 para-professionals and approximately 12 student assistants. Cataloging includes serials, non-book, monograph copy cataloging, and catalog maintenance.

The deacidification workflow includes four steps: identification, deacidification, recording the action in the LMS, and physically marking the volumes. Depending on the type of material (current periodicals, new serial volume receipts, or existing bound volumes) each step is completed at different times and in different units following the established workflow. The Eisenhower library targets those materials that are at risk and have long-term research value. In all cases, volumes printed on clay-coated or super-calendered paper and titles available in micro or electronic format are excluded from the process. In addition, for current periodicals, domestic science titles are not eligible for deacidification because of the probability that these titles will become available electronically. New serial volumes also exclude titles that are not permanently retained. Monographs and serials in the stacks, identified on a retrospective project basis, also exclude volumes with severely damaged bindings.

Volumes are identified as acidic using a pH test pen. If the volume is printed on alkaline paper, the pen mark is purple; yellow if the paper is acidic. Each volume is tested because the quality of paper can vary from issue to issue. Acidic paper loses strength over time as the acid in the paper breaks down the fibers. New materials, even when acidic, are still strong and are ideal candidates for the deacidification process. Once the acid is neutralized there is very little breakdown of the fiber. In retrospective projects the strength of the paper must be determined to assure that the embrittlement process has not deteriorated the paper too much to survive the deacidification process. This is accomplished by completing a fold test. Since deacidification does not change the brittleness of the paper but only stops the paper from further deterioration, it is not cost-effective to deacidify very brittle paper. Those materials are excluded from the process. (A more expensive paper splitting process exists that actually strengthens the structure of the paper.)

Kristine brought deacidified volumes for the audience to examine; most people can feel a difference. At Johns Hopkins acidic journals are sent for deacidification directly from the bindery. The bindery transports the materials to PTI while making other deliveries. For shipments direct to PTI, reusable Rubbermaid containers transport the materials. A timesaving device is a reusable label with one side containing the commercial bindery address and the other side the address of PTI.

Once the volumes arrive at PTI, the books are checked-in and put into a book holder that resembles the agitator of a washing machine. The book holder is then placed into a cylindrical chamber that correlates to the tub used in the washing machine analogy. The agitator holds the books in place with bands so the pages can move freely and allow the solution to impregnate all of the paper. Jeanne described the process as "putting the books into a gentle Jacuzzi." The solution needs to permeate the inner gutter and vents in the side of the "Jacuzzi" in order to distribute the solution throughout the pages. The materials are in the solution for about 25 minutes and then allowed to stabilize. The volumes are then checked, re-packed, and returned to the Milton S. Eisenhower Library. A hand-held sprayer is used for oversized materials and a vertical machine for loose materials.

While the materials are at the bindery and PTI, information noting the deacidification treatment is being recorded in the LMS. MARC tag 583 in the bibliographic record is used to record preservation actions as follows:

583 bb $3v.109:no.1-3 c.1$a mass deacidified; $i liquid; $c19990409; $kPreservation Technologies Inc. $5 MdBj

MARC 583 does not display to the public but does display to staff, and can be searched with a special keyword index. Delimiter *three* ($3) specifies which volumes and copies have been de-acidified. The ANSI standard for holdings information is loosely followed for noting the holdings information. Delimiter *a* ($a) specifies the action performed; delimiter *i* ($i) the method of action; delimiter *c* ($c), the "time of action" subfield, contains the date the note is first added to the record; delimiter *k* ($k) notes the action agent; and delimiter *5* ($5) contains the OCLC holdings symbol. In addition to marking the bibliographic record each volume also is physically marked. Alkaline volumes are stamped at the point of testing with the infinity symbol, the official ANSI symbol; deacidified volumes are stamped with a symbol denoting deacidification either before or after processing. Acidic volumes rejected for treatment are stamped "reviewed for treatment <year>" at the point of testing. Every volume is stamped so it is apparent which volumes have been tested or treated.

The serials unit pulls current periodicals ready to be bound and creates an online item record with the status "at the bindery." The volumes are then transferred to the Binding Unit where the unbound volumes are tested. All volumes are then sent to General Bookbinding of Ohio. Acidic volumes are packed separately in boxes marked for PTI and go directly to PTI after binding. PTI returns the volumes to the library after deacidification. The Binding Unit stamps deacidified volumes and sends volumes to Circulation to be checked-in. A student assistant in Cataloging adds/updates the action note to the bibliographic record. The Acquisitions Serials Unit tests new serial volumes at the time of receipt, flags acidic volumes, and supplies Cataloging with a list of acidic volumes. All volumes are then sent to the Preparations Unit. The Preparations Unit labels all volumes, stamps the acidic volumes, and checks-out the acidic volumes to a pseudo-patron so that staff is at all times aware of the location of each volume. Acidic volumes are then shipped to PTI. A student assistant in Cataloging adds/updates the actions note to the bibliographic record. The Preparations Unit receives deacidified volumes from PTI and sends the volumes to Circulation to be checked-in. Resource Services Librarians in consultation with the Preservation Department identify retrospective serials in the stacks. After identification, the acidic volumes in the stacks are sent to the Binding Office. The Binding Office checks the acidic volumes out to the pseudo-patron and sends the acidic volumes to PTI. The volumes are stamped when returned from PTI and sent to Circulation to be checked-in. A student assistant in Cataloging adds/updates the action note to the bibliographic record.

The challenges for the Milton S. Eisenhower Library are to keep the in-house processing costs low and limit the impact on users. Strategies for limiting user impact are a short turn-around-time, the ability to send small shipments, removing the item only once for both the binding and deacidification processes, and using the online catalog to inform users of the item's unavailability. Turn-around-time for materials sent to the bindery and deacidification averages one month. Materials sent directly to PTI are, on average, unavailable for a two-week period. In-house processing costs are kept as low as possible by incorporating deacidification into the regular workflow, using student assistants for as much processing as possible, and automating the recording of information in the bibliographic record. Serials offer more of a challenge than monographs because of the continual need to add/update notes in the bibliographic record. In NOTIS action notes were added to the bibliographic record based on checkout status without human intervention; Horizon requires custom programming, but this programming is not yet implemented. Until implementation, there needs to be continued reliance on keyboard macros in Cataloging and continued attempts to automate the lists compiled for Cataloging. At the Milton S. Eisenhower Library, the deacidification process has been assumed without additional staff. An important part of this process is the commitment by the Preservation Department to pay for the additional student costs rather than expect the Cataloging Department to assume the additional expense.

Both presenters suggested reasons for having a deacidification plan. A planned approach is a proactive rather than as-needed method of tackling the acid-paper dilemma. Preservation microfilming or photocopying can be two to five times more expensive than deacidification.

Deacidification reduces the need for reformatting and does not result in the loss of utility for users that occurs with reformatting. A deacidification program allows for cooperative resource sharing, and using the MARC record facilitates sharing the information. It may be possible for groups to negotiate for lower per-item prices for deacidification than an individual library could realize.

DISCUSSION

The first question from the audience concerned the relative costs of deacidification and preservation photocopying. On average, preservation photocopying is at least twice as costly as deacidification, even excluding the cost of re-cataloging the item in the new format. A second question requested an estimate of the cost of a deacidification program and Jeanne estimated the outsourcing cost at $13.00 to $17.00 per volume. Jeanne stressed that a buckram binding is only one aspect of preservation; putting a good case on a volume does not stop the degradation of acidic paper. Another individual asked how long the mark from the pH pen remained on the paper; the answer was, usually less than a week. A question was asked about when a partially acidic volume was sent to PTI. At Johns Hopkins a journal is sent for deacidification if it is 50% or more acidic. A final question was asked about deacidifying photographic archives; Jeanne referred the questioner to the Library of Congress and to the bibliography on deacidification of journals (http://www.lib.msu.edu/drewes/Bibliography.htm) provided to each member of the audience. A second handout detailed the deacidification program at the Library of Congress (http:// lcweb.loc.gov/preserv/). Both handouts are in the handout package available from NASIG.

NOTES

1. Ellen McCrady, "The pH of New Library Books, 1976-1993: A Compilation of Survey Results," *The Abbey Newsletter: Preservation of Library & Archival Materials* 21:1 (1997):1-2.
2. Shannon Zachary, "The Permanence of Ephemera: A pH Survey of Current Periodicals in a Research Collection" (research paper, ILS 840, Michigan State University, 1993).
3. For more information on MARC 583 see: *USMARC Format for Bibliographic Data: Including Guidelines for Content Designation* (Washington, D.C.: Library of Congress, Network Development and MARC Standards Office, 1994), 583:1-5.

Organizing Web-Based Resources

Linda Chase
Claire Dygert

Workshop Leaders

Judith A. Johnston

Recorder

SUMMARY. This presentation explored options for providing access to electronic resources, including alphabetical and subject lists on library Websites, full cataloging in the OPAC, and a proposal for creating an access catalog. *[Article copies available for a fee from The Haworth Document Delivery Service: 1-800-342-9678. E-mail address: getinfo@haworthpressinc. com <Website: http://www.haworthpressinc.com>]*

INTRODUCTION

Librarians have been collecting and organizing information for centuries. But the digital age provides a new environment with unprecedented volumes of information available in unprecedented formats.

Linda Chase is Assistant University Librarian, Collections Services, American University.

Claire Dygert is Serials Department and Electronic Resources Librarian, American University.

Judith A. Johnston is Head, Cataloging Unit, University of North Texas.

[Haworth co-indexing entry note]: "Organizing Web-Based Resources." Johnston, Judith A. Co-published simultaneously in *The Serials Librarian* (The Haworth Press, Inc.) Vol. 38, No. 3/4, 2000, pp. 277-286; and: *From Carnegie to Internet2: Forging the Serials Future* (ed: P. Michelle Fiander, Joseph C. Harmon, and Jonathan David Makepeace) The Haworth Press, Inc., 2000, pp. 277-286. Single or multiple copies of this article are available for a fee from The Haworth Document Delivery Service [1-800-342-9678, 9:00 a.m. - 5:00 p.m. (EST). E-mail address: getinfo@haworthpressinc.com].

Formerly, information was scarce and the challenge was to make enough of it available to users. Today's challenge is to identify what is relevant and useful in the mass of too much information. People in and outside this profession are working very hard to meet this challenge.

One reason for the extraordinary expansion of available information is the World Wide Web. The accessibility of HTML and HTML editors makes it fairly easy to produce Websites. Information that was once produced in print for limited distribution is now often simultaneously produced on the Web for almost unlimited distribution. The lack of standards for organizing Web-based resources, however, poses problems for a library user going directly to the Web for information. The Web is like a library where all the books have been taken off the shelves, piled in a big heap and the title pages removed. The information is still there, but it will take some luck to find what is needed. An Internet search resulting in 400,000 hits, like a pile of books without title pages, is not useful.

Librarians can provide better access than this for their users, and in fact, they are doing some helpful things. Librarians are teaching users how to search and evaluate what they find. They are also collecting and organizing reliable resources. Both inside and outside the library profession, people are working on developing common standards to describe information resources. It certainly is a time of transition. As noted in a recent OCLC Institute program of March, 1998 titled, *Knowledge Access Management*:

> We're clearly emerging from one tradition and creating a new one. The analogy is probably with the period between 1850 and 1900, between the first attempts at a union catalog and the cataloging rules of the Library of Congress, published in 1904 or so. . . . Whether these efforts represent the ending of a period or a new beginning remains to be seen . . . but they are events worth attending to in either case.

Some unique challenges are presented when describing and organizing information in digital format. How do we describe multiple resources aggregated into a single database? How do we define "holdings" in a virtual environment? How do we draw the defining line around a resource that links to other resources? How do we manage URLs that frequently change? How do we help users navigate in an environment where the library catalog may no longer be the central gateway to information? How do we incorporate new methods for organizing digital information into our standardized cataloging practices?

DEFINING HOLDINGS

Defining holdings in the print environment has been fairly straightforward. Then computer files, often more difficult to quantify came along. Now there is access to remote databases, and databases which aggregate multiple titles. Does a library "hold" remote resources, or not? When subscribing to databases aggregating many titles, how many titles are counted? What about Websites on a library pathfinder? They are, in a sense, selected resources, but does the library really have them? Is the free online version of a print journal to which the library subscribes one title, or two? If the library gets the same journal from more than one provider, how many times will it be counted?

Libraries are traditionally evaluated on the basis of their collection size. Accrediting agencies, government agencies, and administrators rely on measures to evaluate a library, and size of holdings is one measure of the library. There is also the issue of budget accountability. As libraries buy fewer print objects in favor of electronic resources, they need to be able to demonstrate to their users and administrators that despite having fewer things to count, they are indeed providing access to more information. Thus, the definition of holdings is important to a library. Because industry standards for defining and counting are not yet established, librarians define and count in different ways.

EMBEDDED RESOURCES

Another problem in describing Web-based resources is posed when multiple resources are embedded within an umbrella title. For example, a single subscription to the online database *Gale Business Resources* represents nineteen separate print titles. How do we make these individual titles accessible to our users? For these resources, the cataloging record helps resolve this problem by listing all titles in the table of contents note, as well as giving a title-added entry. It's not always this easy, however, as we'll see with the next example, *Litera-*

ture Online (LION). This is a huge database, which includes, among other things, tens of thousands of full-text English and American poems; twenty different versions of the English Bible; and twenty-four separate contemporary printings of individual plays by Shakespeare. How should the contents of this database be represented to our users in a way that makes them accessible?

A third example of the problem of embedded resources is *Columbia International Affairs Online* (CIAO), which has full-text research reports, working papers, articles, and a number of monographs. Normally, if these monographs were purchased, they would be cataloged, shelved, separately counted, and accessible to users through the catalog. When the presenter's library purchased this resource in March 1998, it included ten digitized monographs. Just before the 1999 NASIG conference, a check of this Website showed that it now included some 200. There is no mechanism for tracking and cataloging these monographs posted at the CIAO Website.

EXTERNAL LINKS

Opposite to the problem of describing information embedded within a Website is the challenge posed by links to information resources external to that resource. Let's say you've identified a scholarly Website on women's health in the developing world, and you want to add it to your collection of resources. Now imagine that this Website links to a video recording on nutrition done by the World Health Organization, as well as to online pamphlets about family planning from the Planned Parenthood Website. Each of these links may be equally important. Should each be separately cataloged? What is the relationship of those different resources to the resource that the cataloger is trying to describe? Where does the cataloger define the line around a document, and what is the relationship between documents? Although the following quote from a 1997 video (*Into the Future: On the Preservation of Knowledge in the Electronic Age*) is about preservation of Web-based resources, it is also true for description:

> The whole concept of linked non-linear documents makes preservation very tricky, because where do you draw the boundary around the document? If my document references sixteen other documents by having links to them, then what does it mean to preserve my document? We also have to preserve all of those

> other sixteen documents, and transitively all of the documents that they reference and point to. . . . You can think of the Web as one huge interlinked connection of documents . . .

Perhaps, then, the solution is simple–we can create one single cataloging record and be done with it!

INSTABILITY OF WEB-BASED RESOURCES

The instability of Web resources also poses a challenge to those attempting to describe and organize them. Certainly, describing a Web resource is more challenging than describing a static physical object. The book on the shelf is the same book cataloged a year ago. But the Web resource cataloged five minutes ago may well look different now; and if it doesn't, it could look different five minutes from now. Some online journals feature continuous updating, but at unpredictable intervals. Unstable elements of Web-based information resources include the summary, scope, contents (what catalogers would call analytics), title, publisher, host, author, amount of coverage, and the URL. This represents a nightmare world for catalogers.

Fortunately, there are some mitigating factors. One is the use of a PURL, the Persistent URL, a kind of location authority. It creates a relationship between the PURL as it appears in the catalog, and the current URL. The user doesn't need to know where the resource currently resides. Other similar technical possibilities exist and are in development. There are other, less technical mitigating steps that can be taken. One is using librarians' judgement to decide what descriptive cataloging to create. If the content of the resource changes frequently, the cataloger will want to create a more general content descriptor. Librarians can take a role in selecting appropriate Web resources that provide stable and authoritative information sources.

FRAGMENTATION OF ACCESS POINTS

One of the greatest challenges that the digital environment poses to library users is the fragmentation of access points to information. No longer can the user rely upon the catalog to provide them access to the bulk of resources held by the library. Libraries offer the OPAC, the library Website, Web lists of resources, pathfinders that may include both freely available Internet resources as well as resources on subscription, and Internet search engines. Libraries also have publisher or vendor Websites. The abstracting and indexing databases to which a library subscribes might come from a particular platform, such as Ovid or Silver Platter. That's fragmented access. Increasingly, faculty and academic departments provide Webpages that provide links to Internet resources. We might think of these pages as departmental libraries–something that academic libraries often frown upon, as they deflect the user away from the greater collection of information.

These multiple access points create a great deal of confusion and frustration for the user and librarian alike. What can we do to re-centralize access to information, no matter where it resides? How can we help our users be more efficient information gatherers? How can we encourage teaching faculty to share the Web resources they identify as valuable with the library, so that we might incorporate them into the collection? Librarians should work to refocus the energy back into the library, so that everyone on campus thinks of the library, even in this new environment, as a place to access good resources, whether they're on the Web or physically in the building. We're going to explore some options of how we might do that.

AVAILABLE OPTIONS

The first option, one common to most libraries, is the alphabetical or subject lists of electronic resources on library Webpages. These lists work with five or six resources, but as new resources are added the lists quickly become unwieldy. Another option is to catalog all Web-based resources, whether they are subscriptions or not, in the OPAC. The third option is to create something called an Access catalog, which complements the OPAC and yet is more than a list. The final option is to use some combination of these three.

WEB-BASED LISTS

Web-based lists of e-resources have several advantages, and seem to be the current primary organizational method of choice. Creating lists is inexpensive. HTML is fairly simple now, and editing programs make it easier. Lists are relatively easy to update, as opposed to editing a catalog record. They also have disadvantages. Lists lack any content searching capability further than the title or maybe a brief description. Using lists also ignores the value of librarians' expertise: librarians have hundreds of years of knowledge in organizing information to make it easily accessible to users. Lists quickly become unwieldy due to length. Lists do not integrate the resources from the OPAC. We know that users like the quick online full-text information that many resources provide, so if they can find something there, especially on the undergraduate level, many will not go to the catalog. Finally, lists also deflect users away from physical library resources.

Earlier in the presentation, we shared a quote suggesting that this time of transition is analagous to that of 1850 to 1900. If we think about how we're organizing Internet resources now, we may see that we're stepping back in time. Consider this 1850 quote from Antonio Panizzi, who was the principal librarian at the British Museum, and instrumental in developing their catalog:

> Almost every one who possesses a library of a few hundred volumes thinks himself competent to draw up a list of them; this he supposes is easily done by copying the titles; and such list he takes for granted constitutes an alphabetical catalogue.

OPAC ACCESS

Access to Web-based resources through the OPAC has many advantages. Our OPACs are extremely well developed tools for getting users connected to information. Users know how to search them, navigate their way through them, and how to interpret the resulting display. The OPAC is also a single entry point to information in all formats, and is the traditional gateway to information. Resources found in the catalog indicate that a collection decision has been made. The MARC record format provides another advantage. MARC is a flexible and useful tool that allows for multiple access points and supports relationships between bibliographic records. The interoperability of MARC standards makes it possible for information created in one catalog to also work in another. The exchange of data made possible over the past decades is a huge advantage. The 856 field is one example of MARC's adaptability. MARC has been one of the major improvements in libraries in this century in fostering the economic and production advantages of shared cataloging. Professionals have spent much time developing and perfecting the OPAC as an excellent tool that employs the knowledge and expertise of librarians.

However, OPAC access also has disadvantages. What library catalogs are designed to do is somewhat different from what is needed in this environment. The traditional functions of the catalog are to provide access and describe an object. In describing an object, the bibliographic record is a surrogate for that object. When describing electronic resources that are unstable and unfixed, the description can no longer serve as a surrogate with any permanency. In any case, the user doesn't need a surrogate, because in the Web catalog, the 856 field links directly to the resource itself. So, if the need for a surrogate is no longer there, part of what catalogs are designed for is less relevant in this environment. Another disadvantage to relying upon the catalog to provide access to Web-based resources is the fact that MARC standards change very slowly, because they are based on cooperative effort and consensus, which takes time. The ongoing debate over how to handle multiple versions is an example. Changes have been proposed to the MARC record to handle Web-based resources, and much work is being done, but the changes are not yet close to universal adoption. Meanwhile, libraries must make electronic resources accessible to users. Finally, input of information into OPACs is more costly than creating lists and, therefore, assumes a long-term commitment and maintenance.

ACCESS CATALOG

The term "access catalog" comes from an article by Terry Hanson. Hanson differentiates an access catalog for electronic, networked resources from the holdings (traditional) catalog. The development of an access catalog would have some advantages. Once set up, it could potentially cost less, depending on what metadata (whether it be MARC, the Dublin Core, etc.) is used, and what level of staff is doing the cataloging. An access catalog could be used to protect the integrity of the holdings catalog. Records for resources that are going to change, or that might not be around after two years, would not be entered in the OPAC. An access catalog offers more flexibility and timely access. Often, important Websites are set up for elections or particular topics in the news. The library wishes to make them accessible to users, but not to create catalog records, because of the maintenance issues and the sites' limited existence. An access catalog also accepts different standards of organizing.

An access catalog makes mediated access to the Web possible. Librarians know how to select valuable resources and organize them in a way that makes them easily accessible. However, in this time of transition, libraries do not collect many things that they would like to collect, because they do not know what to do with them. An access catalog would provide a place to experiment in this rapidly changing environment and be an opportunity to combine traditional expertise with innovation. It would allow catalogers to use their expertise in new and innovative ways. A potential crosswalk to the OPAC could be developed. Ideally, the OPAC and access catalogs would be set up to enable the user to search them simultaneously or separately. Work currently being done to allow MARC data to be translated into other metadata and back will help make this possible. Another advantage of the access catalog is that it could include information on license restrictions and regulations for use.

An access catalog also has disadvantages. It is a new, untried and thus risky approach still in development. It is not certain if it will work or be valuable after 5 years. It is still not a complete resolution of fragmentation. Websites with lists will continue to exist. Implementation requires staff time and training. Staff will need to learn the metadata chosen for use in the access catalog. Additional costs are the software and maintenance of the access catalog. Finally, in this early developmental stage, standards for access catalogs are not yet in place.

The presenters' proposal is to build an access catalog to complement the OPAC and Webpages. They suggest that the use of lists to organize information on library Websites be phased out. The presenters outlined an approach to building an access catalog. First, convene library-wide discussions to draw on staff experience and ideas. Develop a project team. Explore external and internal funding to help with the cost of development, staff training, hardware, software and evaluation. Seek other libraries as partners. Resolution of technical questions is a major need, particularly the creation of the interface or crosswalk between catalogs. The crosswalk is key to the success of this idea. Identify internal library resources such as staff time and responsibility.

To create an access catalog, the library may need to give up something else. Develop policies for selection, organization and maintenance of the electronic resources and access catalog. These policies will require continual updating. It's important to develop policies before you create the access catalog.

BIBLIOGRAPHY

ALCTS Committee on Cataloging: Description and Access. "Task Force on Metadata and the Cataloging Rules: Final Report." (August 21, 1998) *http://www.libraries/psu.edu/iasweb/personal/jca/ccda/tf-tei2.html* (Oct. 1, 1998)

Dentinger, Sue. "The Public Electronic Library: Web-Menuing versus OPAC Cataloging." *Library Hi Tech*: 16:3-4 (1998): 89-94.

Desmarais, Norman. "Chaos–XML: Organizing the Internet." *Against the Grain.* 10:7 (Dec. 98-Jan. 99): 75-84.

Hanson, Terry. "The Access Catalogue Gateway to Resources." *Ariadne.* 15 *http://www.ariadne.ac.uk/issue15/main* (July 23, 1998)

Lewis, John D. "XML: an introduction." *OCLC Systems and Services*. 14:1 (1998): 51-52.

Miller, Paul. "Metadata for the Masses." *Ariadne. 5. http://www.ariadne.ac.uk/issue5/ metadata-masses/#dcextend* (Jan 15, 1998).

Milstead, Jessica, Susan Feldman. "Metadata: Cataloging by Any Other Name . . . " *ONLINE* (Jan. 99) *http://www.onlineinc.com/onlinemag/OL1999/milstead1.html* (May 24, 1999)

Morgan, Eric Lease. "We Love Databases!" *Computers in Libraries.* 18:2 (Feb. 1998): 38-39.

Tennant, Roy. "The Art and Science of Digital Bibliography." *Library Journal.* 123:17 (Oct. 15, 1998): 28-30.

Weibel, Stuart. "The State of the Dublin Core Metadata Initiative April 1999." *D-Lib Magazine.* 5:4 (Apr. 1999) *http://www.dlib.org/dlib/apri199/orweibel.html* (May 3, 1999).

Provocative Public Services: Ways That Serials Public Service Is Changing in the Electronic Era

Robb M. Waltner

Workshop Leader

Marcella Lesher

Recorder

SUMMARY. Robb Waltner's workshop was designed to offer public service librarians an alternative to the many technical service workshops available to NASIG attendees. The intent of this workshop was to provide an opportunity for participants to compare how their own careers have evolved with changes in technology. He also spoke about the importance of interpersonal networking and hoped that the workshop would support that opportunity as participants talked about the similarities and dissimilarities of careers and career paths. *[Article copies available for a fee from The Haworth Document Delivery Service: 1-800-342-9678. E-mail address: getinfo@haworthpressinc.com <Website: http://www.haworthpressinc.com>]*

INTRODUCTION

Waltner began the discussion by taking a poll of the audience regarding the time they spent at the reference desk. Findings from both

---

Robb M. Waltner is Periodicals Librarian, University of Colorado, Denver, Auraria Library.

Marcella Lesher is Periodicals Librarian, Academic Library, St. Mary's University, San Antonio, TX.

[Haworth co-indexing entry note]: "Provocative Public Services: Ways that Serials Public Service Is Changing in the Electronic Era." Lesher, Marcella. Co-published simultaneously in *The Serials Librarian* (The Haworth Press, Inc.) Vol. 38, No. 3/4, 2000, pp. 287-290; and: *From Carnegie to Internet2: Forging the Serials Future* (ed: P. Michelle Fiander, Joseph C. Harmon, and Jonathan David Makepeace) The Haworth Press, Inc., 2000, pp. 287-290. Single or multiple copies of this article are available for a fee from The Haworth Document Delivery Service [1-800-342-9678, 9:00 a.m. - 5:00 p.m. (EST). E-mail address: getinfo@haworthpressinc.com].

sessions conducted at the conference were very similar. The majority of participants indicated that they generally spent 10 hours or less at the reference desk on a weekly basis. A smaller group worked 11-20 hours at the desk, and a very small minority spent more than 50% of their time at the desk. Participants also noted the need to consider the time spent on library instruction as another important element in many public services positions. Most attendees were from academic libraries.

SHIFTING CAREERS

Using a questionnaire to provide focus for the first half of the session, Waltner asked participants to comment on such areas as background preparation, descriptions of current work responsibilities, and future goals and plans. Waltner and several participants described the evolution of their own careers and plans for the future. As in other segments of the library profession, public service librarians have encountered change throughout their careers. Waltner himself discussed his own career path where his responsibilities as periodicals librarian have expanded to include access services and interlibrary loan. A participant noted that electronic journal management had become a public service responsibility. Split positions in technical and public service were mentioned by a number of participants who considered it a way of promoting variety into their careers. Others noted that while responsibilities have changed, job titles remain the same. In looking at future goals and plans, all discussants indicated a desire to remain in academic settings.

Newly created positions without clear definition were another avenue of change for librarians. Several participants talked about the process of moving into newly created positions or long unfilled positions, and having to discover for themselves what their new job responsibilities entailed. One librarian in this situation said she was uncomfortable with her undefined role until she realized that regardless of her confusion, her knowledge was still helpful to patrons. Another participant noted that many types of work experience, including non-library work, were helpful at the reference desk. Employment in restaurants and retail stores, for example, provides good customer service training and develops interpersonal skills vital to reference work.

REFERENCE SERVICE: PROBLEMS AND SOLUTIONS

Waltner then moved the discussion into a new category, which he called: "Things we cannot discuss at my library–yet." He opened the discussion by asking participants to comment on questions such as:

1. How much time can you spend with each user?
2. How much time do you want to spend?
3. Can you "follow-up"?
4. Can you assist users with a variety of resources with a single visit to the library?

The general consensus was that with the variety of information resources now available, time constraints were indeed a factor in providing good service to patrons. Problems such as slow computer response time and differing computer interfaces were identified as having a significant impact on the amount of time devoted to serving individual library users. Providing service to persons not affiliated with the institution was also discussed as a recurring problem. Outside users of the library were often more in need of reference assistance and less familiar with traditional library resources than were the library's regular or "official" users.

Instruction in the use of a large variety of differing interfaces or access points is still often an issue of concern, even when time is available to work with students. Students may not want to take the time to learn how to use the various tools necessary to find the best information for their research queries, a situation that makes it difficult for librarians to provide the best assistance. Librarians find themselves balancing their desire to recommend a comprehensive array of resources with a desire to streamline the information seeking process. Although this streamlining process is designed to match the amount of time that the student may be willing to devote to research and may provide an acceptable answer, it may not necessarily provide the best information.

Several participants described ways time constraints were being addressed at their libraries. These included providing appointment times to give students more one-on-one assistance and the use of online reference assistance to help students at off campus locations. One participant described a formal library instruction course developed at her institution that had successfully provided students with the background and tools necessary to conduct required library research. The need for a more active approach to reference service was also mentioned, as one participant noted that many students needing assistance do not approach the reference desk, and that students sitting at computer terminals are not necessarily using their time efficiently [1]. Another participant noted the importance of working with faculty members in teaching critical thinking skills to better prepare students for research.

Waltner also addressed the issue of human resource allocation by asking whether participants believed that their institutions needed more people to serve in public service positions. Several participants described programs in their libraries intended to deal with staff shortages in public service areas. Such programs included: employing students to assist with basic questions; using computer assistants to help with printing problems or other technical difficulties; cross-training technical services librarians to assist with reference service; and, at one institution, implementing an internal internship program where technical service personnel worked part-time in public service roles. One participant also noted local state requirements for computer literacy had increased resources for user training at his library. Given that para-professionals take on some of the new tasks required to improve public service, Waltner mentioned the need to reward these staff members appropriately when they increase their workloads.

CONCLUSION

In general participants in this session seemed to be embracing change and were looking forward to the challenges of the electronic environment. There was a general awareness that job responsibilities are evolving and that the lines between public service positions and technical service positions are becoming more blurred as librarians take advantage of resources available in the virtual environment. For this session's participants, provocative public service meant welcoming change and responding to the need to acquire new skills as necessary in the electronic era.

NOTES

1. Editor's note: For a recent discussion of active or aggressive reference service, see: Anne Grodzins Lipow, "'In Your Face' Reference Service," *Library Journal*, August 1999: 50-52.

Toward Better Access to Full-Text Aggregator Collections

Yumin Jiang
Jeanne A. Baker

Workshop Leaders

Lynda S. Kresge

Recorder

SUMMARY. Libraries are searching for practical and viable ways to provide users with information about serials titles in electronic aggregator collections. This session offered an overview of Cornell University's experience in developing policies and procedures to provide enhanced access to individual serials titles in databases such as UMI's ProQuest Direct. It also provided an update on recent work by the PCC Task Group on Journals in Aggregator Databases to design an aggregator analytic record, which could be used as a prototype by vendors. *[Article copies available for a fee from The Haworth Document Delivery Service: 1-800-342-9678. E-mail address: getinfo@haworthpressinc.com <Website: http://www.haworthpressinc.com>]*

Yumin Jiang is Cataloging Librarian for Serials and Electronic Resources, Albert R. Mann Library, Cornell University.

Jeanne A. Baker is Head, Serials Cataloging Unit, McKeldin Library, University of Maryland, College Park.

Lynda S. Kresge is Head, Database Management, and Coordinator of OCLC/RLIN Operations for the Harvard College Library, Harvard University.

[Haworth co-indexing entry note]: "Toward Better Access to Full-Text Aggregator Collections." Kresge, Lynda S. Co-published simultaneously in *The Serials Librarian* (The Haworth Press, Inc.) Vol. 38, No. 3/4, 2000, pp. 291-297; and: *From Carnegie to Internet2: Forging the Serials Future* (ed: P. Michelle Fiander, Joseph C. Harmon, and Jonathan David Makepeace) The Haworth Press, Inc., 2000, pp. 291-297. Single or multiple copies of this article are available for a fee from The Haworth Document Delivery Service [1-800-342-9678, 9:00 a.m. - 5:00 p.m. (EST). E-mail address: getinfo@haworthpressinc. com].

AGGREGATOR'S AT CORNELL

Noting that aggregators bring better access to titles but provide many new challenges for librarians, Yumin Jiang described how Cornell librarians are meeting those challenges. Following the library's decision to subscribe to ProQuest Direct in 1997, Jiang was assigned to look into how best to provide enhanced access to individual serials titles in the ProQuest database (1,600 journals in ABI/Inform and 2,000 journals in Periodical Abstracts). She designed a cataloging project, which ran from October 1998 to February 1999, and which ultimately became a cooperative project involving almost every library department, including three technical services processing centers. Her description of the Cornell project covered decisions made on a variety of issues that libraries need to consider when undertaking a similar cataloging project.

Access Options. Since Cornell's OPAC runs on NOTIS, which does not allow hotlinks directly from the bibliographic record, librarians set up a Library Gateway for networked resources on the Web. In addition to listing all Web resources by broad category, the Gateway also provides keyword access [1]. For ProQuest titles, librarians created a searchable title list (including serials title, ISSN, coverage dates, etc.). Cornell chose the single bibliographic record (instead of the separate record) approach for the ProQuest titles, because the library already subscribes to most of the ProQuest titles in print or on CD-ROM, and catalog records for these versions were already in the OPAC.

Catalog Record. Cornell added the following fields to the bibliographic record: 506 (access restrictions), 530 (availability of other versions), and 856 (URL). In order to minimize maintenance, Cornell decided to script the URL to the database level (i.e., use the URL for ProQuest Direct in the 856 instead of the specific URL of the individual serials title). The 899 field (local series) pulls together titles in one aggregator collection (for example "UMIPeriodicalAbs"). In addition, Cornell chose to establish open-ended holdings information, recording the date, volume and issue number of the earliest full-text volume of ProQuest coverage.

Cataloging Process. Cornell catalogers designed an efficient workflow, making heavy use of macros. Student assistants search ProQuest, verify holdings, record the first volume and issue, and perform basic updating on existing NOTIS records. Catalogers revise student work and create copy and original records for titles not already in the OPAC. Title changes are handled by creating linking fields in the bibliographic records and notes in the holdings records. Titles available electronically from several different online collections are recorded on a single bibliographic record by using multiple 856 and 899 fields.

Long-Term Maintenance Problems. Jiang identified potential maintenance problems, including selective coverage of a title by a particular database. She also suggested that database vendors provide more detailed information about title and holdings coverage, because libraries cannot examine every title closely. Also problematic are journal title changes; changes in the years of coverage for individual titles; and changes in the titles included in the aggregator collection.

Project Summary. Cornell saw dramatic increases in use as a result of their ProQuest project. In the first quarter, comparisons with the previous year's use statistics showed that gateway hits doubled on ABI/Inform and quadrupled on Periodical Abstracts. In addition, the number of full-text articles viewed from the two databases tripled in the first year. Librarians believe that a combination of factors is responsible for these statistics: improved cataloging in the OPAC, better user instruction by librarians, and increased familiarity with the collection by users. The success of the ProQuest Project has led to other similar undertakings at Cornell. One hundred and ninety titles in the Springer Link collection were cataloged using the single-record approach; the project was completed in spring 1999. Eighty titles in the ACM Digital Library collection were cataloged, using both single and separate-record techniques for serials and monographs. A cataloging project for 210 titles in the IDEAL Collection is in the planning stage.

Jiang concluded that enhanced access to aggregator collections is both possible and worthwhile, but each collection needs to be evaluated and dealt with individually, depending on its scope and nature. Cataloging projects like Cornell's require considerable resources and long-term commitment. Staff must be flexible and creative, and cooperation across departments is crucial to success. Jiang's advice to libraries considering such projects includes:

1. Study the full-text database and the library's own collections.
2. Investigate all access options and library staff resources while taking into account users' specific needs and the library's policy for processing electronic resources.

3. Design efficient workflow and time-saving strategies for implementing the project.
4. Keep your eyes on the ultimate goal: to provide better access to library collections.

PCC TASK GROUP

Jeanne Baker, member of the PCC Task Group on Journals in Aggregator Databases, led attendees through the Task Group's work to date in defining and designing a useful and cost-effective aggregator analytic record. Details about the group's charge may be found at http://lcweb.loc.gov/catdir/pcc/aggregatortg.html; their Interim Report, dated May 1999, is available at http://lcweb.loc.gov/catdir/pcc/aggupdrpt.html.

A CONSER Task Force survey of CONSER libraries during the summer of 1998 indicated that its libraries were providing access to full-text titles in aggregator collections in a variety of ways: adding single and separate records to OPACs, adding title lists to library Websites, and compiling paper guides. Late in 1998 the Task Force conducted a survey of the broader library community and presented the results at ALA Midwinter 1999. This survey revealed that 71% of libraries want titles in the OPAC for full-text journals in aggregator collections, and 72.6% expressed interest in purchasing record sets. Following this report, EBSCO volunteered to participate in a demonstration project to create and load aggregator records. Consequently, the CONSER Task Force was expanded and became the PCC Standing Committee on Automation (SCA) Task Group on Journals in Aggregator Databases, with "responsibility for recommending vendor record content, for demonstrating the feasibility of automated generation of record sets, and for communicating preliminary specifications to the appropriate vendors" [2]. EBSCO and the Task Group have been working ever since to mount a test file for the demonstration site; their goal is to finish by December 1999.

Baker pointed out that the test file records will be vendor records, not necessarily available through bibliographic utilities like OCLC and RLIN. The Task Group's working assumption is that they are creating a file of electronic records that could stand alone in an OPAC; however, each record will contain enough information to enable a library to develop a matching algorithm to allow the transfer of electronic record information to a print record already in the library's OPAC and/or to enable easy identification and deletion of records if needed. Baker acknowledged that some online systems will require some local customization of the records. For example, the University of Maryland will add an 049 field and a 949 field to these records, since the ILS software expects to load OCLC records. She also pointed out that some maintenance would likely be needed after loading these records. EBSCO's records, for example, may contain both successive and latest entry records for the same title, so a library that has not used latest entry records in its OPAC may want to produce a loader report for all latest entry records (records where S/L = 1).

The Task Group has drawn up a list of proposed data elements, and plans to have a final list available for vendors at the ALA Annual Meeting in June 1999. They also have identified specific issues concerning some of the data elements, including which fields to use for deduplication (or deduping); what encoding level to use; and where to record holdings' information. Baker reviewed several of the key fields in their list:

- Fields identifying the aggregator: Leader 07 (= b, for serial component part); 001 (vendor control number); 003 (identifies the vendor whose control number is in the 001).
- Fields taken from the print record: Encoding level ("2" for records derived from CONSER print records, "z" for others); 1XX, 240, 245 (plus $h computer file), 246, 250, 260, 310, 4XX, some 5XX (not 510), 6XX, 7XX, 8XX.
- Fields needed for deduping: 022 (use ISSN of the print version); 035 (OCLC, RLIN, LCCN).
- Fields indicating electronic aspects: Use 006, 007, and 773 for the title of the aggregator database. Note that subfield "g" is "required if applicable." For many databases this subfield will not be used, because there is no exact physical location in the database where the journal or journal article resides); 856 $3 (use for holdings coverage), $u, $z.
- Fields for records not built from print records: all of the above, but use 653 and 720 for 6XX and 7XX entries not under authority control.
- Fields needed to perform maintenance: Leader 05 for ongoing maintenance ("n" = new, "c" = corrected, "d" = delete); 035 (vendor ID for the file of aggregator records, needed to delete the file as a whole).

Field 130 is not included, because the records are not required to follow AACR2 rules; field 510 also is not included, because it applies mostly to print indexes.

In conclusion, Baker offered the following list of advantages of aggregator records:

1. The library's print holdings are extended by the addition of electronic holdings, giving the patron "one-stop shopping" by using the OPAC as a gateway to electronic resources.
2. The vendor does the tracking in title changes, deletion/addition of titles, and changes in holdings coverage.
3. Maintenance is easier for the library, because it can be automated.
4. Statistics to track database usage can be generated by reports from the OPAC.

The Task Group's next steps include giving presentations at the ALA Annual Meeting as well as at the annual meeting of the American Association of Law Libraries, meeting with other vendors, and soliciting feedback from all audiences. They will be evaluating the demonstration project, and keeping an eye on other developing standards, such as the Digital Object Identifier (DOI). The University of Maryland is planning a separate-record test load of EBSCO's aggregator analytic records. A single-record test load may take place at another institution later this year.

DISCUSSION

General discussion following the presentations focussed on how cataloging decisions are made at the institutional level, where so much depends on staffing goals and financial resources; whether Project Muse and JSTOR fit the new definition of aggregator collections (i.e., any collection put together by a vendor); potential problems for deduping–if the 035 field is already used for other library automation processes, such as the overlaying of records; how to deal with OPACs that don't use USMARC holdings (so the 856 is not represented in the bibliographic record as holdings); problems with titles where coverage is a moving target and libraries have therefore chosen not to trace holdings; and issues with unstable URLs.

NOTES

1. Cornell's Library Gateway may be accessed at: http://campusgw.library.cornell.edu/ Cornell's cataloging procedures for networked resources are available at: http://www.library.cornell.edu/tsmanual/gwcatalog/netcatinst.html.

2. PCC Standing Committee on Automation (SCA), Task Group on Journals in Aggregator Databases. "Interim Report." May 1999. http://lcweb.loc.gov/catdir/pcc/aggupdrpt.html (2 May 1999).

If It's Legal, It's Probably a Serial

Janet McKinney

Workshop Leader

David M. Bynog

Recorder

SUMMARY. Legal materials often have special considerations within a library's collection. A background and understanding of the producers of these materials and the multiple formats available is beneficial to those who work with these items. This workshop presented an overview of these materials as well as information pertaining to collection development and handling of legal items. *[Article copies available for a fee from The Haworth Document Delivery Service: 1-800-342-9678. E-mail address: getinfo@haworthpressinc.com <Website: http://www.haworthpressinc.com>]*

Janet McKinney began by describing this workshop as the culmination of what she had learned in eight years as a law librarian. The workshop was designed to introduce the audience to legal materials and help them understand the abundance of information produced by the government. She started with a brief refresher on the three branches at the federal level and most state levels to illustrate the complexity of and relationships among all sources of law.

Janet McKinney is Director of Collection Resources, Leon E. Bloch Law Library, University of Missouri-Kansas City.

David M. Bynog is Assistant Acquisitions Librarian, Fondren Library, Rice University.

[Haworth co-indexing entry note]: "If It's Legal, It's Probably a Serial." Bynog, David M. Co-published simultaneously in *The Serials Librarian* (The Haworth Press, Inc.) Vol. 38, No. 3/4, 2000, pp. 299-303; and: *From Carnegie to Internet2: Forging the Serials Future* (ed: P. Michelle Fiander, Joseph C. Harmon, and Jonathan David Makepeace) The Haworth Press, Inc., 2000, pp. 299-303. Single or multiple copies of this article are available for a fee from The Haworth Document Delivery Service [1-800-342-9678, 9:00 a.m. - 5:00 p.m. (EST). E-mail address: getinfo@haworthpressinc.com].

GOVERNMENT

The U.S. government comprises three branches: the legislative, the judicial, and the executive. The legislative branch produces multiple versions of bills. These bills, originally produced on sheets of paper, are known as slip laws. When bills are passed, they are then printed and bound in chronological order into session laws. These laws may also be codified into subject groupings, or titles. Thus one bill dealing with different subjects may be located in several titles. Regulatory agencies, such as the Internal Revenue Service, also have the power to create rules and regulations. Proposed and finalized rules are published in the *Federal Register*. When fully finalized they are published in the *Code of Federal Regulations*.

The judicial branch rules on cases based on statutes and laws. Judges use the principle of *stare decisis*, or precedent, to make decisions about points of law based on similar facts and rulings. These decisions are published as slip opinions until the bound volumes appear. Most cases are additionally printed in reporters. Judges can also produce opinions rendering statutes and laws ineffective. Congress may then attempt to pass modified versions of these laws.

McKinney also emphasized that librarians must be extremely careful not to practice law. Even if the librarian holds a JD he may only point the patron to various legal resources but may not interpret or prescribe an appropriate resource. Even advising patrons which legal forms to use falls under this heading of unauthorized practice of law.

FORMATS OF MATERIALS

The nature of the legal system is such that it produces a great amount of legal information. Governments themselves may publish this information, increasingly in electronic formats, or they may turn to commercial providers. Commercial providers may also publish treatises which may include additional commentary and annotations to the law. McKinney underlined the importance of knowing the official and authoritative source of the law. Since laws may be printed in these multiple formats or by multiple sources, it is imperative to provide citations to the official source if you are using one of the various edited versions.

She then discussed the various formats in which legal materials may appear. She supplemented her discussion by showing actual physical copies of several of these items. Bound volumes gather legal information, effective as of a certain date, into one source. Unfortunately, since the law is constantly changing, printing new bound volumes is not always feasible. Many of these bound volumes have slits in the back, which can accommodate supplements called pocket parts, which update the bound volumes. Publishers can continue to issue these until the volume becomes too thick. At this point a new bound volume is needed. Advance sheets are paperback volumes, which are produced between bound volumes and may have citations to the bound volumes. When the information is cumulated into the next bound volume these advance sheets may be thrown away. Softbound supplements may also update bound volumes. Loose-leafs enable easy updating and interchanging of materials in lieu of bound volumes. These are often more complicated than merely inserting new pages; filing instructions must be carefully followed.

In addition to print items, electronic versions are becoming abundant. Subscription type services such as Lexis/Nexis, as well as CD-ROM and Web-based information are proliferating. CD-ROMs are popular, particularly among law firms, and may be updated monthly or quarterly by a cumulative CD-ROM. Web-based products often have the most current information and provide the luxury of being accessible to patrons outside of the library or law office. McKinney concluded the electronic segment by hypothesizing about the role of DVD format for legal materials. Though she knew of no current commercial publishers providing items in this format she mentioned that the Patent and Trademark Office has announced it will move some of its materials to DVD format.

COLLECTION DEVELOPMENT

McKinney indicated that the same criteria for selecting other library materials are important for legal materials. Your clientele, community, and budget are factors, as well as the costs of all materials including updates, new editions, and related materials. McKinney quoted several figures from several resources, which noted the rising cost of legal materials.

When selecting legal materials many sources serve as excellent guides. Traditional resources such as *Books in Print*, book reviews, book stores, and good approval plans are such sources. There are also specialized sources such as "*Law Books and Serials in Print,*" "*Recommended Publications for Legal Research,*" and the Government Printing Office. Electronic resources such as publishers' Webpages and AcqWeb (http://www.library.vanderbilt.edu/law/acqs/acqs.html) are additional resources.

McKinney also gave a list of basic resources that would be useful for most libraries to collect. Primary sources for the law include state statutes and codes, state regulations, the *United States Code*, and the *Code of Federal Regulations*. Because this last item takes up much shelf space she recommended collecting selected titles in specific areas. She also discussed the usefulness of buying annotated sources, which are easy ways to access specific cases. Secondary sources of the law include a law dictionary, treatises, encyclopedias, how-to books, and sample forms. McKinney cautioned that resources should be kept up-to date, or your library could be held liable for any erroneous information. Electronic resources available via the Internet warrant specialized consideration in the selection process. How reliable and authoritative is the information? Is a specific Website stable? She indicated that Websites that end in .gov or a specific state (e.g., .mo or .la) are typically reliable sources.

When purchasing materials, McKinney mentioned that often you might need to go directly to the publisher for certain items. Vendors, both specialized and general, often carry legal materials. McKinney cautioned buyers to pay close attention to the pricing of items when ordering, due to possible additional costs for updating. She recommended trying to purchase comprehensive subscriptions where updates are built into the initial price.

PROCESSING

McKinney briefly discussed problems with cataloging and receiving legal materials. The decision to catalog an item as a serial or a monograph is a concern. The Library of Congress's K schedule, where most legal materials are cataloged, is relatively new. The H and J call numbers also include many legal items. The irregularity of legal materials can make publication patterns of materials difficult to predict. Many libraries have multiple check-in records for the various components of an individual title. Filing, shelving, and the retention of legal materials create added problems. When items are superseded, there may be historical purposes for keeping them, but it is important to clearly mark these materials as superseded, so that patrons do not rely on outdated information.

CONCLUSION

When concluding the workshop, McKinney mentioned that the complex nature of legal materials constantly keeps librarians on their toes. It is important to keep in mind that the mission of libraries is to serve their patrons and that legal material makes up a segment of needed information. Several participants asked McKinney to clarify certain statements. One audience member wanted a further delineation of what constitutes official materials. McKinney stated that while many governing bodies issue authoritative items themselves, as long as they have given a contract to a commercial publisher, then it is considered official. She mentioned that the *Mississippi Code*, which had been officially published by West Publishing, was recently switched over to Lexis Law Publishing by the state. Lexis thus reproduced the code, which duplicated the information most libraries already had in the West volumes. Several audience members mentioned that they are currently holding onto their West editions until Lexis makes further changes, making the purchase of new additions more practical and affordable. Another audience member asked if it was acceptable to give patrons the correct tax form to use. McKinney stated that even this action could be misconstrued as unauthorized practice of law. It is best to merely point a patron in the direction of the forms and let him decide which one is the correct one for his or her needs.

Looking a Gift Horse in the Mouth: Collection Management Following a Statewide Purchase of Electronic Resources

Nancy Newsome
Jill Ellern

Workshop Leaders

Jeffrey S. Bullington

Recorder

SUMMARY. The introduction of a statewide electronic resources collection and its impact on one institution's serial use study is examined. The Hunter Library at Western Carolina University embarked on a serials-use study at the same time that North Carolina introduced a new statewide collection of electronic resources (NCLive) including many full-text serials. This session gave an overview of the serials collection development cycle at WCU, the impact that NCLive will have on that process, and how data is collected, managed, and analyzed for serials collection development. *[Article copies available for a fee from The Haworth Document Delivery Service: 1-800-342-9678. E-mail address: getinfo@haworthpressinc.com <Website: http://www.haworthpressinc.com>]*

Nancy Newsome is Serials Librarian at the Hunter Library, Western Carolina University.

Jill Ellern is Systems Librarian at the Hunter Library, Western Carolina University.

Jeffrey S. Bullington is Social Science Librarian at the University of Kansas.

[Haworth co-indexing entry note]: "Looking a Gift Horse in the Mouth: Collection Management Following a Statewide Purchase of Electronic Resources." Bullington, Jeffrey S. Co-published simultaneously in *The Serials Librarian* (The Haworth Press, Inc.) Vol. 38, No. 3/4, 2000, pp. 305-311; and: *From Carnegie to Internet2: Forging the Serials Future* (ed: P. Michelle Fiander, Joseph C. Harmon, and Jonathan David Makepeace) The Haworth Press, Inc., 2000, pp. 305-311. Single or multiple copies of this article are available for a fee from The Haworth Document Delivery Service [1-800-342-9678, 9:00 a.m. - 5:00 p.m. (EST). E-mail address: getinfo@haworthpressinc.com].

To start, Nancy Newsome provided an overview of the serials collection development process in use at the Hunter Library, Western Carolina University (WCU). Collection development follows a three-year cycle at the Hunter Library, and involves consultation and review with faculty, incorporating cost and inflation review, course review (which includes faculty and librarians), and analysis of local library consortia holdings. Librarians have the final say on serial cancellations, but the faculty is heavily involved in the process.

The Hunter Library shares a common catalog system with two other University of North Carolina System schools, UNC-Asheville, and Appalachia State University. All three institutions participate in a courier service for expedited document delivery and interlibrary loan between campuses. Serials collection development projects completed at the Hunter Library include: the cancellation of *Mathematical Reviews* (replaced with an STN database); the cancellation of *Chemical Abstracts* (replaced with Carl Uncover); and the decision to support two degree programs, a Master of Science in Communication Disorders, and an Education Doctorate, entirely through document delivery (unlimited Uncover and Reveal).

SERIALS USE STUDY

The Hunter Library decided to embark on a major use study of serials to effectively manage the periodical collection and ensure its relevancy to student, faculty, and community needs as well as address budgetary concerns. It was hoped that a use study would indicate titles that received little or no use, titles that received use of current issues only, and titles that received heavy use.

Methodology. The study was designed to take two years and began during the spring 1998 semester, with data sets being collected by semester blocks. Nancy Newsome suggested that one should set and commit to a study time frame in advance, and that a minimum of a one-year study is necessary. To study periodical use, serials were bar-coded (one barcode for each bound volume and one barcode for all current issues in any serial title). The bar-coding preparation, a joint effort between the Cataloging and Serials units, began in the spring of 1997 and took one year to complete. All serials were included in the use study with the exception of some microfilm collections and the Reference/Index titles (Ms. Newsome did note that the

Reference Department now wants to conduct a similar study for the Ref/Index titles.)

Campus cooperation. The Serials Department needed to work with several other campus partners for a successful study. Those partners were Circulation, a statistician, the library Systems Office, and the campus Computing Center. Circulation provided the front line data gathering. Materials were gathered from tables and other library areas and brought to Circulation, where they were counted using the Innopac system's "Count IN-LIBRARY use" function. Print issues of newspapers were excluded from the study, but microfilm was counted. The changes in Circulation workflow required additional staff hours, another workstation in circulation for checking in items, and additional training and orientation for circulation staff. Work with a consulting statistician, a statistics faculty member, was needed to gain some idea of the data types to collect, to help determine data fields and layout, and to work with the library once real data was collected. The Systems Librarian provided knowledge and expertise on database software structure and management (for this study, MS Access), database creation, data loading, report generation, and problem solving. The campus Computing Center helped the library decide on appropriate software for the database, provided technical support for that software, and offered basic training workshops for all appropriate library personnel. Finally, the Serials Unit identified the desired data types, handled problem information and cleanup, and came up with report ideas.

NCLive and its impact on use study. During the spring 1998 semester, shortly after the serials study got underway, the library communities of North Carolina introduced a new statewide consortium of electronic resources, NCLive. Some of the resources included in NCLive, and now available to the WCU community through the Hunter Library, included EBSCOHost, UMI ProQuest, and FirstSearch among others. NCLive is funded as a separate budget item by the North Carolina State Legislature, and is available to academic and public libraries in the state. What impact would NCLive have on the serials use study and on serials collection development in the Hunter Library? What new doors of opportunity would NCLive open up for the library and users?

The decision was made to incorporate NCLive data into the study, and attempt to determine if these new resources had an impact on use patterns for library serials. NCLive information, including titles-available data in Excel format, is available at the NCLive information Website [1]. The Excel file includes data on all serial titles available through the various NCLive resources including start and stop dates for abstracts and full text if available. Nancy and Jill hoped NCLive would be able to provide use or hit count statistics, matching between titles and OCLC numbers, and some additional indications as to a title's audience and content level.

Creating the database. Jill Ellern described creating the database. The important steps in creating the database included the downloading or collecting data, massaging and cleaning up the data, importing it into MS Access, connecting data elements together, creating reports, and adding in or linking to other data. The data is gathered on a semester basis, and makes use of the Innopac system statistics features.

Problems with the data gathered using Innopac include the inability to distinguish data from individual campuses, Innopac cumulates data from all three campuses (WCU, UNC-Asheville, and ASU), and the data is not time-stamped. The system's record-keeping functions were used to create a data set of items with an in-house use (IUSE) greater than zero and with a location at WCU. The needed data was pulled from the bib number, volume, and IUSE and LOC (location) fields for item records. Data was moved from the Innopac machine to a local PC using FTP software. Last fall (1998) the retrieval numbered 7000 records, and this past spring (1999) the retrieval was 8000 records. Data comes from Innopac in a particular format, but needs to be reformatted for importation into the database program [2]. MS Access could not handle tags such as an equals (=) sign and so those tags had to be removed.

Data cleanup. Data was imported into MS Word for cleanup using Word's search and retrieve function. Semester data (e.g., Sp98) was added to the records, and field names added to columns. The data was saved as text, then retrieved into and saved as an MS Excel worksheet. Finally, the worksheet was then loaded into MS Access to create the database [3]. Jill Ellern noted that it takes about 2 hours to cleanup a semester's worth of data. The migration of data through Word and then Excel is desired because Access "likes" Excel data much better than word processing data. Once data has been retrieved from Innopac and cleaned up, the IUSE field in Innopac records is reset back to zero, transfer files are deleted all along the process (in Innopac and local machines), and the data in Access is backed up.

Data collected. Currently, the Access file is at 42 MB and represents one and one-half years of data. Additional data collected from Innopac includes serial cost/price information (collected annually), and department assignments for serials (this was done once, and possibly will not be repeated). Data that was input directly into the MS Access database included full departmental information (department name, number of students and faculty, and departmental contact), the department codes used by the library, and subject headings used to describe serials. MS Access database tables are for title, use, price, department information (dept. code), department assignments, NCLive data (shelf list title key), and subject (shelf list title key.) The tables are indexed by the Innopac B-number (a bibliographic control number, assigned by the library system software, which does not correspond to the OCLC number). There is also a shelf list title index.

Using NCLive data. Making use of NCLive data presented some unique problems and challenges. The NCLive records have no B-number, nor do they make use of the OCLC number, so they had to be matched up to WCU titles via the shelflist index. Of 8059 records in the NCLive list, only 1097 matched exactly to WCU records. Another 475 records were matched with the shelflist title field, but only with corrections. A subject table presents problems as well, many of which are similar to those for the NCLive table. It would be indexed to the title table by the shelflist title field. Matching subject headings and creating a consistent, manageable subject list are two additional challenges. One possibility to handle this is to use a subject file created by the Hunter Library Reference Department that has 65+ subject headings. To date, the subject table has not been loaded or put into use.

Problems encountered so far with using the MS Access data include sorting reports by title; the shelf list field had to be added to make this happen. The problem of multiple bib records attached to an item makes massaging the data challenging. Adding new bib numbers to the database requires keeping an eye out for new titles added to Innopac and adding them directly to the database by hand. A zero-use title cannot divide into the serial cost and provide a cost per use figure (cannot divide a sum by zero). However, shelflist title matching remains problematic.

Cleanup projects underway include fixing prices; there are problems with combinations and with memberships. Zero (null) entries for zero use titles create problems for cost per use figures and still need resolution. Finally, the NCLive titles need to be analyzed and matched to WCU titles by hand.

Reports generated. The presenters next gave the audience a look at some live data views of their database. Nancy Newsome then explained some of the types of collection development reports that are created from the MS Access database. These include reports noting total use per calendar year for titles, total costs per calendar year, cost per use for departments, paper use of NCLive titles, marginal use titles, and full departmental information (including titles). Future uses of the data could include: a printed list of periodicals (would need to gather holdings data for this); a subject list of periodicals (once the subject headings question and table are solved); other types of reports as might be envisioned; and finally, posting data on the Web for others to see (use of MS Access will make this very easy). Examples of three report types (all departments sum of cost and use; Full Text NCLive marginal use titles; and total periodical use) are available for viewing at the WCU library Website [4].

Question period. The session ended with some time for comments and questions. One audience member suggested that setting one as the base figure instead of zero might solve the zero-use problem. Another participant asked whether the presenters had taken the use data to faculty yet, and if so, what their responses have been. To date, they have not shared this data with faculty, because the study is still underway. It will be interesting to hear the results from this study, and how the Hunter Library makes use of the information gained from the study.

NOTES

1. NCLive information is available at: http://statelibrary.dcr.state.nc.us/hottopic/nclive/nclive.htm. The link to the Excel file on titles is available from this page. (July 25, 1999).

2. Nancy Newsome and Jill Ellern, "How the Data Looks from Innopac" and "How We Want the Data to Look," NASIG Presentation SLIDES, http://www.wcu.edu/library/about/internal/presentations/nasig/SLIDES/ppframe.htm (July 25, 1999).

3. Examples of Innopac records and the format desired for importation into MS Access.

INNOPAC Record Format:

RECORD # = b16940568.
INTL USE = 1. LOCATION = cpbgf.

RECORD # = b16940568.
v.14(1980).
INTL USE = 1. LOCATION = cpbgf.

Desired record format for importation into a database program:

b16940568 v.8(1976) 1 cpbgf Sp98

b16940568 v.14(1980) 1 cpbgf Sp98

Bnumber Volume Use Location Semester

4. Nancy Newsome and Jill Ellern, NASIG Presentation REPORTS. http://www.wcu.edu/library/about/internal/presentations/nasig/REPORTS/(July 25, 1996).

Supporting E-Journal Integration Through Standards: The OCLC Reference Services Experience and Experiences from the Field

Deborah L. Bendig
Marjorie Hlava

Workshop Leaders

Marilyn Quinn

Recorder

SUMMARY. The development and use of standards for online systems supports the on-going integration of electronic serials with local library systems. Examples of standards having an impact on digital access are SGML, HTML, XML, the ISSN, Serial Item and Contribution Identifiers (SICIs), Z39.50, standards for serial holdings' statements, and MARC. The DOI (Digital Object Identifier) is also receiving much attention, especially in the area of serials' rights management. OCLC has directed its attention to standards in the development of the new version of its FirstSearch product. Numerous organizations are involved

---

Deborah L. Bendig is Manager, Databases and Collections Section, OCLC Marketing, Reference & Resource Sharing Division, OCLC.

Marjorie Hlava is President and Chairman of Access Innovations, Inc.

Marilyn Quinn is Bibliographic Control Librarian, Rider University.

[Haworth co-indexing entry note]: "Supporting E-Journal Integration Through Standards: The OCLC Reference Services Experience and Experiences from the Field." Quinn, Marilyn. Co-published simultaneously in *The Serials Librarian* (The Haworth Press, Inc.) Vol. 38, No. 3/4, 2000, pp. 313-322; and: *From Carnegie to Internet2: Forging the Serials Future* (ed: P. Michelle Fiander, Joseph C. Harmon, and Jonathan David Makepeace) The Haworth Press, Inc., 2000, pp. 313-322. Single or multiple copies of this article are available for a fee from The Haworth Document Delivery Service [1-800-342-9678, 9:00 a.m. - 5:00 p.m. (EST). E-mail address: getinfo@haworthpressinc.com].

in developing both generic and specialized standards to improve access and linking. *[Article copies available for a fee from The Haworth Document Delivery Service: 1-800-342-9678. E-mail address: getinfo@haworthpressinc.com <Website: http://www.haworthpressinc.com>]*

STANDARDS: DEVELOPMENT AND USE

Marjorie Hlava summarily described many of the schemes in what she called an "alphabet soup" of standards. The picture she presented was of "a very fluid field," in which standards for linking and describing digital documents are evolving steadily, but also more slowly than publishers, database designers, and libraries might wish. Her presentation provided numerous examples of what some of the standards look like in actual practice. Hlava said that ultimately standards will increase the availability of more resources by promoting seamless and less costly access to digital materials; the creation of platform-independent systems and portable data formats; and cheaper production costs.

Many of the standards mentioned in this workshop are concerned with accessibility through content analysis and description, document and issue identification, electronic data interchange for electronic commerce, and rights management. She listed examples of standards already in use: MARC, the ISSN, Z39.50, Serial and Contribution Identifier (SICI), PII, and serial holdings' statements. Newer standards include Standard Generalized Markup Language (SGML) and its derivative, Hypertext Markup Language (HTML), Hypertext Transport Protocol (HTTP), and extensible Markup Language (XML). In addition to the standards currently in use, others are evolving. Organizations such as OCLC (Dublin Core), the International Federation of Library Associations, UNESCO, and the European Union are concerned with creating international standards for metadata (the U.S. term) and data dictionaries (European term).

Most of the standards either in use or evolving are concerned with metadata for text; but metadata for non-textual data is also being developed. Consensus-driven groups working on specialized or generic metadata sets include, the Motion Picture Industry Association; the Song Writers Association; Interoperability of Data in E-Commerce Systems (INDECS); EDItEUR-EPICS; Book and Serials Industry Communications (BASIC) and Serials Industry Systems Advisory

Committee (SISAC); and the World Wide Web Consortium (W3C). INDECS, for example, is working on an overarching, generic structure or model for complex metadata of all kinds. Two other standards in development for non-textual data are the ISAN and the ISWC, both of which will be useful for rights management and for keeping track of work usage. The International Standard Audiovisual Number (ISAN) is being developed by ISO and is closely linked to the DOI initiative. The International Standard Work Code (ISWC) is a code to represent the intellectual content of a work in its original form along with all of its derivative formats.

DOI: DIGITAL OBJECT IDENTIFIER

The Digital Object Identifier (DOI) is another standard being developed which can be used for many applications related to identifying digital works and rights management for publishers involved in electronic commerce. The syntax is under consideration by the National Information Standards Organization (NISO), but there is disagreement over the kinds of material for which the DOI is appropriate. Serial publishers are already making use of DOI and are not willing to wait for all elements of the DOI to be defined. Unfortunately, development has been further complicated and politicized by assigning leadership to an International DOI Foundation (IDF) member who is also employed by Elsevier, as well as by the membership of the IDF board itself.

Hlava provided examples of the DOI "handles" (i.e., records which identify digital objects and Internet resources) and identified their components (i.e., the kinds of information included in the handles). DOI components include: title (of article), agent identifier (publisher), author(s), publication date, type (abstract, full-text, etc.), DOI genre, article identifier (PII, SICI, DOI, ISSN, CODEN), journal issue and pages. The DOI initiative has developed "resolver" software and "interceptor" filters, which allow a number in the "handle" to resolve the data deposited in a metadata database and then bounce data back to the user. In other words, when someone is using a client such as a Web browser, it initiates a link and the browser sends the handle to a handle system for resolution. The handle system contains a database of descriptive data (metadata); and resolution refers to the process whereby the system identifies the data associated with the handle, such as a

URL (e.g., a publisher's Website), and bounces the data back to the user with the interceptor software. One application of this system permits electronic exchange of copyrighted information.

MARKUP LANGUAGES: SGML, HTML, XML

Hlava spent a large portion of her presentation on the markup languages, SGML, HTML, and XML. Standard Generalized Markup Language (SGML) was created to provide a uniform publishing markup language and became an ISO standard (ISO 8879:1988). The standard for its derivative Document Type Definitions (DTDs) is currently being reviewed and is awaiting a vote (ISO 12083). HTML is a specific application and DTD for SGML. It has a limited set of elements, most of which are for formatting and display on the Web. It provides little information about the content, context, and structure of the documents, as well as very little added-value data. Basically, it is intended for Web presentation and does not work well for publishing. XML, on the other hand, is very flexible and portable, even more so than SGML. It works with Web browsers, embraces Unicode, and can provide multi-directional linking (e.g., XLink) to various formats (video, sound, etc.). The DTD for XML is called a schema, and there are distinctive schemas defined for XML (e.g., CDF, OFX). XML is very useful for various Web and industrial applications.

SGML: Hlava mentioned several advantages and disadvantages of SGML.

Advantages:

- It is platform and application independent and can share and repackage information.
- It is portable and flexible enough for international use.
- Front-end application is easy.

Disadvantages:

- SGML is complex and SGML-aware software is complicated, making it a challenge to maintain SGML documents.
- It is not Web friendly, since it lacks a mainstream, supportive browser like Netscape.

- Retrospective conversion of documents into SGML is expensive, bringing its cost close to that of cataloging with MARC.
- Supported style sheets are just coming out.

The basic parts of an SGML document are the SGML declaration of a Document Type Definition (DTD), such as HTML (enabling Web representation), and a document instance represented by a marked up title page. SGML supports a variety of linking styles and accommodates internal and external links. Basic elements of SGML used to mark up a journal article include:

- Structure (beginning and end of the article; chapter vs. section; title vs. content, etc.)
- Content (including information such as phone numbers, author names, title, legal and rights data)
- Added-value information (subject terms, indexing, document type, version, etc.)
- Format (bold, italics, center, etc.)

HTML: HTML is a specific application and DTD for SGML. It has a limited set of elements, most of which are for formatting and display on the Web. It provides little information about the content, context, and structure of the documents, as well as very little added-value data. Basically, it is intended for Web presentation and does not work well for publishing.

XML: XML, on the other hand, is very flexible and portable, even more so than SGML. It works with Web browsers, embraces Unicode, and can provide multi-directional linking (e.g., XLink) to various formats (video, sound, etc.). The DTD for XML is called a schema, and there are distinctive schemas defined for XML (e.g., CDF, OFX). XML is very useful for various Web and industrial applications. The big question is to what extent will the newer, more flexible XML replace HTML. A newer version of HTML, called Dynamic HTML (DHTML), will probably co-exist with XML in the near future. However, XML will probably replace use of SGML [1].

PDF: Another popular way to present data electronically is Portable Document Format (PDF). PDF is Web and user friendly and good at character and font recognition. The viewer is free, and it permits both video and sound. Its disadvantages are numerous, however, including its proprietary format, very limited editing capacity, primitive navigational tools, poor linking functions/ability, and it requires accompanying tools (such as Acrobat software, PDF Writer, Distiller, Postscript, etc.) for producing, viewing, downloading, printing, and manipulating documents.

Hlava concluded her presentation by briefly discussing the journal and database publishers who are providing digital document linking, such as the American Institute of Physics, Silver Platter, Academic Press, Ohiolink, and UMI. She also said that some publishers are using SGML and the DOI, while others, impatient for ISO compliant codes, are creating their own codes/mark-up languages. Standards, Hlava notes, may be evolving quickly, but not necessarily within the official channels of standards making organizations like ISO. Given these circumstances and others, Hlava is skeptical that standards organizations are currently accomplishing all that they should or could be accomplishing. While universal, seamless access to more and more resources is becoming a reality, platform-independent systems and portable data formats are not. While access costs for users appear to be decreasing, production is still expensive. Hlava recommends that librarians put more pressure on standards organizations and publishers to work toward seamless access to electronic resources.

OCLC'S USE OF STANDARDS IN FIRSTSEARCH AND ELECTRONIC COLLECTIONS ONLINE

Deborah Bendig presented OCLC's perspective on the development of "seamless access" to journal articles. She began by describing access in the library environment as a "distributed information model" where "no one owns it all." This environment is characterized by library users with access to virtual union catalogs; multiple vendors–no single vendor can satisfy all information needs; multiple sources of information–the library is not the only place to seek information; hypertext linking among resources, including journals; and the aggregation of information sources through library catalogs and Webpages. This environment is further distributed by the various paths users can follow to access full-text electronic information. These paths include direct links from the OPAC; from bibliographic or abstracting/indexing databases; or from library Web pages, article lists, and electronic reserve systems.

SEAMLESS ACCESS: ISSUES

Having established the environment in which the pursuit of seamless access is taking place, Bendig highlighted current issues influencing the provision of seamless access. These issues include the role of the MARC record, ISSNs, serials holdings' statements, linking strategies, standards, and authentication.

MARC. There are three issues related to MARC records and the quest for seamless access. The single versus multiple record debate: should single MARC records be used to provide access to electronic and print versions of a resource? [2]. Vendor-supplied MARC records versus library produced MARC records. The library community is leaning towards vendor-supplied records as suggested by The PCC (Program for Cooperative Cataloging) task group on defining elements for vendor-supplied records [3]. The use of MARC 856 is also being discussed, particularly definitions of subfields within the 856 [4]. Bendig noted that OCLC's WorldCat Collection Sets are currently being enhanced to provide sets of MARC records on demand for electronic resources, including journals distributed through full-text databases such as ABI/INFORM and OCLC FirstSearch Electronic Collections Online.

ISSN. Bendig discussed the assignment of ISSNs and the recent decision to assign a separate ISSN to the online version of a print serial. She was not entirely happy with this policy, because multiple ISSNs for the same journal title complicate electronic indexing and linking. Issues to consider include (1) whether or not the two versions are equivalent, (2) which ISSN is used in A&I records, (3) which ISSN to which to attach library holdings, (4) how to represent ISSNs in "master serial records." Additionally, given the use of the ISSN to identify and link directly to an online journal, there are problems related to journal title/ISSN changes. What happens to the journal contents under such circumstances? For browsing, does the data stay with the original ISSN in online systems, so users will have to look in two or more places for the entire contents of a journal? Or is it appropriate to move the data to a single location (while keeping the original publication information with each article) to facilitate browsing and retrieval?

Holdings' statements. Serial holdings' statements are another linking component of online journal systems, adding yet more complexity to the issue of linking. There are various sources of holdings' statements currently available to libraries: local system holdings, online union catalog holdings, and locally provided files of serial holdings. Moreover, different systems display different ANSI-specified levels: title-level holdings, volume-level holdings, and issue-level holdings.

Another complication is the availability of numerous options for linking to full-text. One can choose to connect by using native record numbers (e.g., ABI Inform), by using calculated identifiers such as the SICI (e.g., OCLC), by using proprietary linking processes based on bibliographic data elements, and by using the proposed DOI standard, to name only a few. Many questions need to be answered, such as which full-text service is the desired connection, i.e., the problem of the appropriate copy.

Z39.50. The advent of the Z39.50 standard has addressed the problem users have had searching and coping with multiple search systems. Full-text delivery in the Z39.50 environment is managed by an increasing number of enhancements to the Z39.50 protocol. For example, the GRS (Generic Record Syntax) format and record segmentation will help deal with delivery of large and/or complex records, such as PDF-formatted documents.

Seamless linking and full-text delivery will rely on improvements in authentication. IP address and password recognition is too limited and complicated for thousands of users on the Internet. Proxy servers solve some problems with remote access from various locations. Digital certificates and working with existing encrypted identification systems such as Kerberos are new solutions (under consideration at OCLC). The goal is to provide secure, efficient, and remote access to remote full-text.

Bendig continued by describing the OCLC Reference Services, the kinds of full-text availability with these services, and various linking mechanisms used by OCLC. A few examples of the kinds of full-text in the FirstSearch bibliographic databases include Wilson Select and UMI with native full-text, NetFirst and FactSearch with virtual full-text, and H. W. Wilson with a related but not really native full-text. Third party full-text, i.e., linking full-text to unrelated database citations, is also available (Wilson Select, UMI, Electronic Collections Online).

Linking in FirstSearch is currently done using a combination of bibliographic elements: ISSN, volume number, issue number, date of publication, title words, and page numbers. Linking in Electronic Collections Online uses a version of the SICI and does not show dead links to the users. That is, the users see links only when coverage matches their request and they subscribe to the journal. ECO (Electronic Collections Online) is currently linked to secondary databases such as EconLit, MEDLINE, PsycINFO and PsycFIRST, and Social Sciences Abstracts.

OCLC has completely reworked and rewritten the software for the new FirstSearch, which will begin in August. Development will continue, and additional functions and services will be phased in as they are developed. One of the new features is pay-per-view access to specific articles. In the new FirstSearch, OCLC will use SICI's to link all available full-text to all appropriate bibliographic records.

Other issues pertaining to linking have been discovered as OCLC works with linking. One such issue is the management of different representations of articles. This encompasses (1) handling the level of the item represented (e.g., book reviews); (2) data included in titles (e.g., prefixes, suffixes, title enhancements for subject content, collective titles for sections); (3) representation of special characters in titles; and (4) handling various versions/manifestations of the same titles.

Another issue is the provision of different kinds of information in different databases (issue numbers, page numbers, TOC title versus the "real" article title), the accuracy of the information, and the way that title and ISSN changes are handled. OCLC intends to refine the way it uses SICI's to allow for more precise matching and the ability to match articles that have fewer identifiable elements (e.g., no paging).

The future of linking can be seen in many FirstSearch developments. There is more full-text linking between databases. Users can choose between ASCII or image format in some cases. Searches make better use of SICI's and can default to the issue's TOC when an article is not found. There is increasing direct access to articles from external sites (beginning with ISI's Web of Science, and eventually other institutions' and individuals' pages).

The industry is also exploring new ways to find articles that do not have an identifier/locator. New look-up services are being developed to support linking by retrieving resources from outside the original database (e.g., PubMed's PubRef and PubLink for medical and other material).

Bendig recommended a report presented at the Second Workshop on Linkage from Citations to Journal Literature, held in February 1999. A summary is found at *http://www.niso.org/linkrpt.html*, and the complete working group paper is found at *http://www.lib.uchicago.edu/Annex/pcaplan/reflink.html*. This paper includes a discussion of the so-called "Harvard Problem," i.e., enabling a system to retrieve a preferred or appropriate copy of an article, when that article is available from numerous Internet resources.

Bendig concluded by saying, "As information becomes more and more distributed among systems, interoperability among those systems becomes crucial to providing seamless access to users. Creating and following standards is the best way to ensure this interoperability."

The presentations took up much of the allotted time due to the huge amount of information provided. The follow-up discussion, based on questions from the attendees, centered on the MARC holdings format and, specifically, the use of the 856 in the MFHD record. OCLC has worked with the 856 only in the bibliographic record so far, and Bendig recommended attending the NASIG Cataloging Node and reports on the 856 to come at the ALA Conference. It was clear from the discussion that the use and placement of the 856 depends greatly on the capabilities of the local systems.

The presenters stressed that librarians need to pressure standards organizations and publishers to get the work done which is needed to give us seamless access to journal literature.

NOTES

1. Hlava recommended *The SGML/XML Webpage* by Robin Cover as an excellent resource for learning more about these metadata languages: http://www.oasis-open. org/cover.

2. CONSER Working Group. Single or Separate Records? What's Appropriate and When?
http://www.test.library.ucla.edu/libraries/cataloging/sercat/conserwg

3. *Program for Cooperative Cataloging. Standing Committee on Automation. Task Group on Journals in Aggregator Databases Report. May 1999*. Defines minimum set of elements for vendor-supplied records. *http://lcweb.loc.gov/catdir/pcc/*

4. See MARBI Proposal No. 99-08. *Defining URL/URN Subfields in the MARC 21 Bibliographic Format*. May 14, 1999. http://lcweb.loc.gov/marc/marbi/1999/99-08.html

Forging the Future for Archival Concerns and Resource Sharing

Marjorie E. Bloss
Mary I. Wilke

Workshop Leaders

Teresa Arnold

Recorder

SUMMARY. This workshop presented a brief history, current projects, and some future goals of the Center for Research Libraries, which is based in Chicago, Illinois. Participants were invited to share their ideas on the many aspects of consortia development via a questionnaire and discussion. *[Article copies available for a fee from The Haworth Document Delivery Service: 1-800-342-9678. E-mail address: getinfo@haworthpressinc.com <Website: http://www.haworthpressinc.com>]*

Marjorie Bloss began the workshop with a brief overview of the handouts. There was a simple two-page questionnaire on consortia,

---

Marjorie E. Bloss is Vice President for Library Operations, The Center for Research Libraries.

Mary I. Wilke is Head, Acquisitions Department, The Center for Research Libraries.

Teresa Arnold is an account executive, Swets Subscription Service.

[Haworth co-indexing entry note]: "Forging the Future for Archival Concerns and Resource Sharing." Arnold, Teresa. Co-published simultaneously in *The Serials Librarian* (The Haworth Press, Inc.) Vol. 38, No. 3/4, 2000, pp. 323-331; and: *From Carnegie to Internet2: Forging the Serials Future* (ed: P. Michelle Fiander, Joseph C. Harmon, and Jonathan David Makepeace) The Haworth Press, Inc., 2000, pp. 323-331. Single or multiple copies of this article are available for a fee from The Haworth Document Delivery Service [1-800-342-9678, 9:00 a.m. - 5:00 p.m. (EST). E-mail address: getinfo@haworthpressinc.com].

designed specifically for use at the workshop. Participants were encouraged to complete the questionnaire at the workshop because, as Bloss explained, the Center for Research Libraries (CRL) is very interested in learning the wants and needs of their members, which are primarily the large research and university libraries. Also distributed was an informational brochure and fact sheet, both about the CRL, and a brochure for an upcoming conference on cooperative collection development. The conference will be hosted by the CRL and co-sponsored by numerous library groups, and held in mid-November 1999, in Atlanta, Georgia. The audience was also invited to take a decorative coaster, which had been produced in honor of the Center's 50th anniversary.

WHY CONSORTIA?

Both Bloss and Wilke started by commenting on why consortia have come into existence. Although admitting it was a cynical view, Bloss said that libraries cooperate because they need to, not because they want to. Libraries undertake cooperative ventures because of a lack of funds, and not because they want to work together. Bloss said the following reasons contribute to the growth of consortia: (1) the ever-increasing price of serials; (2) the need to purchase print and non-print material such as microfiche, microfilm, CD ROM and digitized material; (3) the growth of publishing in Europe; and (4) the reconfiguration of the Soviet Union which has led to duplication and replication of governmental offices.

Wilke agreed with this, saying that no library has enough money to buy and process everything it wants, a situation that has created a need for resource sharing and cooperation. The skyrocketing number of consortia formed during the past decade is evidence of the strength of this need. Wilke added that while the CRL was not the answer for every need, it may give people, including non-members, peace of mind to know that certain rare materials are being protected and preserved.

HISTORY OF THE CENTER FOR RESEARCH LIBRARIES

Marjorie Bloss continued with a brief history of the CRL. This year the Center is celebrating its 50th anniversary, but the concept goes back to the 1930s. It was then that thirteen mid-western university presidents began to look at the situation with their libraries and the possibility of having one facility. The concerns they had were: a lack of library shelf space; the need for library material in new formats, including microfiche and microfilm; and the desire to coordinate the purchase of new and more expensive reference materials. To address these concerns, the Carnegie Corporation funded a study in the early 1940s to determine the feasibility of such a group.

Because the library directors were somewhat reluctant to give up their materials, it was not until about seven years later that action was taken. By this time, space was really at a premium and a decision was made to pool resources and build off-site storage. It was planned that material in storage at this facility would be freely accessible and available for use when requested by patrons. In 1951 the Mid-West Interlibrary Center (MILC) was opened. It was a state-of-the-art, temperature controlled, closed stacks, compact storage facility. By 1962 the idea had extended beyond the mid-west and libraries across the U.S. wanted to participate. At this time the name was changed to the Center for Research Libraries.

Bloss enumerated the accomplishments of the program. Today the Center houses a large, strong research library collection with comprehensive coverage of various types of material such as foreign dissertations, foreign newspapers, scholarly journals, repository collections, and area study collections. The foreign language (non-English) material is particularly important, because as library budgets shrink, holdings of foreign language materials have decreased. Bloss explained that in most libraries, newspapers, which are printed on very poor quality paper, are held for only six months to one year and then discarded. Having made a commitment to collect unusual materials such as these, the CRL is filling a gap. The Center facilitates expert national collaboration among research libraries, which is evidenced by such programs as their Area Study groups. Another function of the Center is to act as the administrative agent in helping member libraries and groups to obtain grants. The Center is incorporated and therefore can handle the acquisition of grant money for members.

Today the Center has 208 members and a collection of over 5.5 million items. It is both a consortium and a research library, and its members include other consortia. The CRL has focused on collecting materials in paper, microfilm, and microfiche. While there has been a lot of interest in collecting digitized materials, and the Center has explored this option, Bloss pointed out the necessity of focusing on particular goals. Recalling Vicki O'Day's discussion of information ecologies, Bloss said that when faced with implementing new technologies, it is important to look at how the pieces fit together and to ask whether having the new technology is relevant to achieving the desired goals. The Center's limited funds were cited as another reason for maintaining well-defined goals.

AUDIENCE PARTICIPATION IN CONSORTIA

Mary Wilke then asked the audience to comment on their participation in consortia. The majority of the audience participants were members of at least one consortium. One person stated that in addition to being a member of CRL, their institution also had agreements with two other universities. Another audience member said their university library participated in a consortium for electronic resource sharing on a statewide level. This consortium aided their members by providing training guidelines for cataloging electronic resources. An audience member from Great Britain said that their university belonged to a regional consortium, a larger national consortium for higher education libraries, and also shared resources for particular programs such as Nursing. A state university program for sharing materials across fifteen campuses, with an emphasis on digital resources, was described. Bloss noted that there are many types of consortia in existence, categorized by type of library, region, or subject specialty. Their function can be resource sharing, or interlibrary loan, or preservation, or cooperative acquisition and collection development activities. Often these activities overlap.

SPECIAL PROJECTS OF THE CRL

Marjorie Bloss then spoke about the Center's involvement with ICON–the International Coalition on Newspapers. About ten years ago the first symposium on newspaper preservation and access was held in London. One hundred librarians, scholars, and publishers from around the world participated. It was acknowledged that while newsprint was not made to last, newspapers were valuable research materials and it was important to find a way to preserve them. It was not until May 1997, that another symposium on access to and preservation of international newspapers was held. This was a collaborative effort by the CRL, ARL, the Council on Library Information and Resources, and the Library of Congress.

From this symposium a working group developed. The group's first goal was to establish charter members for ICON, who would assume the collective responsibility for the preservation of newspapers, especially foreign newspapers. Letters have recently been sent out to potential charter members for this purpose. The second goal was to develop a Union List of non-United States newspapers. OCLC, a strong supporter of the USNP (United States Newspaper Project) will host the database for the Union List. Bloss explained that normally a contributor to a Union List in OCLC must have both the bibliographic record and the holdings information. However, OCLC now has another option called "group access." With group access, bibliographic records can be added first, and holdings can be added later.

The CRL, acting for ICON, submitted a draft for a grant to the NEH in May of this year. They have received a positive response to the draft, and plan to submit the complete grant proposal in July 1999. Part of the grant will be for a conference in 2000 on the preservation of digital newspapers.

An audience member asked how many titles were expected to be accessible in ICON. Bloss answered that a very rough figure would be 20,000 to 25,000, but at this point it was difficult to determine the amount of overlap. Nine out of the twelve charter members are members of CONSER. Some of the institutions most likely to become charter members are the British Library, the New York Public Library, the Library of Congress, and the National Library of Canada.

ELECTRONIC JOURNAL PROJECT

Bloss went on to describe another project of the CRL. The CIC (Committee on Institutional Cooperation) had begun a project to archive electronic journals. It was to be a closed archive containing approximately 120 titles. Eventually the CIC decided they did not want to continue with the project and the CRL began exploring the possibility of taking it over.

The first thing the CRL did was to determine copyright compliance for the material. They consulted with CRL legal counsel and then sent letters to the publishers of the electronic journals. They received responses for only 40% of the titles; the publishing status of the remaining 60% was unknown.

The project also had to be integrated into the CRL's acquisition process. It was necessary to determine how to keep track of check-in, changing URLs, and the inevitable process of migrating to new technology. The project also contained a broad spectrum of titles, and in the process of deciding whether to take the CIC project, it was suggested that the CRL maintain only those titles that fit with their other collection activities. The project is still under evaluation.

OTHER QUESTIONS

An audience member asked if CRL was planning to work with JSTOR to archive the paper part of their collection. The answer was that this was a possibility and that discussion was taking place, although nothing had been settled yet. Another question, asked by a Canadian, related to whether or not national libraries were going to increase their activities as depositories of library materials. The answer was that due to the logistics, it was unclear at this time. Another person wanted to know what it cost to access rare materials at the CRL. The answer was that members could submit an unlimited number of requests and borrow the material for an unlimited amount of time. For non-members the cost was $25.00 per loan within the U.S., and $30.00 per loan outside of the U.S. Non-members can submit up to ten requests per year and the loan period is four weeks. It was noted that these prices would probably be rising in the near future.

COSTS INCURRED BY CRL

Mary Wilke then brought the audience's attention to the fact sheet handout, which showed ballpark figures for adding and storing materials at the CRL. To add one volume, the cost is $250.00. This included receiving the title, cataloging (not original), and processing. The figure took into account time, staff, and supplies. To add a new volume to an existing title, the cost is $55.00. The annual storage fee per volume is $21.00. These figures reflect the special circumstances of the CRL, i.e., temperatures are kept very low and it is a closed stack collection.

SUPERSEDED REFERENCE COLLECTION

Wilke went on to describe another important function of the CRL, which is to collect and preserve superseded reference materials. She explained that while most libraries retain more than the latest edition of many reference titles, they are often forced to move superseded reference materials from the reference collection to the circulating stacks. The CRL maintains a collection of 25 non-current reference titles. They collect all editions or volumes of each title, from the beginning of publication, but not the most recent edition. This part of the collection is important because it helps CRL to meet its goal of organizing and preserving historical materials for research. In addition, libraries can free valuable space by weeding older editions or volumes of the titles available in this collection.

SRMP: SCIENCE RESEARCH MATERIALS PROJECT

The last project discussed was the very recent SRMP or Science Research Materials Project, an initiative suggested by Patricia Yocum at the University of Michigan. The SRMP departs from the usual CRL focus because it is subject-based rather than format-based (like ICON) or function-based (like CRL's Area Studies programs). The main impetus for this project is the exorbitant cost of STM serials in comparison with arts and humanities serials. While libraries can't cut material from their core collections, they can reduce the number of peripheral materials by coordinating their collections. This is a natural function for CRL to assume, as they have always specialized in collecting peripheral materials. Wilke explained that CRL is the facilitator for this group because they are a legally established entity and can legally act for a group like SRMP, e.g., CRL can apply for grants on behalf of SRMP. They are able to provide an environmentally controlled archive for access and preservation. The CRL enhances the ability of other libraries to build and maintain local collections with the assurance that complementary, rarely held materials are in a safe, secured print and/or electronic archive and are accessible to patrons.

An audience member asked if the parameters for the SRMP project had been established yet. The answer was that this would probably be done on a title by title basis. The group would be meeting in the fall of 1999 to discuss this. For now, they have decided not to include medical titles and to focus on science and technical titles. This project touches all areas of consortium work including preservation, interlibrary loan, collection development and acquisitions.

CRL AND OTHER CONSORTIA

Lastly, Marjorie Bloss stated that the CRL itself belonged to two library cooperatives, OhioLink and Orbis. OhioLink has loaded the holdings of a number of CRL's academic library members into one database. Because CRL's bibliographic file is now integrated with OhioLink, CRL is now following the same lending and borrowing patterns as OhioLink. A new pattern for the CRL is the ability for patrons to borrow hard copy monographs electronically. This is an experiment for the Center and so far it has been working fairly well.

The other consortium CRL has joined is Orbis, which is a group of libraries in Oregon and Washington. This will be similar to OhioLink. It is expected that CRL records will be loaded into that system by late July 1999. CRL is looking for a non-Innovative Interfaces group to join so they can gain experience with a system that is different from their own (both OhioLink and Orbis use an Innovative Interfaces system.)

CONCLUSION

In conclusion, Bloss and Wilke said that the CRL was not just for ARL libraries. They said all members of OhioLink had borrowed from their collection, including community colleges. While this is surprising to some, it seems to prove that patrons of non-research level libraries will use research level materials if access is provided. The CRL will continue to maintain a careful focus on the scope of their collection development. They also intend to move forward with improving the speed of delivery of materials in response to requests. This will be accomplished by improving their capability to scan material, and use e-mail or Ariel as delivery mechanisms. By giving the workshop, Wilke and Bloss said they hoped to underscore some of the current issues in consortia development and to emphasize the need for libraries to work together to meet their common goals.

Audience participation for this workshop was very good. A great deal of information was presented, and the audience interjected with questions at regular intervals throughout the workshop. The material presented was an excellent introduction to CRL and the complex aspects of consortia. In addition, the presenters were very enthusiastic about their subject, and were very receptive to audience participation.

WEB ADDRESSES AND CONTACT INFORMATION

Some publications, membership lists, and information about the collections and holdings can be found on CRL's home page: http://wwwcrl.uchicago.edu/

Information about the Superseded Reference Works Collection can be found at:

http://wwwcrl.uchicago.edu/info/supersededref/full.htm

Contact the Center:

The Center for Research Libraries, 6050 South Kenwood Avenue, Chicago, IL, 60637-2804, USA. Phone: 773-955-4545 Fax: 773-955-4339

Business hours are Monday-Friday, 9:00 AM to 5:00 PM (CST)

The Convergence of User Needs, Collection Building, and the Electronic Publishing Market Place

Jie Tian
Sharon Wiles-Young

Workshop Leaders

Elizabeth Parang

Recorder

SUMMARY. Success in meeting user needs was assessed at California State University, Fullerton, by means of a survey, and at Lehigh University by an examination of database usage statistics. Implications for service provision, user education, and collection building were discussed. *[Article copies available for a fee from The Haworth Document Delivery Service: 1-800-342-9678. E-mail address: getinfo@haworthpressinc.com <Website: http:// www.haworthpressinc.com>]*

INTRODUCTION

This workshop presented the results and discussed the implications of two user-needs assessments at two very different university li-

---

Jie Tian is Reference Librarian, California State University, Fullerton.
Sharon Wiles-Young is Team Leader, Information Organization, Lehigh University.
Elizabeth Parang, Coordinator of Periodicals, Pepperdine University Libraries.

[Haworth co-indexing entry note]: "The Convergence of User Needs, Collection Building, and the Electronic Publishing Market Place." Parang, Elizabeth. Co-published simultaneously in *The Serials Librarian* (The Haworth Press, Inc.) Vol. 38, No. 3/4, 2000, pp. 333-339; and: *From Carnegie to Internet2: Forging the Serials Future* (ed: P. Michelle Fiander, Joseph C. Harmon, and Jonathan David Makepeace) The Haworth Press, Inc., 2000, pp. 333-339. Single or multiple copies of this article are available for a fee from The Haworth Document Delivery Service [1-800-342-9678, 9:00 a.m. - 5:00 p.m. (EST). E-mail address: getinfo@haworthpressinc.com].

braries: California State University (CSU), Fullerton, and Lehigh University. Jie Tian of CSU Fullerton, described the results of her library's assessment of user needs based on a survey, while Sharon Wiles-Young based her comments on an examination of database usage statistics. Both speakers were interested in the convergence of user needs, electronic publishing and collection building. Despite the differences in the institutions and assessment tools, Sharon and Jie identified similar issues, trends, and discussion topics relevant to any library using electronic resources. Overall, Jie and Sharon found that electronic resources challenge librarians to balance competing demands, such as meeting the needs of many general users vs. meeting the more limited needs of specialized users; selecting full-text databases vs. indexes/abstracts; and choosing electronic vs. print materials.

BACKGROUND

Fullerton, one of the largest campuses in the CSU system, serves a mostly undergraduate population–over 21,000 of the more than 25,000 students were undergraduates in 1997/1998. In contrast, Lehigh University enrolled 4,000 undergraduate and 2,000 graduate students in 1998/1999. While the largest of the seven schools at CSU Fullerton are those in business and economics, Lehigh University has strong undergraduate programs in engineering, the sciences, and management, with a strong graduate program in education. Both campuses are "wired," with computer services or hook-ups available in all buildings including the dorms. CSU Fullerton provides access to its Web-based services for all students, including those off-campus, via Titian Access, the university's own Internet network provider.

Both Jie and Sharon noted that the availability of electronic resources has had a great impact on each of their libraries. At CSU Fullerton, the number of public workstations has increased from eight to eighty. The library provides access to 97 electronic resource databases that include indexes, abstracts and some full-text; 500 cataloged electronic journals; and 2,500 current print subscriptions. Lehigh has also increased the number of computers in its library and has upgraded computing equipment. The library provides Web-access to 85 databases–indexes, abstracts and full-text; 2,000 cataloged electronic journals; and 4,000 current print subscriptions.

FULLERTON'S ELECTRONIC RESOURCE USE SURVEY

In discussing user needs, collection building, and electronic publishing, Jie emphasized that while each area can be approached in isolation, it is more valuable to consider them together because they are interdependent. User needs for service and education, are influenced by the library's collection and by the rapid development of electronic publishing. For example, significant increases in the number of electronic resources at Fullerton prompted an electronic resource use survey. The survey was designed to determine what electronic resources were used and how relevant they were to the curriculum. Surveys were distributed during the end-of-semester peak (May 9-23, 1999) at three service points, and the Electronic Resources area.

The 265 survey responses indicated the most intensive users were students from the four largest schools–Humanities and Social Sciences; Business and Economics; Human Development and Community Services; and Communication. The largest user group was made up of students taking 300 level courses followed by those taking 400 level courses. These results correspond to the requests for instruction sessions during the same time period, most of which were made by upper-level students. Goals of the survey included determining what databases were used and if users focussed on full-text databases. Of the 97 databases available, survey respondents used 74. Full-text retrieval was a definite focus; the survey showed that 82% of database usage resulted in the retrieval of articles. Survey respondents used aggregated, full-text, interdisciplinary databases such as Lexis/Nexis and Expanded Academic ASAP most often. Business students were the heaviest users of databases, although they used neither Dow-Jones News Retrieval (available via Telnet at the time of the survey) nor electronic journals. Interestingly, with the introduction of the Web product, Dow-Jones Interactive, and the electronic journal collection JSTOR (both added after the survey), use of these resources has increased. Another goal of the survey was to gauge user satisfaction with electronic resources. Results showed that English majors and lower division students were most satisfied with the full-text databases, while upper-level students (400-level and above) were less satisfied. Upper-level students relied on traditional indexes and interlibrary loan rather than full-text electronic databases.

USAGE STATISTICS AT LEHIGH

At Lehigh, the usage statistics of electronic materials were gathered and analyzed to determine user satisfaction with electronic collection building decisions. These statistics were gathered on a number of electronic products, including Project Muse, JSTOR, Elsevier's PEAK (Pricing Electronic Access to Knowledge) Project, ACS (American Chemical Society), and IDEAL. The type of statistics gathered from each of these resources varies. In the case of Project MUSE, statistics on usage of individual titles were possible, while in JSTOR usage statistics related to subject area not individual titles were availaable. Of the Project MUSE collection, *American Journal of Mathematics*, followed by *Postmodern Culture*, were the titles used most frequently. In JSTOR, economics and business were the subject areas used most heavily, followed by math and history. The ACS package included 25 journals and showed hits on abstracts, tables of contents, and full-text with a breakdown by title. The titles in IDEAL showed little use at the time statistics were gathered, possibly because of server problems. Elsevier's PEAK Project reported statistics on titles used.

Sharon thought the use of JSTOR was high because librarians had featured it in bibliographic instruction sessions earlier in the year. Another factor thought to influence use of electronic journals was having titles cataloged, with records available in the OPAC. Usage statistics showed that as titles of electronic resources were added to the catalog, they were used immediately–even before publicity or promotion. Future projects at Lehigh will include analyzing usage by title; and comparing use of electronic titles with that of print titles.

IMPLICATIONS FOR SERVICE PROVISION

The results of the CSU Fullerton survey presented implications for library services, and suggested a need to expand user education. The survey indicated that many undergraduate students in general courses, such as Current Social Issues, were unable to find full-text resources to support their course work. However, librarians knew general course-work could be supported by the electronic resources at CSU, so they decided to integrate and promote the use of these electronic resources. Consequently, CSU made a change to their staffing in certain service areas; namely, a librarian was removed from the Reference Desk and stationed in the electronic resource area. Another change was the reorganization of instructional librarians into seven teams. Instruction sessions emphasized use of full-text databases and other electronic resources whenever appropriate; electronic resources were publicized; instructional Webpages were created; informal sharing of instruction experiences and instruction assessment was encouraged.

ORGANIZATION/ACCESS ISSUES

Two presentation methods commonly exist for electronic resources: catalog the titles for OPAC access and/or create Webpages. Librarians at Lehigh debated the issue of the Web vs. the catalog because they didn't have the resources to keep both up to date. The systems person developed a program to pull the electronic journal titles out of their online catalog and automatically add them to a Webpage listing of journal titles with URLs. URL maintenance is vital for such lists. However, reference librarians are now doubtful that a list of 2,000+ titles is really useful and are starting to create subject Webpages emphasizing indexes and abstracts.

The question of single versus multiple records should be considered when discussing access issues. Lehigh uses the single record approach whereby a single record is used for a title available in multiple formats. While this approach is convenient, it presents the problem of confusing holdings information, especially when a title is available in an aggregator database. Both Lehigh and CSU Fullerton add holdings statements for electronic journals to the print record if one exists. Jie noted that at CSU Fullerton all electronic journals are cataloged but full-text database titles are not.

Another issue related to access is the technical question of using IP addresses versus password access. Both librarians and vendors consider this issue important. In general, IP addresses are preferred to password access because it requires less effort on the part of the user; and less information has to be maintained for individual databases. Depending on the approach taken, privacy issues may arise; for example, some publishers ask for a great deal of personal information about users before issuing passwords. Use of a proxy server is another very effective method of providing access to databases, especially when student numbers are used as IDs. Proxy servers authenticate authorized students based on an ID and password.

COLLECTION DEVELOPMENT ISSUES

Electronic publishing has implications for collection development. The CSU survey showed that upper-level students were less successful than lower division students in finding appropriate full-text material, as suggested by upper-level students' reliance on document delivery. The survey also showed that certain subject areas were not well represented by electronic resources. These results suggest that more specialized electronic resources are necessary to support the research needs of more students. The value of mega-packages like Dow-Jones and Lexis-Nexis Academic Universe must also be considered by the collections librarian–are these collective databases meeting the needs of diverse user groups?

Duplication of resources is another concern for collection development. With so many aggregate and bundled databases available, an individual journal can be licensed to database producers, subscription agencies, archival services, and indexing/abstracting services. Using the *Harvard Business Review* as an example, Jie noted that it is available electronically in ABI Inform via ProQuest Direct; Business and Company ASAP; Dow-Jones Interactive Abstracts; Expanded Academic ASAP; Ebsco's Masterfile; and Lexis-Nexis. This same title is also available in print, microform, and perhaps as a stand-alone electronic journal. In the face of such choice, the library must decide which form or forms to purchase by examining both its collection development policy and its budget.

DISCUSSION

When asked if access to full-text titles had resulted in a drop in interlibrary loan requests, both Jie and Sharon indicated it had not. The CSU system has a document delivery service. Both faculty and graduate students are getting more interlibrary loans while undergraduates are getting fewer because less specialized material is available in full-text electronic form.

Sharon was asked if, once all JSTOR titles were cataloged, users were more satisfied. She replied that usage certainly went up as titles were cataloged, but that since it was not possible to determine if patrons were accessing the journals from Webpages or the OPAC, the impact of cataloging on user satisfaction could not be determined.

A discussion ensued as to whether libraries are canceling print in favor of full-text. A participant from Lamar University indicated they planned to drop one third of their print subscriptions in order to pay for the electronic access; they examined use statistics for print journals and are canceling those for which use has dropped. The University of Alberta canceled all print subscriptions for titles in Project Muse. The University of Toronto is adding paper subscriptions in science to meet demand; although full-text is available in the Elsevier product, students have to pay to print while document delivery is free.

RELATED RESOURCES

CSU Fullerton

Periodical Services: http://www.library.fullerton.edu/Periodicals_Services/period.html

Electronic journals: http://www.library.fullerton.edu/Ejournals/ejourn.html

California State University (consortia Websites): http://www.co.calstate.edu/irt/SEIR/index.html

Lehigh University

Electronic journals: http://www.lehigh.edu/~intext/ejournals/

New Subject pages: http://www.lehigh.edu/~intech/infodome/

Current Information on Scholarly Electronic Publishing Resources for Electronic Serials: http://info.lib.uh.edu/sepb/sepr.htm

Putting It All Together: The Involvement of Technical Services, Public Services, and Systems to Create a Web-Based Resource Collection

Steve Shadle
Alex Wade

Workshop Leaders

Susan Scheiberg

Recorder

SUMMARY. Steve Shadle and Alex Wade, of the University of Washington Libraries, presented an overview of the development and implementation of the Digital Registry of Web Resources, part of the University of Washington Libraries' Web Gateway redesign. The Registry, an SQL database derived from MARC records exported from the Libraries' cataloging system, also provides innovative services for the libraries' users and staff. The presentation was divided into two parts: Steve Shadle discussed the environment in which the decision was made to develop the Digital Registry and design considerations and de-

---

Steve Shadle is Serials Cataloger, University of Washington.
Alex Wade is Systems Librarian, University of Washington.
Susan Scheiberg is Team Leader, Serials Acquisitions, University of Southern California.

[Haworth co-indexing entry note]: "Putting It All Together: The Involvement of Technical Services, Public Services, and Systems to Create a Web-Based Resource Collection." Scheiberg, Susan. Co-published simultaneously in *The Serials Librarian* (The Haworth Press, Inc.) Vol. 38, No. 3/4, 2000, pp. 341-347; and: *From Carnegie to Internet2: Forging the Serials Future* (ed: P. Michelle Fiander, Joseph C. Harmon, and Jonathan David Makepeace) The Haworth Press, Inc., 2000, pp. 341-347. Single or multiple copies of this article are available for a fee from The Haworth Document Delivery Service [1-800-342-9678, 9:00 a.m. - 5:00 p.m. (EST). E-mail address: getinfo@haworthpressinc.com].

cisions made during its development; Alex Wade then presented implementation issues and functionalities of the Digital Registry, and discussed future projects.

ENVIRONMENT

Beginning in 1990, access to the University of Washington's library catalog and the majority of their bibliographic databases was provided through Willow, a locally developed interface using BRS software and data structures. At that time Willow had several important advantages–it provided a single, simple, powerful user interface to most online resources through a single network of X-terminals that were relatively simple and inexpensive to maintain.

However, several factors have recently caused the Libraries to question the viability of such a model. First, the University of Washington Computing and Communications Office would soon begin to charge for providing support and development for the Willow system, which they previously provided at no cost. Second, the pressures of using a Web-based delivery system were growing, and because Willow was based on a relatively closed tape-loaded system, integration with emerging Web-based services would be difficult and costly.

Perhaps motivated by the lack of organized Web access in the Libraries' online environment, some individual selectors and units developed Webpages of their own. As these pages grew, several problems became evident. There was often an overlap of resources in the various Websites, resulting in duplication of effort when hyperlinks changed or became outdated. Further, because individual selectors had their own preferences and abilities in designing their Websites, there was great variance in style and content. Additionally, the Websites often became too large for individuals to maintain without some assistance. Thus, the Libraries considered a centralized approach to the Libraries' Web presence.

DIGITAL REGISTRY DESIGN

Because electronic journals were a ubiquitous component of the disparate Web spaces, the initial plan was to construct an e-journals database which would not only centralize maintenance and production of e-journal Webpages, but would also support links to library holdings and full-text resources. However, the database was soon reconceptualized to integrate all forms of electronic resources such as abstracting and indexing services, full-text and bibliographic databases, Websites, locally networked CD-ROMS, and other such products.

The design and population of the new database of electronic resources, the "Digital Registry," had to occur in a short time frame–approximately 7 months. Therefore, the developers were required to use existing tools within the current development environment such as the NT server, IIS, MS-SQL, Java, ASP, and VB-Script. Similarly, as there was no budget for personnel to do the additional data entry, the design had to incorporate existing workflows and recycle data as much as possible.

The design decisions for Phase I of the Digital Registry centered on having one data repository and a single record approach. The developers decided to maintain the Innovative database as the repository, and to use a MARC exporter to feed the SQL (Structured Query Language) database. The Digital Registry, however, required the addition of local MARC fields to the Innovative record structure for Registry-specific data elements such as genre, classes, local notes, access control, etc. These added tags allowed for a populated resource upon release, which then could be edited and supplemented by subject experts.

In order to incorporate populating the registry into existing workflow as much as possible, a process was developed in which Public Services personnel and selectors identified resources to add to the Registry through the use of a Web form, which included fields for the resource's URL, title, type, class, and description. The form was then forwarded to the Acquisitions/Cataloging staff, who added and edited the MARC record. The information was then automatically exported into the SQL database overnight, resulting in the resource appearing in the Digital Registry the following day.

The Library Systems staff was responsible for designing the overall architecture for the Digital Registry. They developed such components as Java scripts to call stored procedures and generate HTML, ASP for dynamic querying and page generations, authentication through Patron API to the Innovative patron file, and ASP and Java for the HTML authoring tool kit. These components brought the Registry to full functionality (see Figure 1).

At this point Steve Shadle took a question from the enthusiastic audience. He was asked what the reaction of the Acquisitions/Cataloging Division staff was in regard to the added work of populating the Digital Registry. He replied that overall the staff took it well, though naturally reactions to the increased workload were mixed. However, the administrative decision to designate the modification of the MARC records as a highest-priority project helped ease the process. He also commented that the cross-functional training that ensued has continued to be useful.

CURRENT IMPLEMENTATION

Currently, most pages in the University of Washington Libraries subject directory (http://www.lib.washington.edu/subject) are automatically generated from the SQL database queries, with additional queries to the database producing "by type" lists (for example, "databases"), current awareness lists, etc. Providing access to electronic resources through this gateway is a noticeable improvement, since prior to the implementation of the Digital Registry only about one-half of the subject specialists had developed subject guides.

Another clear benefit of the shared SQL database environment is simplification of link management. Selectors no longer have to check

FIGURE 1

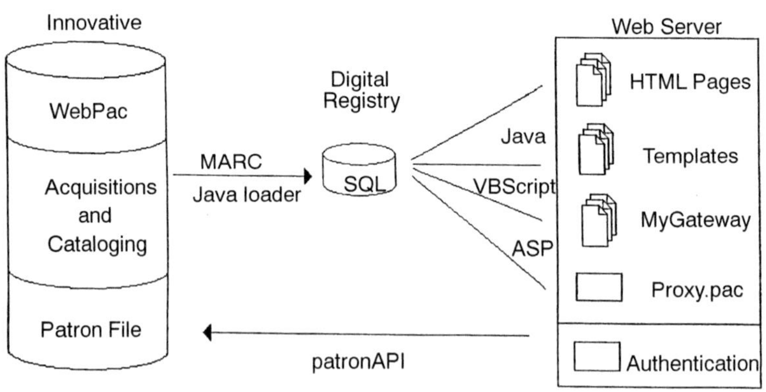

pages regularly to find problematic links; a "spider" program checks URLs every night, and generates reports of broken links. In reply to an audience question, Wade stated that approximately 1200 HTML pages are generated and checked nightly.

Among the innovative features of the Digital Registry is end-user customization through a service called "My Gateway." "My Gateway" allows validated users to perform a variety of tasks to customize their particular gateway into the Libraries' and the University's online resources. Currently one can add one's own resources to the subject lists, subscribe to the University's "News of the Day" information service, and create a roaming bookmark list. Other services such as saved queries, scheduled TOC deliveries and other SDI services, and links to other library and university services are currently being developed.

A further innovative service is template-based Web publishing for selectors. Through "My Gateway" librarians can amend the auto-generated subject pages, create and maintain resource guides, lists of core titles, pathfinders, bibliographies, fragmentary "include" files, and other such tools, which are then linked to and from the main subject pages. This results in "custom" Webpages that are readily available to library users through a well-established access point.

Although the Digital Registry provides clear benefits such as a single input work flow, the modification and use of existing cataloging records, improved content level and uniformity of subject pages, and a built-in support system for new projects, the current implementation also presents some challenges. For example, Wade considered the potential problem that might arise when there are multiple selectors for a subject–he discussed scenarios in which one selector adds or removes a resource without consulting the other, or in which there is disagreement on a particular resource. Naturally, Wade stated, this might create a potentially difficult situation. The existence of the shared Digital Registry necessitates cooperation between multiple selectors, and highlights the need to maintain a collection development policy for selecting and deselecting electronic resources.

In addition, questions of standardization arise. For instance, how should the subject hierarchy be defined, and who should define it? How should the individual subject pages look, and to what extent is control standardized or distributed? These questions are being discussed within the Libraries.

At this point, a participant asked in what manner, and how well, communication occurred throughout the Registry's development and implementation. Shadle indicated that because subject catalogers had to communicate with selectors in order to edit the MARC records correctly, communication has actually improved. The process also allowed selectors to discuss their needs with the other Division staffs, which resulted, according to Shadle, in "difficult benefits." However, Wade pointed out, "cross-pollination" of job responsibilities (in that systems and technical services librarians also act as selectors) enhanced negotiations to a large degree.

Another participant asked how technical services were able to "take control" of the Webpages. Shadle and Wade stated that ultimately what appears on the page comes primarily from public services librarians, and that some of the public services personnel still maintain their own pages. Furthermore, because the time frame for development and implementation was so tight, it was more efficient to use the database maintenance workflow that was already in place in technical services.

A final question was raised–that of including titles from aggregators. Shadle answered that they are not currently adding these titles; they are waiting to see what standards and practices develop in this regard.

FUTURE PROJECTS: LINKING CITATIONS, HOLDINGS, AND FULL-TEXT

Wade resumed, presenting issues that have arisen in the pervasive full-text environment. First, users now have more options for gaining access to full-text documents, which can be quite confusing. Second, split-run problems are beginning to occur, in which a part of journal run is in print, and other parts are either additionally or exclusively online and may be accessed through multiple vendors. Finally, some A & I vendors are now developing link-to-text capabilities, but only provide linkages through their own proprietary full-text or document delivery services, not to holdings from other online or print resources.

Several requirements must be met if the system is to overcome such problems. It must allow for multiple, distributed document providers; accommodate new providers; and be able to rank those providers by various criteria. It must permit multiple linking keys, sustain rule-based selection among the various keys, and support varying levels of granularity in the data (for example, title, issue, or article/page level).

The system must degrade gracefully according to locally established rules, and finally, it must work with a user's Web browser without requiring a custom client or plug-ins.

To meet the above requirements, the UW Library Systems Office prototyped an intelligent proxy that acts as a "pass-through" proxy, which rewrites an HTML page before returning it to the user, thus providing the user with links to holdings and full-text transparently. In doing so, the intelligent proxy parses the page returned from an A & I search, and creates a link to a local resolver program. When the user requests the full-text, the local resolver then uses the citation information to query the Digital Registry to find the appropriate full-text provider, and then fetches the full-text document for the user. The Digital Registry, then, is the cornerstone for the intelligent proxy's work, providing access not only to the electronic resources themselves, but also the mechanisms to maintain URLs for components, userids, and passwords associated with each A & I and full-text provider.

Finally, Wade discussed pertinent questions regarding the further development of the Digital Registry. Current service questions under consideration include the level of linking that should be considered "core service," and whether there should be variability in functionality between vendors, as all vendor systems work differently. Likewise, should vendor solutions to linking be integrated into the Registry, or would this, perhaps, create too great a dependency on the vendor? What, then, is the tolerable level of vendor dependency? Scalability issues are also potentially problematic. For example, new sources require new components to the intelligent proxy, since currently there are no common standards for search, retrieval, or document identification among vendor systems. Similarly, some sites use Javascript to build URLs dynamically or Java Applets to open non-HTTP connections, which increases the complexity of parsing for the proxy. Furthermore, as radical changes in a vendor's system can break components of the proxy, brittleness becomes another factor to consider. Finally, the costs of maintaining detailed holdings information vital to the Registry's success are high for a single institution. When does this cost become prohibitive?

The floor was then opened for final questions. Wade and Shadle were asked how they have measured patron response to the Digital Registry. They replied that in addition to anecdotal evidence such as positive user responses, they recorded a tenfold increase in Website use statistics; future plans to measure patron response include usage studies.

From Catalog Card to MARC: USMARC Bibliographic Self-Defense

Jo Calk

Workshop Leader

Bob Persing

Recorder

SUMMARY. A primer on the USMARC bibliographic format, presented as a narrative of its development. The logic of the MARC field tags is explained, with emphasis on how they reflect the information formerly printed on catalog cards. *[Article copies available for a fee from The Haworth Document Delivery Service: 1-800-342-9678. E-mail address: getinfo@haworthpressinc.com <Website: http://www.haworthpressinc.com>]*

INTRODUCTION

Jo Calk worked at the Library of Congress when the MARC format was being developed. She presented this workshop for serials librarians needing a basic introduction to MARC. Her method was to trace, in narrative format, the logic behind the assignment of the MARC tags.

Jo Calk is Systems Development Supervisor, Blackwell's Book Services.
Bob Persing is Head of Serials, University of Pennsylvania Library.

[Haworth co-indexing entry note]: "From Catalog Card to MARC: USMARC Bibliographic Self-Defense." Persing, Bob. Co-published simultaneously in *The Serials Librarian* (The Haworth Press, Inc.) Vol. 38, No. 3/4, 2000, pp. 349-355; and: *From Carnegie to Internet2: Forging the Serials Future* (ed: P. Michelle Fiander, Joseph C. Harmon, and Jonathan David Makepeace) The Haworth Press, Inc., 2000, pp. 349-355. Single or multiple copies of this article are available for a fee from The Haworth Document Delivery Service [1-800-342-9678, 9:00 a.m. - 5:00 p.m. (EST). E-mail address: getinfo@haworthpressinc.com].

MARC: THE BEGINNING

Before computers, the Library of Congress (LC) had developed an efficient standard method of describing bibliographic entities on catalog cards. With the advent of computers, however, LC staff decided that machine-readable records would make it easier to distribute bibliographic information. To this end, a MARC pilot project, funded by the Council on Library Resources, was undertaken from 1966-1968. Its initial goal was to store card data in machine-readable form, for easy distribution.

From these beginnings, several variations of MARC developed, with USMARC, the most common, being the version used by OCLC and the Library of Congress. The variant forms, such as UKMARC and CANMARC, include characteristics specific to the bibliographic needs of the country where developed. There is currently a project underway to harmonize USMARC and CANMARC into one unified format, called MARC 21.

All MARC records contain three elements: the record structure–the "box" in which the data is transmitted; content designation–which describes what is included in each data element; and the data content itself–the descriptive information formerly on the catalog card. These elements are reflected in the three physical parts of the record. These are the leader, which contains 24 fixed characters representing vital data elements; the directory, which indicates the record's length; and the variable fields, which contain the bibliographic data to describe the item in hand. The variable fields contain the majority of the bibliographic information we associate with cataloging.

VARIABLE FIELD MARC TAGS

For the variable fields, three-character numeric tags were created to identify each type of data. Numbered from 001 to 999, this range allows 999 choices, a number the developers felt was enough to cover all contingencies. The numbers were created to correspond to the paragraphs of an AACR catalog card. Thus, the 1XX fields correspond to the first paragraph (author, corporate body, etc.), the 2XX fields relate to the 2nd paragraph (title, edition).

Calk described the logic used by the MARC creators in the 1960s to pick the tag numbers. To represent main entry, the first paragraph on a catalog card, it seemed logical to begin the corresponding MARC tags with "1." So the numbers 100 through 199 were designated for each type of main entry: 100 for personal name, 110 for corporate name, 120 for geographic name, and 130 for a uniform title main entry.

The developers, however, quickly started making changes to this orderly spacing by tens. The 120 was discarded because geographic names were considered a form of corporate name, which could be represented by the 110 tag. Conferences and meeting names, on the other hand, were considered different enough from corporate names to warrant a tag of their own. Consequently, the 111 (conference name) tag was created. The closeness of the tag numbers signals a relationship between the two tags, while at the same time differentiating them.

To represent the second paragraph of the catalog card (title and edition), the MARC developers logically chose the 200 range of tag numbers. Because they had reached 130 in the first paragraph, and were trying to proceed by tens, the first choice for the title tag was 240. Continuing by tens, the 250 for edition and 260 for publication information were also defined. Law librarians, however, asked where the uniform filing title, which they used for filing, should be placed. Since uniform title preceded title proper on catalog cards, it seemed logical to maintain this arrangement in the MARC record, so the 240 was reassigned for uniform title, and the 245 tag (halfway between the filing title and the edition) was created for the title proper. This explains how the 245, perhaps the best-known MARC tag, came to be assigned an odd number.

When they reached the third paragraph, the developers saw the drawback of counting by tens. If they followed their logic, and began numbering the 3XX tags with 370 (following the 260 tag), they would soon run out of numbers. So they decided to start each new paragraph over at the beginning of the number range. This is why the first tag of the 3XX section is 300, not 370.

The MARC developers also made sure to leave room in some places for future expansion, a strategy that proved important as they began developing tags for other formats such as serials. As they began work on serial's tags, MARC developers quickly found serials had additional descriptive needs requiring even more tags than those required for books. Wherever possible, these additional tags were fitted between and coordinated with existing monograph tags. For example, the 022 tag was chosen for the ISSN, because it was close to the 020 tag for the ISBN. Each subsequent bibliographic format proved to have similar, unique needs, and tags were added as needed.

ADDING AND DIVIDING DATA: INDICATORS AND SUBFIELDS

MARC developers next realized that filing information was necessary for some tags. This data had to be separate from the descriptive information, since different libraries might use different sets of filing rules. To accommodate this associated data, the concept of "indicators" was introduced: two additional numbers, sandwiched between the tag number and the data itself. The first digit provides more specific information about the tag; the second digit describes its usage. For some fields, the values defined for the second indicator were LC-centric, with other libraries relegated to notes in a subfield.

To further divide and parse each field, it was divided into coded subfields. Each subfield was designated by a delimiter character (unprintable by most computers and represented by a dollar sign–$) and an alphabetic character indicating type of subfield. Like the tag numbers, subfield designators were neither intuitive, nor consistent from field to field. Catalogers were expected to refer to a MARC format manual to learn which data belonged in which subfield.

Although bibliographic databases like OCLC display MARC tags and data together, to make records easy to read, MARC records are actually distributed with tag numbers separate from the data–tag numbers are listed in a directory followed by the data. This delivery process was devised to allow the slow, clunky computers of the late 1960s to store and parse the records easily, and it is still in use today. Similarly, the "leader" is still in use as originally designed, being composed of 24 characters representing fixed data, the first element of which is the total record length in characters. Tag numbers follow the leader, with values indicating the number of characters in the record. See Figure 1.

The fixed fields provide a set way to express certain required information for each record. This information is chiefly useful for retrieval, and provides an easy way to limit and refine searches, coded machine-readable data being easier for a computer to read than text. Each bibliographic format has its own fixed fields, since crucial data ele-

FIGURE 1. USMARC format bibliographic record as distributed on tape

($=delimiter ASCII X'1F'; *=end-of-field character ASCII X'1E'; @=end-of-recor
X'1D') For convenience, the tags are underlined in the Directory.

```
01216nam  2200301 a 4500001001800000003000400018005001700022008004100039
035002100080040002400101042001400125043001200139050002200151082002600173
100002300199245015600222260010700378300002800485500002000513504006200533
650006800595650004900663650004800712610007100760700002100831700001900852
710004300871*   94206341 //r96*DLC*19961003091359.6*940513s1994    gaua
   b    001 0 eng d*  $a(OCoLC)30434583 *  $aNdLibC$cNdLibC$dDLC*  $alc
copycat*  $an------*00$aZ692.S5$bM29 1994*00$a025.06/0705/72097$220*1 $a
MacLennan, Birdie.*10$aNASIGNET and beyond :$belectronic networking reso
urces for serialists /$cby Birdie MacLennan and Marilyn Geller ; with co
ntributions from Maggie Rioux.*  $aDecatur, GA :$bThe Electronic Communi
cations Committee, North American Serials Interest Group,$cc1994.*  $a98
 p. :$bill. ;$c28 cm.*  $a"January 1994."*  $aIncludes bibliographical r
eferences (p. 79-85) and index.* 0$aSerial publications$zNorth America$x
Computer network resources.* 0$aLibrary information networks$zNorth Amer
ica.* 0$aInternet (Computer network)$zNorth America.*20$aNorth American
Serials Interest Group$xComputer network resources.*1 $aGeller, Marilyn.
*1 $aRioux, Maggie.*2 $aNorth American Serials Interest Group.*@
```

ments differ from one format to another. This data is recorded in the 008 field of the record. As a sample, Calk walked through the 008 field of a serial record. See Figure 2.

Calk then presented charts showing some of the most common USMARC serials bibliographic tags, heading types and indicators. The purpose of indicators was discussed, with examples ranging from their use in specifying name order for name headings, to defining non-filing characters. Another use for indicators is to add simple but important information. Indicators in series statements, for example, can be sufficiently fine-tuned to specify personal pronouns when required; a tag reading "$a Collected works $v v.4" for a male author can be displayed as "His Collected Works, v.4" through proper indicator coding.

REVISIONS TO MARC

Revisions to the MARC formats are made by MARBI, a joint ALCTS/LITA/RUSA committee, which meets at both ALA meetings [1]. They work with LC, OCLC, RLIN and their host ALA sections to create fields as needed, and to revise existing fields [2]. LC also maintains good descriptive pages about MARC on their website: http://lcweb.loc.gov/marc/bibliographic

MARC HOLDINGS FORMAT

At the request of the audience, Calk added an impromptu discussion of the MARC Holdings Format fields. For general textual strings,

FIGURE 2. 008 fixed-length data elements field:

008 Fixed-Length Data Elements Field

Each of the seven USMARC bibliographic formats has a different set of 008 Fixed-Length Data Elements. The serials 008 data elements are listed below.

Offset /0	Description	Example Value	Definition
00-05	Date Entered on File	860131	31 Jan 1986
06	Type of Date/Publication Status	c	Currently published
07-10	Date 1	1986	Starting date
11-14	Date 2	9999	Open-ended
15-17	Place of Publication, Production, or Execution	pau	Pennsylvania/U.S.
18	Frequency	b	Bimonthly
19	Regularity	r	Regular
20	ISSN Center	1	United States
21	Type of Serial	p	Periodical
22	Form of Original Item	(blank)	Not specified
23	Form of Item	(blank)	Not specified
24	Nature of Entire Work	d	Dictionary, glossary, gazetteer
25-27	Nature of Contents	(blanks)	Not specified
28	Government Publication	(blank)	Not a government publication
29	Conference Publication	0	Not a conference publication
30-32	Undefined	(blanks)	Undefined
33	Original Alphabet or Script of Title	a	Basic Roman
34	Successive/Latest Entry	0	Successive
35-37	Language	eng	English
38	Modified Record	(blank)	Not modified
39	Cataloging Source	d	Not LC

holdings may be stored in the 866–textual holding, basic bibliographic unit. But most local systems have difficulty parsing such textual data. The alternative is to use the 853/863 combination, with the 853 containing the captions, and the 863 containing the related enumeration. Either option may have an impact on system migration, or on future bar-coding efforts since many local systems still do not fully support MARC holdings records. The 852 field shows location and call number. The 856 field is for location information, such as URLs for electronic data.

CONCLUSION

This workshop was a creative way to introduce the MARC format for serials people unfamiliar with it. The historical structure of the presentation kept it from being just a list of tags and indicators. The logic behind the tag numbers, for instance, is not readily apparent without hearing the thinking that went into picking them. Calk's presentation was very entertaining in its description of the somewhat haphazard process of MARC tag number selection. Her descriptions of the developers' debates and discussions were presented as a long narrative, as if in their own words. The tone of this narrative is difficult to capture in a factual report, but it succeeded in humanizing the presentation for the audience.

NOTES

1. MARBI: Machine-Readable Bibliographic Information; ALCTS: Association for Library Collections and Technical Services; LITA: Library and Information Technology Association; RUSA: Reference and User Services Association; ALA: American Library Association.
2. LC = Library of Congress; OCLC: OCLC Online Computer Library Center, Inc.; RLIN: Research Libraries Information Network

Realistic Licensing or Licensing Realities: Practical Advice on License Agreements

Trisha L. Davis

Workshop Leader

Lucien R. Rossignol

Recorder

SUMMARY. As electronic resources become increasingly prolific it is extremely important that librarians, and all interested parties, scrutinize the contents of the often complex license agreements associated with these products. This practical and useful workshop examined the fifteen principles set forth in *Principles for Licensing Electronic Resources*, published in July 1997. *[Article copies available for a fee from The Haworth Document Delivery Service: 1-800-342-9678. E-mail address: getinfo@haworthpressinc.com <Website: http://www.haworthpressinc.com>]*

In July of 1997 a document entitled *Principles for Licensing Electronic Resources* was released by representatives from the American Association of Law Libraries, American Library Association, Associ-

---

Trisha L. Davis is Head, Serials and Electronic Resources Department, Ohio State University Libraries.

Lucien R. Rossignol is Head, Acquisitions Services, Smithsonian Institution Libraries.

[Haworth co-indexing entry note]: "Realistic Licensing or Licensing Realities: Practical Advice on License Agreements." Rossignol, Lucien R. Co-published simultaneously in *The Serials Librarian* (The Haworth Press, Inc.) Vol. 38, No. 3/4, 2000, pp. 357-361; and: *From Carnegie to Internet2: Forging the Serials Future* (ed: P. Michelle Fiander, Joseph C. Harmon, and Jonathan David Makepeace) The Haworth Press, Inc., 2000, pp. 357-361. Single or multiple copies of this article are available for a fee from The Haworth Document Delivery Service [1-800-342-9678, 9:00 a.m. - 5:00 p.m. (EST). E-mail address: getinfo@haworthpressinc.com].

ation of Academic Health Sciences Libraries, Association of Research Libraries, Medical Library Association, and Special Libraries Association [1]. In her workshop, "Realistic Licensing," Trisha Davis of Ohio State University presented a spirited overview of the genesis of the document and explanations of its key points. Davis stressed that the document contains principles, not hard and fast rules; and as such, it should be considered a guide, not a prescriptive resource, for librarians and providers of electronic information as they review or create licenses. What follows are major issues to consider when negotiating a license for electronic materials.

Post-Subscription Access Rights. An important, but often overlooked, feature of licenses is a clause regarding post-subscription access rights. Many librarians fail to recognize the importance of post-subscription access rights for data to which they currently have access. It is crucial that license agreements contain a clause allowing access to data after the license or subscription has expired. Without such a provision, librarians run the risk of unwittingly losing access to data covered by the period of the subscription. These lacunae are the result of the integrated nature of most Websites; it is not possible, in most cases, for providers to limit access to specific years of data. Librarians must ensure that licenses specify access to the data for which they have paid, even after the period of the subscription has expired.

Such assurance may take the form of an intermediary provider, such as OCLC, or may be provided on CD-ROM or other form of electronic storage medium. Even hard-copy subscriptions may be used if they are provided at a reduced cost. Increasingly, providers of electronic media are willing to provide archival copies at the end of a subscription or license expiration. Occasionally it may be necessary to pay an additional fee for the archive but the cost is usually minimal. The license agreement should specify how archival copies will be accessed, who will provide them, and under what conditions they will be provided. Consortial arrangements for uploading archives can sometimes prove beneficial.

Copyright Law and the License. As they review license agreements, librarians should keep in mind that they have rights based on the existing body of copyright law. They should make certain that licenses do not infringe upon their fair use rights in terms of printing, downloading, copying, and interlibrary loan. When negotiating license agreements, it is reasonable to cite the support of major library associations of the United States for these rights.

Fair Use: Rights and Responsibilities. When reviewing licenses to assure fair access to electronic resources, it is very easy for librarians to lose sight of the fact that providers of information as well as other parties also have rights. Information is not free, much as we might wish it so. It is our responsibility to remember the rights of authors and disseminators of electronic information. While vigilance on the part of librarians to recognize the rights of originators and providers of information is necessary, it is impossible to prevent all infringement of these rights. Creators and providers of information must recognize that librarians should not be held liable for unauthorized use of their products, as long as librarians make every effort to implement security measures designed to allow access to authorized users only. One of the most common security measures used is that of limiting access by IP addresses. Another mechanism is to make terms of use appear automatically on the computer screen as part of the sign-on process.

While the rights of providers of electronic data are not universally accepted in the library community, the authors of *Principles for Licensing Electronic Resources* firmly believe that recognition of these rights by purchasers and users is entirely appropriate. It is equally appropriate for librarians to state clearly in the license that they will take immediate and appropriate action to deal with fair use infractions; i.e., to carry out due process, and to make certain that similar infractions are not repeated. Information providers must also give fair warning and allow sufficient time for libraries to take corrective measures before taking punitive action. Librarians should also not be asked to establish security measures that will impede database use by legitimate users.

Termination of Licensing Agreements. Another item vital to any license agreement is the right of either party to terminate the contract. The terms and conditions under which termination of the contract takes place should be explained fully. For example, if a provider changes the content of a database in a way that makes it less useful than it was originally, the library should, at the very least, be granted advance notification of such change, and the right to terminate the contract based on these changes. Of course not all changes are detrimental. Information providers should and do add data to their databases. As long as such changes do not result in additional or hidden charges they pose no threat to the integrity of the contract. Similarly, the license should specify the conditions under which the database provider may terminate the contract.

Indemnification. Although it tends to be a problematic feature of licenses, indemnification is very important. Indemnification can be expressed in very simple language and can serve as an insurance policy to protect one or both parties. A license agreement should require the licensor and the intellectual property or copyright holder to indemnify or hold harmless the licensee in actions based on claims of infringement or other complex legal issues. Librarians should have access to their university's office of legal affairs and should not hesitate to contact legal affairs office staff on any question related to license interpretation, indemnification. Indeed, the office of legal affairs should ideally be a party to the entire process of reviewing a license; they should advise on modifications, and review the final version before signing.

Privacy Issues and Data Collection. Licenses should also address the issues of privacy and use-data collection. While database providers can often improve their product by gathering use statistics, such as peak hours of use, they must respect the laws and institutional policies regarding confidentiality and privacy. Usage statistics are also valuable to the library. When purchasing a product priced by number of simultaneous users, for example, usage statistics can help determine the number that will best meet the library's needs. While usage statistics have a legitimate purpose and may be gathered without infringing on the privacy of library patrons, other usage information is less innocuous. When negotiating a license, the librarian should make clear that information providers have no right to know exactly who is logged on to their database at any given time or the names of individuals using specific databases. Standard clauses in the license agreement should address this issue and should specify that in cases where usage data is being collected, the librarian should be notified and the collected data made available to the library.

Third-Party Agreements. Librarians should guard against being held to agreements entered into by the database provider and a third party. If such arrangements are stipulated in a license agreement and the database provider is unwilling to delete them, it may not be possible for the librarian as a prospective purchaser to actually sign the license agreement. The librarian must review such third party agreements very carefully to make certain that they are compatible with university, state, or other governing body's laws and regulations.

Miscellaneous Tips. Davis concluded the formal portion of her presentation by summarizing the process of license review. Very important and often overlooked is making sure that the license in hand is the correct one. Librarians should determine use parameters by asking if the agreement is for Web-based access, single or multiple users, institutional use, etc. He or she must decide which usage rights are mandatory and therefore must be specified in the license. A team consisting of interested parties is a good way to approach the rights issue. Interested parties might include someone from the serials or acquisitions departments, a reference librarian, and a Web librarian. Finally, the librarian should know exactly who has the right to sign the license agreement. Who has delegated purchasing authority? Is it the librarian, the library director, the head of legal affairs? Whoever does have the right to sign the license agreement must realize that he or she is signing on behalf of not only the library but also the parent institution.

The final portion of the workshop involved a hands-on exercise. Attendees were asked to gather into groups of five or six individuals for the purpose of reviewing a sample license agreement and reporting their conclusions to the larger audience. Regrettably, the complexity of the topic and large number of people attending the workshop did not permit all groups to present their opinions. Overall the workshop was a terrific introduction to licensing agreements.

NOTES

1. *Principles for Licensing Electronic Resources* (1997). Available at the Special Libraries Association Website: http://www.sla.org/govt/diglic59.html

Taming the Octopus: Getting a Grip on Electronic Resources

Nancy Markle Stanley
Angelina F. Holden
Betty L. Nirnberger

Workshop Leaders

Donnice Cochenour

Recorder

SUMMARY. When libraries acquire electronic resources there is often no tangible item received; and managing the selection, ordering, receiving, access to and payments for these resources frequently requires mechanisms different from those used for standard printed resources. This workshop described the rationale, structure and use of the ERLIC database created by the Acquisitions staff at Pennsylvania State University Libraries in an effort to better manage their electronic resources. The workshop was divided into three parts: rationale behind the development of the database, a demonstration of the database, and a discussion period. *[Article copies available for a fee from The Haworth Document Delivery Service: 1-800-342-9678. E-mail address: getinfo@haworthpressinc.com <Website: http://www.haworthpressinc.com>]*

Nancy Markle Stanley is Head of the Acquisitions Services Department, Penn State University.

Angelina F. Holden is a member of the Resources, Systems, and Data Services Team of the Acquisitions Services Department, Penn State University.

Betty L. Nirnberger is a member of the Resources, Systems, and Data Services Team of the Acquisitions Services Department, Penn State University.

Donnice Cochenour is Serials Librarian, Colorado State University

[Haworth co-indexing entry note]: "Taming the Octopus: Getting a Grip on Electronic Resources." Cochenour, Donnice. Co-published simultaneously in *The Serials Librarian* (The Haworth Press, Inc.) Vol. 38, No. 3/4, 2000, pp. 363-368; and: *From Carnegie to Internet2: Forging the Serials Future* (ed: P. Michelle Fiander, Joseph C. Harmon, and Jonathan David Makepeace) The Haworth Press, Inc., 2000, pp. 363-368. Single or multiple copies of this article are available for a fee from The Haworth Document Delivery Service [1-800-342-9678, 9:00 a.m. - 5:00 p.m. (EST). E-mail address: getinfo@haworthpressinc.com].

INTRODUCTION

This workshop reported on the development of a database, the Electronic Resources and Licensing Information Center (ERLIC), created by the Resources, Systems, and Data Services (RSDS) Team of the Acquisitions Services Department at Pennsylvania State University Libraries. Nancy Markle Stanley, Head of Acquisitions, began the workshop by presenting the rationale behind the development of ERLIC; Angelina F. Holden, a member of the RSDS team, gave a demonstration of the database. Betty Nirnberger, also of the RSDS team, led the question and answer period and lively discussion following the presentation. Nirnberger initiated many of the ideas behind the ERLIC project.

IMPETUS BEHIND ERLIC

Stanley stated that the project began due to a critical need to track and claim invoices for electronic products subscribed to by her library system. However, the project quickly grew to also track and share information about license agreements and the status of orders, and to answer many other questions about electronic resources.

With electronic resources, there are multiple stakeholders who need to know a variety of information about the product. For example, acquisitions personnel need to know the status of the order, how the product is funded, overall costs, and when payment is due. Collection development personnel need to know the status of licensing negotiations and what has been negotiated; later they will want to know usage data to determine the value of the product for their users. Public Services personnel need to know who will be able to access the product and how. Systems personnel need to know the schedule of product updates, if the product is loaded locally, and how to guarantee secure access to only authorized users. Everyone needs to know the product's content and coverage, including Cataloging, which must create the bibliographic records and holdings information.

To meet these needs, ERLIC includes information on budget support, access and authentication, current and pending orders, negotiated agreements, payments, and user data. ERLIC tracks complete funding support for each product including collaborative purchases among selectors or shared purchases within a consortium. The programs or disciplines supported by the product are identified, including diversity programs, which enables the creation of attribution reports for accreditation purposes. Access information includes the format of each product, hotlinks for the Web or telnet address if applicable, who can access the product and the associated IP ranges, user name and password if applicable, the domain name, and the number of simultaneous users allowed. Using this information, the database can be utilized to provide several standard reports and statistics.

HOW ERLIC WORKS

Acquisitions staff begin creating an ERLIC record for a new product at the initial point of consideration by entering a brief description of the product (including type of content: citations, abstracts, and/or full-text), the number of records in the product, and scheduled updates. As the order process continues, information is added to include the status of the order (whether the product is under consideration, on trial, a new order, a standing order or has been cancelled), and other typical order information (purchase order number, supplier name and address). As the acquisition process continues, additional information is added to the database. A scanned image of the finalized license agreement is linked to the ERLIC record. Other links are created for the online bibliographic record, the product itself, and any supplier's usage data files. As payments are made, these are added to the record to maintain a three-year payment history, as well as information about when the next payment is due. Thus, the original intent of the database–to track and claim outstanding invoices–is fulfilled.

Following Stanley's description of the development process, Holden demonstrated ERLIC. The database was created using the relational database, Microsoft Access. Holden stressed that some of the information contained within the database is confidential within the organization. For this reason a note was added to the Banner Screen to alert users that license agreements and payment information can be shared only with Penn State faculty and staff. In some cases, specific fields containing sensitive information can be blocked from anyone's view except the staff responsible for maintenance of the database. Holden demonstrated the various relational forms for order status, access status, usage statistics, and payment history. She showed how information could be searched by a variety of data points, and displayed some of the online reports currently available. See Figure 1 for a sample screen image of a record in ERLIC.

THE VALUE OF ERLIC

ERLIC is considered to be a work in progress, but its value has already been proven. It was initially conceptualized as a way to track orders and to anticipate and claim invoices, but has evolved into a centralized information source addressing a much wider range of needs. In addition to centralizing numerous critical details about an electronic resource and the institution's order, ERLIC assists with tracking the license agreement during the initial negotiation and signature process. It has also allowed better access to the terms and conditions of use by those who actually use the product, including making contact information and vendor account numbers available during library service hours when the Acquisitions Services Department staff members are not working. Issues needing further discussion include

FIGURE 1. Sample ERLIC screen for the electronic resource, *Project Muse*

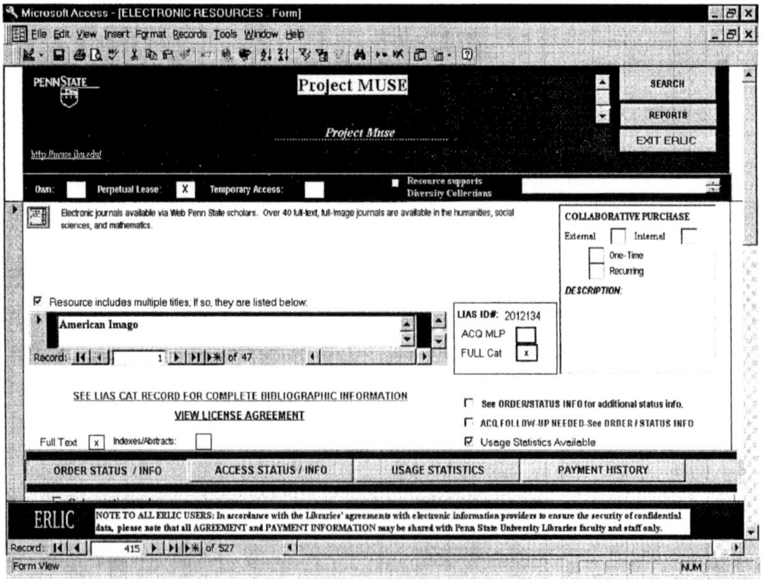

the identification of electronic resources with links to paper subscriptions; ways to improve tracking of free electronic resources; and how to make ERLIC accessible to the 20+ other Penn State locations across the state.

QUESTION AND ANSWER SESSION

Following the demonstration, participants enjoyed a lively question and answer session. Many of the questions were requests for more details about how the database was structured and used. When asked if the creation and use of ERLIC had brought about changes in the team's day-to-day workflow, Nirnberger stated that the Acquisitions staff are aware of new electronic resources very early in the purchase process and the records in ERLIC are created in stages as new information becomes available. She did not indicate any major change in how work was being accomplished, stating only that staff now have a better handle on the elusive aspects of these resources. Nirnberger added that the database provides the capability of allowing e-mail messages associated with the ordering and negotiation stage to be saved as text files and attached to the corresponding record in ERLIC, which improves the complex communication process required to establish an order for an electronic resource.

One participant asked why our integrated library systems (ILS) don't provide for this information in the acquisitions modules, forcing libraries to maintain a separate database to capture this information. Others agreed that this would be a valuable enhancement to most integrated library systems. Stanley noted that the current environment of automated services in their library system is fragmented. One system handles ordering and payment, another handles check-in, and yet another serves as the public catalog. This makes the ERLIC database even more valuable since it creates a central information source for electronic resources. They are investigating methods for importing data from their other systems to reduce the need to re-key data. Nirnberger noted that they might consider the possibility of allowing university officials outside the library to update the status of data elements in ERLIC as items pass through various offices on campus. For example, staff in university purchasing, university accounting, and the attorney's office might update selected fields when they complete their part of the ordering and license negotiation process.

Participants recognized the value of a database such as ERLIC to handle the complex ordering, monitoring and maintenance required by the acquisitions staff for these electronic products now so prevalent in our libraries. The presentation slides are available at *http://www.libraries.psu.edu/iasweb/acq/index.htm*. The handout from the presentation, including several screen shots of the database, is available at *http://www.libraries.psu.edu/iasweb/acq/nasighandout.htm*

14th Annual NASIG Conference Registrants Carnegie-Mellon University June 10-13, 1999

Conference Registrants	*Organization/Institution*
Aaron, Amira	The Faxon Co.
Abaid, Teresa	Florida Atlantic University
Abram, Stephen	Micromedia
Acton, Deena	National Library of Medicine
Aiello, Helen M.	Wesleyan University
Albano, Christine	Cleveland Public Library
Albee, Barbara	The Faxon Co.
Alexander, Whitney	Santa Clara University
Allen, Barbara	CIC
Allen, Norene	The Faxon Co.
Allgood, Everett	New York University
Alvarez, Josefa H.	UTEP Library
Anderson, Iris	International Monetary Fund
Anderson, Vanessa	UnCover
Andrews, Susan	Texas A&M University-Commerce
Anemaet, Jos	Oregon State University
Arnold, Teresa	Swets & Zeitlinger, Inc.
Ashman, Allen B.	Kentucky Union List of Serials
Aufdemberge, Karen J.	University of Toledo
Badics, Joe	Eastern Michigan University
Baia, Wendy	University of Colorado at Boulder
Baker, Carol M.	University of Calgary
Baker, Jeanne	University of Maryland
Baker, Mary Ellen	Cal Poly State University
Balhorn, Kathy	Lawrence Livermore National Laboratory
Ballard, Rochelle	Texas A & M University

Barron, Lucy A.	Harvard University
Barstow, Sandy	University of WY Libraries
Basar, Ivan	National Library of Canada
Basch, N. Bernard	Basch Subscriptions Inc.
Bazin, Paul	Providence College
Becker, Louis	New York Public Library
Bell, Carole R.	University of Maryland
Bellinger, Christina	University of New Hampshire
Bendig, Deborah L.	OCLC
Bennett, Marsha	Boston Public Library
Bentley, Ronald W.	Canadian Agriculture Library
Bernards, Dennis	Brigham Young University
Betts, Anthony	Turpin Distribution Services Ltd.
Bills, Linda	Tri-College Consortium
Blake, Nora	University of Vermont
Blatchley, Jeremy	Bryn Mawr College
Bloom, Randy	EBSCO Information Services
Bloss, Alex	University of Illinois at Chicago
Bloss, Marjorie	Center for Research Libraries
Blosser, John	Northwestern University
Bobich, Marianne	T.C.U.
Bogdanski, Sophie	West Virginia University
Boissy, Robert W.	The Faxon Co.
Boland, Lucye	Manhattonville College Library
Bonn, Maria	University of Michigan
Born, Kathleen	EBSCO Information Services
Boyce, Peter	P. Boyce Associates
Branche-Brown, Lynne	Innovative Interfaces, Inc.
Branham, Janie	Southeastern Louisiana University
Brannon, Kathy	Blackwell's Information Services
Brass, Evelyn	University of Houston
Brautigam, David	Westminster College (PA)
Breed, Luellen	University of Wisconsin-Parkside
Brennan, Molly	Virginia Tech
Bright, Alice	Carnegie Mellon University
Broadwater, Deborah	Vanderbilt University
Broadway, Rita	University of Memphis
Bross, Valerie	UCLA
Brown, David J.	Ingenta, Inc.

Brown, Elizabeth W.	Johns Hopkins University
Brown, Ladd	Newman Library-VPI
Brown, Michael D.	University of Chicago Library
Brown, Michael J.	Technomic Publishing Co.
Bruner, David	Northern Arizona University
Bull, Greg	University of St. Thomas
Bullington, Jeff	University of Kansas Libraries
Bundy, Rosemarie	SUNY Health Science Library
Burk, Martha	Babson College
Burke, David	Villanova University
Butler, Joan M.	University of Michigan
Butterworth, Terry	OCLC
Button, Leslie Horner	University of Massachussetts Library
Bynog, David M.	Rice Universtiy
Byunn, Kit S.	University of Memphis
Calk, Jo	Blackwell's Information Services
Campbell, Cameron J.	University of Chicago Library
Cargille, Karen	UCSD
Carlson, Melvin	U Mass Amherst
Case, Candice	Harrisburg Area Community College
Caspers, Jean S.	Oregon State Univ.
Cassidy, Vincent	Thomas Nelson/Arden Shakespeare
Castellani, Maggie	Cleveland Museum of Art
Castrataro, James	Indiana University
Chad, Barry	Carnegie Library of Pittsburgh
Chaffin, Nancy J.	Ariz State Univ. West
Champagne, Thomas E.	University of Michigan
Chan, Karen	Eastern Washington University
Chang, Bao-Chu	NCSU Libraries
Chang, Hui-Yee	University of California, Santa Cruz
Chang, Ling-li	Loyola University of Chicago
Chase, Linda	American University Library
Chen, Cecilia	CSU Dominquez Hills
Chesler, Adam	Kluwer Academic Publishers
Chressanthis, June	Mississippi State University
Christ, Ruth	University of Iowa
Christensen, John	Brigham Young University
Ciuffetti, Peter	Silver Platter
Clarke, Tracey	Absolute Backorder Service

Cleary, Robert M.	University of Missouri
Cochenour, Donnice	Colorado State University
Cohen, Donna K.	Rollins College
Cohen, Joan G.	Bergen Community College
Cohn, Carolyne	Blackwell's Information Services
Collins, Jill	Boise State University
Conger, Mary Jane	Univ. of NC at Greensboro
Congleton, Robert	Temple University
Connolly, Jo	Blackwell's Information Services
Cook, Eleanor	Appalachian State University
Cook, Karen J.	Bowdoin College
Corbett, Lauren	Old Dominion University
Corrsin, Stephen D.	Columbia University Library
Council, Evelyn P.	Fayetteville State University
Courtney, Keith	Taylor & Francis
Cowhig, Jerry	Institute of Physics Publishing
Cox, John E.	John Cox Associates
Cracknell, Linda	Wilfred Laurier University
Creamer, Marilyn	Haverford College
Crews, Lucy A.	Mary Baldwin College
Crooker, Cynthia	Yale Medical Library
Crowell, Loretta D.	Detroit College of Law at MSU
Cuesta, Emerita	Hofstra University
Curtis, Jerry	Springer-Verlag
Daley, Ray	LEXIS-NEXIS
Dane, Stephen	Kluwer Academic Publishers
Darling, Karen	University of Oregon
Davis, Carroll Nelson	Columbia University
Davis, Eve S.	EBSCO Information Services
Davis, Susan	SUNY Buffalo
Davis, Trisha L.	Ohio State University Libraries
De Blois, Lillian N.	Arizona Health Sciences Library
Dean, Otis A.	Blackwell Publishers
Decker, Karen	Blackwell's Information Services
Deeken, JoAnne	Indiana University
Degener, Christie T.	UNC Chapel Hill Health Sciences
Dekker, Jennifer	University of Toronto
Denda, Kayo	The Institute for Advanced Study
Devlin, Mary	Mary Devlin Associates

Diedrichs, Carol Pitts	Ohio State University
Dinelle, Christine	National Library of Canada
Doig, Rosalind	University of Derby
Dougherty, Kathleen	National Agricultural Library
Douglass, Janet	TCU
Downey, Kay	Cleveland Museum of Art
Drewes, Jeanne	Michigan State University
Drum, Carol	U of FL Libraries
Duhon, Lucy	University of Toledo Libraries
Dujmic, Linda	Carnegie Mellon University
Dunn, Sandra C.	NCSU Libraries
Dusky, Kit	Portland State University
Dygert, Claire	American University
Easton, Christa	Stanford Libraries
Edwards, Jennifer	M.I.T. Libraries
Elie, Carolle	NYPL
Ellern, Jill	Western Carolina University
Ellis, Kathryn D.	University of Tennessee
Emery, Jill	UT-Arlington
Endres, Ellen	Martinus Nijhoff International
England, Deberah	Wright State University
Eonta, Gerald	EBSCO Information Services
Ercelawn, Ann	Vanderbilt University
Ernst, Gordon E.	West Virginia University
Essency, Janet	Minot State University
Fahey, Barbara	University of Wisconsin Oshkosh
Farwell, Anne	EBSCO/CANEBSCO
Feick, Tina	Blackwell's Information Services
Felts, John W.	University of North Carolina, Greensboro
Fiander, Michelle	Indiana University-Purdue University Indianapolis
Fields, Cheryl	National Library of Medicine
Finder, Lisa	New York Public Library
Fisher, Heidi A.	Princeton University
Fitchett, Christine	Vassar College Library
Fitzgerald, Sharon Quinn	University of Maine

Flaccavento, Martine	Canada Institute for Scientific and Technical Information
Fletcher, Marilyn	University of New Mexico
Flynn, Kathryn	Rhone-Poulenc Ag. Co.
Fobert, John	Roger Williams University
Folsom, Sandy	Central Michigan University
Fons, Theodore A.	Innovative Interfaces Inc.
Foster, Connie	Western Kentucky University
Frade, Pat	Brigham Young University
French, Pat	University of Calif., Davis
Fried, Jonathan	R. R. Bowker
Fritsch, David	The Faxon Company
Frohlich, Anne	McNeese State University
Fugle, Mary	Lippincott Williams & Wilkins
Furubotten, Lisa	Texas A&M
Gallina, Thomas	Dawson Illinois Svc Ctr
Gammon, Julia	University of Akron
Garralda, John	UnCover Co.
Gaswick, Carolyn	Albion College
Gatchel, Linda M.	Shippensburg University
Gaydos, Bob	Preservation Technologies, Inc.
Geer, Beverly	University of Texas at El Paso
Geller, Marilyn	
Ghezzi, William	Dartmouth College
Giddings, Denise	Kluwer Academic Publishers
Gilbert, Mary	Towson University
Gill, Carol	Trinity University
Gimmi, Robert D.	Shippensburg University
Glazier, Mary	EBSCO Information Services
Gomes, Debra J.	Elms College
Gonzales-Small, Grace	New Mexico State University
Gordon, Martin	Franklin and Marshall College
Gormley, Alice	Marquette University Library
Grawemeyer, Jane	SIRSI
Green, Carol	University of Southern Mississippi
Greene, Philip	EBSCO Information Services
Greever, Karen E.	Kenyon College
Grenci, Mary	University of Oregon
Grice Coffman, Ila M.	University of Oklahoma

Griffin, Linda Smith	LSU Libraries
Griffin, Lynne	University of Michigan Law Library
Griffith, Joan	Harrassowitz
Grover, Diane	University of Washington
Guay, Beth	University of Maryland
Gurshman, Sandra J.	Dawson Information Services Group
Guzi, Gloria	Cleveland Public Library
Haar, John	Vanderbilt University
Haas, Ruth S.	Harvard College Library
Hagan, Tim	Northwestern University Library
Hamilton, Fred	Louisiana Tech University
Hanks, Nancy	Slippery Rock University
Hanrahan, Kathleen	Cuyahoga County Public Library
Hanus, Norine	U.P.E.I.
Harker, Carol	EBSCO Information Services
Harmon, Joseph C.	Indiana University-Purdue University Indianapolis
Harrell, Deborah	State University of West Georgia
Harrell, Karen M.	Spencer Art Reference Library
Harris, Jay	University of AL, B'ham/Lister Hill Library
Harris, Nancy	The Gale Group
Harrison, John C.	Bates College
Haug, Mary Ellen Y.	USAF Academy
Hawkins, Les	National Serials Data Program
Hawrychuk, Shelley	University of Toronto
Hedberg, Jane	Wellesley College
Heitman, Herrick	Washington State Library
Helmetsie, Carolyn L.	NASA-Langley Research Ctr
Henderson, Charlotte	Southern University
Henderson, Kittie S.	EBSCO Information Services
Hendren, Carol	CCLA
Henjum, Elaine	FCLA
Hepfer, Cindy	SUNY Buffalo & Serials Review
Heras, Elaine	Lewis & Clark College
Herbst, Christine	St. Louis University Health Science Center Library
Hinds, Isabella	Ingenta, Ltd.
Hinger, Joseph	St. John's University Law Library
Hirning, Lorraine	Athabasca University

Hirons, Jean	Library of Congress
Hitti, Angela	Cambridge Scientific Abstracts
Hlava M.K., Marjorie	Access Innovations, Inc.
Hodge, Stan	Ball State University
Hodson, Richard	UKSG
Holden, Angelina	Penn State University
Holley, Beth	University of Alabama
Holliger, Carol	Ohio Wesleyan University
Hopkins, Randall	EBSCO Info. Services, Federal Govt. Division
Horn, Marguerite	SUNY Albany
Howard, Allison	University of Pittsburgh
Howser, Barbara R.	University of Texas at Arlington
Hoyer, Craig	Swets & Zeitlinger
Hranek, Joseph D.	Cambridge University Press
Hughes, Carolyn C.	University of Southern Maine
Hulbert, Linda	SIU-Edwardsville
Hurd, Sandra H.	EBSCO Information Services
Husted, Susie	CUNY-Queens
Inger, Simon	CatchWord
Irvin, Judy	Louisiana Tech University
Isaacs, Kathryn F.	Library of Virginia
Ivins, October	Publist.com
Jackson, Mildred L.	Grand Valley State University
Jaeger, Don	Alfred Jaeger, Inc.
Jaeger, Glenn	Absolute Backorder Service
Janes, Jodith	Cleveland Clinic Foundation
Jedlicka, Beth	University of Georgia
Jiang, Yumin	Cornell University
Jizba, Richard	Creighton University
Johnson, Kay G.	University of Tennessee
Johnston, Judy A.	University of North Texas
Jones, Danny	Harrassowitz
Julian, Gail	University of South Carolina
Kahl, S. Carolyn	University of Texas at El Paso
Kahofer, Stephen	Baker & Taylor
Karabelas, Rhea	Harvard University
Katz, Toni D.	Colby College
Kaufman, Suzanne	University of Pittsburgh Law Library
Kellogg, Martha	University of Rhode Island Library

Kellum, Cathy	SOLINET
Kennedy, Kit	Blackwell's Information Services
Kercher, Marilyn	Harvard Business School
Kern, Kristen	Portland State University
Keys, JoAnn	George Mason University
Kind, Nicholas	Thomas Nelson/Arden Shakespeare
King, James	Naval Research Lab
Kirkland, Kenneth L.	DePaul University
Kirkwood, Hal	Purdue University-Mgmt & Econ Library
Knapp, Leslie C.	EBSCO Information Services
Knupp, Blaine E.	Indiana University of PA
Kortesoja, Sandra	SJMH Medical Library
Kresge, Lynda S.	Harvard University
Krimmelbein, Michael C.	U.S. Postal Service
Krishan, Kewal	University of Saskatchewan
Kropf, Blythe	New York Public Library
Kusma, Taissa	Academic Press
Ladjen, Nadia	New York Public Library
LaFrenier, Douglas	American Institute of Physics
LaGodna, Barbara	West Virginia University
LaGrange, Johanne	Columbia University Health Sci. Library
Lai, Francesco A.	Agriculture & Agri-Food Canada
Lai, Janet	Loyola Marymount University
Lai, Sheila S.	Calif. State U., Sacramento
Lamborn, Joan	University of Northern Colorado
Lamoureux, Selden	UNC-Davis Library
Landesman, Betty	AARP
Lang, Jennifer W.	University of Cincinnati
Lang, Mary	Univ of the Pacific Libraries
Langendorfer, Jeanne	Bowling Green State University
Larocque, Susan	Canada Institute for Scientific and Technical Information
Lawson, Rick	HealthGate Data Corp.
Leadem, Ellen	Nat'l Inst. of Env. Health Sciences
Leathem, Cecilia	University of Miami
Lee, Deborah	Mississippi State University
Lehman, Mary	University of Notre Dame
Leibowitz, Faye R.	University of Pittsburgh
Leiding, Reba	James Madison University

Leister, Susan	George Washington University
Lenville, Jean	University of Richmond
Lenzini, Rebecca	The Charleston Advisor
Lesher, Marcella	St. Mary's University
Lindquist, Janice	Rice University
Linke, Erika	Carnegie Mellon University
Lipecky, Kitsa	Duquesne University
Liu, Ta-chang	Oak Ridge National Laboratory
Loescher, Nancy	DuPont Pharamceuticals Company
Loghry, Pat	University of Nevada-Reno
Long, Nigel	Faxon Canada
Lowe, Chrysanne	Academic Press
Lucas, Ann	Cooley Law School Library
Lucas, John	University of Mississippi Med. Center
Luther, Judy	Informed Strategies
Lutz, Linda	University of Western Ontario
Ma, Leo F. H.	The Chinese University of Hong Kong
Mabe, Michael	Elsevier Science
MacAdam, Carol	JSTOR
MacArthur, Susan	Bates College
Macklin, Lisa A.	Georgia Tech Library
Macomber, Nancy	Queens College/CUNY
Maher, Diane	University of San Diego
Majors, Mary Ellen	University of North Carolina at Pembroke
Makepeace, Jonathan	Indiana University-Purdue University Indianapolis
Malinowski, Teresa	California State University
Malone, Debbie	Ursinus College
Malone, Deborah	University of San Francisco Library
Manuel, Kate M.	George Washington University
Margolis, Merle I.	University of Wisconsin
Marill, Jennifer	National Library of Medicine
Markley, Susan	Villanova University
Markwith, Michael	Swets & Zeitlinger
Martinez, Rebecca	Blackwell's Information Services
Matsoukas, Konstantina	McGill University
Matthews, Karen	Emporia State University
Matthews, Pam	Gettysburg College
Matthews, Priscilla J.	Illinois State University

McCafferty, Patrick	Case Western Reserve University
McCann, Jett	EBSCO Information Services
McCawley, Christine	West Chester University
McClary, Maryon	University of Alberta
McCutcheon, Dianne	National Library of Medicine
McDonald, Lynn	FLICC/FEDLINK
McDougald, Barbara	USPTO
McGrath, Kat	University of British Columbia
McKay, Sharon	The Faxon Co.
McKee, Amy J.	University of NC at Greensboro
McKee, Anne	Blackwell's Information Services
McKinney, Janet	UMKC Law Library
McLaren, Mary	University of Kentucky
McLean, Carrie	NC State University Libraries
McLeod, William	University of Maryland
McManus, Jean	University of Notre Dame
McNair, Richard	FMF Cape Scott, Canadian Navy
McQuiston, Kathleen	Bucknell University
McSweeney, Marilyn	MIT Libraries
Melkin, Audrey	CatchWord
Melnychuk, Dianne	Cedar Crest College
Meneely, Kathleen	Cleveland Health Sciences Library
Mering, Meg	University of Nebraska
Milam, Barbara	Kennesaw State University
Miller, Judith K.	Valparaiso University
Molden, Coleen	Lamar University
Moore, Wendy	University of Georgia School of Law Library
Moran, Sheila E.	Massachusetts General Hospital
More, Susan L.	Northeastern University, Law Library
Moye, Stephanie	National Museum of American Art
Mudrak, Angela	Youngstown State University
Mulak, Tom	Mary Ann Liebert, Inc.
Murden, Steve	Virginia Commonwealth University
Murphy, Edward	Florida Gulf Coast University
Myers, Mary	Joint Bank-Fund Library
Nadeski, Karen	
Nalepa, Laurie R.	John Carroll University
Neal, Stephen	Taylor & Francis
Neilson, Susan H.	American University Library

Nelson, Carol	Ball State University
Nelson, Catherine	University of California, Santa Barbara
Newberry, Michele	FCLA
Newsome, Nancy	Western Carolina University
Nguyen, Hien	National Library of Medicine
Nirnberger, Betty	Penn State University
Nolan, J. Mark	Project MUSE
Nordman, Alan	Dawson ISG
Novak, Denise D.	Carnegie Mellon University
Novak, Paul	Bethel Park High School
Oberg, Steven J.	The University of Chicago Library
O'Connell, Jennifer S.	EBSCO Information Services
O'Day, Vicki	U.C. Santa Cruz
Ogburn, Joyce	Old Dominion University
O'Leary, Susan	EBSCO Information Services
Olson, Andrea	Cleveland Public Library
O'Malley, Terrence	Case Western Reserve University
O'Neill, Jill	ISI
Orme, Marianne	Pratt Institute
Ouderkirk, Jane	Harvard University
Overcash, Gina R.	Davidson College Library
Page, Mary	Rutgers University
Parang, Elizabeth	Pepperdine University
Parker, Laura	Academic Press
Parks, Bonnie	Oregon State University
Pearse, Michelle	Harvard Law School Library
Perry, Sara	Canada Institute for Scientific and Technical Information
Persing, Robert	University of Pennsylvania
Peterson, Jan	Faxon/Dawson
Phillips, Dr. Patricia A.	UTEP Library
Pierce, Louise	York College of Pennsylvania
Pilling, Margy	Williams College
Pitts, Linda	University of Washington
Postlethwaite, Bonnie	Tufts University
Powers, Susanna	Tulane University
Prabha, Chandra	OCLC
Pritchard, Eileen	Calif. Polytechnic State University
Qualls, Jane	The University of Memphis

Quinn, Brian	Texas Tech University
Quinn, Marilyn	Rider University
Rabner, Lanell	Brigham Young University
Radbourne, Margaret	John Wiley & Sons LTD
Rafter, William	West Virginia University
Ragan, Larry	Penn State University
Raines, M. Diane	Westminster College Library (UT)
Randall, Kevin M.	Northwestern University Library
Randall, Michael	UCLA
Rasmussen, Anne	Kent State University
Ray, Tom H.	Library of Virginia
Recko, Alan	General Bookbinding Co.
Richards, Barbara	Carnegie Mellon University
Rieley, Sarah	Wellesley College
Riley, Cheryl	Central MO State University
Rioux, Margaret A.	MBL/WHOI Library
Risser, Irene	Millersville University of Pennsylvania
River, Sandra	Texas Tech University Library
Roach, Dani	Macalester College
Roazen, Ruth	University of North Carolina, Wilmington
Robertson, Wendy	University of Iowa
Robischon, Rose	USMA Library
Rodgers, David	Baylor University
Rodriguez, Adolfo	National University of Mexico
Roesemann, Douglas N.	The Faxon Co.
Rogers, Marilyn	University of Arkansas
Roncevich, Pat	Pittsburgh Theological Seminary
Rosenberg, Frieda B.	UNC-Chapel Hill
Rossignol, Lucien R.	Smithsonian Institution Libraries
Roth, Alison	Blackwell's Information Services
Rothaug, Caroline	John Wiley & Sons, Inc.
Rozum, Betty	Utah State University
Rumph, Virginia A.	Butler University
Ruthenberg, Donnell	Data Research Associates, Inc
Rutkowski, June	Harvard University
Ryckman, Nancy	University of North Carolina of Greensboro
Rymsza-Pawlowska, Ela	Catholic University of America
Sachon, Mark	Carnegie Library of Pittsburgh
Sak, Ludmila	Rutgers University

Salas, Larry	Kluwer Academic Publishers
Salo-Cravens, Maija	St. Hist. Soc. of Wisc. Library
Sanford, Deborah	Bridgewater State College
Sappington, Sue	University of Texas at Arlington
Savage, Stephen M.	Wayne State University
Saxton, Elna	University of Cincinnati
Schatz, Bob	Everetts
Scheiberg, Susan	University of Southern California
Schein, Anna M.	WVU Libraries
Scherer, Jim	General Bookbinding Company
Schimizzi, Anthony J.	Sterne Library-UAB
Schinker, Rose	University of NE Medical Center
Schmidt, Karen	University of Illinois
Schmitt, Stephanie	Yale University
Schneider, Janet	Schoolcraft College
Schulz, Nathalie	Griffith University Library
Schwartz, Marla	American U. Law Library
Scoones, Philippa	Blackwell Publishers
Scott, JoAnne	University of Chicago
Selby, Janet	Radford University
Semancik, Frank	The Faxon Co.
Seminaro, David A.	Blackwell's Information Services
Sercan, Cecilia S.	Cornell University
Shadle, Steve	University of Washington Libraries
Shaw, Ward	CARL
Shea, Marsha	SDSU Libraries
Shontz, Priscilla	Driscoll Children's Hospital
Sievers, Arlene Moore	Case Western Reserve University
Silcox, Stuart	Faxon Canada
Simser, Charlene	Kansas State University Libraries
Sinha, Reeta	HSCL-Emory University
Slaughter, Philenese	Austin Peay State University
Sleeman, Allison M.	University of Virginia
Sleep, Esther	Brock University
Smets, Kristine	Johns Hopkins University
Smith, Angel	University of Evansville
Smith, Merrill	EBSCO Information Services
Smith, Tom	Lawrence Livermore National Laboratory
Smulewitz, Gracemary	Rutgers University

Snyder, Christina	Blackwell's Information Services
Somers, Michael A.	University of North Carolina, Charlotte
Sonka, Bud	National University Library
Spence, Duncan	Publishers Services Ltd.
Springer, Fran	Thunderbird
Sprys, Bonnie	Carnegie Mellon University
St. Clair, Gloriana	Carnegie Mellon University
Stamison, Christine	Blackwell's Information Services
Stangroom, Scott	Boston College
Stanko, Lynn	National Agricultural Library
Stanley, Nancy	Penn State University
Steele, Patrick	Cuyahoga County Public Library
Stefancu, Mircea	University of Illinois at Chicago Library
Stickman, Jim	University of Washington
Stier, David	John Wiley & Sons, Inc.
Stoecker, Dawn	R. R. Bowker
Stokes, Charity K.	University of Nebraska-Lincoln
Stone, Evalyn	Metropolitan Museum of Art
Strother, Kim	The Faxon Company
Sullenger, Paula	Auburn University
Sullivan, Sharon A.	UCLA Biomedical Library
Sullivan, Sherry	Swets Subscription Services
Sutherland, Laurie	University of Washington
Sweeney, Daniel	Wake Forest University
Sweet, Kathy A.	Phoenix College Library
Swetman, Barbara	Hamilton College
Szczyrbak, Gregory	Millersville University, Ganser Library
Taffurelli, Virginia	NYPL-Science, Industry & Business
Tagler, John	Elsevier Science
Tai, I-Chene	Le Moyne College
Talley, Kaye M.	University of Central Arkansas
Tam, Jessie	University of Pittsburgh, Barco Law Library
Tarango, Adolfo R.	University of Nevada, Reno
Taylor, Sally	University of British Columbia
Teaster, Gale	Winthrop University Library
Teel, Kay	Stanford University
Tenney, Joyce	University of MD, Baltimore County
Testa, James	ISI
Thomas, Suzanne	University of Pittsburgh

Thompson, Elizabeth	Swets & Zeitlinger, Inc.
Thompson, Konny	Gonzaga University
Thomson, Sarah	University of Mass. Amherst
Thorne, Kathleen	San Jose State University
Thornton, Christopher	Case Western Reserve University
Thunell, Allen	Michigan State University
Tian, Jie	California State University-Fullerton
Tisack, Rebecca	Carnegie Library of Pittsburgh
Tong, Dieu Van	UAB Sterne Library
Tonkery, Dan	Information Quest
Toussaint, Jo Ann	University of St. Thomas
Tumlin, Markel D.	San Diego State University
Turitz, Linda J.	University of California, Berkeley
Turitz, Mitch	San Francisco State University
Tusa, Sara D.	Lamar University
Van Auken, Gayle J.	Linda Hall Library
Van Schaik, JoAnn	Texas Tech HSC Library
van Sickle, Jennifer L.	Trinity College
Vent, Marilyn	University of Nevada, Las Vegas
Viscuglia, Donna	Harvard University
Vukas, Rachel	EBSCO Information Services
Wade, Alex D.	U. of Washington
Wakeling, Will	Northeastern University
Waldrep, Pam	Eastern Illinois University
Walker, Dana	Harvard College Library
Wallace, Patricia M.	University of Colorado
Wallas, Phillip	EBSCO Publishing
Walravens, Hartmut	Staatsbibliothek
Waltner, Robb M.	University of Colorado, Denver
Wang, Margaret K.	University of Delaware
Ward, Jeannette	University Central Florida
Warner, Susan B.	Covenant Health System
Watson, Barbara	Cornell University ILR
Watson, Virginia	Brigham Young University
Weaver, Christine	Swets & Zeitlinger
Weigel, Friedemann	Harrassowitz
Weiss, Amy K.	Appalachian State University
Weiss, Paul J.	University of New Mexico
Weng, Cathy	Temple University

Wesley, Kathryn	Clemson University
Whiting, Peter	Prairie View A&M University
Whitney, Marla	CARL Corporation
Wiegand, Sue	Valparaiso University
Wilbur, Christie	Harvard University
Wilder, Rayette	Gonzaga University
Wiles-Young, Sharon	Lehigh University
Wilhelme, Judy	University of Michigan Library
Wilhite, Marjorie	University of Iowa Libraries
Wilke, Mary I.	Center for Research Libraries
Wilkins, Cheryl	GlaxoWellcome
Wilkinson, Fran	University of New Mexico
Williams, Geraldine	Northern Kentucky University
Williams, Mary W.	Tarleton State University
Williams, Sheryl L.	University of Nebraska Medical Center
Williams, Tara E.	American Chemical Society
Williams-Jackson,Crystal G.	St. Louis University -HSL
Williamson, Josephine	University of Delaware
Wilson, Sally	University of Pittsburgh, Falk Library
Winant, Joshua	Yankee Book Peddler
Winchester, David	Washburn University
Wishnetsky, Susan	Northwestern University, Galter HSL
Woo, Kathy	University of San Francisco Library
Wood, Kelly Sink	Davidson College Library
Wood, Richard J.	Sam Houston State University
Yanney, Donna	Georgia College & State University
Yaunt, Barbara	Carnegie Mellon University
Young, Naomi Kietzke	Southern Methodist University
Zenga, Johanne	Faxon Quebec
Zhang, Yvonne	Cal Poly Pomona
Zupko, Laura	Chicago Public Library

Index

